Formal Approaches to Slavic Linguistics 9, 2000

Michigan Slavic Publications is a non-profit organization associated with the Department of Slavic Languages and Literatures of the University of Michigan. Its goal is to publish titles which substantially aid the study and teaching of Slavic and East European languages and cultures. The present volume, based on a colloquium held at Indiana University, Bloomington, in February 2000, continues a series of conference proceedings devoted to formal approaches to Slavic linguistics.

Michigan Slavic Materials, vol. 46

Annual Workshop on Formal Approaches to Slavic Linguistics

The Bloomington Meeting 2000

edited by
Steven Franks
Tracy Holloway King
Michael Yadroff

Michigan Slavic Publications
Ann Arbor 2001

collection © Michigan Slavic Publications, 2001
individual contributions © authors

Library of Congress Cataloging-in-Publication Data

Workshop on Formal Approaches to Slavic Linguistics (9th : 2000 : Bloomington, Ind.)
    Annual Workshop on Formal Approaches to Slavic Linguistics. The Bloomington meeting, 2000 / edited by Steven Franks, Tracy Holloway King, Michael Yadroff.
        p. cm. -- (Michigan Slavic materials ; vol. 46)
    Includes bibliographical references.
    ISBN 0-930042-86-7 (pbk.)
    1. Slavic languages--Congresses. I. Franks, Steven. II. King, Tracy Holloway, 1966- III. Yadroff, Michael. IV. Title. V. Michigan Slavic materials ; no. 46.
PG13 .M46 no. 46
[PG11]
491.8--dc21

                                                2001001775

Michigan Slavic Publications
Department of Slavic Languages and Literatures
3040 Modern Languages Bldg.
University of Michigan
Ann Arbor, MI 48109–1275

email: michsp@umich.edu

Contents

Preface vii

Klaus Abels
The Predicate Cleft Construction in Russian 1

Olga Arnaudova
On Two Focus Strategies in Bulgarian 19

Leonard Babby
The Genitive of Negation: A Unified Analysis 39

Željko Bošković
Li without PF Movement 57

Wayles Browne
You Always Forget Something 77

Peter Chew
The Representation of the jers in Russian 99

Barbara Citko & Kleanthes Grohmann
The (Non)-Uniqueness of Multiple WH-Fronting:
German = Bulgarian 117

Eva Hajičová
Status of Focus Sensitive Particles in the Topic-Focus
Articulation of the Sentence 137

Ben Hermans
Compensatory Lengthening in Slovak 155

Sophia Malamud
Centering and Scrambling: Towards a Discourse-Status
Motivation of Russian Word Order 173

Marjorie McShane
One Formal Approach Leads to Another 191

Asya Pereltsvaig
  Syntactic Categories are not Primitive: Evidence from
  Short and Long Adjectives in Russian 209

Ljiljana Progovac
  Clausal Functional Projections in Serbian 229

Adam Przepiórkowski
  Case Agreement in Polish Predicates 257

Elena Rudnitskaya
  Feature Movement Approach to Long-Distance Binding
  in Russian 275

Natalya Strahov
  A Scrambling Analysis of Russian WH-Questions 293

Yuki Takatori
  Inertness of Sonorant [voice] in Polish 311

Masha Vassilieva
  How Russian Commits Comitatives 327

Preface

The present volume represents a selection of papers presented at the ninth annual meeting of Formal Approaches to Slavic Linguistics, which took place 9–10 February 2000 at Indiana University, Bloomington. FASL 9 was sponsored by the following units at Indiana University: the College of Arts and Sciences, the Russian and East European Institute, Research and the University Graduate School, International Programs. The generous support of these offices is gratefully acknowledged.

FASL9 was held in conjunction with two other events. One was a special poster session on Semantics in Slavic Languages, organized by Barbara Partee. A selection of papers from this session will be published as a special issue of the *Journal of Slavic Linguistics*, guest edited by Wayles Browne and Barbara Partee. The other was a meeting on 18 February devoted to the Future of Slavic Linguistics in America, the proceedings of which are being published by Slavica. This meeting was primarily funded by a grant from the US Department of Education, which additional funding by the Duke University/University of North Carolina Slavic, Eurasian, and East European Language Resource Center, as well as the Indiana University Department of Slavic Languages and Slavica Publishers.

In addition, many individuals assisted in the organization of the conference in diverse ways. First and foremost, we wish to thank George Fowler for his help on the organizing committee and during the conference itself. Thanks are also due Leslie Gabriele for her work on the organizing committee. We would like to thank all the reviewers who had to evaluate a large number of high quality abstracts in a short period of time. Finally, we are deeply indebted to many unnamed staff, students, and colleagues at Indiana University who assisted in making FASL 9 a reality by preparing, copying and mailing materials, meeting participants at the airport, helping at registration, and generally dealing with the conference details.

Since its inception by Jindřich Toman, who organized the first FASL at the University of Michigan, FASL has rapidly expanded and become an increasingly competitive conference. Correspondingly, the selection process has become more stringent, with four referees evaluating each abstract this year. The result has been that FASL continues to be the primary forum for Slavic linguists to exchange ideas in the United States and continues to attract linguists from around the world. There were twenty two papers presented at the conference, including sixteen competitive talks, four poster session papers, and invited presentations by Wayles Browne and Ljiljana Progovac.

All participants were invited to submit their papers to the proceedings. Eighteen of the papers presented at the conference appear in these proceedings. The remaining four papers which were not submitted for publication are: Maria Babyonyshev and Edward Gibson "The Role of Nominal Morphology in Sentence Processing"; Sue Brown, "Case Marking and Negative Closure: Arguments for A-Chain Reconstruction"; Martyna Kozlowska-Macgregor, "Polish Aspects within Domains of Syntax"; and Milan Rezac, "Syntactic Conditions on Second Position Clitics". All papers were edited for content and style by the editors before preparation of final camera ready copy. The result, we feel, is an outstanding volume, representing the high quality of current work in formal Slavic linguistics.

The Predicate Cleft Construction in Russian

Klaus Abels
University of Connecticut

1. Introduction

In this paper I will provide a minimalist (Chomsky 1993, 1995, 1999, 2000) analysis of the Predicate Cleft Construction (PCC) in Russian.[1] The construction is familiar from a number of languages (2 Haitian from Lumsden and Lefebvre 1990:765, 3 Hausa ibid:762) and is fairly common in spoken Russian (1).

(1) √ Čitat' (-to) Ivan eë čitaet, no ničego
    read$_{inf}$ (TO) Ivan it$_{fem.acc}$ reads but nothing
    ne ponimaet.
    not understands
    'Ivan does read it, but he doesn't understand a thing.'

(2) √ Se achte ei te achte flè yo.
    it-is buy he PAST buy flowers PL
    'That is BUY that he bought flowers.' (he didn't steal them)

(3) √ Cin abincii da saurii, Aka cee SUN yi.
    eat-VN food with speed indef. say 3rd.Perf do
    'Eating food in a hurry, one said they did.'

In section 2 I present a brief sketch of the semantics of the construction and the basic data. In section 3 I argue that the data is best analyzed in terms of remnant VP fronting. Section 4 provides an implementation of this analysis in terms of the copy theory of movement. In this section the main theoretical conclusions are established: (i) the PCC provides support for the copy theory of movement, (ii) pronunciation of

---

[1] In fact there is quite a bit of speaker variation. In this paper I keep to a consistent set of data collected from a single speaker: Natalia Rakhlin. Discussion of variation among speakers would go beyond the scope of this paper.

Steven Franks, Tracy Holloway King, and Michael Yadroff, eds. *Annual Workshop on Formal Approaches to Slavic Linguistics: The Bloomington Meeting, 2000.* Ann Arbor: Michigan Slavic Publications, 2001, 1–18.

multiple copies of a single element from the numeration is possible, and (iii) under a strictly lexicalist view of morphology, a natural account for the PCC is not possible. Section 5 takes up some problematic data. I argue that object shift/Case checking is obligatorily overt for definite DPs in Russian. Section 6 is a brief summary of the main results.

2 The Data

A typical example of the PCC was already provided in example (1). Descriptively, the example is a string containing a non-finite form of a lexical verb V, the optional discourse particle *to*, followed by a regular main clause with an occurrence of the same verb V in a finite form. Certain examples that do not conform to this description will be discussed below. Not all sentence initial infinitivals will automatically count as examples of the PCC. Fronted complements of verbs that take infinitival complements or sentence initial non-finite adjuncts qualify only if they carry the semantics of the PCC.

I will call the initial part of the clause preceding *to* the *Head* of the cleft; the particle *-to* will be called *TO*; the part following *TO* (or the *Head* if *TO* is absent) will be called the *Body* (cf. 13). The tensed form of the verb in the *Body* will be called the *Finite Verb*, and the uncleft form of the sentence will be called the *Base Line Sentence*. Thus in (1) *čitat'* is the *Head*, *Ivan eë čitaet* the *Body*, *čitaet* the *Finite Verb*. Example (4) is the *Base Line Sentence* corresponding to (1).

(4) √   Ivan   eë   čitaet.
        Ivan   it$_{fem.acc}$ read$_{3rd.sg}$
        'Ivan is reading it.'

Predicate clefting in Russian has clear cut effects on the information structure of a sentence (see Paillard and Plungjan 1993 for discussion). My own view is that the *Head* provides a S(entence)-topic in the sense of Büring (1995). The *Head* is, roughly speaking, a contrastive topic. In line with Büring's theory, a predicate cleft has a set of questions as its topic semantic value. Its ordinary semantic value is one answer to one of the questions in the topic semantic value. Predicate clefts have two intonational nuclei: one on the non-finite form of the verb in the *Head* and one on the *Finite Verb*. These intonational nuclei indicate the focus and the topic domains. A plausible semantic interpretation of (1) is:

(5) Topic semantic value:
{Did Ivan read it?, Did Ivan understand it?, Did Ivan throw it away?, ...}
Ordinary semantic value
Ivan read it.

According to Büring, sentences with S-topics conventionally implicate that the answer given in the ordinary semantic value is not exhaustive, i.e. that certain of the questions in the topic semantic value are still under discussion. This can clearly be seen from the continuation of (1): '...but he did not understand it'. This continuation constitutes an answer to the second question listed in (5).

Furthermore, sentences with S-topics cannot be uttered out of the blue. Unless at least one answer to one of the questions in the topic semantic value was already under discussion, such a sentence cannot be felicitously uttered. Since I am assuming the topic semantic value of the PCC to be a set of yes/no-questions that differ in the verb only, it follows that no other element may be new in the context.[2] These semantics can be used as a diagnostic for predicate clefthood. Space limitations keep me from developing these sketchy remarks further.

The first question to ask with respect to predicate clefting is how general the clefting process is. Is it limited to specific semantic or structural verb classes? The answer is 'no'. An example of a transitive verb was already given in (1). An example with an unergative verb is given in (6), with an unaccusative verb in (7), with a ditransitive in (8), a PP-embedding verb in (9), and a CP embedding one in (10). These examples also exemplify various semantic classes.[3]

(6) (Grammatika Russkogo Jazyka 1960 vol 2.1 p. 404)
Čto √ èto on? streljat' ne streljaet, a ruž"ë deržit.
what √ that he? shoot$_{Inf}$ not shoots, but rifle hold$_{3rd.sg}$
'What's wrong with him? Holds a rifle but doesn't fire?!'

(7) √ Rasti -to Marina rastët, no často boleet.

---

[2] This last fact will become quite important in section 5 of the present paper when indefiniteness and definiteness are discussed.

[3] Example (10) shows that stative/i-level predicates are possible with the PCC in Russian. Larson and Lefebvre (1991) report that this is impossible in Haitian.

grow$_{inf}$ TO Marina grow$_{3rd.sg}$ but often be ill$_{3rd.sg}$
'Marina does grow, but she is ill a lot.'

(8) √ Dat' (-to) ja eë emu dal, no...
give$_{inf}$ (TO) I her him gave, but...
'I did give it to him, but...'

(9) √ Dumat' o ženit'be (-to) on dumaet
think$_{inf}$ about marriage (TO) he think$_{3rd.sg}$
- no nikogda on ne ženitsja.
but never he not marry-self
'He does think about marriage, but he will never marry.'

(10) √ Dumat' čto Xomskij genij on dumaet no čitat'
think$_{Inf}$ that Chomsky genius he thinks but read$_{inf}$
ego knigi ne čitaet. /no znat' ne znaet
his books not reads /but know$_{inf}$ not knows
'He does think that Chomsky is a genius, but he doesn't read his books./ but he doesn't know for sure.'

Having established the full generality of the clefting process, we are in a position to ask questions about the morphology involved. The relevant generalization is as follows: if a *Base Line Sentence* contains an inflected form of a lexical verb, then the infinitive of that verb occurs in the *Head*. The inflected form occurs in the *Body*. All the Russian examples given so far fall under this generalization.[4] Consider however examples like (11) and (12), where the *Base Line Sentences* (11a) and (12b) contain analytic tense forms. In these cases no doubling takes place as shown by the ungrammaticality of (11b) and (12b) and the grammaticallity of (11c) and (12c).

(11) a. √ On budet čitat'.
he will read$_{inf}$
b. * čitat' (-to) on budet čitat'.
read$_{inf}$ TO he will read$_{inf}$

---

[4] The copula is the only clear counterexample I know. It will be discussed in footnote 15.

(11) c. √ čitat' (-to) on budet.
   read_inf TO he will
   'He will read.'

(12) a. √ Dom byl postroen.
   house was build_prt.past.pass
   b. * Postroen (-to) dom byl postroen.[5]
   build_prt.past.pass TO house was build_prt.past.pass
   c. √ Postroen dom byl.
   build_prt.past.pass house was
   'The house was built.'

Put in different terms, if a *Base Line Sentence* has only one exponent of both lexical content of the verb and tense information, then doubling takes place. If a *Base Line Sentence* represents these two pieces of information on independent items, no doubling occurs.

3 The Structure and Derivation of the PCC

Assuming that what I have called the PCC is indeed a coherent phenomenon in Russian, we can now ask how to analyze it. The questions to ask are: What is the structure? How are the sentences derived?

In what follows I will argue for a structure along the lines indicated in (13). A (remnant) VP is moved to a position higher than TP and below CP. The exact nature of the phrase is irrelevant here. The position may or may not be the specifier of the landing site projected by -*to*.[6]

(13) [$_{CP}$ ... [$_{XP}$ [$_{VP}$ ... V_{inf} ...] ... [-to ... [$_{TP}$ ... V_{fin} ...]]]]
   ---- *Head* ----   TO | --- *Body* ---

---

[5] Michael Yadroff (p.c.) accepts this sentence. Jairo Nunes (p.c.) notes that comparable examples are also acceptable in Brazilian Portuguese. Maybe for the speakers who allow doubling of the passive participle, the participle acts as a nominal. In this case the structure is that of a base generated external topic. See below for some discussion of base generated topics in Russian.

[6] I am not aware of any examples where an adjunct can intervene between the *Head* and *TO*, so that the *Head* presumably is the specifier of the phrase projected by -*to* (or in the absence of -*to* some null counterpart).

On this view the *Body* forms a constituent at least the size of TP. The *Head* is also a phrasal constituent. The claim made in (13) that the infinitival verb is structurally below C° can be substantiated quite easily.

(14) a. √ Pëtr skazal čto pročitat' (-to) on eë pročitaet...
       Petr said that read TO he it$_{fem.acc}$ read$_{fut}$
    b. * Pëtr skazal pročitat' (-to) čto on eë pročitaet...
       Petr said read$_{inf}$ TO that he it$_{fem.acc}$ read$_{fut}$
    'Peter said that he would read the book through.'

Example (14) shows that the *Head* can follow the complementizer *čto*, but it cannot precede it. This implies that *čto* is structurally above the *Head*.

The structure in (13) also claims that the *Head* is located above TP. To show this we observe that the *Head* usually precedes the subject of the sentence. It is then higher than the landing site of the subject.[7] If subjects are in the specifier of TP, then the fact that the *Head* precedes the subject shows that the *Head* is higher than the subject.The position of the subject in Russian is contested, however, so a stronger argument is needed.

Ever since Jackendoff (1973) it has been quite widely believed that different classes of adverbs are attached in different structural positions and that sentential adverbs are attached in a particularly high position, above TP (see Stjepanović 1995). If this is true, then (15) shows that the *Head* is above TP. The *Head* precedes the subject, which precedes the adverb, which is, by assumption higher than T°. Sentences where a sentential adverb precedes the *Head* are ungrammatical (cf. 17b).

(15) √ Čitat' (-to) on naverno čitaet, no...
       Read$_{inf}$ TO he probably reads, but...
    'He probably does read, but...'

The two arguments just given indicate that the Head of the predicate cleft is in a structural position between C° and T°. This conclusion is independent of the exact structure of the *Head* and *TO*.

---

[7] I will not concern myself here with the exact position of the subject in a theory assuming a split Infl theory (cf. Pollock 1989, Chomsky 1991 among many others). The *Head* is above TP.

I will argue next that the *Head* plus *TO* are in fact not plausibly analyzed as a constituent. There are two options for analyzing the *Head* plus *TO* as a constituent: (i) the non-finite verb plus *TO* might form a complex head, or (ii) the *Head* plus *TO* might form a phrasal constituent. Although (i) might be the right analysis for some idiolects of Russian which disallow all examples of the type that follows, the idiolect under consideration provides quite strong evidence that the *Head* is not a complex head.

(16) a. √ Dumat'   o   ženit'be (-to) on   dumaet
        think$_{inf}$ about   marriage TO   he   thinks
        - no nikogda on ne ženitsja.
        but never   he not marry-self
    b. * Dumat'   (-to) on   dumaet   o   ženit'be — no...
         think$_{Inf}$ TO   he   thinks   about marriage but...
         'He does think about marriage, but he will never marry.'

The *Head* of the cleft in the grammatical example (16a) is not just a syntactic head, but a phrase, i.e. the verb plus its complement. If the infinitival verb indeed formed a complex head with *TO*, we would expect (16b) to be grammatical and (16a) to be ungrammatical, the exact opposite of the observed pattern. The data are thus inconsistent with analyzing the *Head* plus *TO* as a complex head.

These data however are not sufficient to show that the *Head* plus *TO* do not form a constituent at all. They might still form a phrasal constituent. I am not aware of any direct evidence bearing on the point. However, an indirect argument will be presented after the movement analysis of the PCC has been defended.

We have already seen some evidence in (16) that the *Head* is roughly the size of a VP. Further evidence is easy to adduce. In (17a) for example, a VP adverb is part of the *Head*. As shown in (17b), a sentential adverb cannot appear in the same position.

(17) a. √ Bystro pečatat'   (-to) on   pečataet, no   delaet
         fast   type$_{inf}$ TO   he   types   but   makes
         'He types fast, but he makes a lot of mistakes.'
         mnogo ošibok.
         many errors

(17) b. * Včera   pečatat' (-to) on pečatal, no   sdelal
         yesterday type$_{inf}$ TO   he typed   but made
         mnogo ošibok.
         many errors
         'He did type yesterday, but he made a lot of mistakes'

I therefore assume that the *Head* is indeed a VP.[8]

Having defended the structure given in (13), let me turn now to the task of analyzing the derivation of the PCC. There are at least two conceivable derivations, one in which the *Head* is base generated in its position and one in which it is moved there. Both of these have been suggested in the literature on other languages.[9] If we assume base generation of the *Head* in its position, various questions arise. Why does the observed identity (modulo finiteness) between the *Finite Verb* in the *Body* and the non-finite verb in the *Head* obtain? Why can't the lexical verb be doubled in analytic tense forms (cf. 12)? How is the theta grid of the infinitival verb in the *Head* satisfied in examples like (1) where only one object and one subject occur? The same question arises with respect to (16). In fact, we can complement the paradigm in (16) with (16c) below and (1) with (1b) and ask what rules out these sentences.

   c. * Dumat'   o   ženit'be   (-to) on   dumaet
        think$_{inf}$ about marriage (TO)   he   thinks
        o   ženit'be   —   no   nikogda on   ne   žcnitsja.
        about   marriage   but   never   he   not   marry-self
   d. * Čitat'   eë   (-to)   Ivan   eë   čitaet, no...
        read$_{Inf}$ it$_{Fem.Acc}$ TO   Ivan   it$_{Fem.Acc}$ reads   but...

In other words, the data indicate that as far as theta relations go, the non-finite verb can stand in for the finite verb and vice versa. Furthermore, the two verbs are identical (modulo inflection). Both of these properties are typical properties of movement. This suggests that the PCC ought to be analyzed as a movement phenomenon. Otherwise, a

---

[8] I am not concerned here with establishing the exact size of the *Head* (VP, vP, or something slightly bigger) and will use the term VP as a cover term.

[9] Koopman (1984) is the classic reference for the movement approach. Larson and Lefebvre (1991) argue for base generation for the PCC in Haitian; however, they invoke an additional mechanism of LF VP-movement and replacement of the Head.

good deal of redundancy would have to be introduced into the theory, since there would have to be two ways to derive these properties: movement and whatever is responsible for the PCC. We thus have a theoretical argument from simplicity for a movement analysis of the PCC.

Still, one might be tempted to try to assimilate the PCC to other Russian constructions involving base generation. Base generated topics come to mind as a candidate, especially since the PCC is a structure with an S-topic. However, the PCC behaves quite differently from base generated topics. For some discussion of this, see Franks and House 1982 or King 1995 (esp. 103–106). Example (18) illustrates one of the differences. Unlike the PCC (example 14), base generated topics are a matrix phenomenon in Russian.

(18) a. √ Kniga   on   eë   pročital.
      book$_{nom.sg.fem}$ he it$_{Fem.Acc}$ read$_{3sg.msc.past}$
      'The book—he read it.'

b. Pëtr skazal (*kniga) čto (*kniga) on eë pročital.
    Petr said book that book he it$_{Fem.Acc}$ read
    'Peter said that he had read the book through.'

A second difference, apparent in example (18a), is that the topic usually doubles an argument in the sentence, but there is no requirement that the they both be the same lexical element ('eë' vs. 'kniga') or be otherwise identical (see Franks and House 1982). Furthermore, no material can be scrambled in front of a base generated topic (19a), wheras scrambling in front of the head of a predicate cleft is marginally possible (19b).[10]

---

[10] This kind of scrambling is comparable to scrambling in front of a *wh*-phrase in a real, non-echo question as shown in (i). The similarity provides a further argument for assuming that the *Head* is in a position between TP and CP if Bošković (1999a) and Stepanov (1998b) are on the right track in assuming that *wh*-phrases move to a position between TP and CP in Russian.

(i) (example provided by A. Stepanov p.c.)
    √ Ivan kogo znaet
       Ivan who$_{Acc}$ knows
       'Who does Ivan know?'

(19) a. * On,   Ivana,   ego   vidit.
         he,   Ivan$_{acc}$ him   sees
     b. ? On   čitat'   (-to)   čitatet, no...
         he   read$_{inf}$ TO   reads,   but...
         'He does read, but...'

Finally, on a movement approach to the PCC we expect locality effects to appear, as in fact they do (20). To capture these effects on a base generation approach would require further stipulations which would, once again, have to be redundant with conditions on movement or chains.[11]

(20) * Kupit'   (-to)   ty   skazal čto   ja   èto kupil...
       buy$_{inf}$ TO   you   said   that I   that bought

Predicate clefting out of embedded infinitives is sometimes possible. There is a parallelism with *wh*-movement in Russian, which is also possible out of infinitivals und subjunctives, but not out of full finite clauses. Notice that in order to derive the examples in (20) we would have to move the embedded VP out of the embedding VP.

We have seen that any attempt to analyze the PCC as a base generation phenomenon will end up introducing quite a bit of redundancy into the system, and that the PCC exhibits certain characteristics of movement. Let us take the evidence for movement at face value. If we make the commonly held assumption that movement is to a c-commanding position,[12] we have the missing argument for the structure proposed above and repeated here.

(13) $[_{CP} \ldots [_{XP} [_{VP} \ldots V_{inf} \ldots] \ldots [\text{-to} \ldots [_{IP} \ldots V_{fin} \ldots]]]$

The problem above was that we were missing an argument against treating the *Head* plus *TO* as a constituent. If we assumed now that the *Head* plus *TO* did form a constituent, the moved VP would not c-command its copy in the base position, and the structure should be out

---

[11] I take no stance here on whether chains exist and what properties they have.

[12] Chomsky (1995) essentially stipulates that movement is to a c-commanding position. For some discussion and important qualifications, as well as attempts to derive the relevant facts, see Epstein et al. (1998), Nunes (1996, 1999) among others.

for the same reasons other cases of movement to a non-c-commanding position are out.

To summarize the results of this section, we have seen that the Head of a predicate cleft is a phrasal constituent of roughly the size of VP. This (remnant) VP moves to a position between IP and CP.

4   The PCC and the Copy Theory of Movement

Pre-minimalist generative approaches assumed that when an element is moved it leaves behind a special type of null element, a trace, or nothing at all. Under minimalist assumptions, traces cannot exist as primitive elements. The copy theory of movement is virtually forced by the inclusiveness condition (cf. Chomsky 1995). The properties of traces have to be deduced (cf. Nunes 1996, 1999). Their most salient property is that they are phonetically null. On the face of it, the fact that in the general case a moved element is pronounced in one and only one position speaks against the copy theory of movement (21).

(21) a.   John was arrested (*John)
     b.   What did you eat (*what)

Arguments have been developed (Franks 1998, Bošković 1999a, b) that syntactic movement can at times be obscured because a lower copy of a moved element is pronounced. Nunes (1999) discusses cases where two copies of a moved element are pronounced. Richards (1997) and Abels (2000) discuss examples where it looks as though LF movement can be anticipated in overt syntax. These can be analyzed as pronunciation of an exceptionally high copy. All of these types of examples are expected to exist under the copy theory of movement, but are incompatible with trace theory.

I would like to suggest that the PCC is an example of the second type, where multiple copies of a single element, namely the verb, are phonetically realized. Consider again examples (1) and (12c).

(1) √   Čitat'   (-to) Ivan eë   čitaet, no   ničego
         $read_{inf}$ (TO) Ivan $it_{fem.acc}$ reads   but nothing
         ne   ponimaet.
         not   understands
         'Ivan does read it, but he doesn't understand a thing.'

(12) c. √ Postroen dom byl.
build_prt.past.pass house was
'The house was built.'

The generalization concerning these examples was that the lexical verb is doubled just in case there is no independent exponent of tense and agreement information hosted in Infl. This suggests that the second copy of the lexical verb is realized in order to keep the morphology on Infl from getting stranded. Russian doesn't have *do*-support. The general strategy in Russian is to pronounce the lexical verb in cases where English shows *do*-support. An example of this is VP-ellipsis.[13]

(22) a. √ Ivan čitaet etu knigu každoe voskresen'e, a Pëtr
Ivan reads this book every Sunday, but Peter
ne čitaet [_VP ~~etu knigu každoe voskresen'e~~]
not reads this book every Sunday
'Ivan reads this book every Sunday, but Peter **doesn't**
(read it every Sunday)
b. √ Ivan budet čitat' etu knigu každoe voskresen'e, a
Ivan will read this book every Sunday, but
Pëtr ne budet [_VP ~~čitat' etu knigu každoe~~
Petr not will read this book every
~~voskresen'e~~]
Sunday
'Ivan will read this book every Sunday, but Peter **won't**
(read it every Sunday)

The examples in (22) show that VP ellipsis in Russian patterns with VP-ellipsis in English modulo *do*-support vs. pronunciation of the lexical verb. I have analyzed the PCC as a VP fronting process. We thus expect the same abstract patterning between English and Russian to take place with VP fronting in English. This prediction is borne out. Compare (1) with (23a) and (12c) with (23b).

(23) a. √ John said he would read the book and read the book he **did**.
b. √John promised that the house would be built, and built it was.

---

[13] The source of these examples is Stepanov (1998a). He argues in detail that these examples involve VP ellipsis.

The reason why there is a second copy of the verb in (1) is clear now: to support the inflectional affix in Infl. The pronunciation of the first occurrence of the verb in the moved VP is forced because semantically, it carries the focus, which needs an audible exponent.

A full discussion of an algorithm for pronunciation of moved elements and of the conditions under which multiple copies can be pronounced is beyond the scope of this paper. A number of suggestions exist in the literature (Franks 1998, Bošković 1999, Nunes 1999, Abels 2000).

Note that I have talked about two "copies" of the verb. However, the two instances of the verb are not strictly identical; morphologically one is an infinitive and the other a finite form. Calling these two forms copies of the same lexical element requires a theory of morphology in which lexical items are not inserted into the syntax fully inflected, i.e. a theory assuming actual inflectional affixes, and where lexical insertion takes place late, after the syntax. Consequently, the analysis presented here requires some form of Distributed Morphology (Halle and Marantz 1993). The infinitive occurs as the realization of the default form of the verb.[14]

Indirect evidence that this reasoning is correct comes from the following paradigm where there is an aspectual mismatch between the infinitival in the *Head* and the *Finite Verb* (24a, b).

(24) a. * Čitat' (-to) on eë pročitaet...
  read$_{inf}$ TO he it$_{fem.acc}$ perf-reads
 b. ** Pročitat' (-to) on eë čitaet...
  read$_{perf.inf}$ TO he it$_{fem.acc}$ reads

On the assumption that the aspectual prefix *pro-* heads its own verbal projection in the syntax (see e.g. Fowler 1994) and merges with the verb in the morphology, (24a) is a simple violation of a pied-piping requirement. (24b), on the other hand, is not derivable at all. The principle of Distributed Morphology to insert an element which is maximally specific, compatible with the information present, and never

---

[14] As it stands we actually expect the bare verbal stem to appear in the PCC. However, this is not an option, since the bare stem realizes the imperative in Russian and can otherwise occur only in a limited number of marked constructions. It seems that the bare stem is more marked than the infinitive. I would like to thank Steven Franks (p.c.) for reminding me of these facts.

more specific than the information present in the syntactic tree would have to be violated. This is reflected in the judgments.[15]

In this section we have seen that the movement analysis of the PCC provides indirect arguments for the copy theory of movement and for Distributed Morphology.

5 The PCC, Verb Movement and Object Shift

In this section I will address some examples that seem to undermine the analysis developed so far. The idea that the PCC is derived via VP movement was justified on the basis of examples like (9) and (17a). The *Head* of the cleft indeed looks like a VP in those examples.

However, the examples with nominal complements of the verb (including (1) repeated as (25a)) are systematically not of this general form. DP complements are never part of the *Head* -- at least for the speaker consulted.

(25) a. √ Čitat' (-to) Ivan eë čitaet, no ...
     read$_{inf}$ TO Ivan it$_{fem.acc}$ reads but...
   b. * Čitat' eë (-to) Ivan (eë) čitaet (eë), no
     read$_{inf}$ it$_{fem.acc}$ TO Ivan it$_{fem.acc}$ reads it$_{fem.acc}$ but...
   'Ivan does read it, but he doesn't understand a thing.'

Example (25b) illustrates two points: DP arguments behave like other arguments in that they cannot be doubled; DP arguments are never part of the *Head* of the predicate cleft. The object in this example is pronominalized, but the same kind of pattern holds with full DPs. This pattern is understandable only if the fronted VP is a remnant in (25a). What prompts the DPs to evacuate VP?

One important observation with respect to DP complements is that they cannot be indefinite, as shown in (26).[16]

---

[15] Catherine Chvany (p.c.) points out the following examples:

(i) √est'/*byt' -to on est'...
    is$_{3sg}$/BE$_{inf}$ TO he is...

This example can be accommodated if *byt'* is not the infinitive of *est'* (see Chvany 1996 for discussion of the relevance of this conclusion).

[16] Laurent Dekydtspotter (p.c.) informs me that a similar ban on indefinites is found with the PCC in other languages, too. Judgments vary on the status of (26).

(26) * Čitat' (-to) on kakuju-nibud' knigu čitaet,...
read$_{inf}$ TO he which-NIBUD' book reads,...
'He is reading some book or other, ...'

This fact should not surprise us, since the ban on indefinite arguments follows from the semantics, as pointed out above. To explain why the moved VP is always a remnant, I am led to conjecture that object shift/Case checking is obligatorily overt in Russian. The verb can, but need not move past this object shift position.[17] Whether indefinite objects move to the same position overtly to get Case must be left open here.

Finally, there is another class of examples where the internal argument of a verb is not fronted along with the verb itself, but where we cannot invoke object shift or movement to a Case position as an explanation.

(27) ? Dumat' (-to) on dumaet o pesni, kotoruju pel
think TO he thinks about song which sang
Ivan...
Ivan...
'He does think about the song that Ivan sang, but...'

(28) ? Dumat' (-to) on dumaet čto Xomskij genij no...
think$_{inf}$ TO he thinks that Chomsky genius but...
'He does think that Chomsky is a genius, but...'

Comparing (27) and (28), which, according to Michael Yadroff (p.c.), are perfect if a pause precedes the complement, with the corresponding examples (16a), (16b) and (10) reveals that it is heaviness that allows the complements to appear in final position.

---

[17] It is uncontroversial that there is a certain amount of verb movement in Russian. Just how far the verb moves is unclear. We have already seen some evidence that the verb does indeed leave its base position in Stepanov's VP-ellipsis examples in (22). Further evidence that the verb sometimes moves as high as %P comes from the fact that a yes/no question can be answered in Russian by repeating just the verb and eliding everything else. Martins (1994) argues that this indicates that the verb is in %P and IP is deleted. Finally, John Bailyn (p.c.) points out that the order VS with unergative sentences is most plausibly derived by assuming that the verb moves past the base position of the subject in these sentences. This would entail that the verb moves past the base position of the subject (contra Bailyn 1995).

In this section we have seen that the movement analysis argued for in this paper leads us to conclude that object shift/overt Case checking (at least with definite DPs) is obligatory in Russian and that the verb can optionally move past the object shift position or stay below it.

6 Conclusion

In this paper the basic data concerning the predicate cleft construction in Russian were introduced. The following structure was defended:

(13) $[_{CP} \ldots [_{XP} [_{VP} \ldots V_{inf} \ldots] \ldots [\text{-to} \ldots [_{IP} \ldots V_{fin} \ldots]]]$

The construction was accounted for as an instance of remnant VP movement. This analysis is justified because a whole range of chain properties hold of the PCC: locality constraints, identity of theta relations, identity of content, etc. It was further concluded that object shift/Case movement is obligatorily overt for Russian definite DPs and that the verb optionally moves past this object shift/Case position. The fact that in predicate clefts with synthetic verb forms, two occurrences of the verb appear provides a strong argument for the copy theory of movement. The fact that the two copies of the verb differ morphologically was taken as an argument for late lexical insertion and for a model of morphology along the lines of Distributed Morphology.

References

Abels, Klaus. (2000) "Move?" Ms., U. of Connecticut.
Bailyn, John F. (1995) "Underlying Phrase Structure and 'Short' Verb Movement in Russian." *Journal of Slavic Linguistics* 3(1): 13–58.
Bošković, Željko. (1999a) "What is special about multiple Wh-fronting." Paper presented at NELS 1999.
Bošković, Željko. (1999b) *On the Syntax Phonology Interface—Clitics in South Slavic*. Ms. University of Connecticut.
Büring, Daniel. (1995) *The 59th-Street Bridge Accent—On the Meaning of Topic and Focus*. Ph.D. dissertation, U. Tübingen.
Chomsky, Noam. (1993) "A Minimalist Program for Linguistic Theory." Hale and Keyser, eds., 1–52.

Chomsky, Noam. (1995) *The Minimalist Program.* Cambridge, MA: MIT Press.

Chomsky, Noam. (1998) *Minimalist Inquiries: The Framework.* Cambridge, MA: MITWPL. (MIT Occasional Papers in Linguistics, 15.)

Chomsky, Noam. (1999) *Derivation by Phase.* Cambridge, MA: MITWPL. (MIT Occasional Papers in Linguistics, 18.)

Chvany, Catherine V. (1996) "Syntactic Accessibility and Lexical Storage: The distribution of the Russian infinitive Form 'moč" and Its Theoretical Implications." Olga T. Yokoyama and Emily Klenin, eds. *Selected Essays of Chatherine V. Chvany.* Columbus, OH: Slavica.

Epstein, Samuel D. et al. (1998) *A Derivational Approach to Syntactic Relations.* Oxford: Oxford University Press.

Fowler, George. (1994) "Verbal Prefixes as Functional Heads." *Studies in the Linguistic Sciences* 24(1–2), 171–85.

Franks, Steven. (1998) "Clitics in Slavic." Position Paper presented at the *Comparative Slavic Morphosyntax Workshop.* (http://www.indiana.edu/~slavconf/linguistics/index.html)

Franks, Steven and Richard House. (1982) "Genitive Themes in Russian." *Papers from the Regional Meeting of the Chicago Linguistics Society.* 156–68.

Hale, Ken and Jay Keyser, eds. (1993): *The View from Building 20.* Cambridge, MA: MIT Press.

Halle, Morris and Alec Marantz. (1993) "Distributed Morphology and the Pieces of Inflection." Hale and Keyser, eds., 111–76.

Institut Jazykoznanija–Akademia nauk SSSR. (1960) *Grammatika Russkogo Jazyka.* Moscow: Izd-vo Akademii Nauk.

Jackendoff, Ray. (1972) *Semantic Interpretation in Generative Grammar.* Cambridge, MA: MIT Press.

King, Tracy. H. (1995) *Configuring Topic and Focus in Russian.* Stanford, CA: CSLI Publications.

Koopman, Hilda. (1984) *The Syntax of Verbs.* Dordrecht: Foris.

Larson, Richard K. and Claire Lefebvre. (1991) "Predicate Clefting in Haitian Creole." Proceedings of NELS 21, 247–61.

Lumsden, John S. and Claire Lefebvre. (1990) "Predicate Cleft Constructions and Why They Aren't What You Might Think." *Linguistics* 28(4), 761–83.

Martins, Ana-Maria. (1994) "Enclisis, VP-deletion and the nature of Sigma." *Probus* 6(2–3), 173–205.

Nunes, Jairo. (1995) *The Copy Theory of Movement and Linearization of Chains in the Minimalist Program.* Ph.D. dissertation, U. of Maryland.

Nunes, Jairo. (1996) "On why traces can't be phonetically realized." Proceedings of NELS 26, 211–25.

Nunes, Jairo. (1999) *Linearization of Chains In the Phonological Component and Phonetic Realization of Traces.* Ms., Universidade Estadual de Campignas.

Paillard, Denis and Vladimir A. Plungjan. (1993) "Ob odnom tipe konstrukcij s povorotom glagola v Russkom jazyke." *Russian Linguistics* 17(3), 263–77.

Pollock, Jean-Yves. (1989) "Verb Movement, Universal Grammar, and the Structure of IP." *Linguistic Inquiry* 20(3), 365–424.

Richards, Norvin W. III. (1997) *What Moves Where When in Which Language?* Ph.D. dissertation, MIT.

Stepanov, Arthur. (1998a) "Preliminary Remarks on VP Ellipsis in Russian." Ms., U. of Connecticut.

Stepanov, Arthur. (1998b) "On Wh-Fronting in Russian." Proceedings of NELS 28, 453–67.

Stjepanović, Sandra. (1995) "Short Distance Movement of wh-phrases in Serbo-Croatian Matrix clauses." Ms., U. of Connecticut.

Klaus Abels
Department of Linguistics U-1145
341 Mansfield Road
Storrs, CT 06269
klaus.abels@uconn.edu

Prosodic Movement and Information Focus in Bulgarian*

Olga Arnaudova
University of Ottawa

In this paper, I discuss neutral information focus and Prosodic Movement in Bulgarian. Prosodic Movement is an important tool for encoding focus whenever an item does not carry focus by base generation and is not contrastively focused.

Recent studies (Cinque 1993, Reinhart 1995, Kiss 1998, Zubizarreta 1998) stress the necessity of differentiating between two focus types/strategies, which I will refer to in this paper as *contrastive* and *information* focus. The need to distinguish them reflects a number of differences. There are first of all the interpretative differences: information focus (also called sometimes presentational) is defined as not context-construable (Rochemont 1986) and permits "spreading" of the focus feature, while contrastive focus is often associated with focus particles such as *only* and involves the exclusion of contextually given alternatives. The distinction between contrastive and information focus has also a syntactic dimension: contrastive foci[1] involve chains containing a variable and a feature checking mechanism (Cinque 1990, Rizzi 1997, Kiss 1998) while information foci are interpreted *in situ*. In addition, there is a prosodic difference: information foci use neutral intonation, while contrastive foci are governed by a separate stress rule. Finally, in some languages, such as Spanish and Italian, information foci

---

* I am indebted to María-Luisa Rivero for discussions and suggestions, which have substantially improved the quality of this paper. I thank the editors of this volume, as well as the participants at FASL-9, and in particular, Steven Franks, Tracy Holloway King, Wayles Browne, and Eva Hajičová for their useful comments. All errors remain my own. The preparation of this paper is supported by SSHRC research grants 410-97-0242 / 410-2000-0120 to M.-L. Rivero.

[1] "Identificational focus" in Kiss' terms. In sentences with information focus, I show the stress on the relevant syllable by using capital letters, and to show contrastive focus, I use bold characters. See also the appendix for the F0 contours of the relevant sentences. I thank Jon Wood for his help with extracting the F0 contours.

trigger prosodic movements, which affect the interpretation of the sentence (Zubizarreta 1998, Guasti and Nespor 1998). I claim on the basis of Bulgarian that investigating focus by keeping in mind these distinctive properties is a fruitful enterprise for Slavic. Prosodic Movement (PrM) is shown to be operative in Bulgarian as a non-feature checking process that applies whenever focus and intonation disagree in sentences with neutral intonation.

This paper is organized as follows. In section 1, I outline the semantic properties of Information Focus (IF) and Contrastive Focus (CF) as applied to Bulgarian (Bg), and show the syntactic representation of CF. Inspired by Kiss 1998, I argue that CF in Bg is optionally strong or weak. The existence of contrastive foci with different settings, strong and weak, accounts for the availability of preverbal focused subjects in Bg, which can be used in weak/strong contrastive environments. This accounts for the fact that they can serve as answers to *wh*-questions.

I claim that contrastive foci involve a derivation involving the presence of a functional phrase in the numeration (most likely ΣP, as in Laka 1990 who proposed such a phrase for Negation and (emphatic) affirmation).

In section 2, I discuss IF and PrM in more detail. I present the Nuclear Stress Rule and the Focus Prosody Correspondence Rule, which are responsible for the licensing of information focus in syntax. Prosodic Movement fixes discrepancies between the neutral stress created by the Nuclear Stress Rule and the Focus Prosody Correspondence Principle. I show that PrM has in Bg (at least) two varieties: it applies to derive V-O-S/O-V-S orders and V-PP-O orders. Following Zubizarreta, I propose that PrM occurs because of the need of a constituent to become metrically invisible and of another constituent to receive phonological and semantic prominence.

The analysis developed here accounts for the many positions in which subjects can surface in Bulgarian. For example, post-verbal subjects, when focused, trigger PrM, deriving V-O-S and O-V-S constructions with a metrically invisible object.

Finally, in section 3, I contrast PrM with stylistic movements (Rivero 1994, 1998) occurring in the PF branch of the grammar, such as preposing to *li* in *yes-no* questions. Conclusions are given in section 4.

1. Information Focus and Strong/Weak Contrastive Focus

In this section, I present the semantic differences between information focus and strong/weak contrastive focus. Then, I discuss the syntactic representation of contrastive focus. I propose that with Contrastive Focus, a functional head associated with emphasis/negation is projected in syntax.

The semantic representation of focus is captured by relating focus to presupposition, which is understood as the shared assumptions of the speaker and the hearer (Jackendoff 1972, Rooth 1985, Hajičová, Partee and Sgall 1998, and Zubizarreta 1998). In Zubizarreta 1998, the representation includes hierarchically ordered assertions which are not part of the syntactic or LF component (e.g. by a 'tree splitting' mechanism as in Diesing 1992) but are represented at an abstract interpretative post-syntactic, post-LF level, called Assertion Structure.

1.1. Information Focus

"[Information Focus] simply marks the non-presupposed nature of the information it carries." (Kiss 1998:248). It can be represented in terms of two assertions. The first assertion introduces a variable x, which is found in a presupposed set (= Restrictor, Hajičová, Partee and Sgall 1998), while the second provides an equation relation between the variable defined in the first assertion and a value (=Nuclear scope, Hajičová, Partee and Sgall 1998).

The value assigned in the second assertion is not contrasted with another set of alternative entities and constitutes an existential closure over the free variable in the Restrictor part. In the framework of Rochemont (1986) it is defined as not c(ontext) construable.[2]

Consider now (1). In (1), the subject *Marija* is not contrasted with another potential candidate for the value, and the Restrictor is the presupposition that somebody read the book (free variable).

---

[2] According to Rooth 1985, with focus, an alternative set is always present, which in my view is the case only with contrastive focus. Rooth 1986 however does not include in his study sentences with 'free' focus, e.g., without overt focalizers such as *only*.

(1) Koj pročete knigata?/Who read the book?
Pročete knigata [F MaRIja] V-O-S (PrM)
read-Past book-the Marija
'MARIJA read the book'

Assertion 1: there is an x, such that x read the book

Assertion 2: x = "Marija"

I claim that this sentence involves PrM and the VOS order is derived from a VSO order by scrambling of the object to the left (see section 2 for more details). To anticipate the discussion, one of the characteristics of PrM is the narrow information focus found on the item that is focused (*Marija* in this case). There is no focus ambiguity and the sentence tolerates a list reading.[3] As a result of the PrM, the Nuclear Stress falls on *Marija* rather than on the object *knigata* (the intonation of this sentence is shown in the appendix: figure 1)

In (2a), the focus domain includes the object 'knigata' (2a), or, alternatively, the entire sentence (2b). The possibility of "expanding" the focus domain, as in (2a) vs. (2b) is known as 'focus spreading' or 'focus projection' (see Selkirk 1984 for discussion and section 2). In this paper, I will use the more neutral term "focus ambiguity".

(2) a. Kakvo pročete?/ What did he/she read?
Pročete [F KNIgata.]
read-Past book-the
'He/she read the book'

Assertion 1: there is an x, such that he/she read it.

Assertion 2: x = "book"

---

[3] Nothing prevents the narrow focused subject from being contrasted *later* with a set, as shown in (i).

(i) Pročete knigata Ivan. A ne Ilijan.
read book-the Ivan. And not Ilijan
"IVAN read the book, and not Ilijan."

According to native speakers of Bulgarian, in (ii), *Ivan* carries a non-exhaustive list reading. Therefore, other values (such as *Petâr*) satisfy the variable:

(ii) Pročete knigata Ivan, a sašto Petâr i Ilian i....
read the book Ivan, as well as Peter, Ilijan, and...
"IVAN read the book, and Peter, and Ilijan, and... also read it."

(2) b. Kakvo se sluči? Kakvo napravi?/What happened?/What did he/she do?
[$_F$ Pročete KNIgata]
read-Past book-the
'He/she read the book'

Assertion 1: there is an x, such that it happened.

Assertion 2: x= "(he/she) read the book"

Consider now (3). (3a) and (3b) have a complex topic containing two elements (*Marija, knigata*) and the focus is the entire CP (*ja pročete / pročete ja*[4]), as in (2b). In this case, the complex topic is the subject of the propositional predicate (the comment) and can be either to the left or to the right.

(3) Kakvo stana s Marija i s knigata? What happened to the book and Marija?

	S-O-Cl-V:	COMPLEX TOPIC		COMMENT(=FOCUSED CP)	
a.		Marija	knigata	[$_{IF}$ ja	proČEte]
		Marija	book-the	CL$_{Acc}$	read-Past
	V-Cl-S-O:	COMMENT (=FOCUSED CP)		COMPLEX TOPIC	
b.		[$_{IF}$ ProČEte	ja]	Marija	knigata
		read-Past	CL$_{Acc}$	Marija	book-the

'As for Marija and the book, she READ it.'

Assertion 1: Ivan (y), knigata (z)\ there is an x, such that y did z.

Assertion 2: Ivan (y), knigata (z)\ x (such that y did z)="read (it)"

1.2. Contrastive Focus

CF can have different settings across languages. Here strong contrastive focus corresponds to Kiss' [+contrastive] and weak contrastive focus to her [−contrastive]. With *strong* CF there exists a specified, closed (singleton or otherwise) set of alternative values, while *weak* contrastive focus, sometimes called 'restrictive' focus (Erteschik-Shir 1997), presupposes an unspecified (open) set of alternative values. The values

---

[4] The preposing of the verb to the clitic is a stylistic PF process, discussed more recently in Rivero 1998. I briefly discuss this process in comparison with Prosodic Movement in section 3.

found in the alternative set are then negated and another value is assigned, or no value is assigned at all (if a negative quantifier is used).[5] Alternatively, we can say that the value is selected by "exclusion" (see Kenesei 1997 and Kiss 1998 for discussion). To capture this I propose to include two additional assertions: one, which is the exclusion function negating the value assigned in the alternative set (Assertion 3), and one, selecting a new value (Assertion 4). This is shown in (4).

(4) Koj (li) čete knigata?Who (on earth) is reading the book?
(unrestricted set: "y")
Ivan li čete knigata? /Is it Ivan who is reading the book?
(restricted set: "Ivan")

[F **Marija**] čete knigata (ne Ivan/ne njakoj drug)
Marija reads book-the (not Ivan/not anyone else)
'It is Marija who is reading the book.'

| Assertion 1: there is an x such that x reads the book. |
| Assertion 2: x = "y"/ "Ivan" |
| Assertion 3: x is not "Ivan"/not "y" |

| Assertion 4: x = "Marija" |

Interestingly, contrastively focused subjects in Romance have only a strong setting; the alternative set in this language is always closed and normally contains one or two values. The sentence in (5) cannot be used in fact as an answer to a *wh*-question and is felicitous only when an exclusion function can apply to a closed set of potential members for the value:

(5) *Who ate an apple? Did Piero eat an apple?
[F **Gianni**] ha mangiato una mela (non Piero). Italian
Gianni has eaten an apple (not Piero)
'It was Gianni who ate an apple.'

One of the benefits of adopting different settings for contrastive focus along the lines proposed here is the possibility of uniting preverbal

---

[5] The main difference between IF and is the fact that in the case of IF an alternative set does not exist. The claim advanced here is that in Bulgarian, preverbal focused subjects, as in (4), (and preverbal focused objects (not shown here)) are contrastive foci, as suggested by the cleft constructions in the English translation.

focused subjects across languages under the strategy of contrastive focus. To compare, preverbal focused subjects are analyzed in Zubizarreta 1998 as information foci for English/Germanic but as contrastive foci for Romance. Zubizarreta claims that all the material following the focused subject in English/Germanic is 'invisible', that way escaping the effects of the Nuclear Stress Rule (see next section). According to the hypothesis outlined here, some languages have only a strong contrastive focus setting (such as Italian), while others use both strong and weak settings (such as Hungarian, Bulgarian, and probably other Slavic languages, such as Russian). If we adopt this view, invisibility is not needed and can be reformulated in terms of a weak contrastive setting.

The interpretative differences between IF and CF outlined above are complemented by a different syntactic licensing. In the case of CF, I propose that a focus phrase with uninterpretable features attracts an item in the computation that bears compatible semantic features. In the literature, *li* particles have been primary candidates for carrying a focus feature in the Bulgarian sentence (see Rudin 1985, Rudin et al, 1998, a. o). Krapova and Karastaneva 1999 and Izvorski 1994 propose that *li* is heading a separate functional phrase from the rest of the complementizer positions. I adopt the proposal outlined in Krapova and Karastaneva that focus phrases are located under the phrase hosting *li* (which they claim is the head of a ForceP). In my view, preposing to *li* does not involve checking of a focus feature, e.g. *li* is not a focus particle. Preposing to *li* is a stylistic process as argued in Rivero 1998 (see also section 3 of this paper) and *li* is a question marker. There is evidence that the focus phrase might be identical to ΣP (as in Laka 1990 where ΣP hosts both negative and emphatic elements). The overt marker of negation *ne* is the head of ΣP in negative contexts. ΣP has a strong EPP feature (in the sense of Chomsky 1999) that attracts an element with compatible semantic features in the computation, as shown in (6) and (7).[6]

---

[6] Note that in sentences where both a focused constituent and the negative marker *ne* are present, the stress falls on the focused constituent and not *ne*, contrary to the rule for stress assignment in *ne*-constructions described in Rudin et al. 1998, which states that *ne* always attracts the stress. As shown in the appendix (figures 2, 3 and 4), the stress pattern with constrastively focused XPs and with negated XPs is very similar, with the prominent element being the contrastively focused item in all the cases, regardless of the nature of the element (subject or object) or of the presence of *ne*.

(6) **Marija** ne e pročela knigata
    Marija Neg Aux read-Part book-the
    'It is Mary who didn't read the book.'

(7) **Marija** e pročela knigata.
    Marija Aux read-Part book-the
    'It is Mary who read the book.'

In the presence of contrastive foci (either strong or weak), PrM does not occur because the sentence stress is always attracted by the focused element and the Nuclear Stress Rule, as defined in the next section, does not apply. As I will show below, PrM is directly related to the application of the Nuclear Stress Rule and its interaction with information focus.

2. Information Focus, Nuclear Stress Rule, and Prosodic Movement

The default sentential stress[7] in sentences with IF is computed by a rule, known as the Nuclear Stress Rule (NSR), which was first formulated for English in Chomsky and Halle 1968. More recently, the NSR has been revived as a syntactic rule, which applies by taking into account debt of embedding (Cinque 1993) and asymmetric c-command ordering (Zubizarreta 1998).[8] I adopt the definition given in (8):

(8) *Nuclear Stress Rule (NSR)*
    The lowest constituent in the asymmetric c command ordering in the phrase bears the intonational nucleus (= Nuclear stress) of that phrase.

The Focus-Prosody Correspondence Principle in (9) independently accounts for the fact that Nuclear stress and (semantic/discourse) focus correlate (see Chomsky 1971).

---

[7] The distinction between neutral ("attentional") and "intentional" intonation is outlined in Pierrehumbert & Hirschberg 1996. Tilkov 1981 distinguishes for Bulgarian between "phrasovo udarenie" (phrasal stress) and "logičesko udarenie" (logical stress).

[8] Selkirk 1984 assigns phonological stress only at PF ('late NSR') and the focus marked constituent 'informs' the stress formation. In her framework, PrM could not be explained since syntax and phonology do not interact. When PF is reached, it is too late for syntax to do any revisions and constructions involving PrM cannot be explained.

(9) *Focus–Prosody Correspondence Principle (FPCP)*
The focus-marked constituent of a phrase must contain the word carrying the intonational nucleus of that phrase.

When the FPCP is satisfied, no Prosodic Movement will be needed. Prosodic Movement is a last resort operation, which ensures that the FPCP is not violated.

For Bulgarian, I adopt the general clause structure given in Rivero (1988/1994) which is shared by other Balkan languages such as Greek and Albanian, and, in addition, I argue for a recursive CP (see Rizzi 1997 for Italian and Krapova and Karastaneva 1999 for Bulgarian). In transitive constructions, the subject is in Spec,vP and the object is the complement of the VP. The structure is given in (10). External Topics are dislocated in a CLLD position and at least some internal topics are subsumed under the mechanism of PrM, discussed later:

(10) [CLLD (Subject) [CP če [ForceP li [FocP ne [MoodP da/šte [TP V₁ [... [(Subject) [vP [VP t₁ [Obj]]]]]]]]

When PrM takes place, the object can adjoin to a spec of vP, which I assume is higher than the Spec containing the subject. The nominal (Case and Agreement) features on the substantive categories, the subject located in Spec,vP and the object, are checked by Agree in situ. This can be exemplified by the contrast between (11a) and (11b). In (11a), which is ungrammatical, the subject intervenes between a fronted *wh*-phrase and the verb, e.g., has raised, while in (11b) it surfaces in its base position in spec,vP and the sentence is grammatical. In (11c), which is also grammatical, the subject precedes the wh-phrase, and according to the structure proposed in (10) is base-generated above CP in a CLLD dislocated position.

(11) a. *Kogo Marija vidja?
       whom Marija saw
    b. Kogo vidja Marija?
       whom saw Marija
       'Whom did Marija see?'
    c. Marija, kogo vidja?
       Marija whom saw
       'As of Marija, whom did she see?'

Subjects following contrastive foci, and preceding the verb, as in (12a), are also unacceptable. In my view, this is because subjects have to stay in their base-generated position in Spec,vP (12b).[9] Alternatively, subjects are found in a CLLD position, as in (12c):

(12) a. *Tazi   izložba   Milena   poseti.
　　　　　this   exhibition Milena   visited
　　b. **Tazi**   **izložba**   poseti   Milena.
　　　　This   exhibition visited Milena
　　　'This is the exhibition Milena visited.'
　　c. Milena, **tazi** **izložba**   poseti.
　　　　Milena this   exhibition   visited
　　　'As of Milena, it is this exhibition she visited.'

The phi-features on T (the probe) (Chomsky 1999) remove the case feature on subject (the goal) by the operation Agree, and the light v checks the nominal features of the object. I adopt the idea that the EPP-feature of Tense is checked in some languages by the strong inflectional affix on the verb (Alexiadou and Anagnostopoulou 1998). Crucially, there is no movement of the subject to T to satisfy the EPP or any other condition imposed by T. The verb raises overtly to T for two reasons: to satisfy the EPP and to check the feature on Tense. From this it follows that all preverbal subjects are either dislocated or associated with a projection for negated and contrastively focused elements.[10]

With intransitives, the subject stays in its base position (Spec,vP), and receives sentential stress by the NSR (13). The sentence can have

---

[9] Additional evidence for the fact that subjects are not in Spec,TP is provided by the fact that a number of adverbs can intervene between the subject and the verb:

(i) Petâr včera sled mnogo dâlgi usilija uspja da se spravi s problema.
Peter yesterday after many long efforts managed DA solve problem-the
　"Yesterday, after many long efforts, Peter managed to solve the problem."

If we assume that the verb raises obligatorily to T, the presence of these adverbs cannot be accounted for, if subjects are in Spec, TP.

[10] SVO orders, which are common in Bg, have prompted some authors to claim that subjects in Bulgarian (optionally) raise to Spec,IP (TP) (Motapanyane 1997, Penchev 1998). A VSO treatment for Bg is proposed in King 1994 and Izvorski 1994. Dimitrova-Vulchanova & Hellan 1998 argue that Bulgarian is a VOS language taking as a basic order the one I claim here to be derived by prosodic movement from a VSO structure. The proposal developed here accommodates these various views.

either a narrow scope focus on the subject or a wide-focus scope (shown in the context questions), e.g., it can be used in two contexts:

(13) Koj dojde?/Who came?
Kakvo stana/se sluči? /What happened?
[IF Dojde [IF IVAN]]. V-S
came Ivan.
'IVAN came.'/ 'There came Ivan'

In V-S-O constructions, the object, the lowest element in the c-command ordering, receives the NSR and when it is the actual focus of the sentence, the FPCP will be not violated, as expected. This is shown in (14). When the object is focus marked, it can become the IF of the sentence since then it is contained within the intonational nucleus of the sentence (as the FPCP requires); the CP, when focused, also contains the focus exponent (the object) and the FPCP is satisfied. Note that the subject or the verb in isolation, however, are not permissible information foci, i.e., are not part of the focus set in the sense of Reinhart (1995) because they are not contained within the focus exponent and the FPCP, as a result, cannot be satisfied. Therefore, (15c) and (15d) are not possible continuations of (14), while (15a) and (15b) are.

(14) [F Kupi Marija [F KNIgata]] V-S-O
buy-Past Marija book-the
'Marija read the book.'

(15) a. ... a ne CD-to (and not the CD)
b. ... a ne stana nešto drugo (and it is not the case that something else happened)
c. ... *a ne Ivan (and not Ivan)
d. ... *a ne ja izprati (and she did not send it)

In order to become the (information) focus of the sentence, a subject has to resort to the mechanism of PrM. PrM functions as a focus device so that the neutral intonation can (re)select the subject as the focus of the sentence.[11] The focus obtained through PrM is narrow, i.e., the other elements in the sentence cannot constitute a focus domain. The objects in

---

[11] See figures 1 and 2 in the appendix. The last pitch accent has a H*L pattern, and is the Nuclear stress. The sentence in figure 6 is the basic structure without prosodic movement, where the Nuclear stress is carried by the object *knigata*.

(16a) and (16b) prepose to a higher domain, which is invisible to the NSR:

(16) Koj ste pročete knigata?/ Who will read the book?
??Kakvo šte stane?/??What will happen?
   a. Šte pročete knigata [$_{IF}$ MaRIja]   V-S-O
       fut read book-the   Marija
   b. Knigata šte pročete [$_{IF}$ MaRIja]   O-V-S
       book fut read   Marija
       'MARIJA will read the book.'

I propose a leftward adjunction of the object to vP for (16a), and, to MoodP, for (16b).[12] In both cases, the subject remains *in situ* (Spec, vP), where it checks its features and receives Nuclear stress. The structure for (16) is given in (17).

(17)

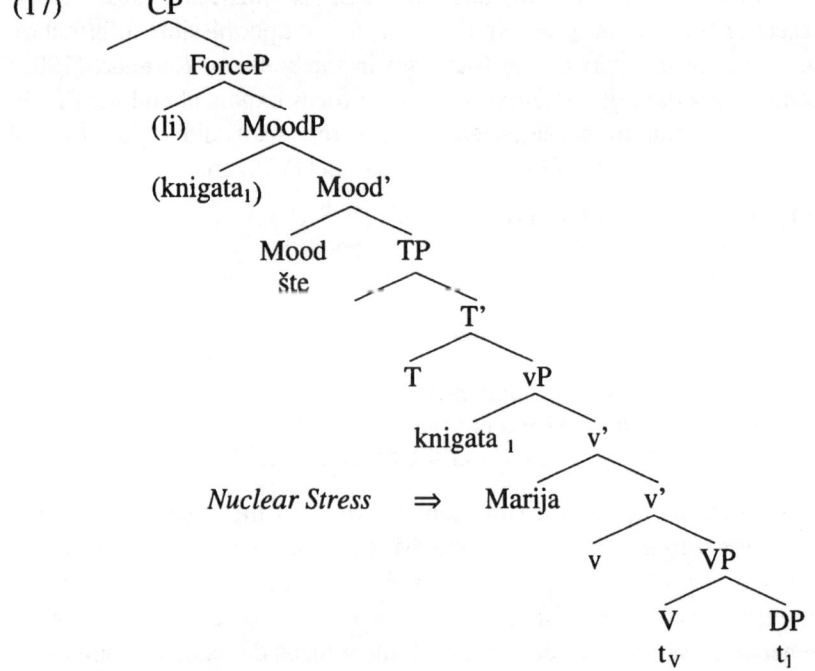

---

[12] The movement of the object to MoodP can also be argued to occur for an independent reason (see Arnaudova 1999)

The fact that the subject is c-commanded by the object can be determined by binding evidence (WCO effects), shown in the contrast between (18a) and (18b): in (18a) the quantified object can be co-referent with the possessive *negovata*, while in (18b), where no PrM has occurred, this binding possibility is not available:

(18) a. Izprati   [vsjako dete]$_i$ negovata$_i$ majka.   PrM
        accompanied each child   his   mother
     b. Izprati   negovata $_{(*i)}$ majka   [vsjako dete]$_i$
        accompanied his   mother   each child.
        'His mother accompanied each child.'

This also shows that subject right-adjunction is not a feasible analysis for (18a) since it would not explain why the binding relations in (18a) would differ from those in (18b).

The movement of the object, as in (16b) above, is traditionally analyzed as a 'topicalization' rather than a focalization device (see King 1994 for discussion). As shown above, "topicalization" in Bg has an effect on focus and should be reexamined. I leave for future research to determine if the triggering force for "topicalization" is in some way directly related to focus and the FPCP outlined above.

In Bulgarian, PrM can also occur in constructions with an initial V-O-PP order[13] when the PP is not focused. The resulting structure is V-PP-O,[14] as in (19). The structure for (19) is given in (20).

---

[13] Prosodic Movement is found also in double object constructions, not discussed here (for examples, see Arnaudova, in press).

[14] There are cases where instead of prosodic movement, a non-focal PP or DP stays in situ (*na masata* in (i) and *knigata* in (ii)) after the focused element:

(i) Kakvo složi na masata?/What did you put on the table?
    Složix   **knigata** na masata.
    put- Past   book-the on table-the
    'On the table, I put the book.'
(ii) Koj pročete knigata?/Who read the book?
     Pročete   **Marija**   knigata.
     read-Past Marija book-the
     "MARIJA read the book."/As for the book, MARIJA read it."

If we propose that prosodic movement alternates with metrical invisibility, as Zubizarreta 1998 proposes for French, then Bulgarian will be exactly like French in this respect. Alternatively, anaphoric DPs can be claimed to be dislocated (as in Spanish). Another

(19) Kakvo složi na masata?/What did you put on the table?
Kakvo stana/se sluči?/*What happened?
Složix   [na masata]₁ ximiKALkata t_i.   PrM
(I) put-Past   on the table   pen-the
'I put THE PEN on the table.'

(20)

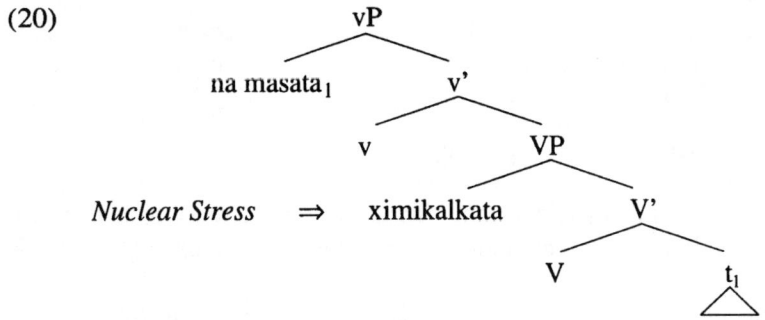

To conclude, Prosodic Movement is a local scrambling operation within the vP which ensures that the Focus Prosody Correspondence Principle is not violated. As discussed, Prosodic Movement is a last resort operation, and is found in Bulgarian in a variety of constructions, such as V-O-S and V-PP-O orders. It selects a focus, which is not initially included in the initial focus set. Binding evidence shows that it has an effect on LF. Therefore we have to postulate that Prosodic Movement occurs before the computation splits into PF and Assertion structure, which is an interpretative level different from LF (see Arnaudova 1999 and Arnaudova, in press for more details).

In the next section I will contrast PrM with stylistic movements, which do not affect LF and occur only when the PF branch is reached.

3. Prosodic Movement and Stylistic Movement to *li*

As already discussed above, in *li*-constructions, such as (21), *li* does not host the focus features but is the head of a ForceP. Note the absence of *li* in declarative contrastive focus constructions, such as (22), which is an indication that focus features are not an intrinsic part of *li*, but reside elsewhere in the sentence.

---

possibility, which seems viable is that in this case the focus is contrastive/emphatic *in situ*, rather than informational (with a weak contrastive setting). I will leave the issue open for further research.

(21) **Marija** li pročete knigata?
　　　Marija Q read-Past book-the
　　　'Was it Mary who read the book?'

(22) **Marija** pročete knigata.
　　　Marija read-Past the book
　　　'It was Mary who read the book.'

In a series of papers, (see most recently Rivero 1998), Rivero discusses movements in which elements, such as the verb in (23), prepose to *li* in order to satisfy interface conditions and not to check formal features. Movements of this type are hierarchical (see Rivero 1998 for examples and discussion) but apply only in the 'pure' PF branch. They do not have in fact any impact on LF.

(23) Pročete li knigata Marija?
　　　read-Past Q book-the Marija
　　　'Did Marija read the book?'

Consider also the fact that *li* can also appear in sentences such as (24):

(24) Ivan utre šte dojde li?
　　　Ivan tomorrow fut come Q
　　　'Will Ivan come tomorrow?'

In (23) and (24), the entire sentence carries information focus and the focus interpretation does is not dependent on the presence of *li*.

Prosodic Movement, as discussed in the previous section, has in common with stylistic movements the fact, that they both do not check features. The major difference between prosodic and stylistic movement, is however that PrM occurs in the syntactic component in conjunction with a stress related PF rule (NSR) and has impact on LF, while stylistic movements occur in the PF branch of the derivation.

4. Conclusions

On the basis of Bulgarian, I argue that each sentence has a focus structure. Focus is computed in syntax in connection with a PF stress rule, the Nuclear Stress Rule, and the Focus Prosody Correspondence Principle, which regulates focus assignment. The focus structure is then interpreted at a post-syntactic interpretative level, Assertion structure, in terms of ordered assertions.

A special instance of the interaction between Nuclear Stress and focus is Prosodic Movement, which ensures that an element becomes the (information) focus of a given sentence. I show that in structures such as V-O-S (*Pročete knigata Marija* 'MARIJA read the book') and O-V-S (*Knigata pročete Marija* 'MARIJA read the book), the subject becomes focus of the sentence (narrow IF) by Prosodic Movement. In addition, I argue that contrastive focus, the counterpart of information focus, is optionally strong or weak. This accounts for S-V-O orders with focused subjects (***Marija** pročete knigata* 'It is Marija who read the book.'), which are interpretively distinct and involve additional assertions, and an alternative set.

References

Alexiadou A. and E. Anagnostopoulou. 1998. Parametrizing Agr: Word order, V-movement and EPP-checking. *Natural Language and Linguistic Theory 16*: 491–539.

Arnaudova, O. 1999. Information Focus versus Contrastive Focus, *Proceedings from the Annual Conference of the Canadian Linguistic Association*, Sherbrooke, 1999. 1–15.

Arnaudova, O. in press. The Interaction between Focus and Prosody in the Bulgarian Sentence. In U. Junghanns and G. Zybatow (eds) *Formale Slavistik 3: Proceedings of the 3rd European Workshop on Formal Description of Slavic Languages* (FDSL-3)

Cinque, G. 1993. A Null Theory of Phrase and Compound Stress. *Linguistic Inquiry* 24: 239–298.

Chomsky, N. 1971. Deep Structure, Surface Structure and Semantic Interpretation. In D. Steinberg and L. Jakobovits, eds., *Semantics: An Interdisciplinary Reader in Philosophy, Linguistics and Psychology*. Cambridge: CUP.

Chomsky, N. 1995. *The Minimalist Program*. Cambridge, Mass: MIT Press.

Chomsky, N. 1999. Derivation by Phase, Cambridge, Mass., MIT *Occasional Papers in Lingustics*.

Chomsky, N., and M. Halle. 1968. *The Sound Pattern of English*. New York: Harper and Row.

Diesing M. 1992. *Indefinites*. Cambridge, Mass.: MIT.

Dimitrova-Vulchanova, M. and L. Hellan. 1996. Clitics and Bulgarian Clause Structure. In *Proceedings of Formal Approaches to South Slavic Languages 1*, ed. by M. Dimitrova-Vulchanova and L. Hellan, 363–409.

Erteschik-Shir, N. 1997. *The Dynamics of Focus Structure*. CUP

Guasti M. T. and Nespor M. *Is Syntax Phonology Free?*, Ms. University of Siena.

Hajičová, E., B. Partee and P. Sgall. 1998. *Topic-Focus Articulation, Tripartite Structures, and Semantic Content*. Dordrecht: Kluwer.

Izvorski, R. 1994. *Yes-no questions in Bulgarian: Implications for Phrase Structure*. Presented at the 9th conference on Balkan and South Slavic Linguistics, Literature and Folklore, Bloomington, Indiana.

Jackendoff, R. 1972. *Semantic Interpretation in Generative grammar*. Cambridge. Mass.: MIT

Kenesei, I. 1996. *On the Syntax of Focus*, Ms.

King, T. H. 1994. *Configuring Topic and Focus in Russian*. Ph.D. Diss., Stanford University.

Kiss, K. E. 1998. Identificational Focus versus Information Focus, *Language* 74: 245–268.

Krapova, I. and T. Karastaneva. 1999, *On the CP field in Bulgarian*, University of Plovdiv, Ms.

Laka, I. 1990. *Negation in Syntax: On the Nature of Functional Categories and Projections*. Ph.D. Thesis. MIT, Cambridge.

Motapanyane, V. 1997. Preverbal Focus in Bulgarian. *Journal of Slavic Lingustics* 5.265–301.

Pierrehumbert, J., and J. Hirschberg. The Meaning of Intonational Contours in the Interpreration of Discourse. *Phonology Handbook*, 271–311.

Penchev, J. 1998. *Sintaksis na sâvremennija bâlgarski knižoven ezik*. Plovdiv.

Reinhart, T. 1982. Pragmatics and Linguistics: An Analysis of Sentence Topics. *Philosophia* 27.

Reinhart, T. 1995 *Interface strategies*. Ms., OTS, Universiteit Utrecht.

Rivero, M.-L. 1988/1994. "Clause Structure and V-movement in the Languages of the Balkans," *Natural Language and Linguistic Theory* 12.63–120.

Rivero, M.-L. 1998. Finiteness and Second Position in Long Verb movement Languages: Breton and Slavic. *Syntactic Categories*, ed. by R. D. Borsley (= *Syntax and Semantics* 32), New York: Academic Press. 295–323.

Rizzi, L. 1997. "The fine structure of the left periphery". In *Elements of grammar*, ed. by L. Haegeman. Dordrecht: Kluwer. 281–337.

Rochemont, M. 1986. *Focus in Generative Grammar*. Amsterdam: Benjamins.

Rooth, M. 1985. *Association with focus*. Ph.D. Diss., University of Massachusetts, Amherst.

Rudin. C. 1985. *Aspects of Bulgarian Syntax: Complementizers and WH Constructions*. Columbus, Ohio: Slavica.

Rudin, C., T. H. King, and R. Izvorski. 1996. Focus in Bulgarian and Russian Yes-No questions" *Proceedings of the Amherst Focus Workshop* 1996, UMOP.

Rudin, C., C. Kramer, L. Billings, and M. Baerman. Macedonian and Bulgarian Li Questions: Beyond Syntax, *Natural Language and Linguistic Theory* 17: 541–586.

Selkirk, Elizabeth. 1984. *Phonology and Syntax: The Relation between Sound and Structure*. Cambridge, Mass: MIT Press.

Tilkov, D. 1981. *Intonacijata v balgarskija ezik*. Sofia.

Zubizarreta M.L 1998. *Prosody, Focus and Word Order*. MIT Press.

Appendix

Figure 1. (V-0-S)

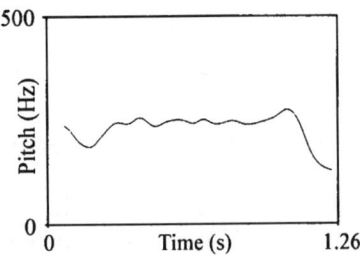

Pročete knigata MaRIja

Figure 2 (S_F-V-O)

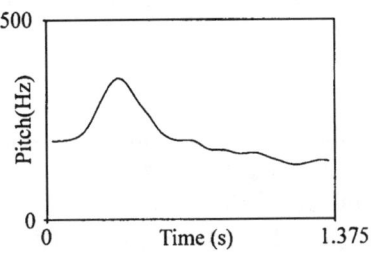

Marija pročete knigata.

Figure 3. (S_F-Neg-V-O)

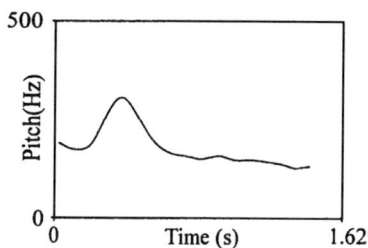

Marija ne e pročela knigata

Figure 4. (O_F –V- S)

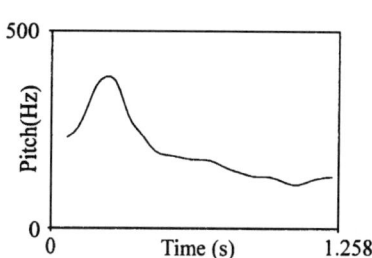

Knigata pročete Marija.

Figure 5. (O-V-S)

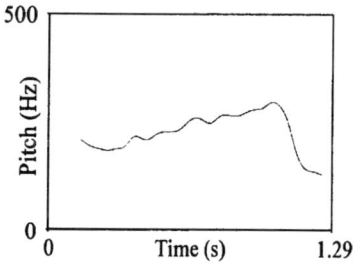

Knigata pročete MaRIja.

Figure 6. (V-S-O)

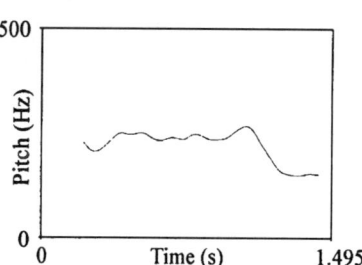

Pročete Marija kNIgata.

Olga Arnaudova
Department of Linguistics, University of Ottawa
70 Laurier Ave East
Ottawa, Ontario K1N 6N5
CANADA

The Genitive of Negation: A Unified Analysis

Leonard H. Babby
Princeton University

1. Introduction

The intuition driving generative analyses of the genitive of negation (GN) is that its syntactic distribution can be accounted for in terms of a single underlying position. I shall argue against the Unaccusative (UNACC) Analysis, which reduces all instances of the GN to the direct object position, by showing that it is empirically inadequate. My hypothesis is that the GN is assigned to available NPs in the scope of VP-negation without regard to their grammatical function (see Babby 1980).

The GN is assigned in three positions: (i) the direct object NP of transitive verbs instead of the ACC (see (1)); (ii) the NP argument in certain intransitive sentences instead of the NOM (see (2)); (iii) bare NP adverbs instead of the ACC (see (3)). The GN is never assigned to the subject NP of transitive verbs, an NP with Quirky Case, or NPs in the scope of constituent negation. (2a) is an affirmative existential sentence (AES) and (2b) is its negated counterpart (NES).

(1) Ona   daže ne   povernula k   nemu golovy.
    she.nom even neg turned   to him   head.gen
    'She didn't even turn her head toward him.'

(2) a. V   našem lesu   rastut   griby.
       in   our   forest grow.pl mushrooms.nom.pl
       'There are mushrooms growing in our forest.'
    b. V   našem lesu   ne   rastet   gribov.
       in   our   forest neg grow.sg   mushrooms.gen.pl
       'There are no mushrooms growing in our forest'
    c. *V našem lesu ne rastut$_{pl}$ gribov$_{gen.pl}$.

(3) a. Togda ja   ne   probyl doma daže pjati dnej.
       then I   neg was   home even 5.gen day.gen
       'I didn't stay home then for even five days.'
    b. Ja   ni   odnoj minuty   ne   dopuskal
       I.nom not one   minute.gen neg allowed
       vozmožnosti,   čto...
       possibility.gen that
       'I did not for one minute allow for the possibility that...'

Sentences like (3b) appear to eliminate the UNACC Analysis since the two GEN NPs *ni odnoj minuty* 'not a single minute' and *vozmožnosti* 'possibility' cannot both occupy the direct object position. However, since it has been proposed that the GEN in (3) may be the partitive GEN (cf. Franks and Dziwirek 1993), I will base my argumentation against the UNACC Analysis on other phenomena (but see Borovikoff 1997 for argumentation that the GEN in (3) really is the GN).

The focus of this paper is the GN in intransitive sentences like (2). I shall assume, based on Babby 1980 and Borschev and Partee 1998, that the NP argument of a negated monadic verb is assigned GEN *only when the sentence is existential*. The crucial question under this assumption is: Are UNACCs the only intransitive verbs used in existential sentences? If UNERG verbs are possible in existentials and their NP argument is assigned the GN, this would constitute evidence against the UNACC Analysis since the NP argument of UNERGs is never in the direct object position at any point in the sentence's derivation.

The following is a central question: Is *gribov* in (2b) the "genitive subject" or is the NOM subject *griby* in (2a) made an *oblique object* when (2a) is negated? It is assumed in the Russian grammatical tradition that, when (2a) is negated, *griby* becomes a GEN object NP and, therefore, that *impersonalization* is the direct result of negating (2a). This claim is plausible in traditional grammar because subject is defined exclusively in terms of NOM Case and verbal agreement: *gribov* in (2b) is GEN and agreement with the verb is impossible (cf. (2c))

The claim that the postverbal NOM *subject* in a AES like (2a) becomes a GEN *object* in the corresponding NES is implausible in theories of syntax that define subject in terms of theta role assignment and *syntactic position* (Case and agreement being nonobligatory subject-coding properties). I will argue below that the syntactic structures of existential pairs like (2a) and (2b) are identical despite systematic differences in Case and agreement, and that *both* sentences are "impersonal" since the postverbal subject NP does not raise to the canonical SpecTP subject position in either.

2 Basic Assumptions

Scope of Negation. An NP can be assigned GEN rather than NOM or ACC only if it is in the scope of VP-negation, which is also referred to as *sentential negation*: [ne [$_{VP}$...NP$_{gen}$...]].

Configurational case. NOM and ACC are Configurational because they are licensed in specific syntactic configurations. In Russian, they are in complementary distribution: An NP is ACC when it is contained in XP, the maximal projection of a *lexical* category X that does not assign Quirky Case to NP (X=V, A, or P). NP is NOM when it is not contained in the maximal projection of a lexical category; for example, canonical subjects are NOM because they are in SpecTP, which is a *functional* projection (see Babby 1994 for details). UNACC verbs are defined as monadic verbs whose initial internal NP argument cannot be assigned ACC and must raise to subject position to receive/check Case.

Definition of subject. An NP is a *theta-subject* if it is assigned the external theta role *i* of a predicate XP$_i$, with which it is in a local (sister) relation (*i* is the index of XP's external theta role, which may be *initially external* (agent) or an *externalized internal theta role* (theme in passives and UNACCs); see Williams 1983). A *canonical subject* is a theta-subject NP that raises to the SpecTP position. English permits non-theta subject NPs headed by an expletive in SpecTP. I assume that Russian has only theta-subjects, i.e., impersonal and existential sentences in Russian do not have null expletives (this assumption is *not* crucial in the analysis I propose below).

Impersonal sentences. The term *impersonal* is used to refer to two different sentence types: (i) Assuming that the theta-subject NP merges directly with a VP$_i$ predicate and then normally raises to SpecTP (see McCloskey 1997, Baker 1997), a sentence is said to be *impersonal* if the NP assigned VP$_i$'s external theta role *i* fails to raise to the canonical SpecTP subject position. (ii) If a Russian verb does not select an external theta role, the *subjectless* sentence it projects is also referred to as *impersonal* (e.g. *Ego tošnilo* 'He$_{acc}$ feels-ill' in Babby 1989 and 1998; the preposed direct object *ego* satisfies the EPP (see Lavine 2000)). Existential sentences are impersonal only in the first definition: *griby* and *gribov* in (2) are both theta-subjects, but they occupy the same "low" (noncanonical) inverted subject position (see section 6 for details).

Affixation of -sja. The primary function of the *-sja* suffix is to eliminate the direct object NP of the transitive verb it is affixed to. This leaves the direct internal theta role (θ_2) unlinked, creating either a derived UNACC verb (e.g., in *sja*-passives, unlinked θ_2 externalizes) or a derived UNERG verb (θ_2 links to the *-sja* suffix itself). For example, reflexive verbs are a subtype of derived UNERGs: *myt'sja* 'to-wash (yourself)') (see Babby 2002: chap. 2; Alsina 1996: chap. 3).

3 Two Approaches to a Unified Analysis of the GN

In this section we examine the two approaches to unifying the GN mentioned above. I argue that, while both are incorrect, each contains essential elements of the correct solution.

The UNACC Analysis makes two crucial predictions (both incorrect): (i) The GN can be assigned only to the *internal* object of UNACC and transitive verbs: never to the VP-*external* subject of UNERG verbs (or to bare NP adverbs) (see Chvany 1975, Pesetsky 1982, Harves 1999, Brown 1999). (ii) The NP argument of UNACC verbs should not raise out of its VP-internal object position when assigned the GN since its externalization is motivated soley by the need to receive/check NOM Case (see Belletti 1988). According to the UNACC Analysis, the internal structure of the VP in (2b) should be the structure in (4).

(4) [$_{NegP}$ ne [$_{VP}$ [$_{V'}$ rastet [$_{NP}$ gribov]]]]

In Babby 1980 I argued that in *intransitive* sentences, GN is assigned only to *inverted subject* NPs of *existential* sentences. This means that in (2b), *gribov* is the GEN *subject*, not the *in situ* GEN direct object. This approach to a unified analysis claims that the inverted subject NP in NESs is assigned GEN rather than NOM because it is in the scope of VP-negation. We see in section 6 that the claim that the GEN NP in (2b) is simultaneously the subject NP (hence VP-external) and in the scope of VP-negation (hence VP-internal) does not involve a paradox or contradiction.

Sentences like (5) demonstrate that the subject of a negated intransitive verb is GEN only when the sentence is *existential*. (5) has many of the properties characteristic of existentials: (i) the subject NP *muskul* is indefinite, postposed, and modified by *ni odin* 'not a single;' (ii) the negated verb is UNACC; (iii) there is a preposed locative adverbial expression. However, *muskul* is nevertheless NOM rather than GEN and agrees with the verb because the sentence does not have the structure of an existential: The assertion in (5) is not that the woman had no muscles in her face during the trial: it is presupposed that she has and asserted that they did not twitch during the trial. (5) is a *declarative*, not an existential sentence (see Babby 1980 for discussion).

(5) Za   vse   vremja suda   u   nee   na   lice
    during whole   time   of-trial   at   her   on   face
    ne   drognul   ni   odin   muskul.
    neg twitched not   one.nom   muscle.nom
    'Not a single muscle twitched on her face during the entire trial.'

The main hypothesis in Babby 1980 can be broken down into two parts: (i) It is only in existential sentences that the subject NP is in the scope of VP-negation, which licenses the GN. (ii) The subject NP's postverbal position and inclusion in the scope of negation are determined by the existential sentence's "scope of assertion," i.e., its *rheme*. Thus the relation between an AES and the corresponding NES was represented in (6) ($[_x...]$ is the sentence's scope of assertion (rheme), which determines the scope of negation [*ne*...]); AESs and NESs have the same syntactic and assertional structures, which are represented in (7) and (8):

(6)   AES: $[_x \text{VP NP}_{nom}]$ > NES: [ne [VP NP_{gen}]]

(7)   V našem lesu $[_x$ [rastut]$_{VPpl}$ [griby]$_{NPnom}$]   (=(2a))

(8)   V našem lesu [ne [rastet]$_{VPsg}$ [gribov]$_{NPgen}$]   (=(2b))

I argue below that the first part of this hypothesis is essentially correct and that the second part is incorrect, i.e., scope of negation is not *determined by* the sentence's rheme.

The two proposals under discussion for unifying the GN are summarized in (9) (=Babby 1980) and (10) (=the UNACC Analysis) (V^n in (9) = VP or V').

(9) $[_x \, V^n \, NP]$ > $[ne \, [V^n \, NP_{gen}]] \, (x = rheme)$

(10) $[[V \, NP]_{V'}]_{VP}$ > $[ne \, [[V \, NP_{gen}]_{V'}]_{VP}]$

The most obvious problem with (10) is that it is empirically inadequate: it cannot unify all instances of the GN (see the details in section 4). While the schema in (9) correctly predicts the distribution of the GN in all three positions identified in section 1.1, it too has a serious defect: the scope of VP-negation and, therefore, the assignment of the GN, is directly determined in terms of the sentence's rhematic structure rather than its syntactic structure. Although there is a regular mapping between syntactic and rhematic structure in Russian existential sentences, the scope of negation, the inverted position of the subject NP, and Case assignment are syntactic phenomena and should be stated in exclusively syntactic terms (which is precisely what the UNACC Analysis set out to do). Therefore, in order to retain the essential insight expressed in (9), x (= rheme) must be replaced by the appropriate *syntactic* category, which we shall do below.

4 The UNACC Analysis

The UNACC Analysis is on the right track in so far as it attempts to unify the GN in syntactic terms. However, it makes a number of incorrect predictions and is thus empirically inadequate:

4.1 Bare NP Adverbs

The UNACC Analysis cannot account for the GN assigned to bare NP adverbs (see (1.1)).

4.2 Unergative Sentences

The UNACC analysis predicts that it should be *impossible* to assign the GN to the NP argument of UNERG verbs because it never occurs in the direct object position at any point in the sentence's derivation. We shall see in section 7.2 that well-formed UNERG sentences with the GN are possible (see example in (19)).

4.3 Existential Sentences

The UNACC Analysis does not account for the following closely related facts: (i) the postposed, indefinite NP argument in negated UNACC sentences like (5) is *not* assigned the GN; (ii) the affirmative sentences corresponding to negated UNACC sentences with GEN NPs all have *obligatorily* inverted subjects (see (2a)); (iii) all negated intransitive sentences licensing the GN have an existential interpretation.

4.4 Derived UNACC Sentences and *-sja*

If an UNACC verb's direct internal NP argument does *not* raise out of VP when it is assigned GEN in the scope of negation (see Belletti 1988), how can we explain the systematic cooccurrence of putative *in situ* GEN direct object NPs and *-sja* in existential passives like (11) if the function of *-sja* is to *remove* the verb's direct object NP (see section 2 and Babby 2002)?

(11) Nikakix opytov s bombami ne
 no.gen experiments.gen with bombs neg
 delalos'.
 were-being-done.n.sg (delalos' < delalo+sja)
 'There were no experiments being carried out with bombs.'

5 Revised UNACC Analysis

Some of the problems with the UNACC Analysis presented in section 4 can be eliminated if it is assumed that the GN is assigned only in negated intransitive sentences that are both UNACC and existential (see Belletti 1988, Borik 1995, Brown 1999). Although this revised Existential UNACC Analysis eliminates the problems in section 4.3, it cannot eliminate the problems in sections 4.1, 4.2, and 4.4. I therefore conclude that all versions of the UNACC Analysis are insufficiently explanatory. Below I propose a unification of the GN that is a revised version of the analysis first proposed in Babby 1980.

6 A Unified Analysis of the GN

The main problem with the unification proposed in Babby 1980 is that the scope of negation is *directly* determined by the sentence's rheme (see (9), repeated here; $[_x...]$ = rheme).

(9) $[_x V^n NP] > [ne [V^n NP_{gen}]]$ (x = rheme)

The advantage of (9) is that it does not make the incorrect predictions that the UNACC Analysis does and it captures the intuition that assignment of GEN in the scope of VP-negation does not depend on the NP's grammatical function. What needs to be done now is to determine which *syntactic category* can replace x in (9) without sacrificing any of its explanatory power. Our first step in reformulating (9) in strictly syntactic terms will be to determine how the inverted subject NP in existential sentences like (2) can be both VP-external (subject) and in the scope of VP-negation.

6.1 The Structure of Affirmative Existential Sentences (AES)

The NOM subject in Russian AESs is *obligatorily* postverbal and agrees with the verb (see (2a)). This suggests that existential sentences in Russian have essentially the same syntactic structure as existentials in English and most other languages, i.e., it is the *inverted word order* that is crucial in determining the unique syntactic structure of existential sentences, not the presence (or absence) of an expletive subject, which will accordingly not figure prominently in the following discussion.

Williams, arguing against Belletti 1988, has demonstrated that the inverted subject NP in existential sentences is *not* in the direct object position: the inverted subject NP is *adjoined to the matrix VP* (see Williams 1994:138; Zubizarreta 1987:154), i.e., the VP in existential sentences has the structure in (12a), not (12b). The structure I propose for the AES in (2a) under the adjunction analysis is (13); the preposed locative PP in Russian existentials has the same EPP-satisfying function as the expletive *there* in English existentials (itself historically a locative adverb):

(12) a. $[[V]_{VP} NP]_{VP}$
 b. $[[V NP]_{V'}]_{VP}$

(13) V našem lesu $[_{VP} [rastut]_{VPpl} [griby]_{NPnom.pl}]$
 'There are mushrooms growing in our forest / In our forest grow mushrooms.'

Expletives in English and preposed locative expressions in Russian permit the subject to occupy a VP-internal position where it is in the domain of existential closure (see Diesing 1992, Brown 1999, Lavine 2000).

Unification of the GN can be represented by (14), which is essentially (9), the crucial difference being that x (= rheme) is replaced by the syntactic category VP. (Recall that V^n = VP or V'.)

(14) $[V^n \text{ NP}]_{VP} > [ne\ [V^n \text{ NP}_{gen}]_{VP}]_{NegP}$

The schema in (14) correctly picks out direct objects, bare NP adverbs, and the subjects of existential sentences, the three positions identified in section 1.1. It correctly excludes subjects of transitive sentences and of UNERG and UNACC verbs in non-existential sentences.

The postverbal subject NP in negated UNACC sentences like (5) is NOM because the sentence is not existential: *ni odin muskul* 'not a single muscle' is *extraposed* (not *inverted*), i.e., it is adjoined to TP (not to VP), which means it is external to VP and, therefore, outside the scope of VP-negation. I shall refer to the NP in [VP NP]$_{VP}$ as an *inverted* subject NP and to NP in [TP NP]$_{TP}$ as an *extraposed* subject NP. Only *inverted* subjects are assigned the GN because only they are in the scope of VP-negation. Note that the subject NP in *[ne* [VP NP$_{gen}$]$_{VP}$] is simultaneously VP-external (with respect to the *lower*, lexically projected VP) and in the scope of VP-negation, which is determined by the *upper* VP.

The crucial [VP NP]$_{VP}$ existential configuration can be derived either by a syntactic rule that lowers the subject NP from its canonical SpecTP position and adjoins it to VP or it can be "base generated," which means that the predicate VP$_i$ merges with the subject NP, forming a predication relation without movement or traces. The latter derivation, which does not involve a lowering operation and is thus conceptually and empirically more appropriate, is schematically represented in (15) (i is the index of the VP's external theta role; read "+" as "merges with" and ">" as "to form"). We define *predicate* is an XP$_i$ with an external theta role i to assign (when V is UNACC, i is an initial internal the role that externalizes *before* VP$_i$ and NP merge). When the external theta role i of VP$_i$ is assigned to NP, VP$_i$ is saturated.

(15) VP$_i$ + NP > [VP$_i$ NP$_i$]$_{VP}$

More precisely, VP$_i$ and NP merge as minimal sisters to form the "adjunction" structure on the right in (15), which is in essence the basic syntactic predication relation (see Epstein et al. 1998:91); in McCloskey's (1997: 221) succinct formulation: "the adjunction relation is the structural correlate of the predicate relation."

Since i of the lower VP_i in (15) is satisfied upon merger with its subject NP, the dominating (upper) VP on the right in (15) does not itself have an external theta role to assign (it is thus not a theta predicate). In English, a finite VP with no external theta role merges with an expletive NP to satisfy the "syntactic" (non-theta) predication requirement (see Rothstein 1985, Kondrashova 1996), which can be construed as the grammaticalization of the EPP. I assume that, in Russian, VPs without external theta roles do not merge with null-expletives, which explains the obligatory sentence-initial position of locative expressions in unscrambled Russian existential sentences: they satisfy the EPP (see Lavine 2000, Babyonyshev 1996).

Russian existential sentences, both affirmative and negated, are thus *impersonal* in the first sense defined in section 2: The matrix VP's external theta role i is assigned to a "lower" inverted subject NP, which does not raise out of $[VP_i\ NP_i]_{VP}$ to SpecTP. The AES in (2a) thus has the minimal syntactic structure represented in (16)

(16) [V   našem lesu   [[rastut]$_{VPi}$ [griby]$_{NPi}$]$_{VP}$]$_{TP}$
     in   our   forest   grow.pl   mushrooms.nom.pl

If NOM Case is assigned to an available NP that is not contained inside the maximal projection of a *lexical* category, as proposed in section 2 (see Babby 1994), assignment of the NOM Case to the inverted subject NP in AESs is entirely predictable: NP in the existential [VP$_i$ NP$_i$]$_{VP}$ configuration is immediately dominated by the *upper* VP, which is not the projection of a lexical head and therefore licenses the NOM Case. (A corollary of this approach to Configurational Case is that, given their ACC Case, direct object NPs and bare-NP adverbial expresssions in affirmative sentences must both be in the projection of a lexically-headed VP, which, however, may be problematic in the case of the bare NP adverbs.)

Subject-verb agreement is perfectly straightforward in Russian AESs: the inverted NOM NP in (15) is in the subject-of relation to VP$_i$ and thus agrees with it in number and person (gender in the past tense), just as canonical subjects do.

6.2 Negated Existential Sentences

The GN in NESs can be accounted for in a maximally simple way in terms of the $[VP_i\ NP_i]_{VP}$ configuration: the inverted, VP-internal subject NP of existential sentences is contained in the scope of VP-negation, and is thus assigned the GN in essentially the same way as direct object NPs (and bare NP adverbs) in transitive sentences, which is precisely what we set out to capture (see (14), repeated here):

(14) $[V^n\ NP]_{VP} > [ne\ [V^n\ NP_{gen}]_{VP}]_{NegP}$

The derivation of the NES in (2b) from the structure underlying the AES in (2a) is represented in (17): the sentence's grammatical relations are *not* altered by the introduction of negation (V^n in (14) = VP in (17)):

(17) V našem lesu [[rastut]$_{VP}$ [griby]$_{NPnom}$]$_{VP}$ >
      V našem lesu [ne [[rastet]$_{VP}$ [gribov]$_{NPgen}$]$_{VP}$]$_{NegP}$

The differences in Case and agreement in (18a-b) thus correspond to systematic differences in syntactic structure, not to the putative *optionality* of the GN (see Bailyn 1997). In (18a), a *declarative* sentence, the subject NP *deti* is not dominated by VP and is thus assigned NOM because it is not in the scope VP-negation. (18b) is existential: the subject NP here is VP-*internal* (prior to scrambling) and thus assigned GEN in the scope of VP-negation.

(18) a. Deti tam ne sideli.
          '(The) children$_{nom \cdot pl}$ weren't sitting$_{pl}$ there.'
      b. Detej tam ne sidelo (< Tam ne sidelo detej).
          'There were no children$_{gen.pl}$ sitting$_{sg}$ there.'
      c. *Detej tam ne sideli.
          'There were no children$_{gen.pl}$ sitting$_{pl}$ there.'

The obligatory absence of agreement with the GEN subject NP in NESs (see (18c)) is not a construction-specific property of existential sentences; it is predictable in terms of the following descriptive generalization: verbs in Russian never agree with subjects whose maximal projection is assigned an oblique Case (cf. Moore and Perlmutter 1999 for discussion).

7 Independent Evidence

In this section we examine evidence supporting the [VP$_i$ NP$_i$]$_{VP}$ analysis of existentials and the unification of the GN in (14) that is based on it.

7.1 Bare NP Adverbs

The schema in (14) correctly predicts that adjunct NPs in the scope of VP-negation are assigned GEN. It remains to be determined whether assignment of the GN to NP adverbs is optional and whether all bare NP adverbs are VP$_i$ internal; I will not pursue these issues here.

7.2 Unergative Sentences with GEN Subjects

The UNACC Analysis predicts that the subject NP of an UNERG verb cannot be assigned the GN because it is never in the direct object position. In contrast, the [VP$_i$ NP$_i$]$_{VP}$ Analysis in (14) predicts that UNERG verbs should be able to have GEN subjects if they are able to head existential sentences, where the subject NP is VP-internal (not VP$_i$-internal) and, therefore, in the GEN-licensing scope of VP-negation. The sentences in (19)-(24) suggest that UNERG existential sentences do in fact occur. (*Skryvat'sja* in (19) is a *derived unergative* verb; the verbs in (20)-(24) are *basic* unergatives.)

(19) Meždu   brevnami   ne   skryvalos'   tarakanov
     between beams   neg   were-hiding.n.sg   roaches.gen.pl
     'There were no cockroaches hiding among the beams.'

(20) Na zabrošennon zavode upal i razbilsja Saša. (Ja tam byl.) Tam (bol'še) ne igraet nikakix detej.
     'Saša fell and was badly hurt at the abandoned factory. (I was there.) There are no longer any children (seen) playing there.'

(21) S tex por kak na ètom zavode sokratili zarplatu, tam ne rabotaet ni odnogo inženira.
     'Since the wages were cut at the factory, there hasn't been a single engineer working there.'

(22) V xorovode ne pljasalo ni odnoj devuški (odni parni).
     'There wasn't a single girl dancing in the round dance (only guys).'

(23) — Peli l' petuxi?
— Ešče ne pelo ni odnogo. (from Potebnja 1968: 397)
'Did the roosters sing?'
'Not one has sung yet.'

(24) Uže byli ne tol'ko kvartiry, no daže celye doma, v kotoryx ne žilo ni odnogo čeloveka. (N. Chukovskij)
'There were not only flats but even entire buildings in which there wasn't a single person living.'

In the derivation of UNERG existential sentences, the initially external subject NP merges with VP_i, producing the $[VP_i\ NP_i]_{VP}$ configuration, just as in the derivation of UNACC existential sentences; the only difference is that i is initially *internal* in UNACCs and initially *external* in UNERGs.

It has been suggested by S. Harves (personal communication) and others (see Pesetsky 1982) that all the UNERG verbs in sentences like (19)-(24) are functioning as UNACCs. If this supposition is correct, the sentences in (19)-(24) would not constitute evidence against the UNACC Analysis; but neither would they count as evidence against my main hypothesis, which is that the postposed NP in Russian existential sentences is in the inverted *subject* position (see (12a)), not in the *object* position (see (12b)).

7.3 Affixation of -sja and the Genitive of Negation

A strong argument against the hypothesis that the postposed GEN NP in NESs is in the direct object position (VP_i internal) comes from the presence of -*sja* in imperfective passive NESs like (25) and (26).

(25) Nikakix   opytov   s   bombami   ne
     no.gen   experiments.gen with   bombs   neg
     delalos'.
     were-being-carried-out.n.sg (delalos' < delalo+sja)
     'There were no experiments with bombs being carried out.'

(26) V universitete po ètim disciplinam ne
 at university in these disciplines neg
 čitalos'   kursov.
 were-being-read.n.sg courses.gen.pl
 'There were no courses being offered at the university in these
 disciplines.' (čitalos' < čitalo+sja)

I have argued (Babby 1975, 2002) that, when -*sja* is affixed to a transitive verb (which is a morpholexical, diathesis-altering operaion), the subcategorized direct object NP position is *eliminated*. (I am distinguishing "affixed -*sja*" from "lexicalized -*sja*" in the case of verbs like *bojat'sja* 'to fear.') If the resulting delinked direct internal theta role is externalized, i.e., linked to the dethematized external NP, a derived UNACC predicate results. This means that -*sja* affixed to a transitive verb functions as a detransitivizing suffix and *affixed* -sja *and an in situ direct object NP cannot cooccur in modern Russian no matter what Case the object NP is assigned*. Given this analysis of -*sja*, the GEN NPs in existential sentences like (25) and (26) must be inverted GEN subjects since they cannot be direct objects.

Negated passive existential sentences like (26) have the following derivation. First, a derived UNACC predicate is formed from a transitive verb (in the lexicon) by affixation of -*sja* (see Babby 1998). Then the UNACC VP_i that V_i+*sja* projects merges with the subject NP (which is thus linked to the externalized theme role of the derived UNACC predicate) to form the $[[V_i+sja]_{VPi} NP_i]_{VP}$ structure that defines existential sentences. The inverted subject NP_i is realized as the GEN subject when this VP merges with *ne* because it is in the scope of VP-negation. If $[[V_i+sja]_{VPi} NP_i]_{VP}$ does not merge with *ne*, NP_i is realized as the inverted NOM subject of the passive AES. In other words, given that affixed -*sja* and the *in situ* direct object NP of a transitive verb are in complementary distribution in Russian, the VP in (26) must have the internal structure in (27), not (28).

(27) $[_{NegP}$ ne $[_{VP} [_{VPi}$ čitalos'] $[_{NPi}$kursov po...]]]
     neg   offered.n.sg+sja courses.gen.pl

(28) *$[_{NegP}$ ne $[_{VP} [_{V'}$ čitalos' $[_{NPgen}$ kursov po...]]]]

Summary. If the analyses of existential sentences and *-sja* that I have proposed in this paper are correct, the syntactic distribution of the GN in Russian can be unified in terms of an available NP that is in the scope of VP-negation (see (14)). There is no need to specify this NP's grammatical function and, therefore, to claim that it occupies the same syntactic position in both transitive and intransitive sentences at the point in the sentence's derivation that *ne* is merged.

References

Alsina, A. 1996. *The Role of Argument Structure in Grammar: Evidence from Romance*. Stanford: CSLI Publications.

Babby, L. 1975. A transformational analysis of transitive -sja verbs in Russian, *Lingua* 35, 297–332.

Babby, L. 1980. *Existential Sentences and Negation in Russian*. Ann Arbor: Karoma.

Babby, L. 1989. Subjectlessness, external subcategorization, and the projection principle. *Zbornik Matice Srpske za Filologiju i Lingvistiku*, XXXII/2, Novi Sad. 7–40.

Babby, L. 1994. Case Theory. In C.P. Otero (ed.), *Noam Chomsky: Critial Assessments (vol. 1: Linguistics: tome II)*. London: Routledge, 630–652.

Babby, L. 1998. Voice and diathesis in Slavic. To appear in the volume of papers from the Comparative Slavic Morphosyntax conference held at Indiana University, June 5–7, 1998. Bloomington: Slavic Publishers.

Babby, L. 2002. *The Morpholexical Foundations of Russian Syntax*. To be published by Cambridge University Press.

Babyonyshev, M. 1996. *Structural Connections in Syntax and Processing: Studies in Russian and Japanese*. Doctoral dissertation, MIT.

Bailyn, J. 1997. Genitive of negation is obligatory. In W. Brown et al. (eds), *Formal Approaches to Slavic Linguistics: the Cornell Meeting*. Ann Arbor: Michigan Slavic Publications, 84–114.

Baker, M. 1997. Thematic roles and syntactic structure. In L. Haegeman (ed), *Elements of Grammar*, Dordrecht: Kluwer, 73–138.

Belletti, A. 1988. The Case of unaccusatives. *Linguistic Inquiry* 19, 1–34.

Borik, O. 1995. *Sintaksičeskij priznak neakkuzativnosti glagola (na materiale russkogo jazika)*. Diplomnaja rabota, MGU, Moskva, 73 pages.

Borovikoff, N. 1997. Negated adjunct phrases are REALLY the genitive of negation. In M. Lindseth and S. Franks (eds.), *Formal Approaches to Slavic Linguistics*. Ann Arbor: Michigan Slavic Publications. 67–85.

Borschev, V., and B. H. Partee. 1998. Formal and lexical semantics and the genitive in negated existential sentences in Russian. In Z. Bošković, S. Franks, and W. Snyder (eds.), *Annual Workshop on Formal Approaches to Slavic Linguitics*. Ann Arbor: Michigan Slavic Publications. 75–96.

Brown, S. 1999. *The Syntax of Negation in Russian*. Stanford: CSLI Publications.

Chvany, C. *On the Syntax of BE-sentences in Russian*. Cambridge,Mass.: Slavica.

Diesing, M. 1992. *Indefinites*. Cambridge, Mass.: MIT Press.

Epstein, S., E. Groat, R. Kawashima, and H. Kitahara. 1998. *A Derivational Approach to Syntactic Relations*. Oxford University Press.

Franks, S., and K. Dziwerck. 1993. Negated adjunct phrases are really partitive. *Journal of Slavic Linguistics* 1, 280–305.

Harves, S. 1999. Unaccusatives as small clauses. Paper presented at AATSEEL, Chicago.

Kondrashova, N. 1996. *The Syntax of Existential Quantification*. Doctoral dissertation, University of Wisconsin, Madison.

Lavine, J. 2000. *Topics in the Syntax of Nonagreeing Predicates in Slavic*. Doctoral dissertation, Princeton University.

McCloskey, J. 1997. Subjecthood and subject positions. In L. Haegeman (ed.), *Elements of Grammar*. Dordrecht: Kluwer, 197–236.

Moore, J. and D. Perlmutter. 1999. Case, agreement, and temporal particles in Russian. *Journal of Slavic Linguistics* 7, 219–246.

Pesetsky, D. 1982. Paths and Categories. Dortoral dissertation, MIT.

Potebnja, A.A. 1968. *Iz zapisok po russkoj grammatike, tom III*. Moskva: Prosveššenie.

Rothstein, S. 1985. *The Syntactic Forms of Predication*. Reproduced by the Indiana University Linguistics Club.
Williams, E. 1983. Against small clauses. *Linguistic Inquiry* 14, 287–308.
Williams, E. 1994. *Thematic Structure in Syntax*. Cambridge, Mass.: MIT Press.
Zubizarreta, M. 1987. *Levels of Representation in the Lexion and in the Syntax*. Dordrecht: Foris Publications.

Leonard H. Babby
Department of Slavic Languages
028 E Pyne Building
Princeton University
Princeton, NJ 08544-5264 USA
babbylh@princeton.edu

Li without PF Movement

Željko Bošković
University of Connecticut

A number of constructions have been suggested to involve PF Movement, e.g., rightward movement and scrambling constructions. In most cases, this is not because such constructions are particularly amenable to a PF Movement analysis, but because they do not fit well in the syntax, given the syntactic apparatus available. Most arguments for PF Movement are thus essentially negative. There are, however, some instances where the case for PF Movement is stronger. Among these, Prosodic Inversion (PI), which moves prosodically deficient elements the minimal distance necessary for them to get prosodic support, stands out.[1] In fact, PI might be the strongest case ever made for PF Movement. The reason for this is that in this instance of putative PF Movement, we are dealing with a clearly defined movement operation, with a precise phonological motivation and explicitly defined locality restrictions sensitive to phonological information, which is generally not a characteristic of other putative examples of PF Movement. Some of the strongest arguments for PI come from Slavic cliticization. A number of those arguments have been seriously undermined. Thus, it has been shown (see Bošković 2000b, in press, Franks 1998, Progovac 1996, and Wilder and Ćavar 1994) that Serbo-Croatian (SC) constructions in (1), often used to argue for PI, not only can be, but in fact must be derived without PI.

---

[1] Halpern's (1995) definition of PI is given in (i).
- (i) For a DCL [directional clitic], X, which must attach to a 4 [phonological word] to its left (respectively right),
  - a. If there is a 4, Y, comprised of material which is syntactically immediately to the left (right) of X, then adjoin X to the right (left) of Y.
  - b. else attach X to the right (left) edge of the 4 composed of syntactic material immediately to its right (left).

(1) a. Lava je Tolstoja čitao.
    Leo is Tolstoi read
    'Leo Tolstoi, he read.'
  b. Skupe   je knjige čitao.
     expensive is books   read
     'Expensive books, he read.'

We are, however, still left with constructions involving *li,* which have been claimed to require PI (see Franks 1998, King 1996, Izvorski et al 1997, and Rudin et al 1999). I will show that even *li*-constructions can be accounted for without PI, which will lead me to question the existence of PI and PF Movement in general, given that PI is one of the strongest cases ever made for the existence of PF Movement.

1. Pronunciation of Non-Trivial Chains

My analysis of *li*-constructions will be based on Franks's (1998, 2000) approach to the pronunciation of non-trivial chains (see also Bošković 2000b, in press, Bošković and Franks to appear, Hiramatsu in press, Pesetsky 1997). It is standardly assumed that only heads of non-trivial chains can be phonologically realized. However, Franks argues that the pronunciation of heads of non-trivial chains is a preference, not an absolute requirement. More precisely, Franks argues that the head of a non-trivial chain is pronounced unless the pronunciation of the head of the chain would lead to a PF violation. If the violation can be avoided by pronouncing a lower copy, the lower copy is pronounced.

In Bošković (2000a) I present evidence for this approach from multiple *wh*-fronting constructions. I will summarize here one of my arguments based on Romanian, which fronts all *wh*-phrases.

(2) a. Cine ce   precede?
       who   what precedes
  b. *Cine precede ce?

Interestingly, the second *wh*-phrase does not move if it is homophonous with the first fronted wh-phrase. (Bulgarian, Russian, and SC pattern with Romanian in the relevant respect.)

(3) a. Ce   precede ce?
       what precedes what
  b. *Ce ce precede?

Following Billings and Rudin's (1996) proposal concerning Bulgarian (Bg), I assumed in Bošković (2000a) that Romanian has a PF constraint against sequences of homophonous *wh*-phrases, which accounts for (3b). What about (3a)? The ungrammaticality of (2b) indicates that there is a syntactic requirement that forces all *wh*-phrases to move overtly in Romanian. (I argue that the requirement is focus.) This should also hold for the second *wh*-phrase in (3a). As a result, (3a) should have the S-structure in (4a). (I am ignoring the lower copy of the first *ce*.) Given the PF constraint against sequences of homophonous *wh*-phrases and Franks's proposal that a lower copy of a non-trivial chain can be pronounced if this is necessary to avoid a PF violation, we can and must pronounce the lower copy of *ce*.

(4) a. Syntax: Ce ce precede ce
    b. PF: Ce ee precede ce?

Under this analysis, the *wh*-in-situ in (3a) undergoes full phrasal movement in overt syntax. As a result, we might expect it to license other elements from the putative raised position, given an appropriate licensing relation. In Bošković (2000a) I show that the expectation is borne out with respect to parasitic gap licensing, as illustrated in (5).

(5) Ce precede ce fără să influenţeze?
    'What precedes what without influencing?'

(6) *What precedes what without influencing?

(7) cf. What did John file without reading?

The fact that, in spite of being pronounced in situ, *ce* in (5) licenses a parasitic gap, just like *what* in (7) and in contrast to *what* in (6), provides evidence that *"ce*-in-situ" does undergo overt *wh*-movement. This is captured by the above analysis, on which the *wh*-phrase in-situ in (5) undergoes full phrasal *wh*-movement in overt syntax which does not differ syntactically in any relevant respect from, e.g, movement of *what* in (7). It is then no surprise that (5) patterns with (7) and not (6).

The pronounce-a-copy analysis can also be profitably applied to Bg and Macedonian (Mac) pronominal clitics. Consider (8).

(8) a. Vera *mi go* dade včera. Bg: OK   Mac: OK
Vera me.dat it.acc gave yesterday
'Vera gave it to me yesterday.'
b. Včera *mi go* dade Vera.   Bg: OK   Mac: OK
c. *Mi go* dade Vera včera.   Bg: *   Mac: OK
d. Dade *mi go* Vera včera.   Bg: OK   Mac: *

The Mac clitics in (8) precede and procliticize to the verb. The Bg clitics, on the other hand, encliticize to the preceding element. They precede the verb unless preceding it would violate their enclitic requirement. In that case they follow the verb, which then provides prosodic support for them. The contrast between Mac and Bg (8c, d) provides strong evidence that placing V in front of a clitic is a last resort strategy invoked when prosodic properties of clitics cannot be otherwise met. This can be interpreted as indicating that PF places the verb in front of clitics, which is exactly what happens under the PI analysis of (8). Under this analysis, the output of the syntax for (8c, d) in both languages has the order clitic-V. Since the Bg clitics in (8) are enclitics, in PF PI places the clitics after the verb, thus satisfying their enclitic requirement. Since the Mac clitics in (8) can procliticize, there is no need to apply PI, hence it cannot apply.

(8) can be accounted for without PI under Franks's approach to the pronunciation of non-trivial chains. Suppose a copy of the clitics is present both above and below the verb. (For the exact location, see Bošković in press.) As discussed, the head of the clitic movement chain is pronounced except when the pronunciation of the head results in a PF violation. In that case, the tail is pronounced, provided that this pronunciation helps satisfy the PF requirement. This approach captures the generalization that the verb can precede a clitic in Bg only when no other lexical material is located in front of the clitic.

Only in this situation will we be able to pronounce the lower copy of the clitic. If there is lexical material preceding the clitic in its raised position, the head of the clitic movement chain must be pronounced.

(9) a. X clitic V ~~clitic~~   b. ~~clitic~~ V clitic

Since in Mac nothing goes wrong in PF if we pronounce the head of the clitic chain, we have to pronounce it. As a result, the V-clitic order is underivable in Mac. The contrast between Bg and Mac (8c, d), as well as the role of phonology in the possibility of the V-clitic order, is thus accounted for. The data under consideration thus follow without appealing to PI or, more generally, PF Movement.

Having shown how the pronounce-a-copy analysis works and how it can be applied to Bg and Mac pronominal clitics, I turn to *li*-constructions, the strongest remaining case for PI. In section 2 I discuss *li* in neutral yes-no questions only. In section 3 I discuss questions in which the element preceding *li* is focalized.

2. *Li* in Neutral Yes-No Questions

Consider (10).

(10) a. *Go vidja li? (Bg)
him saw Q
'Did he/she/you see him?'
b. Vidja li go?
c. Go vide li? (Mac)
him saw Q
d. *Vide li go?

Rudin et al (1999) (RKBB) (see also King 1996 and Izvorski et al 1997) derive (10) by right-adjoining complex head *go vidja/vide* to *li*.

(11) [c li + [go vidja/vide]]...

Recall that Bg pronominal clitics encliticize, while Mac ones procliticize in finite clauses.[2] However, *li* encliticizes in both languages. Given this, only *li* undergoes PI in Mac. Since *go* procliticizes there is no need for it to undergo PI, which is then disallowed. As for Bg (10a, b), since both *li* and *go* are enclitics they both have to undergo PI, which places them following the verb. (Note that PI affects the whole clitic cluster, preserving the order within it.) This gives us (10b). (10a) is ruled out since *go* cannot encliticize.

Although this analysis gives us a principled account of the data in (10) I will show that (10a-d) can be derived without employing PI or any kind of PF Movement. Furthermore, I will show that no appeal to

---

[2] See Bošković (in press) and references therein for cliticization in Mac non-finite clauses, which I ignore here.

rightward head movement, disallowed in Kayne's (1994) system, is necessary if we allow for the possibility of pronunciation of lower copies of non-trivial chains motivated by PF considerations.

Following RKBB, I assume that the complex X^0-element *go vidja/vide* adjoins to *li* in both languages. However, I crucially depart from RKBB in assuming that the movement involves left-adjunction to *li*, instead of right-adjunction, in accordance with Kayne's LCA. The movement leaves behind a copy, giving the structure in (12):

(12) [$_C$ [go vidja/vide]+li] go vidja/vide

In Mac no PF violation occurs if we pronounce the head of the *go vide* chain, which, since preferred, has to be pronounced. We then get *Go vide li*, *Vide li go* being underivable. (10c, d) are thus straightforwardly accounted for. How about (10a, b)? Since Bg pronominal clitics are enclitics *go* cannot be pronounced in the raised position, as in (10a), without a PF violation. The problem is resolved if *go* is pronounced in a lower position. The verb still has to be pronounced in the highest position, where it hosts *li go*. We thus derive (10b).

(13) [$_C$ [go vidja]+li] go vidja

In (13), one chain is pronounced in more than one position. One part of it is pronounced in the head position, and one part in the tail. In Nunes's (2000) terms, we are dealing here with scattered deletion. (13) thus provides evidence that in addition to full deletion, which leads to the pronunciation of either the head or the tail of a chain, scattered deletion is possible. Notice that scattered deletion provides strong evidence for the copy theory of movement. It provides evidence that what is left behind by movement has internal structure, which is readily captured under the copy theory, but not under the trace theory.[3]

Consider now (14), taken from RKBB:

(14). a. *Si   mu   (gi)   dal   li   parite?   (Bg)
          are   him.dat.   them   given   Q   the-money
          'Have you given him the money?'
       b. Dal li si mu (gi) parite?

---

[3] Nunes argues that scattered deletion is less economical than full deletion, hence could occur only if full deletion cannot yield a convergent structure, which is the case in (13).

(14) c. Si   mu   gi   dal   li   parite?   (Mac)
        are   him.dat. them given Q   the-money
       'Have you given him the money?'
    d. *Dal li si mu gi parite?

Under RKBB's analysis, the above constructions have the syntactic structure in (15). PI then places the whole clitic cluster *li si mu gi* after the participle in Bg (each clitic is an enclitic in Bg) but only *li* in Mac (only *li* is an enclitic in this language).

(15) [li+[si mu gi dal]]

Under the current analysis, the complex head *si mu gi dal* left-adjoins to *li* instead of right-adjoining to it. The movement leaves behind a copy. (14a-d) then have the following structure in the syntax:

(16) [[si mu gi dal]+ li] si mu gi dal

Since in Mac, auxiliary and pronominal clitics are proclitics and *li* is an enclitic, nothing goes wrong in PF if we pronounce *si mu gi dal* in the raised position. This pronunciation is then forced.

(17) [[si mu gi dal]+ li] ~~si mu gi dal~~

In Bg we cannot pronounce the higher *si mu gi*. This pronunciation would violate the enclitic requirement on *si mu gi*. The enclitic requirement on *si mu gi* (and *li*) can be satisfied if we do the deletions in (18). As with (13), scattered deletion is the only possibility. What can be pronounced in the highest position is pronounced there.

(18) [[~~si mu gi~~ dal]+ li] si mu gi ~~dal~~

Let us now consider clitic placement in negative *li*-questions.[4]

---

[4] (19a) is acceptable on the irrelevant echo-question reading as a case of the focus *li*-construction, where the element preceding *li* undergoes focus movement. Notice that although itself unstressed, the negative marker causes the following lexically unstressed word to assume stress in Bg. This does not happen in Mac, where *ne* itself is also unstressed.

(19) a. *Ne go vidja li? (Bg)
    neg him saw Q
    'Didn't he/she/you see him?'
 b. Ne go li vidja?
 c. Ne go vide li? (Mac)
    neg him saw Q
 d. *Ne go li vide?

Under the pronounce-a-copy-analysis, the complex X^0-element *ne go vidja/vide* left-adjoins to *li*. (19) then have the following S-structure.

(20) [ne go vidja/vide+li] ne go vidja/vide

In Mac nothing goes wrong in PF if the complex X^0-element preceding *li* is pronounced in the raised position. (Recall that only *li* must encliticize in Mac.) The pronunciation in the raised position is then forced, which gives us (19c).

(21) [ne go vide+li] ~~ne go vide~~

A problem, however, arises in Bg. We should be able to pronounce the whole complex X^0-element *ne go vide* in the raised position, which would incorrectly give us (19a) instead of (19b). The problematic derivation results in the following abstract structure, with two stressed elements preceding *li* in an unmarked yes-no question.

(22) X... Y...   Z li
     +stress +stress

Structures of this kind are quite generally unacceptable in Bg. (The same holds for Mac, see (32). For more examples instantiating (22), see Bošković in press.) To account for this I appeal to the standard assumption that, in contrast to pronominal and auxiliary clitics in the languages under consideration, *li* is a second position (2P) clitic (see also Legendre 2000). I suggest that the abstract structure in (22) is ruled out due to a violation of the 2P requirement: *li* is located in the third instead of the second position of its intonational phrase.[5]

---

[5] See Bošković (2000b, in press) for details of the analysis. Under my (2000b, in press) analysis, where the 2P requirement is treated as a PF requirement, the structure in (22) would be ruled out in PF.

There is evidence independent of *li*-placement in yes-no questions that *li* is subject to the 2P requirement. Consider (23).

(23) [CP Koj [C' li kupuva kolata]]
     who   Q buys   the-car
     'Who on earth is buying the car?'

Rudin (1993) argues that the *wh*-phrase in (23) is located in the Spec of the CP headed by *li*. Rudin (1988) shows convincingly that Bg can locate more than one *wh*-phrase in SpecCP. Thus, she shows that all fronted *wh*-phrases in (24) are located in SpecCP.

(24) [CP Koj kakvo [C' kupuva]]
     who what   buys
     'Who is buying what?'

One of her arguments concerns the lack of *wh*-island effects in (25). Since Bg allows more than one *wh*-phrase in SpecCP, *koja ot tezi knigi* in (25) can pass through the embedded SpecCP in spite of it already being filled by a *wh*-phrase. Notice that the *wh*-island effect is also voided with *wh-li* questions, as in (26), which shows that, like null C questions, *li*-questions allow more than one *wh*-phrase in SpecCP.

(25) Koja   ot   tezi   knigi$_i$ se čudiš   koj   prodava t$_i$?
     which of   these books   wonder.2s who sells
     'Which of these books you wonder who sells?'

(26) Koja   ot   tezi   knigi$_i$ se čudiš   koj   li   prodava t$_i$?
     which of   these books   wonder.2s who Q   sells
     'Which of these books you wonder who on earth sells?'

Significantly, at most one *wh*-phrase can precede *li*.

(27) *[CP Koj kakvo [C' li   kupuva]]?
     who what   Q   buys

Nothing goes wrong with (27) in the syntax. However, (27) can be ruled out in PF due to a violation of the 2P requirement on *li*. I conclude that we independently need the 2P requirement on *li*. Notice also that, under the current analysis, we would expect it to be possible to repair (27) by pronouncing *kakvo* in a lower position of the chain created by its movement to SpecCP. The expectation is borne out.[6]

(28) [CP Koj ~~kakvo~~ [C' li kakvo kupuva]]

Bg (19b) can be derived in the same way:

(29) [ne go ~~vidja~~+li] ~~ne go~~ vidja

Consider now the following constructions:

(30) *Ne li   go   vidja?   (Bg)
      neg Q   him   saw
      'Didn't he/she/you see him?'

(31) (*)Ne li   go   vide?   (Mac)
      neg   Q   him   saw

(30) can be easily ruled out. Given the S-Structure in (29), with *go* assuming stress as a result of it following *ne*, there is no need to pronounce *go* in a lower position. The pronunciation is then disallowed. As for (31), its status is controversial. According to Tomić (1999), it is unacceptable. According to RKBB, it is acceptable. RKBB argue that in addition to functioning as an unstressed proclitic, Mac *ne* can bear stress. They claim that (31) is acceptable with stressed *ne*. (31) can be easily ruled out on a par with Bg (30). The question is whether it can be ruled in, should RKBB's empirical claim turn out to be correct. Suppose RKBB are indeed correct in their claim that (31) should be ruled in with *ne* stressed on the relevant derivation. (31) then has the following structure in the current analysis:

(32) Ne go   vide   li   ne go vide   (Mac)
      +stress +stress

If *ne go vide* is pronounced in the raised position then the 2P requirement will be violated. One of the stressed elements then has to be pronounced in a lower position. Given the discussion in fn. 6, the verb will be

---

[6] As discussed in Bošković (2000a, in press) (see also Bošković and Franks to appear), when determining which part of a non-trivial chain to pronounce the structure is scanned left-to-right. When the element causing a PF violation (*li*) is reached, we back-track locally and delete the element preceding it (*kakvo*).

pronounced in a lower position. The question is where *go* will be pronounced. *Go* in (32) is a verbal proclitic: it must procliticize to the verb in PF. If *go* is pronounced in the highest position then the PF requirement cannot be satisfied. Since *go* would be followed by an element (*li*) that must encliticize to the preceding word (*ne*), *go* could not procliticize to the verb, which follows *li*. To satisfy its PF requirement, *go* then has to be pronounced in a lower position.

(33) [ne ~~go vide~~ li] ne go vide (Mac)

3. Focus *Li*

Another potential argument for PI comes from SC *li*-constructions in which the element preceding *li* is contrastively focused, as in (34).[7]

(34) a. Koga   *li*   Petar   voli?
       whom   Q   Peter   loves
       '**Who** does Peter love?'
    b. Knjige *li*   Ana   čita?
       books   Q   Ana   reads
       'Does Ana read **books**?'

An interesting fact about SC focus *li* is that it is placed after the first prosodic word (1W placement). It cannot occur following unambiguous phrasal material, in contrast to other 2P clitics in the language, which allow both types of placement.

(35) *Kakve/Skupe   knjige *li*   (Ana)   čita?
     what-kind/expensive   books   Q   Ana   reads
     '**What kind of books** does Ana read?'
     'Does Ana read **expensive books**?'

(36) Kakve/Skupe *li* knjige (Ana) čita?

Obligatory 1W environments represent a potential argument for PI. Given PI, the above facts can be accounted for as follows: suppose that

---

[7] In translations I give the focused word in focus *li*-constructions in bold letters.(34a) could be rendered more accurately as "Who on earth does Peter love?" and (34b) as "Is it books that Ana reads?".

in the syntax, the focused constituent is located in the first phrase below *li*. Since *li* is an enclitic, in PF PI places *li* after the first word.[8]

(37) Syntax: [$_{CP}$ *li* [kakve/skupe knjige (Ana) čita]]
 PF: Kakve/Skupe *li* knjige (Ana) čita? (PI applies)

The PI analysis accounts for the 1W restriction on the placement of focus *li*. The argument for PI is, however, not complete. The elements occurring in front of *li* in (36) are syntactically mobile. If PI indeed provides the host for *li* we would expect that syntactically immobile elements could also host *li*. Significantly, this is not possible. (38) is an example of a syntactically immobile element attempting to host *li*.

(38) *Prema   *li*   Mariji   Jovan   trči?
 toward   Q   Marija   Jovan   runs
 'Is Jovan running **toward** Marija?'

Under the PI analysis, nothing rules out the following derivation.

(39) Syntax: [$_{CP}$ *li* [prema Mariji Jovan trči]]
 PF: Prema *li* Mariji Jovan trči. (PI applies)

(38) thus provides evidence that *li* does not acquire its host through PI. The conclusion is confirmed by the following constructions:

(40) a. Lava   Tolstoja   čitam.
  Leo.acc Tolstoi.acc read
  'Leo Tolstoi I read.'
 b. ?Lava   Tolstoj   čitam.
  Leo.acc Tolstoi.nom read
 c. Lav   Tolstoja   čitam.
  Leo.nom Tolstoi.acc read

(41) a. Lava čitam Tolstoja.
 b. *Lava čitam Tolstoj.
 c. *Lav čitam Tolstoja.

---

[8] Franks (1998, 2000) proposes this analysis for Russian *li*, which is also restricted to 1W environments (see King 1994. See also Rudnitskaya 2000 for a recent discussion of Russian *li*). The analysis of SC *li* to be presented below can be extended to Russian *li*.

(42) a. Lava   li   Tolstoja   čita?
       Leo.acc Q   Tolstoi.acc reads
       'Does he/she read **Leo** Tolstoi?'
    b. *Lava   li   Tolstoj   čita?
       Leo.acc Q   Tolstoi.nom reads
    c. *Lav   li   Tolstoja   čita?
       Leo.nom Q   Tolstoi.acc reads

As discussed in Franks (1998) and Bošković (2000b, in press), the first name can be split from the last name by syntactic movement only if both names are properly inflected, i.e. if neither receives the default nominative. The fact that the first name can serve as the host for *li* only when it is syntactically mobile shows that it is syntax which provides the host for *li*, not PI. That PI is not the appropriate mechanism is confirmed by (43), where the constituent split (the split of *Kakve/Skupe knjige* and *Lava Tolstoja*) cannot be accomplished by PI.

(43) a. Kakve/Skupe   li Ana   knjige čita?
       what-kind/expensive Q   Ana   books   reads
       '**What kind of** books does Ana read?'
       'Does Ana read **expensive** books?'
    b. Lava li on   Tolstoja čita?
       Leo Q   he   Tolstoi reads
       'Does he read **Leo** Tolstoi?'

Notice also that only the first element is focused in (36). (44) provides confirmation of the restriction on focus possibilities with *li* since there is no Fyodor Dostoevsky Tolstoi. Notice that *Lava li Tolstoja čita, ili Fjodora* implies a contrast with a hypothetical Fyodor Tolstoi.

(44) *Lava   li Tolstoja   čita ili Fjodora   Dostojevskog?
      Leo.acc Q   Tolstoi.acc reads or   Fyodor.acc Dostoevsky.acc
      'Does he/she read **Leo Tolstoi** or Fyodor Dostoevsky?'

On the PI analysis we would incorrectly expect it to be possible to have focus on the full NPs *Lava Tolstoja* and *Skupe knjige*. Nothing should block the derivation on which the NPs occupy the focus position after *li*, with PI placing *li* after the first word of the NPs.

(45) a. Syntax: *li* [Lava Tolstoja] čita
       PF: Lava *li* Tolstoja čita?   (PI applies)
   b. Syntax: li [skupe knjige] (Ana) čita
       PF: Skupe *li* knjige (Ana) čita?   (PI applies)

A similar problem for the PI analysis is raised by (46), where the element preceding *li* is inherently unfocusable. (Russian patterns with SC in this respect, see Bošković in press.) Under the PI analysis we could derive (46) by having the whole NP *Neka kola*, which is focusable (cf. English *Is it some car that she bought?*), undergo focus movement and then placing *li* after *Neka* in PF by PI.

(46) *Neka   li   kola   kupuje?
      some   Q   car   buys
      'Is he/she buying **some car**?'

The fact that focus is confined to the element preceding *li* is readily accounted for on the analysis on which only syntax can provide a host for *li*. Under this analysis, *li* is the focus licensor in the constructions under consideration, so that only an element that is in the checking domain of *li*, which means preceding *li* in the syntax, can be focused.

I conclude that the 1W restriction on SC *li* does not provide evidence for PI. It is syntactic movement, and not PI, that provides a host for SC *li*. Syntax then must be responsible for the impossibility of placing *li* following unambiguous phrasal material, that is, the ungrammaticality of (35). The question is then how can we account for the 1W restriction on *li* by using syntactic means? If strong features can be lexically specified for the way of checking (by head or phrasal movement), the 1W restriction can be easily accommodated. We could simply say that *li* is lexically specified to require checking through head-adjunction. Notice that the elements that are checking the focus feature of *li* in the good examples in (34)-(43) are all analyzable as non-branching, which in Chomsky's (1995) system means that they are ambiguous X^0/XP elements and therefore can undergo either X^0 or XP movement.[9] Alternatively, we can assume that SC *li* is defective in that it cannot

---

[9] In fact, the two types of movements can be combined. The elements in question could move as XPs and end up adjoined to a head. A variation of this analysis would be phrasal scrambling just below *li* followed by head movement to *li* from this position.

support a specifier, which would rule out the possibility of unambiguous phrasal elements moving to check its focus feature. It is worth noting here that the focus *li*-construction is somewhat archaic. It seems to be disappearing from the language.[10] It is possible that the first step in removing the construction from SC is removing the ability of *li* to support a specifier, which greatly reduces possibilities for checking the focal feature of *li*. This could be interpreted as indicating that checking through head movement is the unmarked option. (Notice that checking through head movement results in shorter movement than checking through movement to Spec.)

There is independent evidence for the analysis that places the element preceding *li* in the C-adjoined position and attributes the 1W restriction on *li* to its inability to support a specifier. Saša Vukić (p.c.) observes the contrast between (35) and (47), involving past tense.

(47) (?)?Skupe knjige *li je* čitala?
      expensive books Q is read
    'Did she read **expensive books**?'

Suppose that *je* in (47) moves to C, right adjoining to *li*. In addition to *li*, C then contains *je*, which is not defective in the above sense.[11]

That the element hosting *li* is located in the C-adjoined position and not SpecCP is confirmed by sluicing constructions. Saito and Murasugi (1990) and Lobeck (1990) claim that only functional heads that undergo

---

[10] Speakers differ with respect to the level of productivity of the construction. Some speakers seem to allow only focused *wh*-elements in the construction.

[11] In Bošković (2000b, in press) I argue that SC clitics are not always located in C. This does not affect the argument, for which it suffices that *je* can move to C, at least in questions. Interestingly, adding a pronominal clitic to *li* does not have the same effect.

(i)   *Skupe knjige *li mu* čita?
      expensive books Q him reads
    'Does he/she read him **expensive books**?'

This could be interpreted as indicating either that pronominal clitics cannot support a Spec and hence do not change anything with respect to the inability of *li* to do so or that pronominal clitics cannot move to C. The latter would mean that pronominal clitics are lower than auxiliary clitics in the syntax. In Bošković (in press) I provide evidence that this is indeed the case. I show that pronominal and auxiliary clitics do not cluster together in the syntax, as syntactic accounts of 2P cliticization assume, the former being lower in the structure than the latter.

Spec-head agreement (SHA) license ellipsis of their complement. The claim is supported by (48a-d), which show that possessive *'s* and +*wh*-C, which undergo SHA, license ellipsis, whereas the non-agreeing functional heads, *the* and *that,* do not.

(48) a. Jim's talk about it was smart but [DP Bill [D' 's e] was boring]
 b. *A single student came because [DP [D' the e] liked the class]
 c. John met someone but I don't know [CP who [C' +*wh*-C e]
 d. *He thinks that she met someone but I don't believe [CP that e]

Significantly, SC *li* cannot license ellipsis of its complement.

(49) Vidi   nekoga. *Koga   li vidi?
 sees   someone   whom   Q sees
 'He/she sees someone. Who?'

This can be interpreted as indicating that *li* does not undergo SHA with the element checking its focus feature, which is readily captured under the C-adjunction analysis. Notice also that sluicing is in principle possible in SC. The null C, which presumably undergoes SHA with the *wh*-phrase in (50), can license it.[12]

(50) Vidi   nekoga. Koga   C vidi?
 sees   someone   whom   sees

Notice also that (49) improves if an auxiliary that can support a specifier is added, as expected under the current analysis.[13]

(51) Vidio je nekoga.   ??Koga li je vidio?
 seen is someone   whom   Q is seen
 'He saw someone. Who?'

Finally, notice that Bg differs from SC in that it allows unambiguous phrasal material to occur in front of *li*, which in our terms means that Bg *li* can take a specifier.

---

[12] In Bošković (2000a) I show that SC *wh*-phrases do not have to move to SpecCP in null-C matrix questions. Nothing, however, prevents them from doing so.

[13] Sandra Stjepanović (p.c.) notes that (51) might involve VP ellipsis, with *je* in Infl.

(52) Novata kola li prodade Petko
new-the car Q sold Petko
'Did Petko sell **the expensive car**?'

Significantly, Bg *li* also allows ellipsis, as shown by (53) (the first three examples are taken from Rudin 1986), which seem analyzable only as instances of ellipsis.

(53) Az li? Kŭštata li? Na masata li? Novata kŭšta li?
I Q the-house Q on the-table Q the-new house Q
Kogo li?
who Q
'Me?' '**The house**?' '**On the table**?' '**The new house**?' '**Who**?'

This is expected. Given that the focused element can be located in SpecCP and thus can undergo SHA with *li*, ellipsis is licensed with Bg *li*. The different behavior of Bg and SC *li* with respect to the ability to follow phrasal material and to license ellipsis thus receives a uniform account under the current analysis.

In conclusion, I have shown that, contrary to what has been previously argued, *li*-constructions do not provide evidence for PI or, more generally, PF Movement. PF can affect word order though not through actual PF Movement. It affects word order by determining which copy of a non-trivial chain should be pronounced. Finally, I have shown that scattered deletion is possible in non-trivial chains.

References

Billings, L., and C. Rudin. 1996. Optimality and superiority: A new approach to multiple-*wh* ordering. In *Formal Approaches to Slavic Linguistics: The College Park Meeting, 1994*, ed. J. Toman, 35-60. Ann Arbor: Michigan Slavic Publications.

Bošković, Ž. 2000a. On multiple *wh*-fronting. Ms., University of Connecticut.

Bošković, Ž. 2000b. Second position cliticisation: Syntax and/or phonology? In *Clitic phenomena in European languages*, ed. F. Beukema and M. den Dikken, 71-119. Amsterdam: John Benjamins.

Bošković, Ž. In press. *On the nature of the syntax-phonology interface: Cliticization and related phenomena.* Elsevier.

Bošković, Ž. and S. Franks. To appear. Phonology-syntax interactions in South Slavic. *Proceedings of Formal Approaches to Balkan and South Slavic Linguistics* 3.

Chomsky, N. 1995. *The minimalist program.* Cambridge: MIT Press.

Franks, S. 1998. Clitics in Slavic. Presented at the Comparative Slavic Morphosyntax Workshop, Bloomington, Indiana.

Franks, S. 2000. Clitics at the interface: An introduction to *Clitic phenomena in European languages.* In *Clitic phenomena in European languages,* ed. F. Beukema and M. den Dikken, 1-46. Amsterdam: John Benjamins.

Halpern, A. 1995. *On the placement and morphology of clitics.* Stanford: CSLI Publications.

Hiramatsu, K. in press. What did Move didn't erase? *University of Connecticut Working Papers in Linguistics* 10.

Izvorski, R., T. H. King, and C. Rudin. 1997. Against *Li* lowering in Bulgarian. *Lingua* 102, 187-194.

Kayne, R. 1994. *The antisymmetry of syntax.* Cambridge: MIT Press.

King, T. H. 1994. Focus in Russian yes-no questions. *Journal of Slavic Linguistics* 2, 92-120.

King, T. H. 1996. Slavic clitics, long head movement, and prosodic inversion. *Journal of Slavic Linguistics* 4, 274-311.

Legendre, G. 2000. Morphological and prosodic alignment of Bulgarian clitics. In *Optimality theory: Syntax, phonology, and acquisition,* ed. J. Dekkers, F. van der Leeuw, and J. van der Weijer, 423-462. Oxford: Oxford University Press.

Lobeck, A. 1990. Functional heads as proper governors. *Proceedings of North Eastern Linguistic Society* 20, 348-362.

Nunes, J. 2000. Linearization of chains and phonetic realization of chain links. In *Working minimalism,* ed. S. Epstein and N. Hornstein, 217-249. Cambridge: MIT Press.

Pesetsky, David. 1997. Optimality theory and syntax: Movement and pronunciation. In *Optimality theory: An overview.* eds. D. Archangeli and D. Langendoen, 134-170. Malden: Blackwell.

Progovac, L. 1996. Clitics in Serbian/Croatian: Comp as the second position. In *Approaching second: Second position clitics and related phenomena,* ed. A. Halpern and A. Zwicky, 411-428. Stanford: CSLI Publications.

Rudin, C. 1986. *Aspects of Bulgarian syntax: Complementizers and wh constructions.* Columbus: Slavica.

Rudin, C. 1988. On multiple questions and multiple *wh*-fronting. *Natural Language and Linguistic Theory* 6, 455-501.

Rudin, C. 1993. On focus position and focus marking in Bulgarian questions. *Proceedings of FLSM* 4, 252-265.

Rudin, C., C. Kramer, L. Billings, and M. Baerman. 1999. Macedonian and Bulgarian *li* questions: Beyond syntax. *Natural Language and Linguistic Theory* 17, 541-586.

Rudnitskaya, E. 2000. The derivation of yes-no *li* questions in Russian: Syntax and/or phonology? In *Formal Approaches to Slavic Linguistics: The Philadelphia Meeting 1999*, ed. T. H. King and I. Sekerina, 347-362. Ann Arbor: Michigan Slavic Publications.

Saito, M., and K. Murasugi. 1990. N'-deletion in Japanese. *University of Connecticut Working Papers in Linguistics* 3, 87-107.

Tomić, O. M. 1999. The Macedonian negation operator and clitichood. Ms., University of Novi Sad.

Wilder, C. and D. Ćavar. 1994a. Long head movement? Verb movement and cliticization in Croatian. *Lingua* 93, 1-58.

Department of Linguistics, U-145
University of Connecticut
Storrs, CT 06269
boskovic@sp.uconn.edu

You Always Forget Something...
(But Here's Something to Jog Your Memory)

Wayles Browne
Cornell University

1. Introduction

The genre of invited talk offers the speaker time and leeway for remarks and personal reflections—even personal remarks. So I will start by saying that as an undergraduate I did not appreciate the scholarly study of Russian literature. When reading Turgenev's *Rudin*, we were asked to discuss the title character as an individual or as a type. I greatly preferred scholarly analysis of the Russian language itself. My university offered a joint major combining linguistics with some other field, so I began to study linguistics and Slavic, and that is still what I combine in my work.

I did not reject artistic literature as a field of endeavor. Let writers write it, and let readers read! But I felt it was not a good field for analysis, because a given literary work depends very much on the author's individual characteristics and proclivities. Being at Harvard, I had the good fortune to study folk literature with Albert Bates Lord. Pieces of folk literature created within a tradition show structures and patterns that one can describe with relatively strict rules. Written literature, in contrast, seemed to me a much worse candidate for analysis: an author might at any moment decide to break out of whatever structures existed in the tradition, seeking to do something misleading and different, to lead the reader around by the nose, whether for fun or to be malicious.

As my reading knowledge of Slavic languages advanced, I began to follow linguistics journals from Slavic countries and see what kinds of articles they contained. One kind, I noticed, had titles resembling "Impersonal sentences in the short stories of Gogol'" or "Upotreba imperfekta u dramskim tekstovima Miroslava Krleže" ('The use of the imperfect in drama texts by Miroslav Krleža'). I tended to classify these as a low genre of linguistics paper. Could such a study yield conclusions valid for modern Russian or normal Croatian? Much better to look for impersonals or imperfects in straight, serious texts like newspapers.

Later I was fortunate enough to spend several years at universities in what was then Yugoslavia. I observed that professors assigned just this sort of topic to students: the occurrence of some phenomenon in a given literary text. A pattern seemed to emerge: together with their MA thesis or *seminarski rad,* students would hand in their collection of examples on slips of paper. It may or may not have been truly representative of the language as a whole, but some of the examples would be useful for a monograph or school grammar. That is, a by-product of these students' papers was a corpus of examples.

In the 1970s I had the privilege of working on the Zagreb University contrastive grammar projects under Prof. Rudolf Filipović (Filipović 1969a, 1969b, 1975). Many of the research papers that these projects produced were based on corpus material. Since we wanted to compare how English and Serbo-Croatian would express the same content, we took an existing corpus of English, the 1-million-word Brown University corpus (Kučera and Francis 1967), cut it in half (due to time and money constraints), and had part of the 500,000 words translated by Belgrade translators and part by Zagreb translators, to get a fair representation of both Serbian and Croatian usage.

Having been a student at MIT, I was familiar with Chomsky's claim that statistical information is unimportant for describing language. However, as my co-workers and I drew examples of this or that phenomenon from the Brown/Zagreb bilingual corpus, I began to notice three things:

First, the frequency with which, for instance, one or another type of English relative clause appeared in the corpus corresponded fairly well with my feelings as a native speaker about how widespread and important this type was in English. So native-speaker intuitions can include intuitions about frequency. Second, the frequency of relative-clause types in the translation agreed fairly well with my feelings about their importance in Serbo-Croatian. So even a second-language speaker can have meaningful intuitions about frequencies. Third, there were always examples on our slips of paper that gave me the Aha! experience: "I would not have thought of that!" So however good my intuitions might be, I would risk forgetting *something* unless and until I looked at large amounts of data.

This gave me a new understanding of the value, not only of examples, but of whole corpora (hereinafter: corpuses). But in the 1970s and 1980s, how could one buy or make one's own corpus? That would take a big project with many employees, like the Zagreb students who were paid by the hour to input a million words of text for the Institut za lingvistiku's frequency dictionary of Croatian. (The dictionary, Moguš et al., finally came out in 1999, after nearly a quarter of a century.)

A paradigm shift in my life as a linguist set in at the beginning of the 1990s. I began to use e-mail and receive letters in various Slavic languages. Then enterprising young people, mostly student volunteers, established free e-mail newspapers to report on the turbulent changes in each of the Slavic countries. I subscribed to Donosy in Polish, RokPress in Slovenian, BosNet (Bosnian and other usages of Serbo-Croatian), Karolina in Czech from Charles University, MakNews in Macedonian, and several lists that forwarded stories from governmental and non-governmental Croatian newspapers. These accumulated on my computer disks, and I had a corpus in Polish, Slovenian, and the other languages just waiting to be searched for words or phrases I—or my language students—were interested in. All these services deserve our thanks. Some still exist in 2000, including Donosy (subscribe by sending e-mail saying "subscribe Donosy-L Imie Nazwisko" to the address listproc@fuw.edu.pl), MakNews (write "subscribe MAKNWS-L firstname lastname" to listserv@listserv.acsu.buffalo.edu), and the Croatian Information Center (write to vijesti@hic.hr).

The World Wide Web became truly worldwide in the mid-1990s. One of its many applications in linguistics was to be a vehicle for corpuses of languages, so that now from my keyboard I can call up a Bosnian corpus in Oslo, a Croatian one in Zagreb, a Czech corpus in Prague, and a Russian one in Tübingen. The present paper will give some examples of questions that these corpuses helped answer and phenomena that they helped me remember or find for the first time. All, I trust, have clear practical applications, and some illuminate theoretical points as well.

2. Understanding case frames.

In Czech I found it odd that the verb *rozumět* 'to understand' really needed the dative on its object. Czechs would correct me when I made a mistake, but I still had the feeling that I had seen the verb with an accusative. When the Czech National Corpus became available on the Web (http://ucnk.ff.cuni.cz/english/pristup.html), I asked for instances of the first person singular present *rozumím*. The CNC provides only 20 at a time (Fig. 1 on the following page), but this was enough to show five different *case frames*, which I have labeled 1 to 5 in the figure. The main frame is indeed No. 1, with a dative object which can be any sort of person or thing or the abstract pronoun *tomu* 'it, that'. No. 2 is a subtype of No. 1, with the reflexive pronoun *si* in its meaning 'each other' standing in the dative and the other person with whom mutual understanding exists expressed as *s* 'with' plus instrumental. No. 3 is what was at the back of my mind: by something$_{Inst}$ I understand (English: I mean) something$_{Acc}$. No. 4 involves the familiar sameness-of-case principle (Bailyn 2000). In the example

(1) *Prohlášení českých a slovenských nezávislých ekonomů, rozumím, nečlenů politických stran*
 'The declaration **of Czech and Slovak independent economists**, that is to say, **of non-members of political parties**'

the first bold phrase is in the genitive and the second is also genitive to match it. Finally frame No. 5 contains an adverb meaning a language. This is not seen in this sample but is found in searching for *nerozumíš* in the Corpus: *nerozumíš česky* 'you do not understand Czech'. The adverb is not a direct object, though our English-speaking students often take it for one.[1]

---

[1] One word about fonts and character sets. The original e-mail newspapers were sent out using just the letters of the English alphabet without diacritics. This was relatively readable for Croatian or Slovenian, even more so for Polish which uses many combinations of letters like *cz, si*. But for a web site like the Czech or Croatian corpus, you need a set of fonts called Latin 2 or Central European (CE): Times CE, Courier CE etc. Thanks to George Fowler and other kind people for supplying these fonts, as well as keyboard layouts to use with them, for the Macintosh. Several web sites offer them free for both Macintosh and Windows operating systems: see Slavic fonts and keyboard drivers at the AATSEEL site http://clover.slavic.pitt.edu/~aatseel/ as well as the many useful links at Syeng-Mann Yoo's Slavophilia site at Ohio State University, http://www.slavophilia.net/computer.htm.

YOU ALWAYS FORGET SOMETHING... 81

[Screenshot of Czech National Corpus web interface "Veřejný přístup" showing search results for the word "rozumím" with 76 occurrences and a concordance listing of the first 20 hits.]

1. rozumím + Dat. (mu, tomu, slovu, pocitu...)
   "I understand (a person, thing, sentence represented by pronoun...)"
2. rozumím + Dat_Refl +s Inst. (každým, Giannim de Michalisem...)
   "a person and I understand each other, get along well"
3. rozumím + Inst. + Acc (chaosem podmínky...)
   "by chaos, I understand (I mean) the conditions of a..."
4. words_any case rozumím words_same case (nezávislých ekonomů, rozumím nečlenů politických stran)
   "of independent economists, I take this to mean: of non-members of political parties"
5. rozumím + adverb (česky...)
   "I understand Czech"

Fig. 1. Examples of rozumím from the Czech National Corpus.

3. A discussion with K. Naylor; the Web as my corpus.

In handouts for my Serbo-Croatian language course in the 70s, I had used *stvar* 'thing, matter' as my sample feminine noun ending in consonant, and given both *stvari* and *stvarju* as its instrumental singular. The late and regretted Kenneth Naylor pointed out that not all consonant-stem feminines in fact have both endings, *-i* and *-ju*. I thought I had seen *stvarju*, but perhaps it just looked logically possible to me. Existing grammars suggest that in general *-i* is more used when a consonant-stem noun is modified by something, for instance *dobrom stvari* 'good thing', and *-ju* more when it is unmodified; their rationale is that *-i* is also the marker for genitive, dative, locative and vocative singular of consonant-stem feminines, as well as for nominative, accusative, vocative, and genitive plural. I tried asking Croatian and Serbian speakers to form an instrumental, but *stvar* is a word of such general meaning that I could not think of a plausible example unmodified by any adjective or demonstrative: "How do you say 'by means of a thing'?"

Recently I returned to the search. The Croatian National Corpus at http://www.hnk.ffzg.hr/korpus.htm at the end of 1999 had 7.6 million words (subsequently increased to over 8 million). As Figure 2 (opposite) shows, it contained no instance of *stvarju*. Are there examples of *stvari*$_{\text{Inst.sg.}}$? Searching pages of results, I found one (Fig. 3 on p. ??):

(2) tendenciji vlasti da vjeru učini posve "privatnom stvari"
tendency of authorities to faith make fully private$_{\text{Inst.sg.}}$
matter$_{\text{Inst.sg.}}$
'the authorities' tendency to make faith a completely "private matter"'

Here *-om* in *privatnom* is the ending for fem. Inst. sg. Are there more such examples? The Croatian National Corpus at present does not provide for searching for a given *combination* of words. However, after I downloaded all 1952 occurrences of *stvari* in their context, I could search through them on my own computer for instances of *-om* followed by *stvari*. There are 11, all of which in fact contain the instrumental singular. (Of course, there might be additional instances of Inst.sg. *stvari* not preceded by an adjective or pronoun.) One sample:

30-milijunski korpus
suvremenoga hrvatskoga jezika

Trenutačni opseg: 7.672.240 pojavnica

Pretraga

Popis različnica

Popis dvorazličnica po čestoti (do čestote 100)
zipped RTF

Hrvatski elektronski tekstovni arhiv

Marko Marulić 67.108 pojavnica

Ivan Gundulić 89.144 pojavnica

Klasici hrvatske književnosti (CD Bulaja) 2.931.091 pojavnica

Ivan Mažuranić

Upit nad 30-milijunskim korpusom:

(Zamjensko pisme: %, npr. sve riječi koje počinju sa *imenic...* : imenic%
; Ako se u upitu nalazi %, pretraživanje korpusa znatno će se usporiti.)

Kodnu stranicu treba podesiti na Central European Alphabet (Windows) (CP 1250)
Oni koji preko tipkovnice ne mogu dobiti: č ć đ š ž neka ih kopiraju s ovog mjesta.

Unesite riječ:

[stvarju]

Odaberite (pot)korpus: [Cijeli korpus] [Pošalji] [Briši]

Izvori

Natrag

Webmaster: Croatian ZZL forces

Tuesday, February 15, 2000   30m pretraga

30m korpus (probna verzija) 15.02.2000 22:45:52
Korpus: 30m_test
Rezultat pretrage: stvarju
Za Airu okolinu pritisnite na ime izvora na desnoj margini --------------------------------->
Takva pojavnica ne postoji u korpusu
Natrag

Fig. 2. The Croatian National Corpus: stvarju not found.

Tuesday, February 15, 2000 Page: 1

30m korpus (probna verzija) 15.02.2000 23:21:34

Korpus: 30m_test

Rezultat pretrage: **stvari**

Za širu okolinu pritisnite na ime izvora na desnoj margini -->

iš bolju kuću, a radiš po 16 sati. Pitanje je koliko ti u	stvari stanuješ u kući. Možeš i u štrajk, no štrajk je	VJ981209i 591
od naslovom »Croatia: A Nation Forged in War«, koja je, u	stvari, bila prva povijest Hrvatske, napisana iz pera neko	VJ981209t 415
vao ni najmanju inicijativu da tamo odem na svoju ruku. U	stvari, moj dolazak u Beograd bio je čisti slučaj! · Niste	VJ981209t 487
li još u Srbiji, na što je on vrisnuo: »Neee, nismo!«. U	stvari, za Hrvatsku sam mislio da se prostire samo duž jad	VJ981209t 526
uposti. Bez ikakve želje za upoznavanjem stvarnoga stanja	stvari, svaka se promjena u Hrvatskoj automatski povezival	VJ981209t 778
ekako bilo jasno da je to toliko dugo čekano priznanje, u	stvari »debelo« kasnilo! · Britanska vanjska politika	VJ981209t 875
loše političke procjene nisu bili previše inteligentni. U	stvari, postupci Foreign Officea najbolje ilustriraju nisk	VJ981209t 903
mačke tvrtke glavni izvođači radova, otkiva da Nijemci, u	stvari, sami plaćaju svoj izvoz. Najveći dokaz da je c	VJ981209t 146
a i ljudi koji slično misle, i ribljih restorana, i mnoge	stvari koje imaju gradovi na moru. Prema tome, Zagreb stva	VJ981209z 515
predsjednikom Tuđmanom, ocijenio je, dodavši da se »neke	stvari mogu rješavati na drugim razinama«. Najavio je i da	VJ9812101 625
s. Na mala vrata uvlače se i prihvaćaju nekoć nezamislive	stvari. Britanski Odbor katoličkih biskupa za bioetiku	VJ981210g 923

Tuesday, February 15, 2000 Page: 4

ali da treba imati realan prikaz i ne treba prejudicirati	stvari«, zaključio je ministar obrane Miljavac.</font></p>	VJ990115up 90
onski omotač i postupanje s proizvodima koje sadrže takve	stvari. Donesena je i odluka o objavi Europske kulturne ko	VJ990115up 14
knjiže, ljudima koji obavljaju zadatke govore samo nužne	stvari, onoliko koliko smiju znati. Time se vlastiti tabor	vj990116g 113
ća, promjena smjera bila je očigledna i radi nekih drugih	stvari. Zbog ranije popularizirane pozicije estradne »obra	vj990116t 218
ali naš politički odnos u smislu da želimo da se te dvije	stvari odijele, a ako se objedinjavaju, to mora biti uz pr	vj990116up 26
ektivni i neobjektivni problemi u poljoprivredi i da neke	stvari mogu biti bolje. No, u toj emisiji u ekstremnom se	vj990117up 19
- je li Papa dobro informiran/ Ako Papa upozorava na neke	stvari, onda sigurno ima razloga i argumenata, odgovorio j	vj99011800 190
ršinskih zbivanja može stvoriti neobjektivnu sliku stanja	stvari i stvoriti pogrešan dojam o naravi nečega o čemu se	vj990118i 109
i općina Republike Srpske, ali me zabrinjava što se ružne	stvari događaju u Brčkom, u gradu pod supervizijom međunar	vj990118sz 84
- je li Papa dobro informiran/ Ako Papa upozorava na neke	stvari, onda sigurno ima razloga i argumenata, odgovorio j	vj990118t 666
govor na postavljeno pitanje: »Ako Papa upozorava na neke	stvari, onda sigurno ima razloga i argumenata, a kako možd	vj990118t 126
kojoj nema ni govora o otpuštanju 600 ljudi te da ih je u	stvari toliko trenutačno u postupku izbora ili reizbora, a	vj990118up 73
dalima unutar Europske unije i njezine Komisije koja je u	stvari neka vrsta europske »vlade« - mogle bi promatrača n	vj990119g 425
rice u stalnom »dijalogu« Hrvatske i Bruxellesa. Okrenimo	stvari naopačke (naravno, samo u igri). Tada bismo mogli o	vj990119g 443
iti isključivo invalidi Domovinskog rata. Jedna od dobrih	stvari koja je krenula vezana je uz kredite za samozapošlj	vj990119i 391
ovima napravljena je velika pogreška, i to zbog sljedećih	stvari. Kredite za samozapošljavanje trebali su dobivati o	vj990119i 406
o ćete nakon završetka utakmice puno i lakše vidjeti neke	stvari, odgovorio je Jelovac. Istina, Zadar je u 33. m	vj990119s 171
e predsjednik Uprave Vjesnika Ivan Božičević. Da će mnoge	stvari biti jasnije u četvrtak, potvrdio je i glavni uredn	vj990119up 13
nskom prostoru. NATO mora Slobodanu Miloševiću reći »	stvari na veoma oštar način« i nakon pokolja u selu Reqaku	vj990119vp 86
ravo na imunitet, te da je riječ o unutrašnjoj čileanskoj	stvari. Na suđenje u London doputovao je iz Madrida s	vj990119vp 13
vakom djetetu. Zato ćemo u ovom tekstu podsjetiti na neke	stvari kako bi se pomoglo onim roditeljima koji iz neznanj	GK9624_k03 93
atehete, jer će u njoj naći kratko i jasno izrečene bitne	stvari, kako crkvene godine tako i pojedinih sakramenata.	GK9625_42 192
izreći, ali te kontracepcijske pilule ubijaju u ženi neke	stvari, pa se sve to negativno odražava na njezin psihički	GK9625_k01 20
unutarnjim odnosima naše države. "Samo slogom rastu male	stvari, a nesloga sve pokvari." Dijalog pak uključuje među	GK9626_01 789
nekoliko uredno ispisanih razglednica Splita. <p>Te su mi	stvari svojevrsni znakovi onoga što ostaje iza Susreta. Do	GK9626_08 151
boravnim ostati ono što je ona sudionica koja je izgubila	stvari marljivo ispisivala i podcrtavala u svojim skriptam	GK9626_08 311
a su se tendenciji vlasti da vjeru učini posve »privatnom	stvari«, da se Crkvu utjera u geto u kojem bi bila osuđena	GK9626_08 634
ako još k tome pod potrebama mislimo samo na materijalne	stvari - onda će se Caritas zaista brzo ugasiti, ali s nji	GK9626_50 289
odine braka Perka i Marko Filipović odricali su se mnogih	stvari, pa i kad su otjerani sa svoga ognjišta, iz sela Pa	GK9626_66 937
j. obasuo svakim dobrom te osobe. I kad se blagoslivljaju	stvari i predmeti i onda se u prvom redu moli za osobe koj	GK9627_36 566
itva za sretnu vožnju ljudi. Tako i blagoslov svih drugih	stvari ili predmeta molitva je za dobro ljudi koji će se n	GK9627_36 593

Fig. 3. Croatian National Corpus: examples of stvari, including one instrumental

(3) ...i to sam, iskreno govoreći, smatrao završenom stvari.
and that Aux sincerely speaking considered finished$_{\text{Inst.sg.}}$ matter$_{\text{Inst.sg.}}$
'and that, frankly speaking, I considered (to be) a finished matter.'

Shall we conclude that Ken was right? At least, it appears that Inst.sg. *stvarju* is an order of magnitude rarer than Inst.sg. *stvari*. But then I decided to use a much bigger corpus. Does the form *stvarju* appear anywhere on any of the Croatian, Bosnian, or Serbian-language web pages in the world? That is a lot more than 7 million words, because it includes back files of newspapers, some literary texts, a lot of rock song lyrics, as well as advertising and *kompjuteraši* showing off their skills.

First I tried my favorite search engine at present, Google (http://google.com). It has a property that we could call *uočljivost:* when it finds a web page containing the search word, it not only lists the title and address of the page, but pulls out the context in which the word appears and shows it with the word itself boldfaced. So if I search for FASL9 and Google finds the site for the conference, it will display the line:

(4) All **FASL9** sessions will be held in Ballantine 005.

Another remarkable Google feature could be dubbed *zmartwychwstanie*. Even if a web page or its server is no longer in existence, Google still has the content and can retrieve it when you click on cached.

Google located many thousands of instances of *stvari*, some Slovenian and some Serbian, Croatian, and Bosnian, less than 1% of which were instrumental case. It neither found nor resurrected any instances of my word *stvarju*. (By good luck, the string *stvarju* is not a word occurring in any of the other languages in which web pages are extant.) However, I did not give in. I opened Metacrawler, http://www.metacrawler.com, which activates several search engines simultaneously (Fig. 4 on the following page). Two of the engines, AltaVista and Infoseek, found a total of 5 occurrences. The title of a 1998 article in the *Godišnjak Pravnog fakulteta u Osijeku* (Annual of the Law School in Osijek, Croatia) is:

No hits on "**stvarju**" (term was not used in search)

Your search - **stvarju** - did not match any documents in this database.

- Make sure all words are spelled correctly.
- Try using fewer words.
- Try using more general keywords.
- Try different keywords.

Copyright ©2000 Google Inc. - About - Search Tips

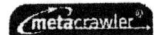

http://www.metacrawler.com (makes several search engines do a search simultaneously)

What are you looking for?
[stvarju]   Search   Search Help
○ any ● all ○ phrase

□ Find books on stvarju at bn.com

View Related

Results for "**stvarju**" 1 to 5 of 5 results
● View by: Relevance | Site | Source   ✉ Email results to a friend

Pravni fakultet "Pravni vjesnik"
    AltaVista : ...ASOPIS dGODI..NJAK PRAVNOG FAKULTETA U OSIJEKUE I/1978. Dragan Cepeli..: Uzdr..avanje
    me..u bra..nim drugovima, Vilim Herman: Slobodno vrijeme (osnovne ...
    Infoseek : Dragan Cepelić: Uzdržavanje medu bračnim drugovima, Vilim Herman: Slobodno vrijeme (osnovne
    napomene), Vladimir Horvat: Usuglašavanje interesa u proširenoj reprodukciji samoupravnim sp ...
    1000, http://zakon.pravos.hr/biblioteka/pravnivjesnik.html (AltaVista, Infoseek)   Hot Work for
                                                                                                     High-Tech Gurus
3 14.01.1994 Odluka o progla..enju Zakona o izmjenama i dopunama Zakona o obvez
    ZASTUPNI..KI DOM SABORA REPUBLIKE HRVATSKE. Na temelju ..lanka 89. Ustava Republike Hrvatske,   Deep discounts on
    donosim. ODLUKA. o progla..enju Zakona o izmjenama i...   over 50k business
    657, http://www.nn.hr/Glasilo/94/33_94.htm (AltaVista)   computing products!
                                                                                                     Solutions4SURE.com
VELIMIR DE..ELI..I SVEU..ILI..NA KNJI..NICA U ZAGREBU
    VJESNIK BIBLIOTEKARA HRVATSKE IZDAJE HRVATSKO BIBLIOTEKARSKO DRU..TVO ZAGREB
    GODINA XXXIII 1990. BROJ 1 .. 4. UDK 027.54 +027.7(497.13-2 Zagreb) : 929...
    471, http://www.ffzg.hr/infos/biblio/nastava/dz/text/dezelic.html (AltaVista)

91 28.10.1996 Zakon o vlasnistvu i drugim starnim pravima
    Home | Clanci | O Burzi | Rekli su o nama | Clanovi | Propisi | Lavsa. ZASTUPNICKI DOM SABORA REPUBLIKE HRVATSKE. Z A K O N. O
    VLASNISTVU I DRUGIM...
    205, http://burza-nekretnina.com/bbo/zakvl.htm (AltaVista)

OD SLOBODE KAO BUNTA DO SLOBODE KAO BICA
    OD SLOBODE KAO BUNTA DO SLOBODE KAO BICA. Episkop Ignjatije (Midic) Sloboda, kao osnovna kategorija ljudskog postojanja,
    moze se shvatiti veoma...
    101, http://www.spc.org.yu/Latin/sloboda.html (AltaVista)

Fig. 4.   Google finds no instances of stvarju; Metacrawler finds five.

(5) Upravljanje suvlasničkom stvarju prema Zakonu o vlasništvu i drugim stvarima.
management co-owned thing$_{Inst.sg.}$according-to Law about ownership and other matters
'The management of property held in co-ownership under the Act on Ownership and Other Matters.'

The second instance, a 1994 amendment to a Croatian law, has almost the same phrase:

(6) ...propisa o upravljanju zajedničkom stvarju u suvlasništvu.
regulations on management joint thing$_{Inst.sg.}$ in co-ownership
'...of regulations on management of joint property in co-ownership.'

The third instance is in an article in the *Vjesnik bibliotekara Hrvatske* (Herald of the Librarians of Croatia), and is of historical interest, since it quotes a document dated 1914:

(7) ...kad su stom [i.e. s tom] stvarju spojili i njegov telegram Strossmajeru.
when Aux with that thing$_{Inst.sg.}$linked also his telegram Strossmajer
'when they linked his telegram to Strossmajer with that matter.'

The fourth is another law text like the first and second, while the fifth is a Serbian bishop's meditation on what God's will does for the world's existence:

(8) ...čini svet dogaŭanjem i dogaŭajem a ne stvarju.
makes world happening$_{Inst.sg.}$ and event$_{Inst.sg.}$ and not thing$_{Inst.sg.}$
'...makes the world a process and an event, rather than a thing.'

As we see, four of the five examples have the ending *-ju* even though this consonant-stem noun is modified by an adjective or demonstrative, so that the form *stvari* would also have been identifiable as an instrumental; the last is unmodified, although it is in a parallel construction with other identifiable instrumental nouns. I greatly regret not being able to show this to Ken.

4. Morphological questions.

4.1 Hungarian.

A Cornell student working on a non-Slavic language, Hungarian, felt the lack of an analogue to *Barron's 201 Polish Verbs* or *L'Art de conjuguer*, and decided to compile a handbook himself. In Hungarian, some verbs have a 'fleeting vowel' in their stems which drops out when an ending is added that begins with a vowel; thus the stem *érez* 'feel' plus the ending *-em* '1.sg.' yields *érzem* 'I feel (with definite direct object)'. In checking the manuscript (Kai Schafft, "A Guidebook to the Conjugation of Common Hungarian Verbs", unpublished manuscript, Cornell 1999), I wanted to know whether this also holds for the verb *énekel* 'sing'. The well-known textbook Bánhidi-Jókay-Szabó 1965 (and later eds.) uses the form *énekelik* for the 3.pl. present (Lesson 7), thus with *e* remaining in place between *k* and *l*, but later mentions this as one of the vowel-elision verbs (p. 207). The Alta Vista search engine http://www.altavista.com proved to have better coverage of Hungarian web pages than Google. Its numerical results for searches for alternative verb forms are large enough to be significant, and show that vowel-dropping is the norm for *énekel*, although vowel retention is also found. Here are results for sample verb forms with and without the *-e-*:

'(s)he sings' (definite object)
énekeli   *énekli*
8 pages found.   194 pages found.

'they sing' (definite object)
énekelik   *éneklik*
29 pages found.   133 pages found.

4.2 Czech.

I wondered about a similar question in Czech. For a long time literary Czech had obligatory přehláska (vowel fronting) of the present tense endings after palatal consonants: thus present stems in *-uj* got *-i* rather than *-u* for 1.sg., and *-í* rather than *-ou* for 3.pl. At present the language is beginning to accept the colloquial forms with *-u* and *-ou* too. Is it doing so to the same extent? We try a sample verb in the Czech National Corpus, *milovat* 'to love', present stem *miluj-*.

miluju	*miluji* 1.sg.
36 instances	37
milujou	*milují* 3.pl.
4 (2 of them identical)	75

It seems clear that the colloquial Czech 1.sg. is accepted in written usage to a much greater extent than the colloquial 3.pl. Can we corroborate this with search-engine data? A Google search on *miluju* gives a very large number of extraneous hits, because this can be a word in Croatian/Bosnian/Serbian too, namely the 3.pl. of *milovati* 'to caress', as well as Slovak if somebody has left out the accent-mark on 3.pl. *milujú* 'they love'. Therefore we search for the group "miluju ji" — the verb with an accompanying word *ji*, which is a word only in Czech (meaning 'her', Acc.sg. fem.), not in Slovak or C/B/S.[2]

miluju ji	*miluji ji* 1.sg.
108 (some are repeat instances)	219
milujou ji	*milují ji* 3.pl.
3	110

Thus we can say that the data from the random corpus of the Web agree with those from the carefully compiled National Corpus to within a factor of 2: *miluju* is much more accepted than *milujou*.

4.3 Serbo-Croatian.

A well-known pedagogical problem in Serbo-Croatian (all standards) is the genitive plural of nouns. For consonant-stem feminines, it is easy: G.pl. in virtually every instance ends in *-i* (traditionally the long vowel *-ī*) thus *stvar: stvarī*. Masculine and neuter nouns in general have *-a* (traditionally a long ending *-ā)* for the G.pl. and can either break up a preceding consonant cluster with another *ā* or not: *objekt* 'object, building' has G.pl. *objekātā*, while *kontekst* 'context' has G.pl. *kontekstā* without cluster-breaking. Only a small number of masculine nouns have

---

[2] *Ji* is a dative sg. form in Slovene, but Slovene does not have present tense forms *miluju, miluji, milujou,* or *milují.*

long -ī, thus *ljudi* 'people, persons': G.pl. *ljudī*. The feminine *-a* stem nouns (this is in fact the majority type of feminine nouns) are another story. If final *a* is preceded by a single consonant, as in *knjiga* 'book', the G.pl. virtually always has long *-ā*. But if a cluster precedes, there are three possibilities: long *-ā*, long *-ā* with cluster-breaking, and long *-ī*, e.g., *djevojka* 'girl' G.pl. *djevojākā*; *tajna* 'secret', G.pl. *tajnā* and *tajnī*.

In writing pedagogical materials, I would want to include the most frequent *-ī* genitive plurals, whether from masculine nouns or feminine *-a* nouns. Neither the Bosnian nor the Croatian corpus has morphological tags at present, so that I cannot simply search for genitive plural nouns. But, considering that nouns are frequently preceded by modifiers which agree with them, I searched the Bosnian corpus for any word ending in *-ih* (the G.pl. ending for adjectives and pronouns) followed by a word in *-i*. At first this yielded many extraneous answers, including some where the first word is the pronoun *ih* 'them'. I therefore required the first word to have at least one initial letter before *ih*, which is expressed (using the notation of 'regular expressions') as ".+ih" in the corpus's search string; and the second word (since the minimal feminine noun in *-a* is three letters long) needs two preceding letters. Therefore we search for ".+ih" ".+.+i", which yields 1465 examples. Many of these are spurious, such as *njih postoji* 'them it exists', but among them we find such genuine, and frequent, masculine nouns as *ljudi, mjesec* 'month' *mjesecī, sat* 'hour' *satī*, and *-a* feminines such as *cigla* 'brick' *ciglī, lampa* 'lamp' *lampī, alga* 'seaweed' *algī, bajka* 'fairy tale' *bajkī, gošća* 'female guest' *gošćī*, plus a good selection of consonant-stem feminines: *nit* 'thread' *nitī, stvar* 'thing' *stvarī, riječ* 'word' *riječī, misao* 'thought' *mislī, noć* 'night' *noćī, strast* 'passion' *strastī*, etc.

5. Syntactic questions.

The Russian word *čej* 'whose' is familiar as a question word. Opinions of Russian grammarians differ as to whether it can be a relativizer; *whose* relatives are most frequently rendered in Russian with the genitive of *kotoryj*, thus 'of which, of whom'

(9) kompozitor, pesni kotorogo vy peli
    composer, songs which-Gen. you sang
    'the composer whose songs you sang'

Can we attest the *čej* relative, and are there any other uses for *čej* that I have forgotten? We search the Russian corpus in Tübingen at http://www.sfb441.uni-tuebingen.de/b1/korpora.html and obtain the results shown in part in Fig. 5 on the following page.[3]

The relative appears in the first example shown; then we see two interrogative instances. In the last line, *ni v č'ix* is the result of splitting the negative word *ničej* 'no one's' with a preposition, a phenomenon studied extensively by Loren Billings (e.g. 1997). The next-to-last is a construction I truly, as a lover of relative clauses, should have thought to investigate: it is the **co**-relative, with a wh-word in the subordinate clause accompanied by a demonstrative or personal pronoun in the main clause.

(10) Net už, č'i kroliki, tot puskaj ix i kormit.
 no already whose rabbits that-one let them also feed
 'Oh no; the one whose the rabbits are should also feed them.'

6. Collocations.

Words in a language do not co-occur entirely freely: each one has some words that it likes to go with and other words that it does not. Such preferred and dispreferred collocations have not been as well studied in general linguistics as they deserve, although the Meaning<—>Text theory of Mel'čuk (1974, 1995, Steele 1990) has mechanisms for describing many types of them. Mel'čuk's dictionary of Russian (Mel'čuk and Zholkovsky 1984) and Benson's of English (Benson et al. 1986) register collocations, the latter with an explicitly pedagogical purpose. Knowledge of collocations is vital for language teaching and learning. Examples from English are the names for a social abuse much debated recently:

---

[3] One can write the Suchausdruck, or expression sought for, either in Russian KOI8-R or Windows 1251 coding, or in Latin transliteration, and the output can be shown in any of these. The corpus uses a transliteration in which ch stands for ч and q for ь, so **chq.*** means чь followed by any letter (.) or any sequence (zero or more) thereof (*), thus covering all declined forms of *čej* apart from *čej* itself.

Uppsala-Korpus

Gesucht wurde: "chq.*"

transformierter Suchstring: chq[A-Za-z]*

Neue Suche

Suchausdruck: [_____] ○ Mit ● Ohne Kontext
[KOI8   ▼] Fundstellen anzeigen? □
Groß- und Kleinbuchstaben unterscheiden? □ [Suchen!] [zuruecksetzen]
Hinweise zu den Suchmoeglichkeiten
Zurueck zur SFB 441-Hauptseite Projekt B1 TUSNELDA

Gefunden in Text SGID0301 (Kogda politikoj zanimajutsja vserqez. Razmyshlenija politicheskogo obozrevatelja. "Moskovskie novosti", 88-12-11 (1.026).)

Татлиев к тому же, видимо, забыл, что, будучи избран в Степанакерте, представляет избирателей Нагорного Карабаха, о чьих требованиях также умолчал.

Gefunden in Text XSKO0101 (Kochnev, M., "Potrjasenie", M., 1964, str. 322-341 (5.010).)

Дурачье вы оба: до сих пор не сообразили, в чьем горшке Одинца искать?

- В чьем?

Дав Ионе досыта назаикаться, пастухи заговорили по очереди: - Нет уж, чьи кролики, тот пускай их и кормит.

Gefunden in Text XSRA0201 (Rasputin, V., Zhivi i pomni, v kn. "Sobranie sochinenij v 2-x tomax", t. 2, str. 8-23 (4.983).)

Я теперь в твоих руках, больше ни в чьих.

Ее всегда раздражали самодеятельные санитары, чья сердобольность позволяет им задержаться в тылу, отстать от тех, кто идет в первой цепи.

Der Suchbegriff wurde in 49 Saetzen gefunden.

michael.betsch@uni-tuebingen.de

Fig. 5. Tübinger russische Korpora at
http://www.sfb441.uni-tuebingen.de/b1/korpora.html
Ask questions in Russian font (KOI8-R or Windows 1251) or in transliteration. In their table, ch means ч and q means ь.

(11) capital punishment   *the capital punishment
      *capital penalty   ?the capital penalty
      *death punishment   *the death punishment
      *death penalty   the death penalty

All of these are equally compositional as far as semantic interpretation goes, but only two are established in the language and hence safe for a learner to use.

A corpus can yield information about favored collocations. If we wish to teach the use of the Bosnian (Croatian, Serbian) word *pitanje* 'question', we need to tell what you do with a question. In English you usually *ask* it, sometimes *bring* it *up* or *raise* it. Not in Bosnian: the chosen verb taking *pitanje* as its object is not *pitati* 'ask' as my students are inclined to believe (searching the Bosnian Corpus shows no examples with *pitanje* coming up to seven words before or after *pitati* and functioning as its object) but *postaviti,* otherwise 'stand something up'. And this is by far the most frequent use of *postaviti* (16 out of 33 occurrences of infinitive *postaviti* are *postaviti pitanje,* and 2 more contain the plural *pitanja*).

A comparison with Polish is of interest. Here too the verb collocating with *pytanie* as its object is *postawić,* but a search shows that this is a comparatively minor use. Lacking a Polish corpus at the time of the FASL meeting (Adam Przepiorkowski later made one available at http://ling.ohio-state.edu/~adamp/searchpage.html which contains more than 10 million words!), I searched the Polish version of the Infoseek search engine at http://info.icm.edu.pl and had to go through more than 50 instances with other things that you can *postawić* ('lay out tarot cards, put a monitor on a computer, set two heroes against each other, build a building or a factory, set up a Bot [= a small computer program that does some task automatically], ...') before encountering a *pytanie.* Polish *postawić* is a member of a thriving system of positional verbs ('put in a standing position' vs. *położyć* 'put in a lying position' and *posadzić* 'put in a sitting position'), while this system is little used in South Slavic, and presumably wider literal use in Polish also leads to wider non-literal use.

7. Government patterns.

When we describe the lexical entry for a verb in a Slavic language, we have to tell what government pattern (case frame or preposition frame) the verb takes. Russian *interesovat'sja* 'to be interested in' needs the instrumental on its object, whereas *ljubit'* 'to love' requires the accusative. There are some generalizations to be made about the semantics of the verbs that take one or another case or preposition+case on their objects, as noted in Laura Janda's presentation (Janda 2000). However the degree to which students or analysts can rely on these generalizations is limited. Even if *Ja interesujus' Annoj*$_{Inst}$ 'I am interested in Anna' in a given instance is another way of saying *Ja ljublju Annu*$_{Acc}$ 'I love Anna', we cannot let our students say **Ja interesujus' Annu*$_{Acc}$. Even if my feeling for Anna contains the "trying to get" semantics which Janda regards as characteristic for the genitive, I should not say **Ja ljublju Anny*$_{Gen}$. Even if I think of offering my love to Anna as a precious gift, she cannot be in the dative case as a recipient: **Ja ljublju Anne*$_{Dat}$.

Linguists have sometimes believed that it is less important to describe the government pattern of nouns and adjectives than of verbs.[4] One claim is that nouns and adjectives can always take a complement in the genitive, so there is no need to describe the government pattern. However a genitive does not always play the same role as a complement in some other form: Russian

(12) podarok molodym xozjajkam
      gift young$_{Dat}$ housekeepers$_{Dat}$
      'a gift to young housekeepers'

(the title of a famous cookbook) does not express the same relationship as

(13) podarok molodyx xozjaek
      gift young$_{Gen}$ housekeepers$_{Gen}$
      'a gift of (= from, by) young housekeepers'.

---

[4] My thoughts on this topic crystallized in the course of discussions with Steven Franks and commenting on his works, but he should not be confused with the "straw" scholar whose claims I will criticize here.

My "straw" interlocutor can argue that the dative is inherited from the verb underlying the noun, namely *dat'* 'to give' which does indeed take a dative for the recipient, so we would not have to mention the dative separately in describing *podarok*.

I would answer by bringing up *ljubov'* 'love', which is derived from the verb *ljubit'* 'to love' to about the same extent as *podarok* is from *dat'*. The complement of *ljubov'* is not genitive (the agent is, but not the object of love); neither is it inherited from *ljubit'*. The construction with the noun in Russian is:

(14) ljubov' k Anne, k nauke, ...
love toward Anna$_{Dat}$, toward science$_{Dat}$, ...

My opponent might say here that *k* + dative 'toward; to [a person]' after *ljubov'* is semantically justified as a way to express the complement. I reply: for one noun you say it can take the genitive, for another noun you say it can take the case inherited from the verb, for a third you say it can take a semantically justified complement. So you need to give a government pattern for each noun just in order to tell which of the three possibilities is realized.

In order to make my counterargument a bit stronger, I decided to compare the patterns taken by the same noun in different Slavic languages. Corpus and web technology makes this much easier. Bosnian, Croatian, and Serbian *k* + dative is similar in semantics to Russian *k* + dative 'toward; to (a person)' but is very rare as a complement to the noun *ljubav*; the noun almost always takes *prema* + dative 'toward, in the direction of; according to' instead, thus *ljubav prema Ani, prema nauci* (Croatian *prema znanosti*). (The Bosnian corpus does turn up a Biblical example *ako imate ljubav k meni* 'If you have love to me' as well as reminding me of a complement type I would have forgotten: *ljubav između ... i ...* 'love between ... and ...'.) Slovenian *k* + dative is even more similar to Russian in its semantics, but search engine data show that the complement to *ljubezen* has to be *do* + genitive 'up to': *ljubezen do Ane, do znanosti*. My conclusion is that 'semantically justified' is not a clear notion when applied to complement types, and one **really** needs to describe each noun's government pattern as part of its lexical entry. Identical claims and arguments can be made for adjectives' and adverbs' lexical entries as well.

8. Remarks on Bulgarian.

By happenstance, none of the above examples have utilized Bulgarian, but I would like to call attention to an excellent set of "Bulgarian research and study materials" gathered by Kjetil RĆ Hauge of Oslo University at http://www.hf.uio.no/east/bulg/mat. These include several small searchable corpuses and the texts of some linguistics dissertations.

Further, Bulgaria has a lively culture of commercialized web search engines, as I found when Loren Billings (personal communication) asked me about the behavior of certain words that end in *-lija*. Three of these are http://www.info.bg, http://netinfo.bg, and http://www.search.bg. All operate in Cyrillic, and font problems arise from time to time in displaying their results, but they can turn up much usable information. Even if one does not have a matching Cyrillic keyboard resource on one's computer, it is still possible to enter a desired search string by using a method similar to the old detective-story cliché—the ransom note made of bits cut from a newspaper. One finds, for example, a Cyrillic *l* somewhere on the engine's display page, cuts and pastes it into the search window, then adds a Cyrillic *i*, then a *ja*, and so on.

9. Instead of a conclusion.

In recent years a subfield of linguistics has taken shape known as corpus linguistics. The present paper, unsophisticated from a statistical viewpoint, has little in it for the CL adept. Rather, its focus is on practical helps for the ordinary working Slavist. May you use them in good health!

References

Bailyn, John. 2000. "Slavic Syntax 2000: GB/Minimalism." Paper presented at SLING2K meeting, Indiana University, Feb. 18, 2000. To appear as "Generative Syntax (GB/Minimalism)" in G. Fowler, ed. (in press). *Slavic Linguistics in the 21st Century*. Bloomington: Slavica.

Bánhidi-Jókay-Szabó. 1965. Bánhidi, Zoltán, Zoltán Jókay, Dénes Szabó. *Learn Hungarian* . 5th ed. Budapest: Tankönyvkiadó.

Benson et al. 1986. Benson, Morton, Evelyn Benson and Robert Ilson. *The BBI Combinatory Dictionary of English: A Guide to Word Combinations.* Amsterdam: John Benjamins.

Billings, Loren. 1997. "Negated Prepositional Phrases in Slavic." In W. Browne, E. Dornisch, N. Kondrashova and D. Zec, eds., *Formal Approaches to Slavic Linguistics* 4, 1995. Ann Arbor: Michigan Slavic Publications.

Filipović, Rudolf, ed. 1969a. The Yugoslav Serbo-Croatian - English Contrastive Project. A. *Reports* 1–. Zagreb: Institute of Linguistics.

Filipović, Rudolf, ed. 1969b. The Yugoslav Serbo-Croatian - English Contrastive Project. B. *Studies* 1-. Zagreb: Institute of Linguistics.

Filipović, Rudolf, ed. 1975. The Zagreb English - Serbo-Croatian Contrastive Project. *Kontrastivna analiza engleskog i hrvatskog ili srpskog jezika. Contrastive analysis of English and Serbo-Croatian* 1–. Zagreb: Institute of Linguistics.

Janda, Laura. 2000. "Cognitive Linguistics." Paper presented at SLING2K meeting, Indiana University, Feb. 18, 2000.

Kučera, Henry, and W. Nelson Francis. 1967. *Computational analysis of present-day American English.* Providence: Brown University Press.

Mel'čuk, I.A. 1995. *Russkij jazyk v modeli "smysl <—> tekst".* Wiener slawistischer Almanach, Sonderband 39. Moscow and Vienna.

Mel'čuk, I.A. and Zholkovsky, A.K. 1984. *Tolkovo-kombinatornyj slovar' sovremennogo russkogo jazyka.* Wiener slawistischer Almanach, Sonderband 14. Vienna.

Moguš et al. 1999. Moguš, Milan, Maja Bratanić and Marko Tadić. *Hrvatski čestotni rječnik.* Zagreb: Zavod za lingvistiku / Školska knjiga.

Steele, James, ed. 1990. *Meaning-Text Theory: Linguistics, Lexicography, and Implications.* Ottawa: University of Ottawa Press.

Wayles Browne
Linguistics, Morrill Hall
Cornell University
Ithaca, New York 14853
ewb2@cornell.edu

The Representation of the Jers in Russian

Peter Chew
Oxford University

1. Introduction

This article has two principal aims. The first is to show that the facts described by the traditional generative account of the jers in Russian can equally well be described by context-free grammar (CFG). This is of interest for three main reasons. First, any CFG is reversible; a theory which can be expressed as a CFG can thus function equally well as a model of both linguistic perception and production. Secondly, it is a straightforward matter to implement a CFG (even a probabilistic CFG) computationally.[1] This allows the grammar to be tested very easily. Thirdly, formulating a working theory in CFG forces one to take into account some important considerations vis-à-vis the representation of the jers. I shall argue that jers must be elements of morphological structure, not constituents of syllable structure or members of the phonological inventory, unless one is to adopt a significantly more unconstrained view of language. The second aim of this article is to show computationally that the traditional account predicts when jers vocalize and delete with a high degree of accuracy. However, as is usual when theories are subjected to the scrutiny which computational verification allows, some clear deficiencies are identified. I shall make suggestions as to how the major deficiencies can be remedied.

This article is organized as follows. Section 2 sets out in detail the standard generative account of the jers which will form the basis for further discussion. Section 3 then demonstrates how this theory can be recast as a CFG, and examines the issues which come to light vis-à-vis the representation of the jers. Section 4 presents the results of testing the

---

[1] There is a transparent relationship between CFGs and Prolog Definite Clause Grammars. For details of the workings of Prolog and DCGs, the reader is invited to refer to a textbook on Prolog, such as Clocksin and Mellish (1981).

theory computationally on a dataset of 2,618 words. In Section 5, the results of this test are discussed, and suggestions are made as to how the standard generative theory might be improved upon, without compromising its context-freeness but reducing the percentage of words to which it incorrectly vocalizes or deletes jers. Section 6 concludes the article by outlining the main findings which come from the work carried out.

2. Russian jers in linear generative phonology

2.1. Havlík's Law and Pesetsky (1979)

Vowel-zero alternations such as that embodied in /dʲenʲ/~/dnʲ/[2] 'day' have been discussed extensively in the phonological literature under the general heading of 'jers'. It is generally believed that in Common Slavic jers were non-alternating short vowels /ĭ/ and /ŭ/ (e.g. Bethin 1998:104). These jers, it is supposed, underwent a change in Late Common Slavic such that word-final jers and jers in a syllable before a syllable with a non-jer vowel (both known as 'weak' jers) were deleted. All other jers (the 'strong' jers) developed into full vowels (in Russian, into /ɛ/ and /o/, respectively). These processes are commonly referred to in Slavic linguistics as Havlík's Law. As Bethin (1998:206) states, a key problem is how the jers should be represented synchronically in Slavic languages.

The traditional approach of linear generative phonology (exemplified by Lightner 1972 and Pesetsky 1979 for Russian; see also Gussmann 1980, Booij and Rubach 1984, and Rubach 1984 for Polish) has been to maintain that the jers are, synchronically, a type of vowel. This approach claims that jers are distinct entities in the phonological inventory, distinguished from non-alternating vowels, in that the former are [+high, –tense] (as opposed to /i/, /u/ which are [+high, +tense] and /ɛ/, /o/, /a/ which are [–high, –tense]). As Bethin (1998:206) notes, this approach also allows Lightner and others to maintain consistency between the

---

[2] I use obliques (rather than square brackets) throughout this paper because I view the 'output' of the jer vocalization and deletion rules as phonemes (/ɛ/ and /o/), which are subject to further phonological rules. In any case, context-free grammar does not distinguish between underlying and surface representations; context-free rules simply add specification to underspecified forms.

explanation of consonantal palatalization before jers and before other vowels (e.g. in the alternation between /stol/ 'table-NomSg' and /stolʲɛ/ 'table-LocSg'), or between /matʲɛrʲijal/ 'material' [noun] and /matʲɛrʲijalʲnij/ 'material' [adjective]).

Although the diachronic reflexes of jers depended solely on whether the following vowel was 'weak' or 'strong', as discussed above, an important insight of Pesetsky (1979) and subsequent followers of Lexical Phonology was that additional factors need to be taken into account in a synchronic analysis. Specifically, in modern Russian, for example, the vocalization or deletion of jers depends on whether they are located in a prefix, suffix, or inflectional ending. Pesetsky suggested that the following rules (which I shall refer to as the 'Lexical Phonology theory') govern the vocalization and deletion of the jers:

(1) a. Jers in inflectional morphemes always delete, because they must either be followed by a word-boundary (as in the masculine nominative singular inflection /O/[3]) or by a non-alternating vowel (as in the feminine instrumental singular inflection /Eju/). (The evidence that these jers exist is their effect on jers in preceding morphemes.)
   b. Jers in root and suffix morphemes always vocalize if followed by a jer, and delete if followed by a (non-jer) vowel.
   c. Jers in prefix morphemes vocalize if followed by a deleted jer, and delete otherwise (i.e., if followed either by a non-alternating vowel or by a vocalized jer).

2.2. Problems with Pesetsky's Approach

A number of problems have been identified with the approach of Pesetsky and subsequent work in the same vein. One of these, on a perhaps trivial level, is that it involves augmenting the phonological inventory. More important, however, it involves (a) postulating phonological entities which never surface in their underlying forms, and (b) absolute neutralization involving these entities (for example, when jers surface as /ɛ/ and /o/ in Russian, they are phonetically indistinguishable from non-alternating /ɛ/ and /o/ respectively). This aspect of traditional generative phonology was criticized, notably in

---

[3] From here on, jers will be represented as E and O.

Postal (1968), Kiparsky (1973) and in Natural Generative Phonology (Hooper 1976), on the grounds that it allows the range of possible phonological theories to become excessively unconstrained. However, it has since been argued, specifically with reference to vowel-zero alternations (in Polish, although of the same type that occur in Russian), that the most natural analysis in some cases does involve postulating abstract entities which never surface (Gussmann 1980:83, Szpyra 1992).

For the time being, however, we will do no more than note these problems. In the next section I shall suggest a context-free model which retains the advantages of Pesetsky's analysis, and, I believe, avoids some of the problems. No extra objects (abstract or otherwise) need to be included in the phonological inventory beyond /ɛ/ and /o/; jers are treated in effect as morphological phrase-structure constituents. At the same time they are part of the lexical representation of morphemes, which reduces the overall size of the lexicon (because, for example, the allomorphs for 'table', /dʲɛnʲ/ and /dnʲ/, do not need to be separately listed).

It should be noted here that there is a significant branch of morphological theory (Zwicky 1992, Bybee 1985, 1988) which would not recognize the last of these points as an advantage. I shall not enter further discussion of this here, save to say that I do view descriptive economy as an advantage in principle. Clearly one would also hope that a linguistic theory would reflect the way native speakers think, but if descriptive economy and psychological reality are irreconcilable, there is no reason to believe that one approach to linguistics is more correct than the other (Chomsky 1970:185-186).

3. The Traditional Theory of the Jers as a CFG

Before proceeding, we need to consider some important factors which will constrain our theory of the jers. First, since jers may sometimes be deleted altogether, it must be the case (assuming that jers can be represented at all in context-free grammar) that jers are represented as part of the pre-terminal hierarchical structure, since rules of the form A → Ø are permitted in CFG, but not rules of the form Ø → A. (Kiparsky 1982:74 explicitly adopts just such a rule for jer vocalization, where zero rewrites as non-zero; Kiparsky's solution is unacceptable, since his phonology must be more powerful than context-free.) The second constraint is that jers must be specified as part of the dictionary entry of each morpheme. If this were not the case, there would be no means of differentiating between, for example, ласк /lask/ 'weasel' (where there is an altern-ation) and ласк /lask/ 'caress' (where there is no alternation):

(2) ласка /laska/ 'weasel-NomSg'
 ласок /lasok/ 'weasel-GenPl'

 ласка /laska/ 'caress-NomSg'
 ласк /lask/ 'caress-GenPl'

In terms of context-free grammar, this means that jers must be given as one of the constituents of the rules for individual entries in the morphological inventory.

The only way in which these two constraints can be reconciled is if jers are morphological, rather than phonological, objects. This means that they are not, strictly speaking, vowels; it would be more accurate to say that they are morphological objects which can surface as vowels. An example is in the specification of the left edge of morphemes in Russian, which will shortly be discussed. Thus, for example, Figure 1 gives the representation for the root morpheme in ласка /laska/ 'weasel-NomSg' (cf. ласок /lasok/ 'weasel-GenPl'), as distinct from the root of ласка /laska/ 'caress-NomSg', which does not alternate in the genitive plural (cf. ласк /lask/ 'caress-GenPl').

Figure 1. Representation of /lask/~/lasok/ 'weasel'

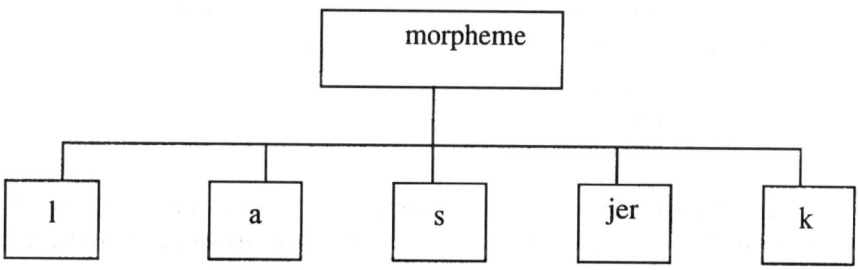

Now, Russian (like any other language) is subject to the constraints of both morphology and syllable structure. In phrase-structure grammar terms, this can equate to the language being generated by the intersection of two grammar modules at their terminal elements.[4] It follows from this that if jers are pre-terminal morphological objects, then they cannot also be pre-terminal objects in syllable structure. To illustrate this, consider the representation in Figure 2, which shows both the morphological and the syllable structure of /lasok/ 'weasel-GenPl':

Figure 2. Representation of ласок /lasok/ 'weasel-GenPl'

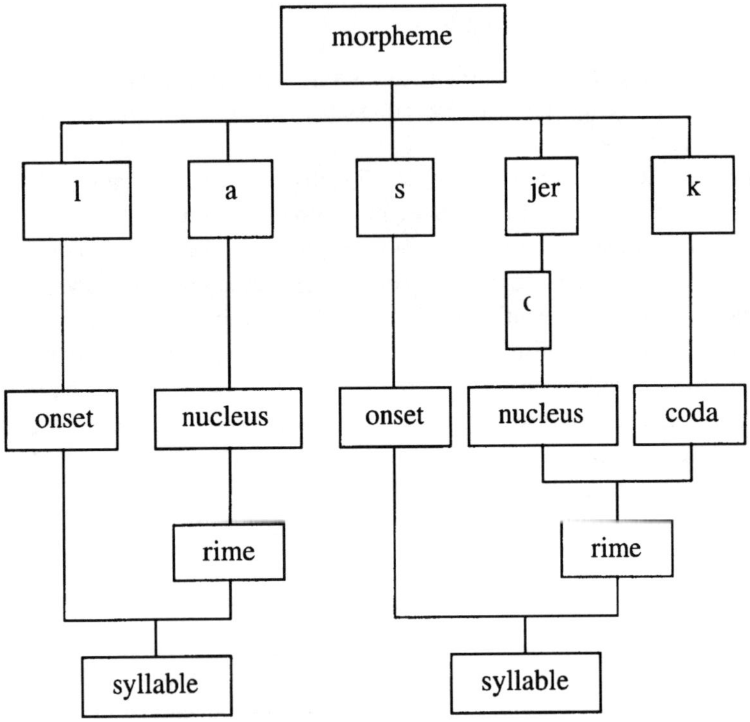

```
                         morpheme
        ┌──────┬──────────┬──────┬──────┐
        l      a          s     jer     k
                                 │
                                 (
        │      │          │      │      │
      onset  nucleus    onset  nucleus  coda
               │                  │      │
               rime               rime
               │                  │
            syllable           syllable
```

Note that the 'jer' constituent differs from the constituents /l/, /a/, /s/ and /k/ in that Note that the 'jer' constituent differs from the constituents

---

[4] It is best to adhere to the constraint that the grammar modules should intersect only at their terminal elements, as this maintains simplicity and allows one to draw transparent conclusions about the power of the overall grammar. For ex-ample, if one of the intersecting grammar modules is finite-state and the other context-free, then the language defined by the intersection is also context-free (see Chomsky 1963:380 for proof of this).

/l/, /a/, /s/ and /k/ in that the latter are terminal symbols in the morphological component and are thus directly subject to the syllable structure grammar. The component 'jer', on the other hand, is a pre-terminal symbol in the word-formation grammar, dominating /o/ (which is the terminal symbol). One consequence of this is that jers are represented lexically, but do not play a direct role in syllable structure. In this way, jers are fundamentally dissimilar from the phonemes /l/, /a/, /s/, /o/, and /k/. This, in essence, is the reason that jers should not be included in the phonological inventory..

Now, this analysis is not yet explicit about when jers vocalize and when they delete. The context-free rules governing this will clearly have to be able to tell whether a jer is 'strong' or 'weak', and this in turn will involve looking at the content of following morphemes. I have already outlined in (1) what the relevant rules are. The only remaining problem is how to encode these in context-free grammar (in which the ordering of rules should not matter), given that Pesetsky and subsequent researchers in Lexical Phonology propose a model which uses cyclic rules and therefore hinges on rule-ordering.

To account for jer vocalization and deletion, I shall suggest that it is sufficient to incorporate four features into a context-free word-formation grammar. These features are [±strong], [±tense], [±high], and [left:X]. The feature [±strong] follows the terminology traditionally used by Slavists ('strong' jers vocalize and 'weak' jers delete: cf. Isa_enko 1970), and should not be confused with the strong/weak distinction in metrical phonology (cf. Liberman 1975). The feature [±tense] is introduced to differentiate between jers and (non-jer) vowels (in conjunction with [±high]), following Gussmann (1980), Rubach (1984), and others. However, this is not to imply that additional segments are to be included in the phonological inventory, as Gussmann and Rubach suggest. The feature [±high] is used with the same meaning as in Chomsky and Halle (1968), and the meaning of the feature [left:X] will become clear in the ensuing discussion.

First, we shall consider the distribution of [left:X] in the terminal rules. In this case, X stands for the feature matrix [a tense, b high], which unifies with the specifications of a morpheme's first constituent which is either a vowel or a jer. (It is assumed that these features spread across any intervening consonants.) Thus a morpheme is [left:[+high, −tense]] if it contains a jer, and no vowels occur to the left of the jer within that morpheme.[5] Accordingly, terminal rules of the type shown in (3) are obtained.

(3) inflection → /O/ 'MascNomSg'
    [left: [+high,
            –tense]]

    inflection → /am/ 'DatPl'
    [left: [–high,
            –tense]]

    root → /lasOk/ 'weasel'
    [left: [–high,
            –tense]]

Next, we turn to the distribution of [±strong]. This is the feature which encodes the actual phonological interpretation of jers (whether they vocalize or delete): a jer in a [+strong] morpheme vocalizes, and one in a [–strong] morpheme deletes. Reflecting the fact that there are three ways in which jers behave (depending on whether they occur in inflectional endings, roots or suffixes, or prefixes), there are three basic distributional possibilities.

First, inflectional morphemes must always be [–strong] in accordance with (1a). Thus in these morphemes the only feature which can vary is the feature [left:X].

Secondly, we shall consider the distribution of [±strong] in roots and suffixes. The facts can be captured only if we allow [±strong] to percolate up to pre-terminal symbols in the tree. In other words, not just morphemes, but whole stems need to be specified for [±strong]. We shall stipulate that a stem is [α strong] if its rightmost constituent is also [α strong]. (Because the word-formation rules are all left-embedding, this constituent must be a terminal symbol.) The *leftmost* constituent's specification for [±strong] is then determined by the specification of the suffix for [left:X]: if the suffix's leftmost vowel is a jer, then the leftmost

---

[5] There are two exceptions to this, which will be dealt with below.

constituent is [+strong]. Otherwise, it is [–strong]. These facts are encoded in the rule schemata in (4).

(4) stem → stem suffix
 [α strong] [+strong] [α strong, left:[+high, –tense]]

 stem → stem suffix
 [α strong] [–strong] [α strong, left:[+tense]]

 stem → stem suffix
 [α strong] [–strong] [α strong, left:[–high]]

The distribution of features is exactly the same if the rightmost constituent is an inflectional ending instead of a suffix, except, as already stated, the inflectional ending must be [–strong]:

(5) X → stem inflection
 [+strong] [–strong, left:[+high,–tense]]

 X → stem inflection
 [–strong] [–strong, left:[–high]]

 X → stem inflection
 [–strong] [–strong, left:[+tense]]

We then have to consider the distribution of [±strong] in the prefixation rules, which, as we know from (1c), is different again. As Pesetsky (1979) pointed out, the relevant issue here is not whether there is a jer in the following root morpheme, but whether there is a non-vocalized jer. The jer in the prefix /podO/ 'under' surfaces as a vowel in /podO+ʒEg+l+a/ 'set light to-Fem' because there is a jer in /ʒEg/ 'burn', and *it has deleted*. It fails to surface in /podO+ʒEg+l+O/ 'set light to-Masc', however, because the jer in /ʒEg/ has vocalized.

I would propose that these facts should be accounted for not in the word-formation rules, but in the lexicon as a fact about root morphemes. This is the first of the two exceptions referred to in footnote 5. For root morphemes whose first vowel is a jer, the morpheme's specification for [left:X] can be made dependent on its specification for [±strong].

Specifically, if the morpheme is [+strong], its jer vocalizes and it is treated as a morpheme whose leftmost vowel is not a jer (with the result that any jer in the prefix to its left will delete). If the morpheme is [–strong], its jer deletes and it is treated as a morpheme whose leftmost vowel is a jer (with the result that any jer in the prefix to its left will vocalize). The following rules for /ʒEg/ 'burn' exemplify this.

(6) noun-root   →   /ʒ   E   g/
     [left: [–high,   [+strong]
             –tense]
     +strong]

     noun-root   →   /ʒ   E   g/
     [left: [+high,   [–strong]
             –tense]
     –strong]

Adopting this approach means that the prefixation rule schemata are similar to those in (4) and (6). The actual rule schemata are as follows:

(7) stem   →   prefix   root
     [α strong]   [+strong]   [α strong,
                                          left:[+high, –tense]]

     stem   →   prefix   root
     [α strong]   [–strong]   [α strong,
                                          left:[+tense]]

     stem   →   prefix   root
     [α strong]   [–strong]   [α strong,
                                          left:[–high]]

Finally, we need to consider the other exception referred to in footnote 5. If a morpheme contains neither jers nor non-altern-ating vowels (for example, the suffix /l/ in Pesetsky's example /podO+ʒEg+l+a/ 'set light to-Fem', we want the feature [left:X] to spread leftwards from the *following* morpheme. For example, in /podO+ʒEg+l+a/, the reason the jer in /ʒEg/ 'burn' deletes is that the next vowel is /a/, so /l/ should share the feature [left:X] with /a/. This can be modeled if the lexical rule for /l/ is as shown in (8).

(8) suffix   →   /I/
     [left: [α high,
              −tense],
      α strong]

It needs to be underlined that the rules in (4), (5) and (7) are rule schemata: they describe the distribution of [±strong] and [left:X] in pre-existing CFG morphology rules.

Because the jers are themselves morphological constituents, the word-formation grammar must contain rules to make explicit when they vocalize and when they delete. These rules are now given in (9).

(9)   O   →   /o/
       [+strong]

          E   →   /ε/
       [+strong]

         O and E   →   / /
       [−strong]

4. A Computational Test of the CFG Theory of the Jers

For this test, the rule schemata outlined above were incorporated into a word-formation grammar and used to process a sample of 2,618 word-forms, each of which contained at least one jer.

Now, although the vocalization and deletion of jers is presented in traditional generative phonology and Lexical Phonology as a process with ordered rules, it in fact turns into a parsing and generation problem in CFG: it can be viewed this way because, as noted above, CFGs are always reversible. The grammar should generate only those forms in which the jers vocalize and delete in the correct places, if the theory which it embodies is correct. At the same time, the grammar should parse (or accept) only those forms which have vocalized and deleted jers in the correct places, and reject all other forms. Thus one way of testing the grammar is to present it with a list of forms grouped as follows: each entry in the list consists of both the well-formed and ill-formed versions of a given word (e.g. дня /dnʲa/ 'day-GenSg') versus *деня /dʲenʲa/; день /dʲenʲ/ 'day-NomSg' versus *днь /dnʲ/ and *дне /dnʲɛ/). (Here, the latter examples in each case are 'ill-formed' only in that jers are vocalized or deleted in the wrong places.) If the grammar is accurate, it should accept all words in the former category and reject all words in the latter category.

The results of the test were as follows. In 2,381 cases (90.95%[6] of the total), the form with jers correctly vocalized and deleted was accepted and all ill-formed alternatives were rejected. In the remaining 237 cases (9.05%), the correct form was rejected and one of the ill-formed alternatives was accepted. In no case was more than one alternative of the same form accepted, because in any given position (according to the rule schemata as formulated above) there is no optionality as to whether a jer deletes or vocalizes. These results show that the theory advanced by Lexical Phonology makes broadly the correct predictions (since the grammar tested does no more than implement the existing theory proposed by Pesetsky in context-free grammar).

5. Discussion of Results

It is interesting to look more closely at the 9.05% of cases that were incorrectly processed by the grammar, to determine whether there are any common factors which might enable these exceptions to be explained. Of these 237 forms, 88 had jers which had been incorrectly deleted in prefixes. For examples, see Table 1 opposite. All of the starred forms in Table 1 are historically attested in Russ-ian (Barxudarov et al. 1975), and in one case the predicted form still exists, but with a different meaning (свет /sv^{j}et/ 'society'). In contemporary Russian, doublets of the /sov^{j}et//sv^{j}et/ type are quite common: in each case, the member of the pair which exhibits 'exceptional' jer-vocalization is historically a borrowing from Old Church Slavonic (OCS), a South Slavic dialect, while the other member of the pair is a native Russian (East Slavic) word. Usually, the two will also be distinguished semantically, with the former more likely to relate to abstract concepts (e.g. событие /sobit^{j}ijε/ 'occurrence') and the latter more likely to belong to the vernacular vocabulary (e.g. сбытие /sbit^{j}ijε/ 'sale').

---

[6] This percentage and all others quoted henceforth are significant to two decimal places.

Table 1. Examples of words incorrectly processed by the CFG

Actual form	Predicted form	Lexical form	Gloss
совесть /sovʲestʲ/	*свесть /svʲestʲ/	/sO+vʲestʲ+/	'conscience'
собираться /sobʲiratʲsʲa/	*сбираться /sbʲiratʲsʲa/	/sO+bʲir+a+tʲ+sʲa/	'to gather'
совет /sovʲet/	*свет /svʲet/	/sO+vʲet+/	'council'
событие /sobitʲijɛ/	*сбытие /sbitʲijɛ/	/sO+bitʲ+ij+ɛ/	'event'
возраст /vozrast/	*взраст /vzrast/	/vOz+rastʲ+/	'age'
воскликнуть /vosklʲiknutʲ/	*вскликнуть /vsklʲiknutʲ/	/vOs+klʲik+nu+tʲ/	'to exclaim'

These doublets could be accounted for in the current framework by specifying each word-form as morphologically [±OCS] (a feature which was proposed in Lightner 1972). This feature would then percolate down to the prefix, with the grammar rules making explicit the fact that jers in [+OCS] prefixes vocalize no matter what follows.

A further 72 of the 237 exceptions seem to motivate a rule of epenthesis. In these cases, the form predicted by the Lexical Phonology theory has a deleted jer, and an unsyllabifiable consonant cluster. All of the cases which fall unambiguously into this class involve the nominalizing suffix /Estv/. Examples are given in Table 2:

Table 2. Further examples of words incorrectly processed

Actual form	Predicted form	Lexical form	Gloss
общество /obʃtʃʲɛstvo/	*общство /obʃtʃʲstvo/	/obʃtʃʲ+Estv+o/	'society'
множество /mnoʒestvo/	*множство /mnoʒstvo/	/mnoʒ+Estv+o/	'multitude'
существо /suʃtʃʲɛstvo/	*сущство /suʃtʃʲstvo/	/suʃtʃʲ+Estv+o/	'being'

What these examples suggest is that it would be wrong to rule epenthesis out entirely as playing a role in jer vocalization. Although the Lexical Phonology theory of the jers accounts correctly for 90.95% of cases, its coverage of the data would be increased to at least 93.70%[7] if a rule were included to vocalize jers where an unsyllabifiable cluster would otherwise result. Clearly, though, these figures demonstrate that epenthesis is at most a minor factor in explaining jer deletion and vocalization.

One might question how the epenthesis rule could be encoded within the current framework, given our earlier stipulation that jers are not syllable structure constituents. A solution to this problem can be found if one substitutes the probabilistic rules in (10) for the non-probabilistic ones in (9):[8]

(10)   O   →   /o/
         [±strong, probability:X]

         E   →   /ɛ/
         [±strong, probability:X]

         O and E   →   / /
         [–strong, probability:Y]

(where Y > X)

With these rules, the morphology will generate two possible forms wherever there is a [–strong] jer. In one of these, the jer will have vocalized, and in the other, the jer will have deleted. Based on the morphology alone, the form in which the jer has deleted will always be more probable than (preferred to) the one in which the jer has vocalized. However, when the syllable structure grammar rules out the form to which the morphology grammar assigns a higher probability, the overall grammar will revert to the form with the vocalized jer instead.

---

[7] The increase in coverage could be even greater, because some forms like сознание /soznanijɛ/ 'conscience' could be accounted for *either* by epenthesis *or* by the [OCS] modification to the grammar proposed above.

[8] For further discussion of the use of probabilistic rules in CFG, see for example Coleman and Pierrehumbert (1997).

6. Conclusions

In this article, I have shown that the traditional account of the jers in Russian can be reinterpreted declaratively in the framework of CFG, by incorporating the features [left:X], [±strong], [±tense], and [±high] into a more general word-formation grammar. In this grammar, jers are morphological constituents, not syllable structure constituents, and in this respect they are fundamentally different from phonemes. A computational test of the CFG also revealed that the ideas embodied in the traditional account are, by and large, accurate. However, the error rate of the theory can be significantly reduced by incorporating a mechanism to deal with borrowings from OCS (the introduction of the feature [±OCS]). It can be reduced yet further if one modifies the grammar to incorporate a way of accounting for epenthesis, and I suggested that this should be done by means of probabilistic rules whereby [–strong] jers can either vocalize or delete, but prefer to delete. In this way, the context-freeness of the grammar overall would not be compromised. While the resulting grammar would not necessarily be exceptionless, it would still account correctly for over 96% of the dataset tested.

References

Barxudarov, S. G. et al. (eds.). 1975. *Slovar' russkogo jazyka XI–XVII vv.* Moscow: Nauka.

Bethin, Christina Y. 1998. *Slavic Prosody: Language Change and Phonological Theory.* Cambridge: Cambridge University Press.

Booij, Geert and Jerzy Rubach. 1984. Morphological and Prosodic Domains in Lexical Phonology. *Phonology Yearbook* 1, 1-27.

Bybee, Joan L. 1985. *Morphology: a Study of the Relation Bet-ween Meaning and Form.* Amsterdam: John Benjamins.

Bybee, Joan L. 1988. Morphology as Lexical Organization. In Hammond and Noonan (eds.). *Theoretical Morphology: Ap-proaches in Modern Linguistics.* San Diego, CA: Academic Press, Inc. 119-141.

Chomsky, Noam. 1970. Remarks on Nominalization. In Roderick A. Jacobs and Peter S. Rosenbaum (eds.). *Readings in English Transformational Grammar.* Waltham, MA: Ginn & Co. 184-221.

Chomsky, Noam, and Morris Halle. 1968. *The Sound Pattern of English.* New York: Harper & Row.

Clocksin, William F., and Christopher S. Mellish. 1981. *Programming in Prolog.* Berlin: Springer-Verlag.

Coleman, John S. and Janet Pierrehumbert. 1997. Stochastic Phonological Grammars and Acceptability. In *Computational Phonology. Third Meeting of the ACL Special Interest Group in Computational Phonology*, 49-56. Somerset, NJ: Association for Computational Linguistics.

Gussmann, Edmund. 1980. *Studies in Abstract Phonology.* Cambridge, MA: MIT Press.

Hooper, Joan B. 1976. *An Introduction to Natural Generative Phonology.* New York: Academic Press.

Isačenko, A. V. 1970. East Slavic Morphophonemics and the Treatment of the Jers in Russian: a Revision of Havlik's Law. *International Journal of Slavic Linguistics and Poetics* 13, 73-124.

Kiparsky, Paul. 1973. Phonological Representations. In Osamu Fujimura et al. (eds.). *Three Dimensions of Linguistic Theory.* Tokyo: TEC. 1-136.

Kiparsky, Paul. 1982. Lexical Morphology and Phonology. In The Linguistic Society of Korea (ed.). *Linguistics in the Morning Calm: Selected Papers from SICOL-1981.* Seoul: Hanshin Pub-lishing Company. 3-91.

Liberman, Mark. 1975. *The Intonational System of English.* Ph. D. dissertation, MIT.

Lightner, Theodore M. 1972. *Problems in the Theory of Phonology*, volume 1. Edmonton: Linguistic Research.

Pesetsky, David. 1979. *Russian Morphology and Lexical Theory.* (Unpublished manuscript, MIT, Cambridge, MA.)

Piotrowski, Marek. 1992. Polish Yers in Non-Linear Phonology. In Wolfgang U. Dressler, H. C. Luschützky, O. E. Pfeiffer, and J. R. Rennison (eds.). *Phonologica 1988: Proceedings of the Sixth International Phonology Meeting.* Cambridge: Cambridge Uni-versity Press. 215-227.

Postal, Paul M. 1968. *Aspects of Phonological Theory.* New York: Harper & Row.

Rubach, Jerzy. 1984. *Cyclic and Lexical Phonology: the Structure of Polish*. Dordrecht: Foris.

Rubach, Jerzy. 1986. Abstract Vowels in Three Dimensional Phonology: the Yers. *The Linguistic Review* 5, 247-280.

Spencer, Andrew. 1986. A Nonlinear Analysis of Vowel Zero Alternations in Polish. *Journal of Linguistics* 22, 249-280.

Szpyra, Jolanta. 1992. Ghost Segments in Nonlinear Phonology: Polish Yers. *Language* 48, 277-312.

Zwicky, Arnold M. 1992. Some Choices in the Theory of Morphology. In Robert Levine (ed.). *Formal Grammar: Theory and Implementation*. New York and Oxford: Oxford University Press. 327-371.

University of Oxford Phonetics Laboratory
41 Wellington Square
Oxford, OX1 2JF, U.K.
pachew@linguist.freeserve.co.uk

The (Non)-Uniqueness of Multiple WH-Fronting: German = Bulgarian

Barbara Citko
SUNY/Stony Brook

Kleanthes K. Grohmann
ZAS-Berlin

1. Introduction

Since Wachowicz 1974, it has been known that Slavic languages front all Wh-phrases overtly in multiple Wh-questions. This is illustrated in (1) for Bulgarian and (2) for Serbo-Croatian (henceforth, SC).

(1) Koj kogo vižda?   *Bulgarian*
    who whom sees
    'Who sees whom?'

(2) Ko je šta kupio?   *Serbo-Croatian*
    who is what bought
    'Who bought what?'

Rudin (1988) showed that Bulgarian and SC represent different types of languages, differing in the surface order of fronted Wh-elements and their behavior with respect to the Superiority Condition (Chomsky 1973). In Bulgarian-type languages (such as Romanian), the order of fronted Wh-phrases is fixed, whereas in SC-type languages (such as Polish or Russian), the order appears to be free.[1]

(3) *Kogo koj vižda?   *Bulgarian*
    whom who sees

(4) Šta je ko kupio?   *SC*
    what is who bought

---

[1] There are many complicating factors that are not going to be crucial for the discussion that follows. For example, the ordering between the second and third Wh-phrase in Bulgarian Wh-questions is free (see e.g. Bošković 1997, Richards 1997).

Steven Franks, Tracy Holloway King, and Michael Yadroff, eds. *Annual Workshop on Formal Approaches to Slavic Linguistics: The Bloomington Meeting, 2000.* Ann Arbor: Michigan Slavic Publications, 2001, 117–136.

Our goal is to show that overt multiple Wh-movement is attested outside of the Slavic family of languages, and in parti-cular that German, contra standard assumptions, is a language with overt multiple Wh-movement. The main evidence for this claim comes from the correlation between overt movement and the availability of Single Pair and Pair List readings in multiple Wh-questions. We show how analyzing German as an overt Wh-movement language allows for a straightforward partition of languages with respect to the availability of Single Pair and Pair List readings in multiple Wh-questions. We conclude with examining the consequences and predictions of this improved partition for the analysis of multiple Wh-movement in Slavic.

2. Proposal: A Tripartition of Wh-Question Formation

2.1. Pair List versus Single Pair Readings

In addition to variation in the syntax, languages differ in the range of interpretations they allow for multiple Wh-questions. In principle, multiple Wh-questions are ambiguous between P(air) L(ist) and S(ingle) P(air) readings. An SP answer consists of a single proposition, whereas a PL answer consists of sets of propositions.

(5) a. Mary bought a sweater. *(Single Pair answer)*
 b. Mary bought a sweater, Jane bought shoes,
 Anne bought a skirt... *(Pair List answer)*

The availability of SP and PL readings is subject to cross-linguistic variation (Bošković 1998b, Hagstrom 1998). For example, English contrasts with Japanese in that it disallows SP readings in multiple Wh-questions. Thus, in the scenario given in (6), which calls for an SP answer, only a Japanese multiple Wh-question is felicitous (infelicity marked by '#').[2]

---

[2] Presumably, the only way to ask a question in this situation in English would be to use a conjoined question.

(6) *Scenario I:* John is in a store and off in the distance sees somebody buying an article of clothing, but he does not see who it is and neither does he see exactly what is being bought. He goes to the shop assistant and asks:
    a. #Who bought what? *English*[3]
    b. Dare-ga nani-o katta no? *Japanese*
       'Who bought what?'
    c. Mary bought a sweater.

Since the most obvious difference between languages like English and languages like Japanese lies in whether the Wh-phrases undergo overt movement or not, Hagstrom (1998) and Bošković (1998b) establish a correlation between overt syntactic movement (in a sense yet to be defined) and the availability of SP readings. The contrast between Japanese and English illustrated above suggests that overt syntactic move-ment forces PL readings, and consequently that SP readings are allowed only in Wh-in situ languages.

The following shows that this correlation is on the right track.

(7) *(Scenario I from above)*

a. #Koj	kakvo	e	kupil?	*Bulgarian*
who	what	is	bought	
b. Ko	je	šta	kupio?	*SC*
who	is	what	bought	
c. Šta	je	ko	kupio?	
what	is	who	bought	

In Bulgarian, a multiple Wh-question is infelicitous in a situation that calls for an SP answer (hence the degraded status in (7a)). Interestingly, SC patterns with Wh-in-situ languages in that it allows an SP answer. This brings further support for Bošković's (1997) claim that Wh-phrases in SC do not involve Wh-movement (where by Wh-movement we mean movement to an extended C-projection), but focus-driven scrambling to some position contained within TP. We will come back to SC in section 4.

---

[3] It is possible to ask a D-linked Wh-question in English in a situation described in (6); thus (i) is felicitous. We will mention related facts below in passing.
    (i) Which item did which customer buy?

In situations that call for PL answers, further distinctions emerge. Consider the following scenario.

(8) *Scenario II:* John sees Jim finishing off his daily sales. He sees a bunch of people that he knows walk away and Jim stacking his left-over merchandise, so he asks him:
    a. Ko je šta kupio?   *SC*
       who has what bought
    b. #Šta je ko kupio?
       what has who bought
    c. Dare-ga nani-o katta no?   *Japanese*
       who-NOM what-ACC bought Q
    d. #Nani-o dare-ga katta no?
       what-ACC who-NOM bought Q
    e. Wer hat was gekauft?   *German*
       who has what bought
    f. Was hat wer gekauft?
       what has who bought

This pattern shows that in Wh-in situ languages such as Japanese and, on current assumptions SC, a PL reading is lost if the lower Wh-phrase is scrambled over the higher one. We will follow Bošković (1998b), and refer to the loss of PL reading in an otherwise grammatical question as *Interpretive Superiority*.

2.2. A Typological Tripartition

Furthermore, the data in (8) show that German presents a puzzle. First, German does not obey superiority, since both orders, *subject > object* and *object > subject*, are possible. The lack of superiority is standardly attributed to scrambling (cf. Müller and Sternefeld 1993). However, if scrambling really is responsible for the availability of both orders, it is not clear why German does not pattern with other scrambling languages like Japanese or SC in that it loses the PL reading in a scrambled version (cf. (8f)). This contrast is going to be crucial for our analysis of multiple Wh-movement in German.

The table given in (9) offers an initial partition of languages with respect to the availability of SP/PL readings, taken straight from Bošković (1998b), who explores Hagstrom (1998) further. Beyond the examples above, a comprehensive discussion of the data that lead to this typology can also be found in Grohmann 2000. Relevant is that German is odd regarding WH2 > WH1, given the Hagstrom-Bošković approach.

(9) *Table 1:* Quasi-tripartition à la Bošković-Hagstrom[4]

If a language has:	It allows readings:	But:
Wh-in situ (Japanese, Chinese, Hindi, SC, Polish, French II…)	WH1 > WH2: PL/SP WH2 > WH1: SP (such as Wh-scrambling)	
Singular Wh-movement (English, Italian, French I, German, …)	WH1 > WH2: PL WH2 > WH1: SP[5] (such as D-linking)	**German: WH2>WH1:PL**
Multiple Wh-movement (Bulgarian, Romanian…)	WH1 > WH2: PL WH2 > WH1: PL[6] (such as D-linking)	

The data examined so far raise the following questions, which we attempt to provide answers for in the remainder:

1. Why is there a correlation between syntactic movement (such as scrambling) and availability of SP interpretation in Wh-in situ languages?

---

[4] See Grohmann 2000 for detailed exposition. French I refers to the construction pattern found in English, where one Wh-phrase moves, while French II denotes the strategy where all Wh-phrases can be left in situ (see Bošković 1998a, Boeckx 1999)

[5] Barss (1992) notes that in D-linked questions, only SP answers are possible:

(i) Which woman did which man see?

Again, while judgments might be fuzzy, we assume this here, but refrain from a more detailed discussion pertaining to issues of D-linking (cf. Pesetsky 1987).

[6] In Bulgarian, D-linked Wh-questions allow violations of superiority. Furthermore, the preferred reading is a PL reading (Roumyana Izvorski, p.c); the same applies to Romanian (Ileana Comorovski, p.c.):

(i) a. Koga kniga koj čovek e kupil? *Bulgarian*
       'Which book did which person buy?'
    b. La care cînd te ai gîndit? *Romanian*
       'Which one have you thought of when?'

2. Why does German not pattern with other 'singular' Wh-movement languages (such as English, Italian, standard French etc.) or other 'scrambling' languages such as Japanese or SC with respect to the availability of PL readings in WH2 > WH1 multiple questions?
3. Do Slavic languages like Polish or SC always pattern with Wh-in situ languages?

What is particularly puzzling is the German pattern. Note that if German were a multiple Wh-movement language, we would get a real tripartition, as shown in (10), a state of affairs we argue for explicitly here (also Citko and Grohmann 2000).

(10) *Table 2:* An improved tripartition

If a language has:	*It allows readings:*
Wh-in situ (Japanese, Chinese, Hindi, Polish, SC, French II...)	WH1 > WH2: PL/SP WH2 > WH1: SP
Singular Wh-movement (English, Italian, French I, ...)	WH1 > WH2: PL WH2 > WH1: SP
Multiple Wh-movement (Bulgarian, Romanian, German ...)	WH1 > WH2: PL WH2 > WH1: PL

The answer to the first question follows from the semantics for Wh-questions provided by Hagstrom (1998), and further developed by Bošković (1998b). Their solution crucially relies on the universal existence of a Q-particle responsible for interrogative clause-typing. In English-type languages, the Q-particle is a covert counterpart of an overt morpheme found in Wh-in situ languages like Chinese or Japanese (cf. Cheng 1991). As Hagstrom (1998) and Bošković (1998b) argue, the position of a Q-particle correlates with the availability of SP/PL readings.

2.3. Homing in on Q and F

The Q-particle originates in a clause-internal position and moves to C, thus typing the clause interrogative. Movement can take place from two positions: from the lower Wh-phrase, correlating with PL reading

(11a), or from a position above all Wh-phrases, correlating with SP reading (11b).

(11) a. $[_{CP} [Q]\text{-}C^0 \ldots [_{TP} (\ldots) \text{WH1} \ldots \text{WH2-}\sout{[Q]} \ldots]]$
 b. $[_{CP} [Q]\text{-}C^0 [_{FP} \sout{[Q]}\text{-}F^0 [_{TP} (\ldots) \text{WH1} \ldots \text{WH2} \ldots]]]$

For reasons of space, we will not go into the semantic details, but refer the reader to Hagstrom (1998) and Bošković (1998b), or Citko and Grohmann (2000) for further discussion. Suffice it to say that SP readings correlate with the variable left behind by Q-movement (bold strikethrough), scoping over all Wh-phrases, and PL readings correlate with it scoping over a lower Wh-phrase only. Our critical assumption is the existence of FP, which we take to be a low, C-related functional projection (assuming a split C-structure, e.g. à la Rizzi 1997).

These two options are attested in Wh-in situ languages, which explains why both SP and PL readings are allowed (see (6) above). With high Q, the choice function computed over the variable (i.e. the boldfaced Q-position; cf. (11b)) ranges over all Wh-phrases in situ (yielding SP), whereas with low Q it ranges only over WH2 (yielding PL, as in (11a)).

Note however, that in languages where WH2 scrambles over WH1, even a low Q is going to end up having both Wh-phrases in its scope; the variable only gets created once Q moves to C^0. This results in a configuration comparable to (11), which accounts for why scrambling results in the loss of a PL reading (*Interpretive Superiority* effect illustrated in (9) above):

(12) $[_{CP} [Q]\text{-}C^0 \ldots \text{WH2-}\sout{[Q]} [_{TP} (\ldots) \text{WH1} \ldots \sout{\text{WH2-}[Q]} \ldots]]$

If the loss of a PL reading is indeed the effect of scrambling of a lower Wh-phrase over a higher one, the only way to account for why German WH2 > WH1 questions retain PL readings is to resort to a Q-stranding mechanism which would allow WH2 to scramble over WH1, but leave the Q-particle in situ. This is indeed the line of thought taken by Hagstrom (1998) and Bošković (1998b). The resulting configuration looks like (13), where, unlike in (12), WH2 and Q move separately:

(13) $[_{CP} [Q]\text{-}C^0 \ldots \text{WH2} [_{TP} (\ldots) \text{WH1} \ldots \sout{\text{WH2-}[Q]} \ldots]]$

The Q-stranding mechanism strikes us as somewhat ad hoc, thus we will argue for an alternative explanation. It is not clear, for example, why Q-stranding should be allowed in German, but not in Japanese (such as illustrated by the contrast in (8)).

We have seen above that in singular Wh-movement languages, SP readings are in principle disallowed.[7] Given the correlation between the scope of Q and the position of Wh-phrases, it becomes clear why this should be the case. Simply, the configuration needed for an SP reading, in which Q has scope over both Wh-phrases, never arises. Wh-movement always displaces one Wh-phrase to a position out of the scope of (the trace of) Q, even if Q is generated high (in F).

(14) $[_{CP}\ [Q]\text{-}C^0 \ldots [_{FocP}\ WH1\ [_{FP}\ \cancel{[Q]}\text{-}F^0\ [_{TP}(\ldots)\ \cancel{WH1}\ WH2]]]]$

Similarly, in multiple Wh-movement languages, Wh-phrases escape the scope of Q, which destroys the SP reading:

(15) $[_{CP}[Q]\text{-}C^0 \ldots [_{FocP}WH1\ [_{FP}WH2\cancel{[Q]}\text{-}F^0\ [_{TP}\ WH1\ \cancel{WH2}]]]]$

This rests on the rather natural assumption that one Wh-phrase targets [Spec, FP], the specifier of the projection hosting high Q. Leaving aside more specific motivation (such as the possibility of a focus feature involved, as sometimes argued), we build on the intuitive connection between F and Wh-properties in the sense that clause-typing properties must be identified in the finer grained C-domain of the clause (cf. Chomsky 1995, Rizzi 1997 and others). As such, we assume clause-typing proper to take place in C, hence motivating movement of Q to C in a straightforward manner. Yet introducing a high occurrence of Q—justified at least on semantic grounds (à la Hagstrom-Bošković)—raises the question of a clausal position. Generating low Q on the lowest Wh-phrase follows from the Hagstrom-Bošković approach. We believe it also follows if high Q is generated not only above all Wh-phrases, but more specifically in a position belonging to the C-system of the clause (responsible, among others, for clause-typing, discoursal effects such as topic or focus, and the like). We assume, following much recent work, a finer structure of the C-domain consisting of a force-indicating CP, topic

---

[7] We are abstracting away here from D-linked questions, which might involve a very different mechanism.

and focus projections (TopP, FocP) and at least a "low" C-head, here identified as F (cf. Uriagereka 1995; see also Agr1P of Cardinaletti and Roberts 1991 or FinP of Rizzi 1997, and discussion in Grohmann 2000). Given that this low head may host complementizers (which may undergo further movement to C; cf. Rizzi 1997 and references), it is not implausible to assign it the property of licensing Q (which undergoes further movement).

So much for motivating not only the existence of F but also its connection to C and Q. In what follows, we argue that this assumption, fitting in neatly with the Hagstrom-Bošković approach, allows for justification of a split as proposed in table 2 (i.e. (10) above). We first show how this approach can be implemented in German, and then address Slavic-related issues.

3. Integrating German

3.1. German as a Multiple Wh-Fronting Language

If German really were a multiple Wh-movement language, as suggested in section 3.1 on interpretive and in section 3.2 on typological grounds, we would expect certain grammatical reflexes, such as syntactic evidence for this very high occurrence of all Wh-elements as found in Bulgarian, for example. In this section we show that such evidence indeed exists and revolves around the relative placement of adverbs and quantifiers with respect to the Wh-phrases in the clause. We illustrate with binary Wh-questions, as throughout, focusing on Wh-arguments; Grohmann (1998, 2000) extends the discussion to further instances, including Wh-adjuncts.

Given what we have said so far, under a multiple Wh-movement analysis of German we would expect all Wh-phrases to appear in some C-related position at the point of Spell Out, i.e. all Wh-phrases obligatorily move into the C-domain in the overt syntax.[8] Following, but

---

[8] There are two issues to note. Firstly, without further ado we assume a head-initial analysis of German clause structure, in the spirit of Zwart (1993) or Kayne (1994), for example. As a result, many argument positions automatically shift higher up, certainly beyond the V-domain. Secondly, note that while it is widely acknowledged that the highest Wh-phrase has indeed moved to a C-position (whether one may want to call it CP, FocP or something else), the standard assumption about subsequent Wh-phrases in German is that they stay in situ or move at most to some Agr-projection. The data

not necessarily relying exclusively on, the assumption that FocP is the default host for overtly moved Wh-phrases, FP is a possible host for the Q-particle (if high, and also for subsequent Wh-elements).

Apart from the syntactic evidence introduced presently and the typological considerations we have based our discussion on so far, there are other "grammatical reflexes" worth men-tioning. One is semantic in nature and follows the approach sketched out in section 2, namely the role of SP/PL interpre-tations following the Hagstrom-Bošković line. Another is prag-matic in nature and was first explored by Grohmann (1998). It focuses on the observation that the discoursal requirements, which make asking a multiple Wh-question in German felicitous to begin with, are different from those applying to English or even more closely related Dutch.

3.2. Quantifier interaction

Beck (1996) observes that some quantifiers may appear in between two Wh-phrases, whereas others may not. We cannot review the details of her analysis here nor delve further into the patterns (cf. Boeckx 1999, Grohmann 1998, 2000, Hagstrom 1998, Pesetsky 2000, and references cited). What is of interest for us is the pattern that emerges. Consider the following:

(16) a. Wer hat gestern wo alle/viele/die meisten/
who has yesterday where all/many/the most
mehr als drei Bücher gekauft?
more than three books bought
'Who bought all books where?'
b. Wer hat gestern wo kein Buch/wenige/die
who has yesterday where no book/few/the
wenigsten/weniger als drei Bücher gekauft?
fewest/ fewer than three books bought
'Who bought no book where?'

From (16) we can deduce that there are no Wh/quantifier-restrictions as such; when following the Wh-phrases, any quantifier may appear.[9] (Same facts shown here and below hold of all kinds of multiple Wh-questions, regardless of Wh-argument or adjunct status.)

When the quantifiers are placed in between the Wh-phrases, however, only those displayed in (16a) are grammatical, for convenience cut down to one instance in (17) and below.[10]

(17) a. Wer hat alle Bücher wo gekauft?
       who has all books   where bought
       'Who bought all (the) books where?'
   b. #Wer hat kein Buch wo gekauft?
       who has no   book where bought
       'Who bought no book where?'

The contrast in (17) allows for a generalization along the following lines. Monotone increasing quantifiers may appear between two Wh-phrases, decreasing ones may not. Rather than following Beck's (1996) approach and tie this generalization in with additional assumptions on LF-movement of Wh-phrases (argued against by, for example, Hornstein 1995) or a reintroduction of (artificial) barriers, we build on the operations assumed here independently: all Wh-phrases overtly move into the C-domain to FocP and FP. Following Rizzi (1997) and others, iterative topic phrases TopP may appear in between these two. It follows from this architecture that anything in between two Wh-phrases must sit in TopP—if all German Wh-phrases do indeed move overtly into the C-domain. Returning to our generalization, we could say that only topicalizable quantifiers may occur between two Wh-phrases. As it happens, increasing quantifiers fit this condition, while decreasing ones do not. Consider the following data:

---

presented below are intended to make the case for a particular high occurrence of all Wh-elements, namely within an articulated C-domain.

[9] We illustrate with the temporal adverb in between the two Wh-phrases, which may sound more natural to most speakers. Given that we identify the specifiers of FocP and FP as the positions for the two Wh-phrases, the adverb must occur in between, e.g. in TopP, (by generation or movement); we will not discuss this further.

[10] This extends to separation constructions, such as partitives, *was für*-split, etc.

(18) a. VIELE Bücher hat Peter gelesen.
many-FOC books has Peter read
'It is many books that Peter read.'
b. Viele Bücher hat Peter gelesen.
many books has Peter read
'Many books, Peter read.'

(19) a. WENIGE Bücher hat Peter gelesen.
few-FOC books has Peter read
'*It is few books that Peter read.'
b. *Wenige Bücher hat Peter gelesen.
few books has Peter read
'*Few books, Peter read.'

German is a verb second language. As (18) shows, virtually any maximal phrase may appear in initial position, whether focused or not. Commonly, the first element is referred to as "topic," but as seen in (18a), it need not be a "topic" and is not one when focused. However, decreasing quantifiers may not appear in initial position, unless they are focused. Given that focused phrases may move to a specific FocP in the C-domain, which moreover is unique (cf. Rizzi 1997), the contrast in (19) and our modified generalization follow immediately.

3.3. Adverb placement

A similar "intervention" effect can be found with adverbs: some adverbs may appear in between two Wh-phrases, others may not. Again, it can be independently shown that the illicit configurations arise with non-topicalizable adverbs.

Manner adverbs, rather low in the structure, must follow the object, unless the object is focused:

(20) a. Peter hat das Buch kaum/gerade gelesen.
Peter has the book barely/just read
'Peter barely read the book.'
b. Peter hat kaum/gerade das BUCH gelesen.

In combination with multiple Wh-phrases, these adverbs may not appear in between the two. This might strike us as a surprise, given that focus is commonly construed with Wh-phrases. It follows, however, if both Wh-phrases are in the C-domain (as opposed to a non-interrogative object as in (20)) and such adverbs may not be topicalized.

(21) a. Wer hat was kaum/gerade gelesen?
      who has what barely/just read
      'Who barely read what?'
   b. #Wer hat kaum/gerade was gelesen?
   c. *Was hat kaum/gerade wer gelesen?

Indeed, manner adverbs, as opposed to sentential adverbs, are not topicalizable. (22) illustrates the contrast, where the object is topicalized also to force a topic-reading of the fronted adverb, rather than a high occurrence in the T-domain. (Again, the same contrasts can be found in embedded contexts.)

(22) a. Wahrscheinlich hat das Buch Peter gelesen.
      probably   has the book Peter read
      'Probably, Peter read the book.'
   b. *Kaum hat das Buch Peter gelesen.
   c. ..., daß <*gerade> Peter <wahrscheinlich> das Buch <wahrscheinlich> <gerade> gelesen hat.
      'Probably/*Barely, Peter read the book.'

Regarding sequences of Wh-phrases and certain "inter-vening" elements, if an interpretation can be construed at all it is the SP reading only for the #-marked cases in (17b) and (21).

In sum, certain elements are not topicalizable and hence predicted not to appear in between two Wh-phrases under the assumption that both Wh-phrases have moved very high, into the C-domain. This prediction is empirically borne out and it is hard to imagine how to account for these facts straightfor-wardly, without further assumptions or stipulations, under the standard approach to (multiple) Wh-question formation in German. (See also Grohmann 2000, Citko and Grohmann 2000 for more discussion and data on topicalizability in German.) We can schematize the relevant structures as follows (where IQ and DQ stand for increasing and decreasing quantifier, respectively):

(23) a. $[_{CP} [Q]-C^0 [_{FocP} WH [_{TopP} IQ [_{FP} WH [_{TP} ...]]]]]$
    a'. $[_{CP} [Q]-C^0 [_{FocP} WH [_{FP} WH [_{TP} ... IQ ...]]]]]$

b. *[$_{CP}$ [Q]-C^0 [$_{FocP}$ WH [$_{TopP}$ **DQ** [$_{FP}$ WH [$_{TP}$ ...]]]]]
b'. [$_{CP}$ [Q]-C^0 [$_{FocP}$ WH [$_{FP}$ WH [$_{TP}$ ... DQ ...]]]]]

What occurs in between two Wh-phrases must sit in TopP (qua our analysis of CP) and as such must be topicalizable.

4. A Slavic Perspective

4.1. Wh-fronting in Serbo-Croatian

In the final part of this paper, we examine the consequences of the Hagstrom/Bošković semantics for the analysis of Slavic multiple Wh-movement. We have seen above that SC patterns with Wh-in situ languages in the availability of SP/PL readings. Thus, (24a) can have both an SP and a PL interpretation, whereas (24b) can only have an SP interpretation.

(24) a. Ko   je   šta   kupio?   (SP/PL)
        who   is   what   bought
     b. Šta   je   ko   kupio?   (SP/*PL)
        what is   who   bought
        'Who bought what?'

Bošković (1998b) shows that this pattern receives a straightforward explanation on the assumption that Wh-phrases in SC do not undergo movement to check Wh features (to [Spec,F] on our assumptions) but rather focus-driven movement to some position within the T-domain (e.g. Stjepanović 1995, Bošković 1997a). For concreteness, let us assume that the relevant positions are specifiers of the two agreement projections, or the equivalents thereof in more recent versions of the Minimalist Program.

(25) [$_{CP}$ C^0...[$_{FP}$ Q-F^0 [[$_{AgrSP}$WH1... [$_{AgrOP}$WH2 [$_{AgrOP}$[$_{VP}$]]]]]]]

Since Wh-fronting in SC never crosses Q, the availability of SP readings is to be expected.

Bošković gives a number of additional arguments for non-Wh-feature driven movement of Wh-phrases in SC. For example, Wh-phrases have to move even in echo questions, where the Q feature is clearly not involved.

(26) ?*Jovan je kupio šta? (Bošković 1997b:12)
   Jovan is bought what
   'John bought what?'

The interaction of fronted Wh-phrases with adverbs sheds some light on the exact location of the moved Wh-phrases. An adverb like *wisely* is in principle ambiguous between a manner and a sentential reading. The two readings are standardly correlated with the different positions for the adverb, TP-adjoined vs. VP-adjoined, for example. In SC, when *mudro* 'wisely' intervenes between the two fronted Wh-phrases, it can either be interpreted as a sentential or a manner adverb.[11]

(27) Ko mudro kogo savjetuje? (Stjepanović 1995)
   who wisely whom advises
   '??Who is it wise of to advise whom?'
   'Who advises whom in a wise manner?'

However, when the adverb follows the two fronted Wh-phrases, the only possible reading is the manner reading. This we take to show that the second Wh-phrase has to occupy a fairly low position within the clause, [Spec,AgrO] in Bošković's analysis, which compels him to the assumption that manner adverbs can adjoin to AgrOP).

(28) Ko koga mudro savjetuje?
   who whom wisely advises
   '*Who is it wise of to advise whom?'
   'Who advises whom in a wise manner?'

For our purposes, what is crucial is the fact that moved Wh-phrases in SC never leave TP, thus never cross Q. This explains why SC patterns with Wh-in situ languages with respect to the availability of SP and PL readings.

4.2. Superiority Effects in Serbo-Croatian

The generalization of the previous section that in SC fronted Wh-phrases never leave the T-domain is not without exceptions, which makes an interesting prediction concerning the availability of SP/PL readings.

---

[11] The slightly degraded status of (27) follows from the general incompatibility of sentential adverbs with questions (Bošković 1996).

Bošković (1997) shows that in certain contexts SC has real Wh-movement, that is movement to the C-domain, which correlates with the emergence of superiority effects. Interestingly, the contexts in which SC exhibits superiority are the contexts in which French has obligatory Wh-movement: embedded Wh-questions and long-distance matrix questions, illustrated in (29).

(29) a. *Pierre a demandé tu as embrassé qui.
Peter has asked you have kissed who
'Peter asked who you kissed.'
b. Pierre a demandé qui tu as embrassé.
Peter has asked who you have kissed

(30) a. Jovan i Marko ne znaju ko je koga istukao.
Jovan and Marko not know who is whom beaten
'Jovan and Marko don't know who beat whom.'
b. *Jovan i Marko ne znaju koga je ko istukao.
Jovan and Marko not know whom is who beaten

(31) a. Qui Jean et Marie croient que Pierre a embrassé?
who John and Mary believe that Peter has kissed
'Who do John and Mary believe that Peter kissed?'
b. *Jean et Marie croient que Pierre a embrassé qui?
John and Mary believe that Peter has kissed who

(32) a. Ko si koga tvrdio da je istukao?
who are whom claimed that is beaten
'Who do did you claim beat whom?'
b. *Koga si ko tvrdio da je istukao?
who are whom claimed that is beaten

Since in long-distance matrix questions, SC patterns with English-type languages with respect to superiority, it is also predicted to pattern with English with respect to the availability of SP/PL readings i.e. to only allow PL in these contexts. While a more careful investigation into the data is necessary, the judgments do appear to confirm this prediction.

4.3. Polish/Russian vs. Serbo-Croatian

Polish and Russian are standardly analyzed as belonging to this group, however if we examine them closer, important differences emerge. Polish and Russian differ from SC in that they never show superiority effects (Citko 1998, Stepanov 1998).

(33) a. Ivan i Petr ne pomnjat kto kogo pobil.
Ivan and Peter not remember who whom beat
b. Ivan i Petr ne pomnjat kogo kto pobil.
Ivan and Peter not remember whom who beat
'Ivan and Peter don't remember who beat whom.'

(34) a. Kogo kogda ty xočeš čtoby ja priglasil?
whom when you want that I invite
'Whom do you want me to invite when?'
b. Kogda kogo ty xočeš čtoby ja priglasil?
when whom you want that I invite

(35) a. Jan i Maria nie wiedzą kto kogo lubi.
John and Mary not know who whom likes
'John and Mary do not know who likes whom.'
b. Jan i Maria nie wiedzą kogo kto lubi.
John and Mary not know whom who likes

(36) a. Kogo kiedy chcesz żebym zaprosiła?
whom when want that.I invite
b. Kiedy kogo chcesz żebym zaprosiła?
when whom want that.I invite
'Who do you want me to invite when?'

Since Polish and Russian long distance Wh-questions behave just like matrix questions with respect to superiority, they should also exhibit the same behavior with respect to the availability of SP/PL. In particular, they are predicted to allow both SP and PL. Again, this prediction appears to be confirmed.[12]

---

[12] For some Russian speakers, SP readings are infelicitous. Interestingly, for the same speakers, orders violating superiority are degraded.

5. Conclusions

To conclude, we have shown that overt Wh-movement pattern is attested outside of the Slavic family of languages, in particular that German is a language with overt multiple Wh-movement. We have furthermore shown that analyzing German as a multiple Wh-movement language allows for a neater partition of languages with respect to the availability of SP/PL readings in multiple Wh questions. Finally, we have shown that there is a finer distinction within the Slavic family of languages with respect to the availability of SP/PL readings.

References

Barss, Andrew. 1992. Questions: Determining Binding and VP-adjunction. Talk given at the University of Connecticut, April 1992.
Beck, Sigrid. 1996. Quantified Structures as Barriers for LF-Movement. *Natural Language Semantics* 4: 1-56.
Boeckx, Cedric. 1999b. Decomposing French Questions. In Jim Alexander, Na-Rae Han and Michelle Minnick Fox, eds. *Proceedings of PLC 23. University of Pennsylvania Working Papers in Linguistics* 6.1: 69-80.
Bošković, Željko. 1997a. Fronting Wh-phrases in Serbo-Croatian. In Martina Lindseth, and Steven Franks, eds. *Formal Approaches to Slavic Linguistics: The Indiana Meeting*. Ann Arbor, MI: Michigan Slavic Publications, 67-86.
Bošković, Željko. 1997b. Superiority Effects with Multiple Wh-fronting in Serbo-Croatian. *Lingua* 102: 1-20.
Bošković, Željko. 1998a. LF Movement and the Minimalist Program. In Pius Tamanji and Kiyomi Kusumoto, eds. *Proceedings of the 28th Meeting of the North East Linguistic Society*. Amherst, MA: GLSA, University of Massachusetts, 43-57.
Bošković, Željko. 1998b. On the Interpretation of Multiple Questions. *Chomsky Celebration Website*. [available online at http: //mitpress.mit.edu/celebration]
Bošković, Željko. 2000. Sometimes in Situ, Sometimes in SpecCP. In Roger Martin, David Michaels and Juan Uriagereka, eds. *Step by Step*. Cambridge, MA: MIT Press, 53-87.

Cheng, Lisa. 1991. *On the Typology of Wh-Questions.* Doctoral dissertation, Massachusetts Institute of Technology, Cambridge.

Chomsky, Noam. 1973. Conditions on Transformations. In Stephen R. Anderson and Paul Kiparsky, eds. *A Festschrift for Morris Halle.* New York: Holt, Reinhart and Winston, 232-286.

Citko, Barbara. 1998. On Multiple WH Movement in Slavic. In Željko Bošković, Steven Franks and William Snyder, eds. *Formal Approaches to Slavic Linguistics: The Connecticut Meeting.* Ann Arbor, MI: Michigan Slavic Publications, 97-114.

Citko, Barbara and Kleanthes K. Grohmann. 2000. A New Argument in Favour of a Syntactic Focus Projection. Paper presented at the *Focus Workshop of GLOW 23*, University of Deusto, Bilbao. April 19, 2000

Grohmann, Kleanthes K. 1998. Syntactic Inquiries into Dis-course Restrictions on Multiple Interrogatives. *Groninger Arbeiten zur germanistischen Linguistik* 42: 1-60.

Grohmann, Kleanthes K. 2000. *Prolific Peripheries: A Radical View from the Left.* Doctoral dissertation, University of Maryland, College Park.

Hagstrom, Paul. 1998. *Decomposing Questions.* Doctoral dissertation, Massachusetts Institute of Technology, Cambridge.

Hornstein, Norbert. 1995. *Logical Form.* Oxford: Blackwell.

Kayne, Richard S. 1994. *The Antisymmetry of Syntax.* Cambridge, MA: MIT Press.

Müller, Gereon and Wolfgang Sternefeld. 1993. Improper Movement and Unambiguous Binding. *Linguistic Inquiry* 24: 461-507.

Pesetsky, David. 1987. Wh-in situ: Movement and Unselective Binding. In Alice G.B. ter Meulen and Eric Reuland, eds. *The Representation of (In)definiteness.* Cambridge, MA: MIT Press, 98-129.

Pesetsky, David. 2000. *Movement and Its Kin.* Cambridge, MA: MIT Press.

Richards, Norvin W. 1997. *What Moves Where When in Which Language?* Doctoral dissertation, Massachusetts Institute of Technology, Cambridge.

Rizzi, Luigi. 1997. The Fine Structure of the Left Periphery. In L. Haegeman, ed. *Elements of Grammar: A Handbook of Generative Syntax.* Dordrecht: Kluwer, 281-337.

Rudin, Catherine. 1988. On Multiple Questions and Multiple WH Fronting. *Natural Language and Linguistic Theory* 6: 445-502.
Stepanov, Arthur. 1998. On Wh-Movement in Russian. In Pius Tamayi and Kiyomi Kusumoto, eds. *Proceedings of NELS 28*. Amherst, MA: GLSA, 453-467.
Stjepanović, Sandra. 1995. Short Distance Movement of Wh-Phrases in Serbo-Croatian Matrix Clauses. Manuscript, University of Connecticut, Storrs.
Uriagereka, Juan. 1995. Aspects of the Syntax of Clitic Placement in Western Romance. *Linguistic Inquiry* 26: 79-123.
Wachowicz, Krystyna. 1974. Against the Universality of a Single Wh-Question Movement. *Foundations of Language* 11: 155-166.
Zwart, C. Jan-Wouter. 1993. *Dutch Syntax. A Minimalist Approach*. Doctoral dissertation, University of Groningen.

Barbara Citko
SUNY
Department of Linguistics
Stony Brook, NY 11794
USA
citko@hotmail.com

Kleanthes K. Grohmann
ZAS
Jägerstr. 10-11
10117 Berlin
Germany
kleanthes@punksinscience.org

Status of Focus Sensitive Particles in the Topic-Focus Articulation of the Sentence

Eva Hajičová
Charles University

1. Introduction

1.1 Motivation

A detailed empirical analysis of negation in Czech and some other (typologically different) languages has led us to the claim (Hajičová 1973; 1975; Sgall, Hajičová and Panevová 1986) that the semantics of (linguistic) negation should be studied and described in relation to the topic-focus articulation (TFA, information structure) of the sentence. The main objective of the present contribution is to show that the properties of the so-called focus sensitive particles (focalizers, rhematizers; see Rooth 1985, and several empirical observations e.g. in Taglicht 1984, König 1991, etc.) should also be analyzed, both in Czech and in English, from the point of view of their position in the topic (T) or in the focus (F) (more precisely, on the boundary between T and F) of the sentence. Here TFA is understood as a hierarchy present at the level of the representation of the meaning of the sentence, rendered in the surface structure by such means as surface word order, sentence prosody, specific syntactic constructions, or morphemic forms. In the framework of TFA we subscribe to (for a more detailed discussion, see Sgall et al. 1986), T can be informally characterized as that part of the sentence the sentence is 'about', F being that part of the sentence that 'speaks' about T. In addition to the dichotomy of T and F, the underlying order of nodes of the representation of the meaning of the sentence (specified in terms of dependency trees rather than constituency relations) is recognized, comparable to the traditional notion of the hierarchy of communicative dynamism (see Firbas 1992).

1.2 A Note on Terminology

The study of what is now often referred to as the information structure of the sentence has a very long tradition in Czech linguistics, though under different names and within different methodologies the most prominent of which are the terms 'functional sentence perspective' (which is Firbas' translation of the original Czech term 'aktuální členění větné' coined by Mathesius in the twenties and used after him by Firbas and his students), and 'topic-focus articulation' as developed by Sgall and his followers within an explicit, formal theoretical framework of functional generative description. The inquiry into the communicative function of the sentence was gradually accepted and further developed by a wider linguistic community; let us mention here esp. A.M.K. Halliday with his distinction between 'given' and 'new', i.e. the information structure on the one hand, and the 'theme'—and, correspondingly, the 'rheme'—on the other, the studies on 'logical stress' in Russian linguistics, and numerous inquiries carried out by German linguists from the times of G. von der Gabelentz, H. Paul, A. Wegener to the more recent studies by J. Jacobs, D. Büring, T. Höhle and many others.

In modern trends of theoretical linguistics, a counterpart of the dichotomy of topic and focus can be found in Chomsky's distinction of presupposition and focus; it should be also noted that crucial examples in the discussions between the so-called interpretative (Chomskyan) and generative (Lakoffian) semantics (such as 'Everybody in this room knows at least two languages' vs. 'At least two languages are known by everybody in this room', or 'Many people read few books' vs. 'Few books are read by many people') differ in their TFA (the fact that has not been explicitly mentioned by the proponents of these approaches but that is self-evident from the perspective of those who are used to work with the TFA analysis).

Decisive role in the dissemination of the notion of 'focus' has come with Rooth's (1985) notion of 'association with focus'. In spite of the fact that his notion of focus is rather narrow and concerns what might be called 'prosodic focus', i.e. that item of the sentence that carries the main stress (intonation center), his PhD thesis and further studies strengthened the interest of the formal semantics community in this domain and has made it possible to integrate the recent results of the Prague School research in TFA within those of the formal semantics inquiries (see esp. Partee 1991 and Hajičová, Partee and Sgall 1998 where previous developments both in structural and in intensional semantics are discussed).

1.3 Elementary Examples

Let us add a few introductory examples, pointing out what is meant by 'TFA' in our approach and how its basic properties are handled. We start with Czech examples the English translations of which exhibit a parallel expression of TFA (in all our examples, we indicate the placement of the intonation center by capitals; for the sake of transparency, we add here and in some examples in the sequel a 'bracketted' version of the sentences indicating by subscripts T and F, which part under the given reading belongs to the topic and which to the focus, respectively; English translations are given in the form of glosses; we add real English equivalents only in cases when we consider this to be important for the issues under discussion or when glosses are not sufficient for the understanding of the Czech sentences):

(1) Táta   PŘIŠEL.
 father has-come
 $[táta]_T$ $[přišel]_F$

(2) TÁTA přišel.
 father has-come
 'FATHER has come.'
 $[přišel]_T$ $[táta]_F$

On its prototypical reading, (1) is 'about' father, and says about him, that he has come. Sentence (2), on the contrary, speaks about the event of 'coming', and says that he who has come is father (it can used e.g. as an answer to the question 'Who has come?').

A similar analysis can be presented for (3) and (4). A possible preceding context for (3) may be the question 'What kind of weather did we have in Prague yesterday?' indicationg that both Prague and yesterday are given by the context and as such 'spoken about'. On the other hand, it would be weird to use (4) in such a context: a good context for (4)—not disrupting the coherence of the given discourse segment—would be e.g. 'Where did it rain yesterday?'

(3) Včera   v Praze   PRŠELO.
    yesterday in Prague rained
    'Yesterday, it RAINED in Prague.'
    [včera v Praze]$_T$ [pršelo]$_F$

(4) Včera   pršelo v PRAZE.
    yesterday rained in Prague
    'Yesterday, it rained in Prague.'
    [včera pršelo]$_T$ [v Praze]$_F$

The high degree of 'grammaticalization' of word order prevents English in some cases to place the focus at the end of the sentence (see (5)), or necessitates a change of the (syntactic) structure of the sentence (as in (6)); Czech, however, offers such a possibility:

(5) Přišel   TÁTA.
    has-come father
    'FATHER has come.'
    [přišel]$_T$ [táta]$_F$

(6) Tu   knihu vydal   KLUWER.
    that book   published by-Kluwer
    'That book was published by KLUWER.'
    [tu knihu vydal]$_T$ [Kluwer$_F$]

2. Focus-sensitivity in Relation to Truth Conditions

Partee (1991) recognizes several degrees of focus-sensitivity that span the pragmatic-semantic range; her findings can be summarized as follows:

The pairs of sentences given below under (7) through (14) differ only in their TFA; their different TFA is acompanied by the following differences ; in most cases, we accompany English examples by their Czech counterparts and number them with primes):

(i) Differences in contextual felicity with no differences in presuppostion or truth-conditions proper:

(7) (a) KENNEDY has been killed.
(b) Kennedy has been KILLED.

(7') (a) Zabili KENNEDYHO. (or: KENNEDYHO zabili.)
(b) Kennedyho ZABILI.

Both (a) and (b) carry the same presuppositions and truth conditions proper, but they differ in contexts in which they can be used: while (a) can appear as a 'hot news' (as well as in a context that can be modelled by such a question as 'Who has been killed?'), (b) is, in the prototypical case, an utterance 'about Kennedy' (answering, e.g., a question such as 'What has happened to Kennedy?').

(ii) Differences in presupposition with no differences in truth-conditions proper: in a given situation one utterance may be true and the other undefined, or one undefined and one false, but not one true and the other false (Hajičová 1984), cf. (8) and its Czech counterpart in (8').

(8) (a) This time John's cousin (didn't) cause(d) our DEFEAT.
(b) This time our defeat was (not) caused by John's COUSIN.

(8') (a) Tentokrát Janův bratranec (ne)způsobil naši PORÁŽKU.
(b) Tentokrát naši porážku (ne)způsobil Janův BRATRANEC.

Both (a) and (b) in their affirmative form trigger the entailment 'We were defeated'; however, under negation, if the expression triggering this entailment ('our defeat') is included in the focus of the sentence (as in (a)), the entailment is undefined: we might have been defeated but it is also possible that we have not; this may be illustrated by two possible continuations of (8)(a), namely (8)(c) and (d):

(8) (c) ... He played better than most of the OTHERS (but yet we did not manage to win the game).
(d) ... He played so well this time that he helped to our VICTORY.

(iii) Differences in truth conditions if 'invited' exhaustive listing is included in truth-conditional content, and/or differences in truth conditions with respect to some contexts of evaluation but not others, as in (9) and its Czech counterpart (9').

(9) (a) English is spoken in the SHETLANDS.
    (b) ENGLISH is spoken in the Shetlands.
    (c) English is spoken only in the SHETLANDS.

(9') (a) Anglicky se mluví na Shetlandských OSTROVECH.
    (b) Na Shetlandských ostrovech se mluví ANGLICKY.
    (c) Anglicky se mluví jenom na Shetlandských OSTROVECH.

Both in English and in Czech, the (a) sentence is understood as to be 'about' English, or 'about' speaking English, while the (b) sentence is 'about' the Shetlands. The sentence (a) is (in the world referred to) conceived of (at least) as weird: its structure somehow implies that English is spoken (only, or at least most importantly) in the Shetlands. An implicit focalizer is present in (b) as well, but there the interpretation with 'only' or at least 'most importantly' does not lead to a weird reading: it is true that the language spoken in the Shetlands, is (mostly) English.

What is concerned here is Kuno's (1971, 345; 1972, esp. 307) exhaustive listing, discussed in more detail in Sgall et al. (1980, p. 82). The authors propose, as an answer to the question which structures invite exhaustive listing, that the exhaustive listing interpetation concerns the position of the relevant item in the Focus of the sentence and is particularly apparent if the verb is included in the Topic (as a contextually bound element). Exhaustive listing is also present if the verb has a 'general' meaning, it is semantically close to the topic (e.g. 'carry out', 'perform', ...) or if the verb 'adds' only a little to the Topic, having a 'general' meaning (e.g. 'carry out', 'perform', ...) or coming semantically close to the Topic (as e.g. in (9)(a) above).

The difference between the interpretation with an explicit focalizer like 'only' as in (9)(c) and (9')(c) and without it (as in the (a) examples) lies in the fact that in the Focus of the (a) examples the countries which interest us are listed (and the weirdness of this sentence lies in the fact that as for speaking English we are interested in 'more important' places) while using 'only' in the Focus of the (c) sentences, in addition to the above interpretation, the speaker excludes 'cases completely not interesting'. It should be added that the (a) sentences can be used in some specific contexts (when "speaking about English"), as in that illustrated by (10).

(10) (Why should Adam learn English?)
Well, English is spoken in the SHETLANDS and he wants to GO there.

(10') Anglicky se mluví na Shetlandských OSTROVECH, a on tam chce JET.

The above observations are supported by numerous other examples in different languages, as exemplified in (11) and (12); unless a specific context is present, the sentence (11)(a) seems rather weird (as if one has to smoke when passing the hallway), while the (b) sentence is pretty natural (meaning: if you want to smoke, go to the hallway).

(11) (a) In the hallway, one SMOKES.
(b) One smokes in the HALLWAY.

With (12), the situation is similar: (12)(a) is true if Tom was too busy with other things during the day so that only in the evenings he was free to concentrate on his disseration; on the other hand, with (12)(b) the reported situation only concerns the evenings, so that (12)(b) is true even if most of Tom's dissertation was written during the days.

(12) (a) Tom psal disertaci po VEČERECH.
Tom wrote dissertation in evenings
(b) Po večerech Tom psal DISERTACI.
in evenings Tom wrote dissertation

(iv) Differences in truth-conditions proper: situations in which one assertion is definitely true and the other definitely false; see ex. (13) taken from Rooth (1985).

(13) (a) John only introduced Bill to SUE.
(b) John only introduced BILL to Sue.

The cases illustrated by this example will be discussed in detail below, in Section 4. Before we pass over to this core issue of our present paper, we have to summarize first our results in the analysis of negation, to substantiate our claim that negation behaves in a similar vein way as focus sensitive particles.

3. Negation and TFA

A detailed empirical analysis of the semantics of (linguistic) negation in Czech and some other—typologically different—languages (see Hajičová 1973, 1975; Sgall, Hajičová and Panevová 1986) has shown that this issue should be studied and described in relation to TFA. In the prototypical case, what is negated is the assignment of the focus (F) to the topic (T) of the sentence: while the positive sentence may be understood as F being predicated of T (i.e. F(T), cf. Peregrin 1994; 1996), its negative counterpart corresponds to non-F(T).

The following cases have to be distinguished:

(i) The verb is in F and the whole F of the sentence is under negation, see (14) and (15):

(14) (Which works by Milan Kundera have you reviewed?) I have reviewed most of his novels but I have not read any POEMS by him.

(15) (a) No blond Albanians study at HARVARD. (Do any blond Albanians exist at all?)
(b) Blond Albanians do not study at HARVARD. (They prefer to do other things.)

In (14), the expression referring to poems is included in F; one of the entailments triggered by the affirmative form of the sentence ('... I have read POEMS by him'), namely that Milan Kundera has written poems, is no longer triggered by the negation of the sentence; this is a similar case as with the defeat in the ex. (8)(a) above; in contrast to presupposition, which is valid both in the affirmative as with the negative statement, such an entailment has been called allegation, cf. Hajičová (1984).

Allegation rather than presupposition is also present in (15)(a), which can be characterized as a topicless sentence, constituting the F (see the 'hot news' reading of (7)(a) above) and as such being under negation as a whole. As the continuation in the brackets indicates, one can ask about the existence of blond Albanians. In (15)(b), on the contrary, the expression referring to blond Albanians is in T and as such is outside the scope of negation; the sentence is connected with a presupposition of the referential accessibility of blond Albanians.

(ii) The verb is in T and the event it identifies is not negated; again, what is negated here, is the assignment of F to T, see (16):

(16) John didn't come late because he was too BUSY.

(16') Jan nepřišel pozdě, protože byl příliš ZANEPRÁZDNĚN.

The sentence (16) may continue e.g. by 'but because his train was late' (Cz. 'ale protože jeho vlak měl zpoždění').. The interpretation then is that the event identified by the main clause is not negated (in spite of the fact that grammatically, the verb is in a negative form, cf. the Czech sentence in (16')) and what is negated is only the fact that his late-comming was caused by his being too busy: he came late, but might not have been too busy.

(iii) The verb is in T and the event it identifies is negated; what is in F, is outside the scope of negation, see (17):

(17) (Why didn't John come?) John didn't come because he was too BUSY.

As the question in the brackets indicates, John's not-coming is given by the context; the interpretation of the sentence is that he was too busy, which was the cause of his not coming.

It is interesting to compare (16) and (17) with regard to the entailment triggered by the causal clause in F ('because he was too BUSY'). In (16) this clause is under the scope of negation; it triggers an allegation since it is neither necessarily the case that he was too busy, nor is his heavy preoccupation negated; the entailment triggered by this clause is again an allegation. For (17), however, the only possible interpretation is that he was too busy; the entailment triggered by this clause is thus valid both in the affirmative counterpart of (17) ('John came because he was too BUSY') as well as in (17) itself, i.e. it is a presupposition.

(iv) The only "new" information in the sentence is the negative modality; the whole sentence except for the modality is in T (Koktová 1987):

(18) (Did John come late?) No, John DIDN'T come late.

In complex sentences, the scope of negation is confined to the clause containing negation (and the clauses embedded in it), as demonstrated by (19):

(19) Jim told me that John didn't come because it RAINED.

The main clause of (19) is outside the scope of negation, but otherwise the ambiguity of (19) due to the different possible scopes of the negation in the embedded that-clause is parallel to the difference between (16) and (17). Two interpretations are thus possible:

(i) The verb 'come' is in T and the event it identifies is not negated: the sentence (19) may continue e.g. by 'but because he wanted to meet Mary'. What is negated is only the fact that his coming was caused by the bad weather: the weather might, but need not have been bad..

(ii) The verb 'come' is in T and the event it identifies is negated; the rest of the sentence, i.e. the F, is outside the scope of negation, as in (19'), and on this reading, the sentence entails that it rained:

(19') (Why did Jim tell you about the reason why John didn't come?)
Jim told me that John didn't come because it rained.

The ambiguity of negation illustrated by examples (16) through (17) above can be documented also by other Czech examples:

(20) Jim nespí ÚNAVOU.
     Jim not-sleep because-of-tiredness

(20') Jim nespí, protože je UNAVEN.
      Jim not-sleep, because (he)-is tired

Ex. (20) (as well as (20')) has the following readings:

(i) It is not true about Jim that he sleeps because he is tired.

(ii) Jim does not sleep because he is tired (but because he took sleeping pills, i.e. he sleeps but not because he is tired).

(iii) Jim does not sleep because he is tired. (i.e. the reason for his being awake is that he is tired)

While (20)(iii) entails that Jim is tired (this entailment is its presupposition, see above the discussion about ex. (17)), in (20)(ii) no such presupposition is present: Jim might have been tired but this need not be the case (i.e. this entailment is an allegation; see above the discussion of ex.(16)).

A similar situation can be observed in German (Zemb 1968; see also the 'commentary test' 'es stimmt nicht' of Posner 1972), in Dutch (Kraak 1966; Seuren 1967), in Russian (Paducheva 1969; Manukjan 1972; Borschev and Partee 1997), and is supported also for example by the analysis of the positions of the negative morpheme 'hanii' in Navajo (Perkins 1978; Hajičová 1996).

4. Prototypical Position of Other Focus Sensitive Particles in the TFA Structure

4.1 Positions of Focalizers in English

The behaviour of negation described in the previous section has been compared to the behaviour of focus sensitive operators (Koktová 1987; Hajičová, Partee and Sgall 1998). It can be concluded that negation functions as one of these particles (focalizers). Let us illustrate this claim on the English sentence (21)(a) and its three readings in (21)(b), where the three possible positions of the boundary between T and F is indicated by % and illustrated by the three readings (i) through (iii); let us add that the ambiguity of English sentences with such a particle as 'only' has been noticed already by Jespersen (1949).

(21) (a) John only travelled from Prague to LONDON.
    (b) John % travelled % from Prague % to LONDON.
    (i) John only travelled from Prague to LONDON.
       (He didn't stay in Germany.)
       [John]$_T$ [only travelled from Prague to LONDON]$_F$
    (ii) John travelled only from Prague to LONDON.
       (He didn't travel from Vienna to Edinburgh.)
       [John travelled]$_T$ [only from Prague to LONDON]$_F$
    (iii) John travelled from Prague only to LONDON.
       (He didn't travel from Prague to Edinburgh.)
       [John travelled from Prague]$_T$ [only to LONDON]$_F$

4.2 Prototypical Positions of Focalizers in Czech

A prototypical position of a focalizer in a Czech sentence with the intonation center (IC) at the end (indicated by the capitals) can be illustrated by examples (22) to (25) (a lit. translation and the context is given in the brackets):

(22) Honza koupil babičce jenom KYTKU.
Honza bought grandmother-Dat. only flower-Acc.
(... but not a gift.)

(23) Honza koupil jenom babičce KYTKU.
Honza bought only grandmother-Dat. flower-Acc.
(... but he didn't buy newspapers for his grandfather)

(24) Honza jenom koupil babičce KYTKU.
Honza only bought grandmother-Dat. flower-Acc.
(... but he didn't come to wish the best to his grandfather.)

(25) (Nothing happened.)
Jenom jedna paní přišla s poplašnou ZPRÁVOU.
Only a woman came with alarming news

It should be noticed that in Czech, as opposed to English, the focalizer 'jenom' (only) is placed (not only in the surface word order, but also from the point of view of TFA and the semantic interpretation of the sentences) on the boundary between the topic and the focus.

4.3 Sentences with a marked position for IC

A prototypical position of a focalizer in TFA is exhibited also by sentences with a marked position for the intonation center (denoted by capitals):

(26) Jenom KYTKU koupil Honza babičce.
only flower bought Honza o-grandmother

(27) Honza koupil jenom BABIČCE kytku.
Honza bought only to-grandmother flower

(28) Honza jenom KOUPIL babičce kytku.
Honza only bought to-grandmother flower

Ex. (26) can be followed e.g. by 'ale ne dárek' ('but not a gift'), and it is then synonymous with (22). Ex. (27) is synonymous e.g. with 'Honza koupil kytku jenom BABIČCE', with the interpretation 'he bought a flower to nobody else than his grandmother'. Ex. (28) can be followed e.g. by 'Nepřinesl jí kytku ze své zahrádky' ('He didn't bring a flower from his garden'); another word order variant (an unmarked one, with the intonation center at the end of the sentence) with the same TFA is 'Honza babičce kytku jenom KOUPIL.'

4.4 TFA and the Choice of Alternatives

A comparison with the so-called choice of alternatives (Rooth 1985) offers itself when analyzing the TFA of the above examples: the set of alternatives consists of the possible answers to questions determining the TFA of these sentences. Thus e.g. for (22), the relevant question is 'What did Honza buy for his grandmother?' and the set of alternatives includes 'H. bought a present', '... a box of chocolates', '... a sweater', '...a scarf', '... a flower'. etc.; for (23), the relevant question is 'What did Honza buy for whom?' and the set of alternatives consists of 'H. bought his grandfather cigarettes', '... his wife a scarf', '... his grandmother a flower', etc. The sentence itself can then be understood as the alternative chosen. In sentences with focus sensitive particles, this choice is further specified by the lexical meaning of the particle ('jenom': restriction, 'také': additive meaning, etc.).

4.5 Focalizers in Complex Sentences

In sentences with embedded clauses the situation gets more complicated; (29) can be used both in the context of (30)(a) and of (30)(b):

(30) Jirka   nám řekl, že   Honza jenom koupil
     Jirka   us   told   that Honza only   bought
     babičce   KYTKU.
     grandmother-Dat.   flower-Acc.)

(30) (a) What did Jirka tell you that Honza had done?
     (b) What did Jirka tell you?

In the context of (30)(a), the boundary between the topic and the focus of (29) is placed before that part of the sentence that is 'associated' with the focalizer 'jenom', i.e. the topic of that reading of (29) is 'Jirka nám řekl, že Honza' ('Jirka us told that Honza'), and the focus consists in 'jenom koupil babičce kytku' ('only bought grandmother-Dat. flower-Acc.'). If the 'associated' part together with the focalizer is called the focus of the focalizer (ff), then we can say that—similarly as with the above prototypical examples analyzed in Sect. 4.2 and 4.3—the focus of the focalizer (ff) equals the focus (F) of the sentence.

In the context of (30)(b), the boundary between the topic and the focus of the sentence lies between the subject of the main clause and the rest, i.e. the topic of that reading of (29) is 'Jirka nám řekl' (lit. 'Jirka us told'), and the focus consists of 'že Honza jenom koupil babičce kytku' ('that Honza only bought grandmother-Dat. flower-Acc.'). On this interpretation, the focus of the focalizer (ff) equals the local focus of the embedded clause rather than the focus (F) of the whole complex sentence.

5. Secondary Positions

In certain specific secondary (non-prototypical) cases, a focalizer can occur in the topic of the sentence (see Krifka's 1995 'second occurrence'); this is a further support for the claim that it is necessary to distinguish between the 'focus' of a focalizer and the focus of the sentence.

In the context of (31)(a), the focus of both (31)(b) and (c) is 'Jirka'; the focalizer 'i' is in their topic rather than on the boundary between T and F. The focus of the focalizer (ff) is 'his enemy'.

(31) (a) Who can support even his enemy if he is right?
    (b) I   svého nepřítele   dokáže podpořit JIRKA.
        Even his   enemy-Acc can   support JIRKA-Nom.
        [I svého nepřítele dokáže podpořit]$_T$ [JIRKA]$_F$
    (c) Podpořit i   svého nepřítele   dokáže JIRKA.
        Support even his   enemy-Acc can   JIRKA-Nom

It is, however, possible to find examples with more than a single focalizer, as in (32):

(32) I svého nepřítele dokáže podpořit jenom JIRKA.
      Even his enemy-Acc. can support only Jirka-Nom.
      [I svého nepřítele dokáže podpořit]$_T$ [jenom JIRKA]$_F$

Here, the F of (32) is constituted by 'jenom Jirka' ('only Jirka', the focalizer 'jenom' ('only') stands in a protypical position, it is a part of F. The ff of 'jenom' equals F (see above, Sect. 4.2). The second focalizer 'i' ('even') is in T, in a similar vein as in (31)(b) or (c) above.

In connection with approaches working with focus as based on the choice among a set of alternatives, the so-called 'scope of focalizers' is specified, which is understood to be that part of the sentence that is relevant for the choice of the alternative. Thus in (22) through (26), the scope of the focalizer 'jenom' ('only') would be constituted by the whole sentence; in (29) in the context of (30)(a), the scope of the focalizer would be constituted by the embedded clause (the choice of the alternative is determined by the fact that Honza bought something to his grandmother). In terms of a dependency-based description, the scope of focalizer is the maximal projection of the head of the focalizer (i.e. all nodes that depend—directly or indirectly—on this head).

We can thus conclude that it is possible to specify the focus of the focalizer (ff) as follows:

(i) if the focalizer is a part of the focus (be it 'local' or 'global'), then ff consists of that part of the representation of the meaning of the sentence (its tectogrammatical representation, TR) that follows the focalizer in the underlying order of elements of the TR;

(ii) if the focalizer is included in the topic, then ff covers that part of the topic of the sentence that follows the focalizer in the underlying order of elements of the TR up to (and including the) item that is the contrastive topic.

6. Conclusion

In the present paper, we have briefly characterized the framework presented in Hajičová, Partee and Sgall (1998), based on an in-depth analysis of examples which exhibit interesting semantic relations connected with focus sensitive particles, and on an apparatus working with the dichotomy of topic and focus. We have attempted to show that this framework, including the notion of contextual boundness and that of the underlying order of elements of TR's, offers convenient tools for a sufficiently detailed description of the sentence structure containing the so-called focus sensitive operators. In addition, we have documented by our previous analysis of the semantics of negation that negation exhibits similar properties in relation with TFA as focus sensitive particles.

This is supposed to serve as another support for the claim that the representations of the meaning of the sentence, the TR's, can be conceived of as a starting point for a procedure delimiting, by means of general rules, a transition from the language system (level of literal meaning) to the domain of cognitive content.

References

Borschev, V. and B.H. Partee. (1997) Formal and Lexical Semantics and the Genitive in Negated Existential Sentences in Russian. In: *Formal Approaches to Slavic Linguistics*, The Connecticut Meeting (eds. . Boshkovich, Steven Franks and W. Snyder). Ann Arbor: Michigan Slavic Publications.

Bosch, P. and R. van der Sandt, eds. (1995) *Focus and Natural Language Processing. IBM Working Paper* 7. Heidelberg: IBM Deutschland,

Boguslavskij, I.M. (1996), *Sfera dejstvija leksičeskix edinic.* Moscow: Škola "Jazyki russkoj kul'tury".

Firbas, J. (1992) *Functional Sentence Perspective in Written and Spoken Communication.* Cambridge:Cambridge University Press.

Hajičová, E. (1973) Negation and Topic vs. Comment. *Philologica Pragensia* 17: 18–25.

Hajičová, E. (1975) *Negace a presupozice ve významové stavbě věty.* Praha:Academia.

Hajičová, E. (1984) Presuppositions and Allegation Revisited. *Journal of Pragmatics* 8: 155–167.

Hajičová, E. (1996) Topic-Focus Articulation—A Matter of Langue or Parole? The Case of Negation. In: *Theoretical linguistics and grammatical description* (ed. Robin Sackmann), Amsterdam: John Benjamins, 167–175.

Hajičová, E., Partee, B.H. and P. Sgall (1998) *Topic-Focus Articulation, Tripartite Structures, and Semantic Content.* Dordrecht: Kluwer.

Jespersen, O. (1949), *A Modern English Grammar on Historical Principles. Part VII, Syntax.* Copenhagen.

Koktová, E. (1987) On the Scoping Properties of Negation, Focusing Particles and Sentence Adverbials. *Theoretical Linguistics* 14:173–226.

König, E. (1991) *The Meaning of Focus Particles.* London and New York: Routledge.

Kraak, A. (1966) *Negatieve Zinnen. Een Methodolosche en Grammatische Analyse.* Hilversun.

Krifka, M. (1995) Focus and/or Context: A Second Look at Second Occurrence Expressions. Deliverd at the conference *Context-Dependence in the Analysis of Linguistic Meaning,* Prague, February 11–15, 1995.

Kuno, S. (1971) The Position of Locatives in Existential Sentences. *Linguistic Inquiry* 2:333–378.

Kuno, S. (1972) Functional Sentence Perspective. *Linguistic Inquiry* 3:269–320.

Manukjan, Ž. K. (1972) Aktual'noe členenie i otricanie (na materiale armjanskogo jazyka). *Naučno-texničeskaja informacija,* Serija 2, No. 9: 45–52.

Padučeva, E.V. (1969) Semantičeskij analiz otricatel'nyx predloženij v russkom jazyke. In: *Mašinnyj perevod i prikladnaja lingvistika* 12: 5–35.

Partee, B.H. (1991) Topic, Focus and Quantification. In: S. Moore and A. Wyner (eds.) *Proceedings from Semantics and Linguistic Theory* I. *Cornell Working Papers in Linguistics* 40. Ithaca, N.Y., 257–280.

Partee, B.H. and P.Sgall, eds. (1996) *Discourse and Meaning: Papers in Honor of Eva Hajičová.* Amsterdam/Philadelphia: Benjamins.

Peregrin, J. (1994) Topic-Focus Articulation as Generalized Quantification. In: Bosch and van der Sandt (1994), 379–388.

Peregrin, J. (1996) Topic and Focus in a Formal Framework. In: Partee and Sgall (1996), 235–254.

Perkins, E.T. (1978) *The Role of Word Order and Scope in the Interpretation of Navajo Sentences,* PhD diss.

Posner, R. (1972) *Theorie des Kommentierens.* Frankfurt.

Rooth, M. (1985) *Association with Focus.* Amherst: University of Massachusetts. PhD dissertation.

Seuren, P.A.M. (1969) *Operators and Nucleus*. Cambridge: Cambridge University Press.
Sgall, P., Hajičová, E. and E. Buráňová (1980) *Aktuální členění věty v češtině*. Prague: Academia.
Sgall, P., Hajičová, E. and J. Panevová (1986) *The Meaning of the Sentence in Its Semantic and Pragmatic Aspects*. Dordrecht: Reidel and Prague: Academia.
Taglicht, J. (1984) *Message and Emphasis. On Focus and Scope in English*. London:Longman.
Zemb, J.-M. (1968) *Les structures logiques de la proposition allemande*. Paris: O.C.D.L.

Eva Hajičová
Charles University
Prague
Czech Republic
hajicova@ufal.mff.cuni.cz

Compensatory Lengthening in Slovak

Ben Hermans
Tilburg University

1. Introduction

Slovak has a process whereby a yer triggers lengthening of a preceding vowel. Intuitively it is attractive to analyze this phenomenon as an instance of compensatory lengthening (CL), because it would then be possible to explain the lengthening as being caused by the loss of the yer. However, there seem to be two problems with this view. The first problem has to do with the representation of yers. Yers are not linked to a mora (or an X-slot). This being the case, the theory of CL, as developed in Hayes (1989), would predict that yers cannot trigger CL, because only moraic segments can trigger it. In this article I refer to this problem as the *representational* problem. The second problem is explicitly mentioned in Rubach (1993). According to Rubach the lengthening process triggered by yer cannot be an instance of CL, because in certain cases the position of the lengthened vowel cannot be explained under this view. I will refer to this problem as the *derivational* problem.

In this article I argue that in Optimality Theory (OT), developed in Prince and Smolensky (1993), both problems can be solved. OT, then, allows us to maintain the attractive hypothesis that yer induced length really is CL. This article is structured as follows. In the next section I discuss the structure of yers. I will argue that yers are moraless. In the third section I discuss the representational problem. In the fourth section I propose a solution to the derivational problem. In the last section the results are summarized.

2. The Structure of Yer

Like all Slavic languages Slovak has a set of vowels, called yers, that alternate with zero. Some examples are given in (1). Like all examples in this article, they are taken from Rubach (1993).[1]

---

[1] An acute accent indicates vowel length.

(1) nom. sg.   gen. sg.
    liter   'litre'   litr+a
    bobor   'beaver'   bobr+a
    blázon   'fool'   blázn+a

There has been extensive debate whether it is possible to predict the presence of yers. It has turned out that this is not the case. The alternation above cannot be treated as epenthesis in the environment C-C], because in this environment the presence of a yer is contrastive. Examples illustrating this are given in (2).[2]

(2) a. *no yer appears in the environment C-C]*
       falš   'foul'
       park   'park'
       pôct   'distinction'
    b. *a yer does appear in the environment C-C]*
       nom. sg.   gen. sg.
       faloš   'dishonesty'   falš+e
       Turek   'Turk'   Turk+a
       ocot   'vinegar'   oct+u

It has also become clear that the alternation in (1) cannot be explained in terms of deletion of a vowel, because in the context C-CV], there is a contrast between the absence and presence of yers.

(3) a. *the vowel is deleted in the environment C-CV*
       nom. sg.   gen. sg.
       semester 'semester'   semestr+a
       kotol   'cauldron'   kotl+a
    b. *the vowel is not deleted in the environment C-CV*
       nom. sg.   gen. sg.
       jeseter   'sturgeon'   jeseter+a
       atol   'atoll'   atol+u

The fact that the alternation in (1) is neither an instance of epenthesis nor deletion has led to the generally accepted view that yers are vowels which are not linked to a mora (Kenstowicz and Rubach 1987, Rubach 1993 on Slovak; Szpyra 1992 on Polish; Yearley 1995 on Russian).

---

[2] The diacritic over *o* indicates that *o* is realized as the rising diphthong [uo].

One variant of this view is developed in Yearley (1995) working in the framework of OT. In her analysis the underlying contrast between yers and stable vowels (of the same quality) looks as follows.

(4) *the underlying representation of yers and stable vowels*

front yer	back yer	stable *e*	stable *o*
		μ	μ
		|	|
e	o	e	o

Consider *Turek/Turk+a*. The realization of the second vowel in *Turek* implies that a mora has been inserted. This violates the constraint DEPENDENCY-μ (DEP-μ). Yearley proposes that insertion of the mora is triggered by NOCOMPLEXCODA (NOCOMCOD), which penalizes a complex coda. The fact that a mora is inserted to avoid a complex coda entails that NOCOMCOD dominates DEP-μ. [3]

(5) NOCOMCOD » DEP-μ

turEk	NOCOMCOD	DEP-μ
☞ turek		*
turk	*!	

In *Turk+a* there is no threat of a coda cluster, because *k* is located in the onset of the second syllable. Hence, realization of the yer is not required. A moraless vowel is not allowed (Yearley 1995:540).There are two ways to get rid of a moraless vowel; we can either delete it, or we can insert a mora. Since the first option is preferred, DEP-μ is ranked higher than MAXIMIZATION-V (MAX-V).

(6) DEP-μ » MAX-V

turEka	DEP-μ	MAX-V
tureka	*!	
☞ turka		*

The question arises as to why a coda cluster can only be broken up by a yer and not by a *new* vowel. Insertion of a vowel violates DEPENDENCY-V (DEP-V). Apparently, then, this is worse than a coda cluster. This indicates that DEP-V dominates NOCOMCOD:

---

[3] In underlying forms a yer is represented with a capital letter.

(7) DEP-V » NOCOMCOD

falš	DEP-V	NOCOMCOD
☞ falš		*
faleš	*!	

Combining all the relevant rankings we get the following hierarchy:

(8) *The phonology of vowel/zero alternation*
    DEP-V » NOCOMCOD » DEP-µ » MAX-V

According to this hierarchy a yer is deleted, unless this leads to a coda cluster. Furthermore, a coda cluster can only be split up by a yer, not by a vowel which is not underlying.

In this section I have shown that yers are moraless vowels. Embedded in the hierarchy of (8), taken essentially from Yearley (1995), this leads to the well known vowel/zero alternation. In the next section I propose an analysis of yer induced lengthening. I show that this phenomenon is problematic for the theory of CL developed in Hayes (1989), but that it can easily be explained in OT.

3. Yer induced length; the representational problem

In Slovak the final vowel of the stem is lengthened in the gen. plur. of feminine and neuter nouns. Examples are given in (9).[4]

(9) *nom. sg.*   *gen. plur.*
    fabrik+a 'factory'   fabrík
    čel+o   'forehead' čiel
    kol+o   'circle'   kôl

Rubach (1993) shows that the gen. plur. suffix consists of an underlying yer. Another affix which is similar to the gen. plur. is the diminutive:

(10) *base form*   *dim. nom. sg.*
     hlav+a   'head'   hláv+k+a
     sirot+a 'orphan'   sirôt+k+a
     čel+o   'forehead'   čiel+k+o

---

[4] Lengthened mid vowels are diphthongized to [ie], resp. [uo], orthographically ô. (cf. also footnote 2).

In the forms on the right, the root is followed by the diminutive -*k*, which according to Rubach contains a yer. Rubach gives many more examples of suffixes that are similar to the diminutive and the gen. plur. in the sense that they trigger lengthening and also contain a yer. Obviously this is not a coincidence. It is for this reason that Rubach postulates a rule which lengthens a vowel if it is followed by a yer. Length alternations of the type illustrated in (9) and (10) have all the characteristics of CL: the loss of the underlying vowel (i.e. the yer) is compensated for by the length of the adjacent vowel. Although this informal description of yer induced lengthening clearly suggests that this phenomenon is an instance of CL it seems problematic to formally implement this idea. This will be shown in the next section.

3.1. Why Yer Induced Length Cannot Be CL

The problem is that, according to Hayes (1989), only the loss of *moraic* segments is compensated for. The derivations in (11), taken from Hayes' article, illustrate this hypothesis.[5]

(11) *In Early Latin s is deleted before an anterior sonorant; its deletion is*

compensated for		not compensated for
μ μ μ μ | | | | k a s . n u s	initial structure	μ μ μ | | | s n u . r u s
μ μ μ μ | | | k a . n u s	s-deletion	μ μ μ | | | n u . r u s
μ μ μ μ \ / | | k a . n u s 'gray'	CL	—— 'daughter-in-law'

In the initial representation on the left the *s* is linked to a mora, because in Latin closed syllables are heavy. This means that after the elimination of *s* a mora is left behind, which is then filled by the vowel. In the initial representation on the right, on the other hand, no mora is left behind,

---

[5] The dot represents syllable boundaries.

because a segment in onset position is not moraic. Consequently, deletion cannot have a lengthening effect in this environment. Asymmetries of this type lead Hayes to the hypothesis that only moraic segments can trigger CL.

According to this theory yer induced lenghtening cannot be interpreted as CL, because the vowel which is deleted is a yer, and a yer does not have a mora, as we have seen in the preceding section. The problem is further illustrated by the following derivation.

(12) *The representational problem*

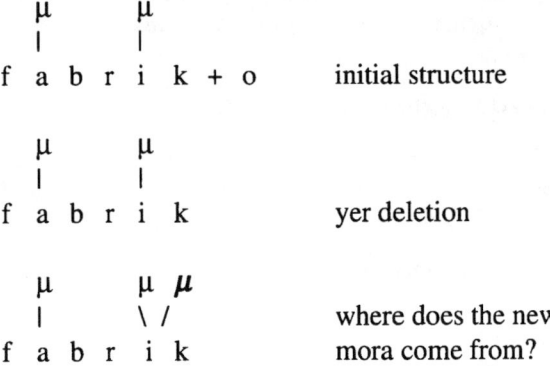

It is clear, then, that the commonly held view of yers as moraless vowels, combined with Hayes' theory of CL, blocks an analysis of yer induced lengthening in terms of CL. A priori two conclusions can be drawn from such a states of affairs. One conclusion would say that yer triggered lengthening in Slovak is not an instance of CL, simply because the theory does not allow it. The alternative conclusion would say that the process is an instance of CL, and that the theory of CL is not correct. Interestingly, the second option is impossible if we assume that phonology is *derivational* in nature. In a derivational theory a deleted segment can still have an effect on adjacent segments *only if it leaves a trace*. This can only happen if it is linked to a mora, because then the mora serves as the trace. However, if we assume that phonology is *non-derivational*, as we do in OT, then the second option described above becomes a real possibility. We might then indeed say that the classical theory of CL is not correct, because it cannot account for yer induced length. It is this strategy which I will follow in the next section.

3.2. Yer Induced Lengthening as CL

Let us first consider the gen. plur. Following Rubach I assume that this morpheme consists of a (back) yer. Underlyingly, then, a form like *fabrík* (cf. (9)) has the following representation:

(13) μ   μ
      | |
    f a b r i k + o

The hierarchy in (8) cannot account for the loss of yer and the accompanying length on the preceding vowel, as is shown in (14).

(14) fabrikO	DEP-V	NOCOMCOD	DEP-μ	MAX-V
1 fabriko			*!	
2 ☞ fabrik				*
3 ☞ fabri:k			*!	

Since the candidates 1 and 3 contain an extra mora compared to the input, they violate DEP-μ. The second candidate just violates MAX-V. Since the elimination of the yer does not lead to a consonant cluster in coda position, the second candidate should be the winner, as is indicated by the reversed pointing finger. It is clear, then, that the hierarchy in (8) must be modified in order to account for the fact that the loss of a yer lengthens the preceding vowel.

As a first step I propose that the constraint DEP-μ in the hierarchy in (8) be supplemented by the constraint HEAD-DEP-μ. This new constraint penalizes the insertion of a new mora, if and only if the insertion site is the *head position* of the syllable. The constraint DEP-μ is moved to the right of MAX-V. We thus get the following system:

(15) *The phonology of vowel/zero alternation; second version*
    DEP-V » NOCOMCOD » HEAD-DEP-μ » MAX-V » DEP-μ

If we now evaluate the candidates in (14) according to the new standards we get the right results.

(16) fabrikO	DEP-V	NOCOM COD	HEAD-DEP-μ	MAX-V	DEP-μ
1 fabriko			*!		*
2 fabrik				*!	
3 ☞ fabri:k					*

The first candidate violates both DEP-μ and HEAD-DEP-μ, because a mora is inserted, and it is inserted in the head position of the (third) syllable. The latter violation is fatal. The second candidate violates MAX-V, because the yer is deleted. Again, this is fatal, because in the new hierarchy MAX-V dominates DEP-μ. The third candidate is optimal, because it only violates DEP-μ. Crucially, it does not violate HEAD-DEP-μ, because the new mora is a non-head mora; it is the dependent half of a long vowel. Neither does it violate MAX-V, because the root node of the yer is not deleted; it corresponds to the root node which is linked to the non-head mora.

Before we can accept this analysis several points must be made explicit. The first one concerns the representation of long vowels. Notice that the lengthened vowel must have two root nodes each linked to a separate mora, as in (17A), rather than one root node linked to two moras, as in (17B). The indices represent the correspondence relations holding between the root nodes of vowels.

(17) input   output A   output B   output C
     (=16.3)

       μ   μ   μ   μ μ   μ   μ μ   μ   μ
       | | | | | | \ / | |
      •₃   •₂ •₁   •₃ •₂ •₁   •₃   •₂   •₃   •₂
       | | | | \ / | | | |
     f a b r i k o   f a b r i k   f a b r i k   f a b r i k

The representation in (17B) violates MAX-V, because the root node of the gen. plur. yer is deleted. Formulated more precisely, it has no correspondent in the output. In addition to this, it also violates DEP-μ, because the output has more moras than the input. If we claim that long vowels have a (multiply linked) single root node, then we cannot explain the lengthening effect triggered by yers. The reason is that, under this view, the configuration in (17B) is always less harmonic than (17C) (=

16.2)), because the former violates MAX-V and DEP-μ, whereas the latter only violates MAX-V. Hence, in this theory of vowel length (17B) can never be optimal. On the other hand, if we assume that, at least in Slovak, long vowels have two root nodes, then we do understand why a lengthened vowel is more harmonic than a deleted vowel. The reason is that, under this view, (17A) (= (16.3)) is more harmonic than (17C) (= (16.2)), because the former violates DEP-μ, whereas the latter violates MAX-V, and in the revised hierarchy of (15) MAX-V is ranked higher than DEP-μ. This shows that we have to stick to the two root-node theory of vowel length, at least with respect to Slovak.

The second point concerns the loss of the place features of the underlying yer. The representation (17A), which in our view is the output of compensatory lengthening, shows that more is going on in the transition from input to output. Notice in particular that all place features of the yer are removed. This shows that IDENTITY[PLACE] (IDENT[PL]), the constraint which penalizes any difference between two corresponding segments at the level of the place features, must be ranked below MAX-V. This is demonstrated in the following tableau.

(18) MAX-V » IDENT[PL]

fabrikO	MAX-V	IDENT[PL]	DEP-μ
fabrik	*!		
☞ fabri:k		*	*

The first candidate in (18) (= (17C)) violates MAX-V, because the yer does not correspond to a segment in the output. In the second candidate in (18) (= (17A)) the root node of the yer corresponds to the root node in the dependent position of the long vowel. Hence, it does not violate MAX-V. However, it does violate IDENT[PL], because the place features that are linked to the root node of the yer (cf. the input representation in (17)) have been replaced by the spreading features of the segment in head position (cf. (17A)). Given the fact that IDENT[PL] is lower in the hierarchy than MAX-V, the candidate which preserves the root node, but removes the original place features, is more harmonic than the candidate which removes the root node. This explains why the candidate with the lengthened vowel is the optimal candidate.

This brings us to the third point. Why are the place features of the underlying yer deleted? Obviously, the reason is that diphthongs are avoided in Slovak. The constraint penalizing diphthongs, NODIPHTHONG, must therefore dominate IDENT[PL]. This is shown in the following tableau:

(19) NODIPHTHONG » IDENT[PL]

fabrikO	NODIPHTHONG	IDENT[PL]
fabriok	*!	
☞ fabri:k		*

I will assume that the same constraint also rules out various other types of complex structure. For instance, it will rule out all candidates with some sort of *light* diphthong, i.e. a representation where a mora is linked to two root nodes, or to two separate sets of place features. Naturally, a full analysis has to make explicit all these possibilities. Within the limited space of this article, however, I cannot go into the details. I will therefore use NODIPHTHONG as a convenient abbreviation for all the constraints that rule out various types of complex structure.[6]

There is one final point which deserves explicit treatment. This is the fact that only an *affix* yer can have a lengthening effect; a yer located in the root never lengthens the preceding vowel. Relevant examples have already been given in (1). Two of them are repeated below:

(20) *no lengthening in the domain of a root*
    liter 'litre'   litr+a   (*lítra)
    bobor 'beaver'   bobr+a (*bôbra)

The roots in (20) must have a yer, because the consonant cluster is broken up. Given the hierarchy in (15) we expect that, if an inflectional

---

[6] The fact that NODIPHTHONG is active in Slovak does not mean, of course, that this language does not allow diphthongs. In fact, diphthongs come in two types: they can be underlying and they can be the result of lengthening. The lengthened mid vowels *e* and *o*, for instance, are realized respectively as [ie] and [uo], as we have seen before. These facts, however, do not contradict NODIPHTHONG. What they do show, however, is that this constraint must be properly ranked with respect to the relevant faithfulness constraints. Again, a full analysis has to take into consideration all these aspects of the phonology of Slovak length. In this article, however, it is impossible to do this, due to lack of space.

ending is added, the yer is retained in the form of a lengthened vowel. Yet, this does not happen, as the forms in the column on the right demonstrate.

Notice that in the analysis proposed here a yer which triggers length on the preceding vowel leaves its original position in the string; it hops over the consonant on its left. This becomes clear if we take a closer look at the underlying representation of a form like *fabrík* and compare it with its realization at the surface.

(21) input   output

$$\begin{array}{ccccccc} & \mu & & \mu & & & \\ & | & & | & & & \\ \bullet_7 & \bullet_6 & \bullet_5 & \bullet_4 & \bullet_3 & \bullet_2 & \bullet_1 \\ | & | & | & | & | & | & | \\ f & a & b & r & i & k & o \end{array} \qquad \begin{array}{cccccc} & \mu & & & \mu\ \mu & \\ & | & & & |\ \ | & \\ \bullet_7 & \bullet_6 & \bullet_5 & \bullet_4 & \bullet_3\ \bullet_1 & \bullet_2 \\ | & | & | & | & \backslash\ / & | \\ f & a & b & r & i & k \end{array}$$

If we compare the correspondence relations holding between the root nodes, vowels and consonants alike, we note that the yer moves over the consonant on its left. Changing the linear order of the string violates the constraint LIN(EARITY). We can now explain the absence of lengthening in the root if LIN(EARITY) is relativized to the domain within which it applies. Specifically, I propose that the constraint (*Root*)LIN is ranked above MAX-V, which in its turn is ranked above the general constraint LIN. The effect of (*Root*)LIN is that the linear order of two segments that are both located in the root morpheme is preserved, whereas the linear order of two segments, one of which is located in an affix, can be changed. This is an instance of the universal tendency that root morphemes are more faithful to their underlying representation than affixes (cf. in particular McCarthy and Prince 1995). Incorporating (*Root*)LIN into our system of constraints we get the following revised hierarchy:

(22) *Vowel/zero alternation and lengthening; third version*
DEP-V » NOCOMCOD » HEAD-DEP-µ , (*Root*)LIN » MAX-V » LIN, DEP- µ

The analysis proposed in this section shows that it is perfectly possible to analyze yer induced lengthening as CL, even though a yer does not have a mora. This is a consequence of the fact that the analysis is cast in the framework of OT. We have seen that a derivational theory cannot possibly analyze yer induced lengthening as CL, because in such a theory input-output mappings are carried out by a series of (ordered) rules. In such a theory, information which is lost at stage n is irrecoverable at stage n+1. OT is crucially non-derivational, because in this theory input and output are seen as parallel representations which are related to each other by a set of faithfulness constraints. Given the parallel nature of input and output representations, information which is present in the input is always recoverable in the output. A segment which is present in the input can therefore always be referred to in the output. Exactly this is the reason why, in OT, it is possible to analyze yer induced lengthening as CL, even though a yer is a moraless segment. We can thus conclude that we have solved the representational problem: even though yers are moraless segments, yer induced lengthening can be analyzed as CL, because in OT it is no longer expected that *only* moraic segments can trigger CL.[7] Let us now turn to the second reason why it is seems difficult to analyze yer triggered lengthening as CL.

4. Yer Induced Length: The Derivational Problem

In his book (1993:145) Rubach is sympathetic to the idea that yer induced lengthening in Slovak is an instance of CL. However, ultimately he rejects it, because in his opinion it cannot always account for the interaction between yer induced lengthening and another important phenomenon, known as the Rhythmic Law.

---

[7] This does not mean that in OT it is expected that *every* segment which is present in the underlying representation can trigger CL. That would be a very bad result, of course, because it would imply that it is impossible to set up a restrictive theory of CL in OT. Such a theory is necessary, however, as is evident from the fact that the loss of a segment in onset position never leads to length on a neighboring vowel (cf. the Latin case in (11)). In fact, in OT it is also possible to explain why segments in onset position do not trigger length if they are deleted. It can be explained in terms of the theory of prosodic faithfulness, recently proposed in McCarthy (1997). Due to lack of space I cannot fully develop this suggestion. I want to point out, however, that it is not important for the main line of this article. Our main point is that in OT we are not forced to maintain the hypothesis that only moraic segments can trigger CL. Moraless segments can also have this effect, at least in principle.

In Slovak yer triggered lengthening is blocked if the vowel to be lengthened is preceded by a long vowel. This is a consequence of the Rhythmic Law.

(23) RHYTHMIC LAW
Two adjacent long vowels are not allowed

The blocking effect of the Rhythmic Law is illustrated by the following examples:

(24) *nom. sg.*   *gen. plur.*
  vedr+o 'bucket'   vedier
  krídl+o 'wing'   krídel

According to Rubach both root morphemes contain an underlying yer. In the gen. plur. the root yer is followed by the yer of the affix. In the first example the final vowel of the gen. plur. is long, a consequence of the lengthening effect of the suffix yer. In the second example, however, the suffix yer does not lengthen the final vowel. This is due to the RHYTHMIC LAW.

Notice that in our analysis the long vowel in *vedier* is not much of a problem. The yer of the root is realized in head position in order to avoid a complex coda. The yer of the gen. plur. is realized in the dependent position, making the final vowel long. The second form *krídel* is not very problematic either, but only if the RHYTHMIC LAW is ranked above MAX-V. This is shown in the following tableau:

(25) RHYTHMIC LAW » MAX-V

krídElO	RL	MAX-V
krídiel	*!	
☞ krídel		*

According to Rubach there is one particular environment where the analysis of yer triggered lengthening in terms of CL runs into severe problems. This happens when a long vowel is followed by three consecutive yers. A relevant example is the form *krídel+iec*, the gen. plur. of the diminutive of *krídl+o*. Underlyingly this form has the structure /krídEl+Ec+O/. Rubach shows that a CL analysis cannot derive the correct form. I do not wish to go into the details of Rubach's derivations here. For our purposes it is sufficient to note that Rubach's argument is based on the fact that yer triggered lengthening is *cyclic* (which is why I refer to it as the derivational problem).

It is indeed true that a form like *krídel+iec* is very problematic for the analysis as it has been developed so far. In fact, it turns out that not only the environment mentioned by Rubach (three consecutive yers following a long vowel) is problematic, all sequences of three consecutive yers are problematic. Let us go through the relevant cases. Consider first *krídel+iec* (the gen. plur. of *krídel+c+e*).

(26) krídElEcO	NoCom Cod	Head-Dep-μ	RL	Max-V	Dep-μ
krídielec		**!	*		***
☞ krídeliec		**!			***
☜ krídlec		*		**	*
krídelec		**!		*	**
krídliec		*	*!	*	**

The tableau in (26) shows that our analysis cannot derive the correct output. It predicts that ill formed **krídl+ec* is optimal, because Head-Dep-μ and RL block the realization of two yers.

An example showing that our analysis suffers form the more general problem that it cannot handle *any sequence* of three yers is *vedier+ec*, the gen. plur. of *vedier+c+e*, the diminutive of *vedr+o* (cf. (24)). This is illustrated in the following tableau:

(27) vedErEcO	NoCom Cod	Head-Dep-μ	RL	Max-V	Dep-μ
viederec		**!			***
vederiec		**!			***
☞ vedierec		**!			***
☜ vedriec		*		*	**
viedriec		*	*!		***

Here the analysis developed so far predicts that **vedr+iec* is optimal, which is entirely incorrect. It is evident, then, that something is missing in the system we have developed so far.

What our system misses is Rubach's important observation that yer induced lengthening is *cyclic*. In OT cyclic effects can be derived from correspondence relations holding between output forms. Let us see whether this constraint family can save our analysis. Consider the following forms:

(28)   *nom. sg.*   *gen. plur.*   *wrong outputs*
      krídel+c+e   krídel+iec   *krídl+ec
      vedier+c+e   vedier+ec   *vedr+iec

Comparing the gen. plur. forms with the nom. sg. we note that in the middle column the morphological base of the diminutive is identical to the one in the nom. (*krídel*, respectively *vedier*). The base of the forms on the right, however, differs from the one in the nom. It is clear, then, that the nom. sg. determines the structure of the gen. plur. This is one reason why, according to Rubach, yer triggered lengthening is cyclic. In OT this is expressed by postulating a correspondence relation between the nom. sg. and the gen. plur. (Benua 1997). Due to lack of space I have to formulate the family of Output-Output constraints as a monolithic block, leaving aside the question as to which member of this family is needed to derive the cyclicity effects attested here.

(29)   OO-FAITHFULNESS
      The structure of the morphologically basic form is preserved in the morphologically related form

The basic form (the nom. sg.) is not problematic for the system developed so far. To see this consider the example *vedier+c+e*.

(30) vedErEce	NOCOM COD	HEAD-DEP-μ	MAX-V	DEP-μ
☞ vedierce		*		**
vederece		**!		**
vederce		*	*!	*

In the optimal candidate *vedier+c+e* both yers are realized, one in the head position, in order to avoid a complex coda cluster, and the second in the dependent position of the syllable created by the first yer.[8] To account for the fact that this candidate determines the structure of the gen. plur. OO-Faith must be ranked higher than HEAD-DEP-μ.

(31) OO-Faith » HEAD-DEP-μ

Base vedierce Input vedErEcO	OO-Faith	HEAD-DEP-μ	MAX-V	DEP-μ
☞ vedierec		**		***
vedriec	*!	*	*	**

The tableau shows that *vedier+ec* is optimal, because it is more faithful to the morphologically basic form, the nom. sg. Concretely, the analysis runs as follows: since the basic form contains the string *vedier*, the affixed form must contain the same string, even at the cost of an extra violation of HEAD-DEP-μ.

The same solution also explains why *krídel+iec* is more harmonic then **krídl+ec*.

(32)

Base krídelce Input krídElEcO	OO-Faith	HEAD-DEP-μ	MAX-V	DEP-μ
☞ krídeliec		**		***
krídelec		**	*!	**
krídlec	*!	*	**	*

Since the base contains the string *krídel*, the gen. plur. should also have this string. Furthermore, since the base ends in a short vowel the medial yer of the gen. plur. is realized in the final syllable, thereby lengthening the *last* vowel.

In this section I have shown that Rubach is entirely right, in the sense that yer triggered lengthening must be cyclic. We have also shown, however, that this does not necessarily mean that this phenomenon

---

[8] One might wonder why *vedier+c+e* is more harmonic than the candidate *vedr+iec+e*, which is neglected in the main text. In this candidate it is also the case that both yers are realized: one in head position, and the other in the dependent position. Consequently, both candidates seem to fare equally well under the constraints considered in (30). It is clear, however, that the candidate *vedr+iec+e* is less harmonic than *vedier+c+e* for reasons having to do with syllable structure. *vedr+iec+e* contains a complex onset, whereas *vedier+c+e* does not have a complex syllable node.

cannot be interpreted as CL. Indeed it is perfectly possible to analyze the lengthening process as an instance of CL, on the precondition that cyclicity is incorporated in OT in the form of OO-Faithfulness.

5. Summary

I have discussed two arguments against the view that yer triggered lengthening in Slovak is a case of CL. The representational argument is solved if CL is analyzed in OT. The derivational problem can be solved in terms of the correspondence relations holding between morphologically related forms. We may thus conclude that Slovak lengthening is an instance of CL.

References

Beckman, J.N., L. Walsh Dickey and S. Urbanczyk. 1995. *University of Massachusetts Occasional Papers in Linguistics 18: Papers on Optimality Theory*. University of Massachusetts, Amherst: GLSA.
Benua, Laura. 1997. Transderivational Identity: Phonological Relations between Words. Doctoral dissertation, University of Massachusetts, Amherst.
Hayes, Bruce. 1989. Compensatory Lengthening in Moraic Phonology. *Linguistic Inquiry* 20: 253-306.
Kenstowicz, Michael and Jerzy Rubach. 1987. The Phonology of Syllabic Nuclei in Slovak. *Language* 63: 463-97.
McCarthy, John. 1997. Faithfulness and Prosodic Circumscription. To appear in *The Pointing Finger; Conceptual Studies in Optimality Theory*, eds. J. Dekkers, F. van der Leeuw and J. van de Weijer. Amsterdam, HIL.
McCarthy, John and Alan Prince. 1995. Faithfulness and Reduplicative Identity. In J.N. Beckman et al., eds., 249-384.
Prince, Alan and Paul Smolensky. 1993. *Optimality Theory: Constraint Interaction in Generative Grammar*. Ms. Rutgers University, New Brunswick, and University of Colorado, Boulder. [To appear, Cambridge, Mass.: MIT Press.]
Rubach, Jerzy. 1993. *The Lexical Phonology of Slovak*. New York: Oxford University Press.

Szpyra, Jolanta. 1992. Ghost Segments in Nonlinear Phonology: Polish Yers. *Language* 68: 277-312.
Yearley, Jennifer. 1995. Jer Vowels in Russian. In J.N. Beckman et al., eds., 77-136.

Tilburg University
Grammatical Models Group
P.O. Box 90153
NL-5000 LE-TILBURG
The Netherlands
b.j.h.hermans@kub.nl

Centering and Scrambling: Towards a Discourse-Status Motivation of Russian Word Order

Sophia Malamud
University of Pennsylvania

1. Introduction

A definition of scrambling already poses a problem in a study that shuns commitment to a syntactic framework. One clear definition I have found for the term "scrambling" is strongly framework-specific: "A process that re-orders maximal projections internally within clauses moving them further to the front of the clauses" (Radford 1997). I shall use the term to denote, vaguely, a process by which two grammatical clauses differing only in the order of their constituents may be formed in a language.

A number of works investigating the phenomenon have appeared in the past decade, mostly in the generative tradition (Mahajan 1990, King 1993, Bošković and Takahashi 1995, Miyagawa 1997, and many others). The main problem that has been noted for these analyses was the apparent lack of motivation for this type of movement. In fact, for most cases of scrambling, no purely syntactic or semantic motivation could be found (Kondrashova 1997, Bošković and Takahashi 1995, King 1993, inter alia). Thus, we turn to pragmatics (focus structure, other aspects of information packaging, discourse salience) for motivations of scrambling (e.g. King 1993, Kondrashova 1997, partially Bailyn 2000).

This paper considers a possible pragmatic motivation for ordering of noun phrases in Russian narrative. In particular, it argues that noun phrases may scramble so as to allow for a smoother transition between clauses within a discourse segment. Centering Theory (Brennan, Friedman, and Pollard 1987, Walker, Iida and Cote 1994) allows us to formalise the notions of "smoothness" and "transition," based on the salience of discourse entities.

The hypothesis set forth in this paper is that Russian scrambling directly affects the smoothness of inter-sentential transitions, and that its motivation is to effect a smoother transition than would otherwise be produced.

To test this hypothesis, I performed a Centering analysis of narrative discourse segments in a tale by Nikolaj Nosov *Neznajka and his friends*, a translation of an essay "On Fairy Tales" by J.R.R.Tolkien, a novel by Mikhail Bulgakov *Master and Margarita*, a biography of Swift by Mikhail Levidov, a short story by Chekhov, and a documentary-style *Gulag Archipelago* by Aleksander Solzhenitsyn. The works were selected to represent a variety of narrative styles, and to contain a sizeable number of narrative segments. Simple past-tense narrative was chosen as the discourse type that is least affected by considerations of poetic style - that is, the breaking of the pragmatic norms to achieve an artistic effect.

The results of this study show that discourse salience is indeed affected by word order in Russian and in turn, affects the smoothness of inter-sentential transitions. Therefore, producing a more coherent discourse arises as a motivation for scrambling.

This paper is organised as follows: in sections 2 and 3 I present the background information on Russian word order and the Centering theory, respectively. Theoretical discussion specific to this study follows in section 4. Section 5 consists of the description of data and analysis in this study, with discussion and conclusions in section 6. Finally, references and an example analysis of a data sample follow as sections 7 and 8.

2. Background: Russian word order

Russian is a "free" word order language. This means that the word order in Russian does not encode "who did what to whom." Instead, the word order and suprasegmental phonology are used to encode different pragmatic and grammatical factors in an utterance.

In a Russian simple transitive "John killed Mary" theoretically all six permutations of the words yield grammatical sentences. However, a random association of a permutation with a discourse context typically yields infelicity. Intonation contours also constrain the use of different word orders.

In her monumental 1986 study of Russian word order, Olga Yokoyama argues that the mechanisms of encoding the pragmatic and grammatical information in an utterance depend most heavily on the "speaker's subjective evaluation of the discourse situation" (Yokoyama 1986, p.331). That is, the word order and suprasegmental phonology that are used in Russian to encode this information depend on the speaker's assessment of the "knowledge" and "current concern" sets for those involved in the discourse.

Yokoyama's study[1] was concerned with spoken discourse, and her most definite conclusions dealt with Type I ("neutral") intonation contour for the utterances. Her work has partially formalised the Prague school's "theme-rheme condition" (Lenerz 1977, p.63), which suggests that "an NP may scramble over less rhematic NP" (non-literal translation in Rambow 1993).

The multiplicity of factors affecting Russian word order have been explored in a very principled way by Yokoyama. It seems, nevertheless, to be an exceptionally difficult task to formalise the process of "subjective evaluation of the discourse situation." The need for such formal description has been the motivation for this study. Centering Theory is a formal framework that allows to capture the above notions.

3. Background: the Centering theory

3.1 The Centering Transitions

The Centering Theory was proposed in Grosz, Joshi, and Weinstein 1983 as a model that accounted for the use of different types of referring expressions. The ideas were subsequently developed and expanded both by the original authors, and by others (Brennan, Friedman, and Pollard

---

[1] The items in the knowledge set of shared common concern seem to approximately correspond to the "theme"; the items more recently promoted to this set (or not promoted yet) are the more rhematic ones.

Yokoyama suggests two ordering rules for Russian utterances. The ordering of the discourse-initial statements with Type 1 intonation is

$Ca \wedge Cb$ Verb $Ca \wedge (B-Cb)$ $A \wedge (Ca-B)$,

where A and B are the knowledge sets of the speaker and the addressee, respectively, and Ca and Cb are the corresponding subsets of their current concern (p. 234).

For the non-discourse-initial utterances, "the primary dichotomy in word order is determined by the preceding utterance" (p. 326). Knowledge items found in $Ca \wedge Cb$ after preceding utterance must be placed in the beginning in utterances with Type I intonation; the rest of the knowledge, which is found in $A \wedge (Ca-B)$ must appear at the end of the utterance. Within these sections the discourse-initial rule applies (Yokoyama1986).

1987; Walker, Iida, and Cote 1994; Walker, Joshi, and Prince 1998, inter alia).

This theory allows us to compute the smoothness of transition between utterances based on the salience ranking of entities in a discourse.

Definition 1: In each utterance, the set of discourse entities evoked in it is the set of forward-looking centres (**Cf**).

Centres are semantic entities that are part of the discourse model (see Heim 1983), or items in the set of shared current concern (Yokoyama 1986).

Definition 2: There is a special member of this set called the backward-looking centre (**Cb**). This is the entity that is most central in the utterance (Walker and Prince 1994), the file card you're writing on (Heim 1983), approximately corresponding to "the utterance theme" (Reinhart 1981, Horn 1986). The Cb links the current utterance with the previous discourse.

The set of forward-looking centres is ranked according to discourse salience, or "activatedness". The factors that determine ranking are the crux of the theory. If any centres are evoked in the next utterance, the highest-ranked of them is the Cb of that utterance.

Definition 3: The highest-ranked centre is the preferred centre (Cp). It predicts what the next utterance is going to be about.

The interaction between Cb and Cp determines smoothness of transition from one utterance to the next as shown in the table 1 below. When the most central entity in an utterance ($Cb(U_n)$) is the same as the most central entity in the previous one ($Cb(U_{n-1})$), and the same item is also predicted to be central in the next utterance ($Cp(U_n)$), the resulting discourse is very coherent, and the transition is Continue. On the other hand, when the Cb from a previous utterance is retained as such, but not predicted to be as salient in the next utterance, the transition type is Retain. The two Shifts result when the most central entity changes: the Smooth-Shifts predicts that it should not change again in the next utterance, while the Rough-Shift does (Table 1).

Table 1. *Transitions from* Un-1 *to* Un.

	Cb(Un) = Cb(Un-1)	Cb(Un) ≠ Cb(Un-1)
Cb (Un) = Cp (Un)	**Continue**	**Smooth-shift**
Cb(Un) ≠ Cp(Un)	**Retain**	**Rough-shift**

Un – *nth utterance,* Cb(Un) – *the backward-looking centre of the nth utterance,* Cp(Un) – *the preferred centre of the nth utterance.*

The transitions, smoothest to roughest are, thus: Continue, Retain, Smooth-shift, and Rough-shift (Walker & Prince 1994). Centering analyses have shown that smoother transitions are preferred over rougher ones within a discourse segment (Di Eugenio 1990, Rambow 1993, inter alia).

3.2 The Ranking

The ranking of entities determines the Cp of the current utterance, and the Cb of the next one. The ranking principle arrived at by most Centering analyses (e.g. Di Eugenio 1998, Miltsakaki 1999), is based on the grammatical function of the entities, which are ranked as follows: EMPATHY > SUBJECT > OBJECT > OTHER. Here, "empathy" denotes either phrases grammatically marked as "empathic" (e.g., in Japanese), or otherwise clearly emphasising the experiencer (e.g., in the dative subject constructions (Yokoyama 1986)).

Studies of Italian (Di Eugenio 1998), Turkish (Hoffman 1998), and Greek (Miltsakaki 1999) have shown that this ranking indeed correctly predicts full noun phrase, pronoun, or zero-pronoun usage, and is independent of the utterance word order in these languages.

However, a study of German (Rambow 1993) showed that whereas topicalisation interacts with Centering in an ambivalent way, scrambling directly affects the ranking: "the Cf (ordered set of forward-looking centres) of an utterance is the list of constituents of the Mittelfeld in that order."

3.3 An Example.

Here is a constructed English example of a discourse containing all four transition types. The entities are ranked by grammatical function; no internal segmentation is assumed. The members of the Cf are listed from highest-to-lowest ranked.

> John is a small boy.
> Cf = {John}
> Cp = John
> Cb = none
> Transition = none
> He is now preparing to go to school.
> Cf = {John, school}
> Cp = John
> Cb = John
> Transition = none
> He puts a pencil-box and a notebook in his backpack, and sets out.
> Cf = {John, pencil-box, notebook, backpack}
> Cp = John
> Cb = John
> Transition = Continue
> A girl Mary meets him on his way to school.
> Cf = {Mary, John, school}
> Cp = Mary
> Cb = John
> Transition = Retain
> Mary likes to talk to John.
> Cf = {Mary, John}
> Cp = Mary
> Cb = Mary
> Transition = Smooth-Shift
> Mathematics is often the topic of John's conversations.
> Cf = {Mathematics, John, conversations}
> Cp = Mathematics
> Cb = John
> Transition = Rough-Shift

4. The Centering Study of Russian Scrambling.

The hypothesis of this study concerns precisely the ranking of discourse entities. When the order of noun phrases differs from the basic one (subject, object, other), I hypothesised that the ranking would go by word-order: left to right. Thus, a reordering of noun phrases may be prompted by the transition preference of the speaker or writer.

4.1 The Segment and the Utterance

Centering is a model of the local discourse structure: it operates within "discourse segments." Hence, it is important to know how to determine the segmentation of a discourse. However, determination of segment boundaries is a separate question of much current investigation. I therefore assume no a priori segmentation in a written discourse.

Within each segment, the Centering Theory calculates the Cf list for every "utterance" – another notion in need of formal definition. Early Centering analyses seem to assume the utterance to be approximately the tensed clause (Kameyama 1998). In a later investigation (Miltsakaki 1999), this was revised, and "utterance" was defined as a full sentence, i.e., "the main clause and its accompanying subordinate and adjunct clauses" (Miltsakaki and Kukich 2000). I follow here the revised definition.

As a further strategy for defining the structure of a discourse, Webber (1991) proposes an algorithm for incremental clause-by-clause construction of a discourse tree, where relations between clauses-nodes are based on their intuitive discourse purpose. A pilot study on an English text has shown that Centering seems to apply between the sister nodes and down each branch, but not upward across levels of the resulting discourse tree. That is, the algorithm does not calculate the correct transition between the last utterance of the embedded segment and the first utterance of the next higher-level segment.

When Webber's strategy is applied to complex sentences containing several subordinate clauses, it becomes clear that Centering can apply between the coordinated subordinate clauses. Miltsakaki 1999 argues that the ordering of subordinate and main clauses does not affect Centering. Thus, unless there were two or more coordinated subordinate clauses, everything but the main clause was ignored in the utterance.

4.2 Further Ranking Assumptions

There has been much variation as to the correct ranking of entities within a complex noun phrase (e.g., possessive). I am following, rather arbitrarily, the convention of Di Eugenio (1998), where the animate possessor is ranked higher than the possessee; for inanimate possessors, the animate possessee is ranked higher, and the inanimate possessee lower. Other variations include left-to-right ranking of entities and shall be tried in my further work.

Otherwise, I have performed data analysis using two different rankings: first, by grammatical function within the main clause and, subsequently, by word order within the main clause.

5. Data and Results

5.1 Control Data

The main source of data in this study was the online library of Russian literature (www.lib.ru). To provide a measure of the true proportions of different transitions in Russian texts, a full short story "Pyat' minut vzajmy" was chosen and analysed. A total of about 70 transitions was calculated. Since of the 78 sentences containing 24 transitive clauses with overt arguments only 4 were scrambled, the ranking was performed by grammatical function only. Discounting the Rough-Shifts in the opening and closing paragraphs of the story as "necessities of artistic considerations," the analysis has shown that Rough-Shifts constituted 10% of all the transitions, with the remaining comprising 34 Continues, 16 Retains, and 13 Smooth-Shifts.

5.2 The Rough-Shift Measure

In order to check the validity of the left-to-right ranking hypothesis, I have chosen a number of literary narrative segments containing scrambled sentences. Computerised search was used to select the scrambled sentences from electronic books and to find the segments containing these sentences. A total of 44 analysable segments of two or more sentences were found, each containing at least one scrambled sentence.

The Centering analysis of this data was done manually twice (see the Appendix). The first analysis utilised ranking by grammatical function and produced 50 Continues, 46 Retains, 16 Smooth-Shifts, and 17 Rough-Shifts out of 129 total transitions. Then, using the left-to-right ranking hypothesis, the second analysis was performed, producing 49

Continues, 46 Retains, 21 Smooth-Shifts, and 13 Rough-Shifts (see Table 2).

Table 2. The transitions in the data.

	# in 1st analysis	% in 1st analysis	# in 2nd analysis	% in 2nd analysis	% in control data set
Continue	50	38%	49	38%	49%
Retain	46	36%	46	36%	23%
S-Shift	16	12%	21	16%	19%
R-Shift	17	13%	13	10%	10%

In their 2000 Centering study, Miltsakaki and Kukich argue that "in general, Continues, Retains, and Smooth-Shifts do not yield incoherent discourses" (Miltsakaki and Kukich 2000). Therefore, only the presence of a Rough-Shift signals a significant incoherence. The number of Rough-Shifts and the presence of Rough-Shifts in a perceptually coherent discourse were therefore the first factors considered in this study.

Statistical tests were then run on these numbers, with the transition percentages from the short story analysis serving as controls, i.e., the *norm*. The z-test was used to measure the probability that observed differences in a *single variable* (the number of Rough-Shifts) are the result of chance variation. The test has shown that the number of Rough-Shifts produced by the first analysis has a 23% chance of being *normal*, compared with about a 98% chance for the second analysis. The difference of four in the number of Rough-Shifts produced by the two analyses is significant with more than 75% percent probability. In order to achieve higher degrees of certainty, a larger data sample needs to be accumulated. Meanwhile, a qualitative evaluation of data was performed.

A closer examination of the transitions has indicated that of the 17 Rough-Shifts produced by the first analysis, 6 were Smooth-Shifts in the second. One of these could have been a Continue changing to Retain in the second analysis, depending on the judgement of the main clause boundaries. The remaining 11 were Rough-Shifts in the second analysis as well.

At the same time, out of the 13 Rough-Shifts produced by the second analysis, 2 were found to be Smooth-Shifts in the first. Neither of these, however, was a clear case. One transition could have been actually a Smooth-Shift in the second analysis if a "mop... kicking and striving for the window" could be considered animate. The other transition could have been a Continue in the second and Retain in the first analysis if Webber's segmentation/segment level strategy were assumed. Overall, therefore, it seems that the word-order dependent ranking provides a more accurate measure of coherence for the data. Since ranking the subject higher shows more discourse segments to be incoherent, it is patent that an unscrambled sentence may produce an incoherence where a scrambled one would not.

5.3 Incorporating the Verb: Refining the Hypothesis

The two analyses have produced approximately the same number of Continue and Retain transitions. Moreover, both analyses have "improved" and "worsened" about the same number of these transitions. This suggests that the original hypothesis does not sufficiently account for the more coherent data. A motivation for reordering that results in the above transitions has to be found.

In the original hypothesis of this investigation, no consideration has been given to the verb. However, it has been noted for many languages, including Russian, that the pre-verbal and post-verbal positions in an utterance have very different informational functions (Yokoyama 1986, Rambow 1993, Kiss 2000, inter alia). Therefore, the position of the verb was traced in the 34 scrambled transitive sentences with overt arguments, for which the two analyses give different transitions. For 15 of them the word-order dependent ranking (second analysis) produced a smoother transition, whereas for the remaining 19, the other analysis did.

Crucially, 12 of the former sentences had OVS order, whereas 16 of the latter had the order OSV (see table 3). It becomes obvious, thus, that simply scrambling the object to the sentence-initial position in Russian doesn't affect its discourse salience, but serves some other purpose. When, however, the subject is simultaneously demoted to the post-verbal position, the salience of both entities is affected.

Of the remaining 3 sentences "confirming" the left-to-right ranking hypothesis, two were the only VOS utterances in the data, and one more depended on the possessor-possessee ranking. At the same time, of the remaining 3 sentences contradicting the initial hypothesis, all were OVS.

However, two of them were a part of the 6-utterance parallel construction segment, and one more a part of a segment in which calculation of segment boundaries and, therefore, of the Cbs was very difficult.

Table 3. Ranking preference in scrambled transitive sentences.
Number of utterances with a certain word order and ranking preference is marked at the intersection of the corresponding column and row.

Preferred ranking ?	Word Order		
	OVS	OSV	VOS
Word-order Dependent	12	1	2
By grammatical function only	3	16	0

Thus, the new hypothesis is formulated as follows: *the entities in Cf are ranked left-to-right in scrambled sentences, except when scrambling is limited to bringing the object to sentence-initial position.* This revised hypothesis was used for the final analysis of the data. The analysis produced only 11 Rough-Shifts, 20 Smooth-Shifts, 35 Retains, and 63 Continues. These are the smoothest resulting transitions yet. The chi-squared test was used to measure the probability that the observed differences in *all the variables* (the number of occurrences of each transition type) are the result of chance variation. In this test, the significance of the Rough-Shift measure is somewhat downplayed, since each variable is given the same significance in the calculation of the chi-squared value. Again, the percentages from the short story analysis were used as controls. As is evident from table 4, the new hypothesis provides a significantly more normal analysis of the scrambling data (60% probability that the scrambled data is the same as the control, all variation due to chance).

Table 4. The chi-squared test.

Ranking hypothesis	Chi-squared value	Probability
By word order	12.69	Less than 1%
By gram. Function	16	About 0%
The new hypothesis	2.07	60%

Thus, indeed the type of scrambling that "topicalises" the object while leaving subject-verb order intact does not affect the salience ranking of entities. In this, it patterns like the German topicalisation to the *Vorfeld* (Rambow 1993) with respect to Centering. At the same time, all the other types of scrambling in Russian behave exactly like the German scrambling of constituents in the *Mittelfeld*.

6. Discussion and Conclusions.

The above result suggests that Centering and word-order are interdependent phenomena. Thus, if one follows the main claim of the Centering Theory that inter-utterance transitions are ordered by preference (Continue>Retain>Smooth-shift>Rough-shift), where a Rough-Shift signals a breach in coherence, then a motivation for scrambling arises.

A study of spoken narrative must be done to test the applicability of the above results. The data collection for such a study is under way now. In addition, a formal model of Russian word order and information structure incorporating the above insights is needed. An attempt at such a model, based on a Set-Combinatory Categorial Grammar proposed for Russian by Nygren 1999, is currently in progress.

On the other hand, the actual smoothness of transitions and complexity of scrambling will be reflected in language processing. Thus, a self-paced reading experiment could show the effects of rougher transitions, and if so, the effect of scrambling on Centering.

References

Bailyn, J. F. (2000). Does Russian Scrambling Exist? Ms. SUNY at Stony Brook, *International Conference on Word Order and Scrambling*, Tucson, AZ.

Bošković, Ž., Takahashi, D. (1995). *Scrambling and Last Resort*. Ms., University of Connecticut and Graduate Study Centre, CUNY.

Brennan, S., Friedman, M., Pollard, C. (1987). A Centering approach to pronouns. *Proc. 25th Annual Meeting of the ACL*, Stanford, CA.

Chomsky, N. (1995). *The Minimalist Program*. Cambridge, MA: MIT Press.

Grosz, B., Joshi, A., Weinstein, S. (1995). Centering: a framework for modelling local coherence of discourse. http://www.cis.upenn.edu/~ircs.

Di Eugenio, B. (1998). Centering in Italian. In Walker, M., Joshi, A., Prince, E. (eds.). *Centering Theory in Discourse.* Oxford: Oxford University Press.

Freedman, D., Pisani, R., Purves, R. (1998). *Statistics.* 3rd ed. New York: W.W. Norton & Company.

Heim, I. (1983). File change semantics and the familiarity theory of definiteness. Bauerle, R., Schwarze, C., von Stechow, A. (eds.). *Meaning, use and the interpretation of language.* Berlin: Walter de Gruyter.

Hoffman, B. (1998). Word Order, Information Structure, and Centering in Turkish. Walker, M., Joshi, A., Prince, E. (eds.). *Centering Theory in Discourse.* Oxford: Oxford University Press.

Kameyama, M. (1998). Intrasentential Centering: A case study. Walker, M., Joshi, A., Prince, E. (eds.). *Centering Theory in Discourse.* Oxford: Oxford University Press.

King, T. (1993). Configuring Topic and Focus in Russian. Ph.D. Dissertation, Stanford University.

Kondrashova, N. (1997). 'Generativnaja grammatika i problema svobodnogo poryadka slov.' Kibrik, A., Kobozeva, I., Sekerina I. (eds.). *Fundamental'nye napravlenija sovremennoj amerikanskoj lingvistiki. [Fundamental Trends of Modern American Linguistics.]* Moscow: MSU Press.

Lenerz, J. (1977). *Zur Abfolge Nominaler Satzglieder im Deutchen.* Tubingen. As cited in Rambow 1993.

Mahajan, A. (1994). *Toward a unified theory of scrambling.* Berlin: Walter de Gruyter&Co.

Miltsakaki, E. (1999). Dissociating discourse salience from information structure: Evidence from a Centering study in Modern Greek and Japanese. *Computational Linguistics in the Netherlands, CLIN '99.*

Miltsakaki, E., Kukich, K. (2000). 'Automated Evaluation of Coherence in Student Essays.' To appear in *Proceedings of ACL 2000.* www.ling.upenn.edu/~elenimi/grad.html.

Moshkow, M. On-line Russian Library. www.lib.ru.

Prince, E. (1981). Toward a taxonomy of given/new information. P. Cole (ed.). *Radical pragmatics.* New York: Academic Press.

Radford, A. (1997). Syntactic Theory and The Structure of English - A Minimalist Approach. New York: Cambridge University Press.

Rambow, O. (1993). Pragmatic Aspects of Scrambling and Topicalization in German: A Centering Approach. Unpublished Manuscript, University of Pennsylvania.

Reinhart, T. (1976). The syntactic domain of anaphora. Ph.D. dissertation, MIT.

Walker, M., Prince, E. (1996). A bilateral approach to givenness: A hearer-status algorithm and a Centering algorithm. T. Fretheim, J. Gundel (eds.). *Reference and referent accessibility.* Philadelphia: John Benjamins.

Walker, M., Iida, M., Cote, S. (1994). Japanese discourse and the process of Centering. *Computational Linguistics* 21.

Walker, M., Joshi, A., Prince, E. (eds.) (1998). *Centering Theory in Discourse.* Oxford: Oxford University Press.

Webber, B. (1991). Structure and ostension in the interpretation of discourse deixis. http://www.ling.upenn.edu/~ellen/bonnie.ps.

Yokoyama, O. T. (1986). *Discourse and Word Order.* Philadelphia: John Benjamins.

Appendix: Some Worked Examples

Consider the following segment from Bulgakov, in which the second sentence is scrambled (The Cb of the previous utterance is K.):

K. svistnul.
K. let-out-a-whistle.
'K. let out a whistle.'

$Cf = \{K.\}$
$Cp = K.$
$Cb = K.$

Ètogo svista Margarita ne uslyšala, no ona ego uvidela v
Of-this whistle Margarita not heard, but she it saw at
to vremja, kak ee vmeste s gorjačim konem brosilo
that time, as her together with hot horse it-threw
saženej na desjat' v storonu.
sažens for ten to side.

'Margarita didn't hear this whistle, but she saw it at the same time when she, together with her hot-tempered horse, was thrown several meters to the side.'

Analysis 1: ranking by grammatical function.
Cf={Margarita, whistle, horse}
Cp=Margarita
Cb = whistle
Transition = Rough-Shift

Analysis 2: ranking by word order.
Cf = {whistle, Margarita, horse}
Cp = whistle
Cb = whistle
Transition = Smooth-Shift

Here is another segment from Bulgakov. Again, the second sentence is scrambled. The Cb at the start is the referent of "ego", Berlioz.

Serdce ego stuknulo i na mgnoven'e kuda-to provalilos',
Heart his banged and for moment somewhere fell,
potom vernulos', no s tupoj igloj, zasevšej v nem.
then returned, but with blunt needle, stuck in it.

'His heart banged and for a moment fell somewhere, then returned, but with a blunt needle stuck in it.'

Cf = {Berlioz, heart, needle}
Cp = Berlioz
Cb = Berlioz
Transition = Continue

Krome togo, Berlioza oxvatil neobosnovannyj, no stol'
Besides that, Berlioz-ACC. Overcame groundless, but such

sil'nyj strax, čto emu zaxotelos' totčas že bežat'
strong fear, that to-him it-wanted immediately to-run

s Patriaršix bez ogljadki.
from P.-place without looking-back.

'Besides, Berlioz was overcome by a groundless fear so strong that he wanted to run from P.-place immediately without looking back.'

Analysis 1: by grammatical function.
Cf = {fear, Berlioz, P.-place}
Cp = fear
Cb = Berlioz
Transition = Retain

Analysis 2: word-order dependent.
Cf = {Berlioz, fear, P.-place}
Cp = Berlioz
Cb = Berlioz
Transition = Continue

The next segment is from Levidov. The first sentence is scrambled; the Cb at the start is Swift.

Knigu Iova, samuju pečal'nuju i samuju nasmešlivuju iz
Book of-Job the most sad and most sarcastic of

vsex knig čelovečestva, on čitaet – snova sviftovskaja
all books of-humanity, he reads — again swiftean

pričuda – každyj god v den' svoego roždenija, 27 nojabrja.
fancy — every year in day of-own birth, 27 November.

'The book of Job, the saddest and most sarcastic of all the books of humanity, he reads – again a Swiftean fancy – every year on his birthday.'

Analysis 1: by grammatical function.
Cf = {Swift, book of Job, November 27, Swift's birth}
Cp = Swift
Cb = Swift
Transition = Continue

Analysis 2: word-order dependent.
Cf = {book of Job, Swift, November 27, Swift's birth}
Cp = book of Job
Cb = Swift
Transition = Retain

S	pečal'nym	nasmešnikom,	avtorom	ètoj	knigi,	bylo	by
With	sad	scoffer,	author	of-this	book,	was	would

o	čem	pobesedovat'	dekanu	sobora	sv.	Patrika.
about	what	to-converse	for-dean	of-cathedral	of-St.	Patrick.

'The dean of St. Patrick's cathedral would have what to say to the sad scoffer, the author of this book.'

Analysis 1: by grammatical function.
Cf ={Swift, St. Patrick's cathedral, book of Job, the author of the book}
Cp = Swift
Cb = Swift
Transition = Continue

Analysis 2: word-order dependent.
Cf = {author of the book, the book of Job, Swift, St. Patrick's cathedral}
Cp = author of the book
Cb = book of Job
Transition = Rough-Shift
(or Smooth-Shift if we allow the book to be ranked higher than its author here)

Sophia Malamud
University of Pennsylvania
smalamud@babel.ling.upenn.edu

One Formal Approach Leads to Another

Marjorie McShane
New Mexico State University

1. Introduction

This paper takes a fresh look at nominal declension in Polish and argues that the notion PARADIGM must be defined according to the application at hand. It shows how the complexities of Polish inflection were handled in one computational application (building a morphological analyzer using machine learning) and suggests that the highly explicit approach required by that application could be exploited in other realms as well— e.g., to comprehensively describe Polish inflection and to lighten the cognitive load for humans attempting to master it.

The question of paradigm delineation in Polish arose in connection with the following task: testing the morphological learner in a knowledge elicitation system intended to cover any natural language.[1] The morphological learner takes as input paradigms supplied by a language informant. On the basis of these paradigms—and only these paradigms— the learner creates rules of inflection that are iteratively tested and refined in a test-debug loop. The process works as follows: the informant provides all the forms for the so-called Primary Example for Paradigm 1; the morphological learner generates rules to cover these word forms; the informant lists a few more words that he believes belong to the paradigm; the learner produces the inflectional forms of those words based on its first round of rules; the informant corrects any mistakes; the learner relearns its rules based on those corrections; the informant tests

---

[1] The project in question, Expedition, is being carried out at the Computing Research Laboratory of New Mexico State University (http://crl.nmsu.edu/expedition). The goal of Expedition is to create the tools to quickly ramp up translation systems from lesser-studied languages into English (Nirenburg and Raskin 1998). The morphological learner is part of the knowledge acquisition module, called Boas (Nirenburg 1998; Oflazer and Nirenburg 1999; Oflazer, Nirenburg and McShane, forthcoming).

the new rules with more words he attributes to the paradigm; and so on, until the informant believes the rules are robust enough to cover all the slight inflectional variations present in Paradigm 1 as he envisions it. Then he proceeds to Paradigm 2. The informant may create as many or as few paradigms as he deems necessary to cover all regular patterns of inflection in his language. It is irrelevant for the learning program whether the informant splits words into many narrowly specified paradigms or bunches them into more broadly defined paradigms. However, there is one absolute constraint: all inflectional forms of all words in a paradigm must be unambiguously predictable based solely on the spelling of the citation form.

Delineating machine tractable paradigms can be a formidable challenge, especially if: (i) the language has complex inflectional patterns; (ii) there are no grammars of the language or the paradigms described in grammars are computationally unsuitable; (iii) the language informant is not a linguist (a likely scenario for the Expedition project). Polish is a particularly difficult case in point because nominal inflection is affected by a dizzying array of phonological, spelling, and semantic rules, not to mention significant irregularity and unpredictability. Furthermore, the small number of paradigms posited in traditional treatments are unsuitable for machine learning because they rely on knowledge beyond that conveyed by the spelling of the citation form. Therefore, the current task required dissecting traditional paradigms and creating new ones based on more exacting common denominators.

Section 2 discusses the complexities of nominal inflection in Polish, the types of knowledge presupposed in traditional treatments, and what types of phenomena can and cannot be conflated in a paradigm for machine processing. Section 3 presents a subset of the masculine paradigms used to test the morphological learner. Section 4 concludes the paper.

2. Polish Nominal Declension: The Basics

Polish nouns inflect for seven cases (Nom., Acc., Gen., Dat., Loc., Instr., Voc.) and two numbers (Sg., Pl.). A survey of Polish grammars revealed that there is no widely accepted inventory of paradigms of the type found, for example, in Russian grammars.² However, the following list approximates the intersection of what Polish grammars consider the basic inventory of paradigms (numerous small groups are omitted).

Table 1. Traditional Paradigm Delineation

Paradigm Description	Example	Gloss
Masc./Neut. alternating	*herb*	coat of arms
Masc./Neut. non-alternating	*kraj*	country
Masc. mixed	*kolega*	colleague
Fem. alternating	*gazeta*	newspaper
Fem. non-alternating	*koszula*	shirt
Fem. in a consonant	*rzecz*	thing

Positing broadly defined paradigms like these presupposes rules from various components of the language system, including the following.

2.1. Semantic Rules

Some inflectional rules derive from the inherent semantic features of nouns. For example:

- VIRILE NOUNS: For Masc. nouns denoting men, the Acc. Sg./Pl. coincides with the Gen. Sg./Pl. In addition, more than one Nom. Pl. ending is often possible for a given lexical item.
- ANIMAL, ETC. NOUNS: For masculine nouns denoting animals and a rather obscure conglomeration of other semantic classes (cigarettes, dances, games, units of currency, vehicles, fruits, vegetables), the Acc. coincides with the Gen. in the Sg. but not in the Pl.³

2.2. Phonological and Spelling Rules

Polish consonants are traditionally divided into hard (*b, p, f, w, m, n, s, z, t, d, r, ł, sł, st, zm*), soft (*ć/ci, dź/dzi, ś/si, ź/zi, ń/ni, ki, gi, chi, li, bi, fi, wi mi*), and functionally soft, which are phonologically hard but take soft

---

² The traditional delineation of paradigms in Russian is: 1st declension (Masc./Neut. with a hard or soft stem); 2nd declension (Fem. with a hard or soft stem); 3rd declension (Fem. ending in a soft sign).

³ See Westfal 1956 for discussion of the masculine Gen. Sg. in Polish.

endings (*c, dz, sz, ż, c, sz, l, rz, cz, dż, cz, dż*).[4] Rules of inflection are generally written using these categories as a point of reference. Alternating consonants soften in some inflectional forms. In contrast, non-alternating consonants are not subject to softening: they either originate soft and remain soft or originate hard and remain hard. For computational purposes, the alternating/non-alternating dichotomy is in part useful but in part misleading. It is useful in that alternating and non-alternating consonants take different endings in certain forms and therefore should be split into different paradigms. It is misleading in that the grouping is based on phonetics, not spelling, so some alternating consonants are spelled the same in all inflectional forms, while some non-alternating consonants are spelled differently in different inflectional forms.

Consider, for example, the Loc. Sg. of Masc. nouns—an inflectional form in which alternating consonants show their alternations. Whereas *b* and *p* alternate but show no spelling mutations (*herb* ~ *herbie* 'coat of arms', *sklep* ~ *sklepie* 'store'), *ń* and *ść* do not alternate but do show spelling mutations (*koń* ~ *koniu* 'horse', *liść* ~ *liściu* 'leaf').[5] The two traditional rules of Loc. Sg. formation that cover these four words correspond to three machine rules of a completely different type (the machine rules are conveyed approximately):

- Traditional rule for *herb* and *sklep*: **add -e** [the canonical ending for alternating consonants] **and soften consonants as necessary** [so *b bi* and *p pi*].
- Traditional rule for *koń* and *liść*: **add -u** [the canonical ending for non-alternating consonants] **and incorporate spelling rules** [so *ń + u niu* and *ć + u ciu*].
- ➢ Machine rule for *herb* and *sklep*: **add -ie**.
- ➢ Machine rule for *koń*: **ń n and add -iu**.
- ➢ Machine rule for *liść*: **ć c and add -iu**.

---

[4] The vowel *i* is used to show the softening of certain consonants when they precede a vowel; e.g., soft *b* preceding *e* is spelled *bie*. In linguistic sources, the soft *b* itself is often conveyed as *bi* (or, alternatively, *b'*).

[5] I define "mutation" as one character changing into another character; so *ń* n is a mutation.

In short, while the traditional classification of alternating/non-alternating is linguistically appropriate and in part useful for machine processing, it masks a spelling problem that must be handled explicitly in the computational system at hand.

1.3. Lexical Idiosyncrasy

A number of inflectional properties of Polish nouns are unpredictable and must be listed explicitly in the lexicon. For example, the Gen. Sg. ending for alternating inanimate nouns can be *-u* or *-a*; the Nom. Pl. ending for alternating virile nouns can be *-owie* and/or *-y/-i*; the Gen. Pl. ending for non-alternating Masc. nouns is largely unpredictable, and often more than one form is possible for a given lexical item.

Another example of lexical idiosyncrasy involves what I will generically call vowel shifts: the insertion, deletion, or changing of a vowel in the final syllable of an inflectional form. As shown in Table 2, it is often not predictable whether a word will or will not undergo a vowel shift—that is, without resorting to incomplete and computationally intractable generalizations concerning consonant clusters and the like.

Table 2. Examples of Lexical Idiosyncrasies

Alt.	Used?	Example	Gloss
ó → o	yes	gróbNOM.SG grobuGEN.SG	grave
	no	mózgNOM.SG mózguGEN.SG	brain
ą → ę	yes	żołądźNOM.SG żołędziuLOC.SG	acorn
	no	pociągNOM.SG pociąguLOC.SG	train
ę → ą	yes	rękaNOM.SG rąkGEN.PL	hand
	no	potęgaNOM.SG potęgGEN.PL	might
Ø → e	yes	perłaNOM.SG perełGEN.PL	pearl
	no	liczbaNOM.SG liczbGEN.PL	number

Because [± vowel shift] is lexically stipulated, words with and without vowel shifts must be assigned to different paradigms: the rules for one paradigm will always include a vowel shift, while the rules for the other paradigm will not. Different types of vowel shifts can be conflated into a single paradigm as long as each vowel undergoes a predictable shift and each shift is explicitly taught to the morphological learner using an example.

The classes of factors discussed above—alternating/non-alternating stems, phonological rules, spelling rules, and lexical idiosyncrasies—must be explicitly accounted for by the paradigms the language informant feeds to the morphological learner.

Now that the complexity of Polish nominal inflection is clear, let us proceed to the concrete matter of building a morphological analyzer to deal with it. Although only a small subset of Masc. paradigms will be discussed, they represent all the problems presented by Masc., Fem. and Neut. nouns in Polish.[6]

2. Computationally Tractable Paradigms

Table 3 (opposite) lists most of the productive patterns of inflection for Masc. nouns in Polish, grouped in a computationally tractable manner.[7] The primary diagnostics are listed in the middle three columns: whether the stem ends in an alternating or a non-alternating consonant; what the Gen. Sg. ending is; whether or not there are vowel shifts.

One could, of course, split the paradigms much more finely, creating a paradigm for every slight inflectional variation and ending up with a hundred or more nominal paradigms. This solution would be perfectly acceptable for the morphological learner, but might be unwieldy for human use. The idea of this experiment was to create a relatively small number of robust paradigms that could be manipulated by both humans and machines. Since the morphological learner first generalizes on the basis of consonants and vowels, then produces consonant- and vowel-specific rules if conflicts occur, letter-specific behavior can be collapsed into a single paradigm as long as examples are provided for each letter in question.

The subsections below focus on the data and conceptual issues related to the four shaded paradigms from Table 3, which cover most of the tricky issues raised by Polish nominal inflection. Vocative forms

---

[6] McShane, forthcoming, develops this approach to paradigm delineation for all open-class parts of speech in Polish.

[7] These paradigms were among those used to test the morphological learning program. The architecture of the learner, the testing procedure, and a detailed account of the results for a subset of Polish Masc. nouns are described in Oflazer, Nirenburg, and McShane, forthcoming.

Table 3. Computationally Tractable Masc. Paradigms

Animacy	Alt.?	Gen. Sg.	Vowel Shifts?	Example	Gloss
inanimate	+	-u	-	telefon	telephone
inanimate	+	-u	+	grób	grave
inanimate	+	-a	-	gram	gram
inanimate	+	-a	+	ząb	tooth
inanimate	-	-u	-	garaż	garage
inanimate	-	-u	+	pokój	room
inanimate	-	-a	-	bicz	whip
inanimate	-	-a	+	nóż	knife
animal	+	-a	-	krab	crab
animal	+	-a	+	wół	ox
animal	-	-a	-	koń	horse
animal	-	-a	+	wąż	snake
virile	+	-a	-	pasierb	stepson
virile	+	-a	+	majster	master
virile	-	-a	-	słuchacz	listener
virile	-	-a	+	cudoziemiec	foreigner
mixed	+	-y	-	poeta	poet
mixed	-	-y	-	kierowca	driver
etc.					

excluded from the test data because the nascent system is primarily intended for journalistic prose, where relatively few vocative forms are expected to occur. In addition, inflectional forms that might not be semantically valid (e.g., plurals for collectives) were permitted; this bit of overgeneration is irrelevant since Polish text will be only be analyzed, not generated, by this system.[8]

---

[8] I must emphasize that the morphological analyzer of Polish built through the Boas knowledge-elicitation system is not intended to compete with morphological analyzers designed expressly for Polish. Polish is simply being used as a test case for a system that is intended for languages for which there are few or no available machine resources.

2.1. Paradigm 1

Paradigm 1 includes *alternating inanimate Masc. nouns with Gen. Sg. in -u and no vowel shifts*. The Primary Example (used as the first, fully-specified example provided to the morphological learner) is *telefon* 'telephone', whose inflectional forms are shown below.

Sg.	Nom.	telefon	Pl.	Nom.	telefony
	Acc.	telefon		Acc.	telefony
	Gen.	telefonu		Gen.	telefonów
	Dat.	telefonowi		Dat.	telefonom
	Loc.	telefonie		Loc.	telefonach
	Instr.	telefonem		Instr.	telefonami

All inflectional forms in this paradigm are trivial except:

- The Loc. Sg. depends upon the stem-final consonant, some of which undergo alternations.

Final Consonant	Loc. Sg. Ending	Consonant Alternations
b, p, f, w, m, n, s, z	-ie	
t, d, st, zm	-ie	t c, d dz, stść, zm źm
ł, r, sł	-e	ł l, r rz, sł śl
g, k, ch	-u	

- The Instr. Sg. depends upon the stem-final consonant; two velars have an idiosyncratic ending.

Final Consonant	Instr. Sg. Ending
b, p, f, w, m, n, s, z, t, d, st, zm, ł, r, sł, ch	-em
g, k	-iem

- The Nom. Pl. depends upon the stem-final consonant; two velars have an idiosyncratic ending.

Final Consonant	Nom. Pl. Ending
b, p, f, w, m, n, s, z, t, d, st, zm, ł, r, sł, ch	-y
g, k	-i

Based on just the Primary Example, the learner knows nothing about the inflectional details presented in the bulleted list above; therefore, more examples must be provided. It is not necessary to provide all the inflectional forms of each additional example—only those that cannot be predicted based on the forms of the Primary Example. Therefore, the paradigm specification for Paradigm 1 will consist of a fully-specified Primary Example plus partially specified additional examples. Once the necessary data have been provided, the morphological learner creates rules which then must be tested on a series of new examples that cover each of the slight inflectional variations found in the paradigm.

Preparing for the teach-test-debug cycle required collecting letter-specific examples that decline precisely alike—inventories not found in available resources. A subset of the words collected for Paradigm 1 is listed below, arranged in a four-tier manner based primarily on the form of the Loc. Sg.

The group labeled LOC. SG. IN -IE contains consonants that alternate phonetically but not graphotactically; their Loc. Sg. ending is -*ie*. Words ending in all of these consonants should be covered by the rules generated for the Primary Example. However, there is one complication: since this paradigm will ultimately contain certain letter-specific rules for the Loc. Sg. (described below), the generalization of rules to any consonant gets corrupted during the process of machine learning. Therefore, Loc. Sg. examples for at least one other stem-final letter from this first group had to be added as a control during the test-debug loop.

The group labeled CONSONANT ALTERNATION AND LOC. SG. IN -IE contains words with letter-specific consonant alternations; their Loc. Sg. is -*ie*. At a minimum, the following three forms had to be provided for a word ending in each letter: the Nom. Sg. (the base form), the Loc. Sg. (the unpredictable, mutated form), and at least one other non-mutated inflectional form, which counters overgeneralization of the mutation.

The group labeled CONSONANT ALTERNATION AND LOC. SG. IN -E contains more words with letter-specific consonant alternations; their Loc. Sg. is in -e (as opposed to -ie, as above). The data requirements for the previous group apply here as well.

The final group contains words with stem-final velars, which have the following special properties, referred to hereafter as VELAR PECULIARITIES: Loc. Sg. in -u; Instr. Sg. in -iem for stem-final g/k but in -em for stem-final ch; and Nom. Pl. in -i for stem-final g/k but in -y for stem-final ch.[9]

Loc. Sing. in -ie

b	p	f	w	m	n	s	z
pogrzeb	sklep	aperitif	motyw	tłum	telefon	adres	nakaz
herb	postęp	klif	krzew	film	egzamin	autobus	obraz

Consonant Alternation and Loc. Sing. in -ie

t/c	d/dz	st/ść	zm/źm
akcent	sad	most	komunizm
plakat	wypad	list	socjalizm

Consonant Alternation and Loc. Sing. in -e

ł/l	r/rz	sł/śl
artykuł	teatr	pomysł
kawał	kolor	zmysł

Velars

g	k	ch
pociąg	bank	dach
brzeg	atak	śmiech

Apart from being machine tractable, this method of paradigm organization has a number of interesting properties relating to language

---

[9] In order to preserve clarity of presentation, some glosses have have been moved to footnotes. Letter-by-letter glosses for this set of examples are as follows: **b**: funeral, coat of arms; **p**: store, ruse; **f**: aperitif, cliff; **w**: motive, bush; **m**: crowd, film; **n**: telephone, exam; **s**: address, bus; **z**: order, painting; **t**: accent; poster; **d**: orchard, outing; **st**: bridge, letter; **zm**: communism, socialism; **ł**: article, chunk; **r**: theater, color; **sł**: idea, sense; **g**: train, bank; **k**: bank, attack; **ch**: roof, laughter.

description, teaching, and learning. First, since each group is so highly specified, even someone who knows nothing about Polish could decline any of the words in this paradigm based on the Primary Example plus the description of each group. Second, having multiple examples for every stem-final letter provides rich material for practice (for reasons of space, only two examples were listed for each stem-final consonant, but many more were collected for this project). Third, the four-tier layout of this paradigm organizes the notable letter-specific variations in a visually memorable way. Finally, this highly precise definition of a paradigm reinforces the factors that affect paradigm membership in Polish: alternating/non-alternating, animate/inanimate, vowel shifts/no vowel shifts, etc.

I am not suggesting that linguistically insightful generalizations be dismissed in the descriptive and pedagogical realms. Rather, I am suggesting a division of labor of the type that has long been discussed with respect to the one-stem verb system in Slavic: it is good and helpful to know the theory, but when it comes to brute memorization and the mysterious process of internalizing a second language, simple rote patterns have their place.

2.2. Paradigm 2

Paradigm 2 includes alternating inanimate Masc. nouns with Gen. Sg. in -*u* and vowel shifts. The Primary Example is *grób* 'grave':

Sg.	Nom.	grób	Pl.	Nom.	groby
	Acc.	grób		Acc.	groby
	Gen.	grob**u**		Gen.	grob**ów**
	Dat.	grob**owi**		Dat.	grob**om**
	Loc	grob**ie**		Loc.	grob**ach**
	Instr.	grob**em**		Instr.	grob**ami**

This paradigm has all the same properties as Paradigm 1 except that there are vowel shifts whose occurrence is not predictable based on the citation form (e.g., *grób* has vowel shifts but graphotactically similar *mózg* does not). The vowel shifts occur in all inflectional forms except the Nom. Sg. and the Acc. Sg., which are identical. It was not possible to find examples representing all consonant alternations in combination with all vowel shifts; therefore, this paradigm currently covers only the combinations for which examples were found.[10]

Vowel Shifts

Nom./Acc. Sg.	Other Forms
ó	o
e	
ie	
a	e

Loc. Sg. in -*ie*

b	p	w
grób → grobie dąb → dębie	półwysep → półwyspie	parów → parowie rów → rowie

n	z
len → lnie sen → śnie	mróz → mrozie nawóz → nawozie

Consonant Alternation and Loc. Sg. in -*ie*

t	d/dzi	zd/ździ
obrót → obrocie odwrót → odwrocie	lód → lodzie błąd → błędzie	dojazd → dojeździe najazd → najeździe

Consonant Alternation and Loc. Sg. in -*e*

ł/l	r/rz
stół → stole dół → dole	bór → borze cukier → cukrze

Velars

k	g	ch
budynek → budynku pakunek → pakunku	róg → rogu okrąg → okręgu	mech → mchu

---

[10] Glosses for the next set of examples are: **b**: grave, oak; **p**: peninsula; **w**: ravine, ditch; **n**: sleep, flax; **z**: frost, fertilizer; **t**: revolution; retreat; **d**: ice, mistake; **zd**: approach, invasion; **ł**: table, pit; **r**: forest, sugar; **k**: building, package; **g**: horn, circle; **ch**: moss.

2.3. Paradigm 3

Paradigm 3 includes *alternating virile nouns with no vowel shifts*. The Primary Example is *pasierb* 'stepson':

Sg.	Nom.	pasierb	Pl.	Nom.	pasierb**owie**
					pasierb**i**
	Acc.	pasierb**a**		Acc.	pasierb**ów**
	Gen.	pasierb**a**		Gen.	pasierb**ów**
	Dat.	pasierb**owi**		Dat.	pasierb**om**
	Loc.	pasierb**ie**		Loc.	pasierb**ach**
	Instr.	pasierb**em**		Instr.	pasierb**ami**

In this paradigm, all of the consonant alternations and velar peculiarities discussed above are still in effect, making the four-tier system of presentation relevant. (I omit the examples here as this convention has been amply illustrated in the earlier paradigms.) This virile paradigm differs from inanimate Paradigm 1 in the following ways:

- The Acc. Sg./Pl. coincides with the Gen. Sg./Pl.
- The Nom. Pl. ending depends both upon the word-final consonant and on idiosyncrasies of the word itself. There are five possibilities: (i) *owie*, (ii) *i* (iii) *y*, (iv) *owie* or *i* (v) *owie* or *y*.[11]

Word-final consonant	Nom. Pl. endings
b, f, w, m, n, z, t	*owie* or *i* or both
p, ch	*i* only
d, ł	*owie* only
r, k, g	*owie* or *y* or both

Which of the Nom. Pl. endings will be valid for a given word is largely unpredictable, as shown by the sample words below (grammar books of Polish often present conflicting information regarding licit variants). The rest of the alternating consonants in this paradigm show a similar degree of unpredictability.

---

[11] Two points deserve mention. First, *i/y* are allomorphs in complementary distribution. Second, although there are no *letters* that exclusively permit *y*, there are *words* ending in *r, k,* and *g* that exclusively permit *y*.

	Cit. Form	*owie*	*i*	Gloss
b	Arab pasierb	Arabowie ——	Arabi pasierbi	Arab stepson
p	biskup chłop	—— ——	biskupi chłopi	bishop peasant
f	filozof szef	filozofowie ——	—— szefi	philosopher boss
w	Nowakow Bogusław	Nowakowie ——	—— Bogusławi	*proper names*
m	kum agronom	kumowie agronomowie	—— agronomi	godfather agronomist
n	kapitan kuzyn piastun	kapitanowie —— piastunowie	—— kuzyni piastuni	captain cousin guardian

For purposes of the morphological learner—and, later, the morphological analyzer—this unpredictability raises no problems: both variants (*owie* and the correct one of the *i/y* allomorphs) will be permitted for every word. This bit of overgeneration is irrelevant since the analyzer will only be analyzing, not producing, inflectional forms. However, since the morphological learner has no way to predict which of the *i/y* allomorphs is used with a given word-final consonant, explicit examples of the Nom. Pl. for each word-final consonant had to be provided. As regards human consumption, no method of paradigm delineation can ease the brute memorization required to produce *filozofowie* in the same breath as *szefi*.

2.4. Paradigm 4

Paradigm 4 includes non-alternating inanimate Masc. nouns with Gen. Sg. in -a and no vowel shifts. The Primary Example is bicz 'whip':

| *Sg.* | *Nom.*
Acc.
Gen.
Dat.
Loc.
Instr. | bicz
bicz
bicz**a**
bicz**owi**
bicz**u**
bicz**em** | *Pl.* | *Nom.*
Acc.
Gen.
Dat.
Loc.
Instr. | bicz**e**
bicz**e**
bicz**y**
bicz**om**
bicz**ach**
bicz**ami** |

Unlike alternating consonants, non-alternating consonants show no Loc. Sg. mutations, making the four-tier system of organization unnecessary. However, a spelling rule comes into play: word-final letters written with a diacritic lose their diacritic and are followed by *i* when a vocalic ending is added.

ń + u niu	ć + u ciu
ń + owi niowi	ć + owi ciowi
etc.	*etc.*

One other complication arises in this paradigm: the Gen. Pl. ending depends upon both the final consonant and the lexical properties of the given word, just as we saw for the Nom. Pl. of virile nouns in Paradigm 3. For purposes of testing the morphological learner, I limited the Gen. Pl. endings to one for each stem-final consonant; however, building a complete analyzer would require the same type of overgeneration allowed in Paradigm 3.

Final Cons.	Gen.Pl. End.	Cit. Forms	Glosses
cz	y	klucz, bicz	key, whip
sz	y	kapelusz, klawisz	hat, key (of a piano)
rz	y	ołtarz, korytarz	altar, corridor
ż	y	krzyż	cross
l	i	parasol, badyl	umbrella, stalk
ść	i	liść	leaf
ń	i	kamień, strumień	rock, stream
j	ów	kij, liszaj	stick, lichen
ch	ów	brzuch, kielich	stomach, glass
szcz	ów	płaszcz	overcoat

This paradigm emphasizes the need to deal with spelling conventions, not just phonetic properties of words, when establishing paradigms. It also reinforces the need for creating an inventory of letter-specific examples to teach and test the morphological learner.

3. Discussion

The rules created through this machine learning process are bi-directional, meaning that they can be used for generation as well as parsing. However, generation imposes a restriction that analysis does not: for generation, each word must be associated with one and only one paradigm.[12] Accordingly, nominal entries in computational lexicons of Polish would have to be expanded to ensure unambiguous paradigm assignment. One option would be to create a full inventory of inherent features and mark each noun in the lexicon for the relevant ones: MASC / FEM / NEUT; INANIMATE / ANIMATE NON-VIRILE / VIRILE; GEN.SG. IN A / U; ALTERNATING / NON-ALTERNATING, etc. The specific combination of inherent features, in conjunction with the spelling of the citation form, would place a noun in a specific paradigm. Another option would be to first create the full inventory of paradigms then manually assign each noun in the lexicon to one of them. Irregular or truly unpredictable forms would have to be listed as exceptions under either approach.

The paper has shown that although the computational approach increases the number of paradigms used to describe Polish declension, it circumvents the necessity of incorporating layers of umbrella rules. Thus, the computational canvas is much larger, but also much clearer. I believe that this degree of clarity and explicitness could be fruitfully incorporated into formal descriptions of, and pedagogical approaches to, Polish inflection.

---

[12] For parsing, the important thing is that the correct analysis is among those posited. Therefore, having multiple analyses is not necessarily problematic, especially since various means can be use to filter the analyses. Of course, having a single analysis is best and could be achieved using the type of lexical expansion described here. However, the task of fully specifying the entire lexicon would be too time consuming for the typical user of our system.

References

McShane, M. Forthcoming. "Polish inflection fit for man and machine," in *Memoranda in computer and cognitive science, Computing Research Laboratory,* New Mexico State University.

Nirenburg, S. 1998. "Project Boas: 'A linguist in a box' as a multi-purpose language resource," in *Proceedings of COLING '98.*

Nirenburg, S. and V. Raskin. 1998. "Universal Grammar and Lexis for Quick Ramp-Up of MT Systems," in *COLING-ACL '98* (36th Annual Meeting of the Association for Computational Linguistics), vol. II, 975-979.

Oflazer, K. 1996. "Error-tolerant finite-state recognition with applications to morphological analysis and spelling correction," in *Computational Linguistics,* 22(1):73-90.

Oflazer, K. and S. Nirenburg. 1999. "Practical Bootstrapping of Morphological Analyzers," in *Proceedings of the Workshop on Computational Natural Language Learning at EACC '99,* Bergen, Norway.

Oflazer, K., S. Nirenburg, and M. McShane. Forthcoming. "Bootstrapping morphological analyzers by combining human elicitation and machine learning," in *Computational Linguistics.*

Westfal, S. 1956. *A study in Polish morphology: the Genitive singular masculine.* The Hague, Mouton.

Computing Research Laboratory
Box 30001/MSC 3 CRL
New Mexico State University
Las Cruces, NM 88003
marge@crl.nmsu.edu

Syntactic Categories Are Not Primitive: Evidence from Short and Long Adjectives in Russian

Asya Pereltsvaig
McGill University

1. Introduction

In this paper, I investigate the distinction between short and long adjective forms in Russian (henceforth, SAs and LAs), illustrated in (1) below, and propose a lexical alternative to Bailyn's (1994) syntactic account.

(1) a. Maša umnaja.   b. Maša umna.
       Masha smart$_{LA}$ Masha smart$_{SA}$
       'Masha is smart.'   'Masha smart.'

In particular, I argue that the distinction is encoded in the lexicon through different feature matrices: LAs are specified for case and animacy feature(s) which are not present in SAs.

On the theoretical plane, the major question considered in this paper is whether syntactic categories are primitive notions or whether they are convenient shortcuts for bundles of primitive features. I will argue that the latter position is in fact correct. Thus, SAs and LAs belong to the same syntactic category as far as their thematic properties are concerned, but to different categories if their agreement features are taken into consideration. Furthermore, I will propose that the set of lexical categories is not universally determined. In conclusion, I will suggest that the loss of the distinction between SAs and LAs across Slavic and in Russian in particular is a result of the mismatch in the way the two sets of features define syntactic categories.

2. The Theory of Syntactic Categories

In the mainstream GB theory, little attention has been paid to the theory of syntactic categories. The main achievement has been to analyze lexical categories in terms of binary features [±N] and [±V]. However, there are two problems with this analysis. First, as noted in Baker (2000), these features have little (if any) content within the mainstream GB theory; therefore, the analysis of lexical categories in terms of these features amounts to restating that there are four major lexical categories. This brings up another problem with the GB analysis, namely, that it restricts the set of possible lexical categories to four universally present categories: Noun, Verb, Adjective and Preposition (in fact, Adposition, but I will stick to the traditional terminology). It is not obvious that this claim is universally true. For example, it leaves Adverbs outside the range of lexical categories. Furthermore, the claim that there is a universal set of syntactic categories has been challenged by Culicover (1999). As will be shown in this paper, this distinction between four lexical categories fails to account for the SA/LA distinction in Russian.

The Minimalist Program of Chomsky (1995) provides little new insight into the problem of lexical categories (in fact, neither "lexical categories" nor "syntactic categories" has an index entry in Chomsky 1995). However, Chomsky (1995:244) reiterates an earlier idea that lexical items are sets of features. The next obvious question is which features determine the syntactic category of an item.

According to Baker (2000:15), the combinations of features [±N] and [±V] must be reinterpreted as referring to thematic properties of the lexical category. For him, "only verbs are true predicates, having the power to assign theta-roles to elements in their specifiers", and "only nouns can bear a referential index". Adjectives are analyzed as "essentially the 'default' category" and prepositions – as non-lexical categories. This is summarized below:

(2) Noun is +N = 'has a referential index'
Verb is +V = 'has a theta grid' (of a particular kind)
Adjective is –N, –V
Preposition is part of a different system (functional)

On the whole, I adopt Baker's idea that categorial features of lexical categories are a shortcut for their thematic properties. However, I make two important revisions to Baker's proposal.

First, assuming the DP-Hypothesis (Abney 1986), I will suggest that a referential index is introduced by the $D°$, not by $N°$ (an investigation of the consequences of this claim is outside the scope of this paper; it is to be undertaken in future research). This makes the distinction between Nouns and Adjectives murkier than ever. One possibility is that Nouns and Adjectives differ in the type of properties they denote: as mentioned in Milsark (1977), nouns tend to denote individual-level properties, whereas adjectives tend to denote stage-level properties. Given the problematicity of assigning a referential index to a Noun directly, I will leave the question of what exactly distinguishes thematic properties of Nouns from those of Adjectives open for further research. In what follows, I will use the bundles of features [± N] and [±V] as a convenient shortcut for thematic properties of a given lexical category.

The second revision concerns about the universality of the system proposed by Baker (2000). According to him, the thematic properties of the Adjective define the set of environments where an adjective can appear, including "attributive modification position, as the complement of degree heads, and as resultative secondary predicates" (Baker 2000:15). However, grouping Russian SAs and LAs into one category Adjective fails to account for their distribution: there are no adjectival resultatives in Russian, both SAs and LAs can appear as complements of degree heads, but only LAs can appear in attributive modification position. Thus, it appears that Russian distinguishes more lexical categories that the three identified by Baker (2000). On the other hand, it seems highly unreasonable to claim that languages like English distinguish between SAs and LAs since this distinction never shows up in the language. Furthermore, as discussed in section 5 below, the distinction between SAs and LAs appears to be unstable in the long run, which suggests that languages tend to have three major lexical category systems.

At this point we reach the conclusion that relying on features referring to an item's thematic properties is not enough to distinguish all syntactic categories. In the next section, I show in detail that thematic properties are not enough to distinguish between SAs and LAs in Russian.

3. Long vs. Short Adjectives in Russian

In this section, I consider the properties of SAs and LAs that are relevant for determining their category. Traditionally, three types of tests are used to determine the syntactic category of an item: its meaning (the most traditional of all tests; here to be amended by the thematic properties identified by Baker 2000), its distribution, and its morphology. For most languages, the three types of tests coincide in their results. For example, the Italian lexical item cadranno 'fall.FUT.3.PL' is identified as a verb because: (i) it refers to an event and can assign a thematic role to its specifier, as shown by the grammaticality of ne-cliticization, as in (3a), and the ungrammaticality of da parte di-construction with the nominalized form of cadere 'to fall', as in (3b) from Samek-Lodovici (1999); (ii) it exhibits verbal morphology, including future (or irrealis) morpheme -r-, and 3rd person plural subject agreement morpheme -anno; and (iii) this item (in its infinitival form) can appear in causative construction, as in (3c).

(3) a. Ne   cadranno molti.
       of-them will-fall many
       'Many of them will fall.'
    b. ?? l'interminabile caduta da parte dei paracadutisti...
       the endless   falling by part of-the paratroopers
       intended: the endless fall by the paratroopers'
    c. Marco mi ha fatto cadere.
       Marco me has made to-fall
       'Marco made me fall.'

In this section, I look at these three types of tests as they apply to SAs and LAs and show that Russian adjectives provide another interesting case for a paradox discussed by Culicover (1999:36): on the one hand, they seem to belong to the same syntactic category, but on the other hand, "attributing to them membership in some traditional category [i.e., Adjective]" does not account for their syntactic and morphological behavior. Rather, they "appear to belong to two ... categories at the same time" (Culicover 1999:36). In section 3.1., I show that both SAs and LAs are unergative predicates that cannot "assign theta-roles to elements in their specifiers" and "need help from a ... category Pred to do this" (Baker 2000:15). In sections 3.2. and 3.3., I show that despite their thematic similarity, SAs and LAs have different distribution and different morphology. Then, in section 4, I will propose an analysis that explains the syntactic differences between SAs and LAs in terms of the morphological differences between them.

3.1. Thematic properties of Russian adjectives

Baker (2000) has examined the thematic properties of adjectives and comparable (stative) verbs across languages (like hungry and hunger) and concluded that adjectives differ from stative verbs in that they cannot assign their theta-role directly to their specifiers. Instead, adjectives require help from Pred°, which assigns the theta-role semantically associated with the adjective to the [Spec, PredP]. Thus, the structures associated with a stative verb and an adjective are as follows:

(4) a. STATIVE VERB   b. ADJECTIVE

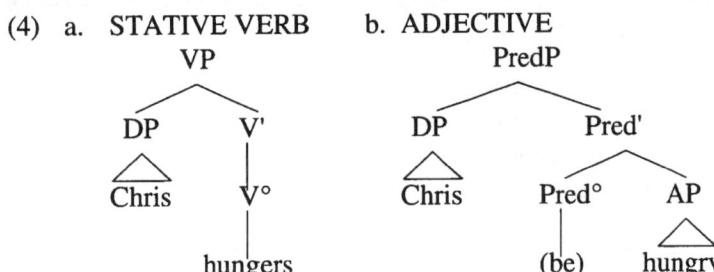

One of the diagnostics used by Baker (2000) to support his claim that stative verbs are unaccusative, while (synonymous) adjectives are unergative is the Genitive of Negation. As discovered by Pesetsky (1982), the Genitive of Negation applies to unaccusative predicates, but not to unergative predicates. When applied to both SAs and LAs, this test shows that both types of adjectives in Russian are unergative. In contrast, stative verbs are unaccusative:

(5) a. *(...čtoby) ni   odnogo   rebenka   nikogda ne   bylo
            that   not one$_{GEN}$ child$_{GEN}$ never   not   was
        golodnogo / golodnym
        hungry$_{LA.SG.M.GEN}$/$_{SG.M.INSTR}$
        intended: '...that no child would ever be hungry'

   b. *(...čtoby) ni   odnogo   rebenka   nikogda ne   bylo
            that   not one$_{GEN}$ child$_{GEN}$ never   not   was
        golodny / golodno
        hungry$_{SA.3.PL}$ / hungry$_{SA.3.SG.N}$
        intended: '...that no child would ever be hungry'

   c. (...čtoby) ni   odnogo   rebenka   nikogda ne   golodalo
            that   not one$_{GEN}$ child$_{GEN}$ never   not   hunger$_{V.3.SG.N}$
        '...that no child would ever hunger'

To sum up, both SAs and LAs exhibit similar syntactic behavior as far as their thematic properties are concerned. In the next section, I will show that despite their thematic similarity, SAs and LAs have very different distributions.

3.2. The distribution of SAs and LAs

It has long been noted that SAs and LAs have very different distributions. Even though both can appear in post-copular positions, as in (6), and as complements to degree heads, as in (7), only LAs can function as prenominal modifiers, as in (8).

(6) a. Dom   novyj.
      house.$_{NOM}$ new$_{LA.NOM}$
      'The house is new.'
   b. Dom   nov.
      house.$_{NOM}$ new$_{SA}$
      'The house is new.'   [Moro 1997:54, (81a)]

(7) a. Maša očen' umnaja.
      Masha very smart.LA
      'Masha is very smart.'
   b. Maša očen' umna.
      Masha very smart$_{SA}$
      'Masha very smart.'

(8) a. Novyj   dom   stoit na gore.
      new$_{LA.NOM}$ house.$_{NOM}$ stands on hill
      'The new house stands on a/the hill.'
   b. *Nov   dom   stoit na gore.
      new$_{SA}$ house.$_{NOM}$ stands on hill
      'The new house stands on a/the hill.'

This distribution can be summarized as follows: both LAs and SAs can be used as predicates, and both types of adjectives can appear with degree heads, but only LAs can be used as attributive modifiers.

Another construction distinguishing SAs and LAs in Russian is the inverse copular construction (ICC). Importantly, ICC must be distinguished from topicalized copular construction (TCC). In ICC the pre-copular XP is associated with the presupposition of existence (and not only with a topic-like interpretation). These constructions also exhibit a variety of properties that distinguish them from TCC (e.g., extraction, binding, availability of pro-predicative clitic lo in Italian, etc.). An example of ICC in English is given in (9a) and an example of TCC in (9b). For a further discussion of these two constructions the reader is referred to Pereltsvaig (in press).

(9) a. The problem is John.
    b. Problematic is John's behavior (not John's attitudes).

In Russian, ICC exhibit NOM-NOM pattern, whereas TCC exhibit INSTR-NOM pattern.

(10) a. Durak   byl   Oleg.   ICC
        fool$_{NOM}$ was Oleg$_{NOM}$
        'The fool was Oleg.'
     b. Durakom   byl   Oleg.   TCC
        fool$_{INSTR}$ was Oleg$_{NOM}$
        'It was Oleg who was a fool.'

Nominative-marked LAs can appear as the pre-copular XP in ICC, whereas SAs cannot. If SAs appear in the pre-copular position, the sentence exhibits properties of TCC).

(11) a. Krasnoe   –   golova.   ICC
        red$_{LA.NOM(N)}$ head$_{NOM(F)}$
        'The red (thing) is a head.'
     b. *Krasna / krasno – golova.
        red$_{SA.F}$ / red$_{LA.N}$ head$_{NOM(F)}$
        'The red (thing) is a head.'
     c. Široka strana   moja rodanja...   TCC
        wide$_{SA}$ country my   native
        'It is wide that my native country is.'   [Lebedev-Kumač]

As argued in Pereltsvaig (in press), the pre-copular phrase in ICC is in [Spec, IP], whereas the pre-copular phrase in TCC is in [Spec, CP]. This means that LAs can appear in [Spec, IP], whereas SAs cannot.

Thirdly, LAs but not SAs can undergo substantivization, in which case they appear in nominal positions. One test to distinguish nouns from

LAs is modification: nouns can be modified by adjectives, but not by nouns:

(12) a. *kamen' dom   b. kamennyj dom
      stone house $stone_{LA}$ house

Using this test, we can distinguish (at least) two classes of substantivized adjectives: those that can still function as adjectives and those that cannot. Some examples of these two classes are given below:

(13) a. beremennaja   'pregnant (woman)'
       glasnyj   'vowel (sound)'
       politexničeskij 'Polytechnic (institute)'
    b. lešij   'goblin'   soxatyj   'elk' (lit. 'horned')
       zodčij   'architect'   zapjataja 'comma'
       nasekomoe 'insect'   mesjačnye 'periods' (lit. 'monthly')

The forms listed in (13a) can be used either followed by a noun or not, whereas the forms listed in (13b) cannot be followed by a noun.

(14) a. Ivan postupil v politexničeskij (institut).
       Ivan was-accepted in Polytechnic (institute)
       'Ivan was accepted in the Polytechnic institute.'
    b. Na poljanu vyšel soxatyj (*los').
       to glade came-out horned elk
       'To the glade came out an elk.'

For the former class of items, one can argue that the LA form does not change its syntactic category, but rather modifies a phonetically null noun the content of which is understood from the context (in line with Bailyn's 1994 analysis of all LAs in Russian). However, the same analysis seems to be unreasonable for the second class of substantivized adjectives, namely those that can never function as adjectives. These nouns are best analyzed as a special class of nouns with adjectival type inflection. Crucially for the argument of this paper, the process of substantivization discussed above does not apply to SAs, but only to LAs.

To sum up this section, LAs are like Nouns in that they can appear in nominal positions: either as substantivized adjectives or as subjects in the inverse copular constructions. However, unlike Nouns, LAs can modify nouns. Once again, we see that grouping LAs and SAs into one syntactic category does not account for their distribution.

3.3. Morphological properties of SAs and LAs

One crucial difference between SAs and LAs is their distinct morphology. In particular, in modern Russian only LAs are marked for case (and therefore, animacy, which is involved in determining case paradigms in Russian: for animate nouns and LAs that modify them the accusative form is the same as the genitive form; in contrast, for inanimate nouns and LAs that modify them the accusative form is the same as the nominative case). In older stages of the language, SAs were marked for case, which is reflected by the forms in the following idiomatic expressions:

(15) a. sred'   bela   dnja
       in-the-midst-of white$_{SA.GEN}$ day$_{GEN}$
       'in full daylight'
   b. ot   mala   do velika
       from small$_{SA.GEN}$ to big$_{SA.GEN}$
       'people of all ages'
   c. na bosu   nogu
       on bare$_{SA.ACC}$ foot$_{ACC}$
       'barefoot'

In the modern language, however, SAs are marked only for number and gender (in the singular). For example, a SA 'red' has only four forms: krasen 'red$_{SA.M.SG}$', krasna 'red$_{SA.F.SG}$', krasno 'red$_{SA.N.SG}$', and krasny 'red$_{SA.PL}$'. On the other hand, a LA 'red' has a large number of case forms.

To recap, in modern Russian LAs are marked for case (and animacy), whereas SAs are marked only for number and gender. Like LAs, Nouns are marked for Case and animacy. In the next section, I will propose an analysis that connects the lack of case morphology on SAs with their restricted distribution (compared to LAs), discussed in the previous section.

4. Analysis

In the previous section, I have shown that Russian adjectives present the following interesting paradox. On the one hand, they have the same thematic properties, and therefore (according to Baker 2000) must be grouped into the same syntactic category – Adjective. On the other hand, distributional and morphological differences between SAs and LAs suggest that they should be separated into two different syntactic categories. Here, I propose to resolve this paradox in the following way: thematic properties of a given lexical category are only a subset of the features that determine the category's syntactic behavior. In other words, lexical categories are distinguished on the basis of a larger set of features, including both thematic properties (as argued by Baker 2000) and morpho-logical features (and possibly selectional restrictions as well, as proposed by Culicover 1999). Crucially, the distinction between three major lexical categories identified by Baker (2000), namely Nouns, Verbs, and Adjectives, is only "the tip of the iceberg." Only including finer distinctions allows us to account for all patterns of syntactic behavior of lexical categories. In this section, I show that taking into account the specifications for morphological features (such as agreement features and case) allows to account for the syntactic distribution of SAs and LAs in Russian.

4.1. On the nominal nature of LAs

In section 3, we saw that LAs exhibit more "noun-like" distribution (compared to SAs). Moreover, we have seen that like nouns, LAs are specified for the all the nominal features, including Case and animacy. I propose that the two facts are related, namely, that LAs can appear in nominal positions because, like Nouns, they are specified for all the nominal features. Consider a possible explanation for the substantivization facts, described in the previous section. The substantivizing morpheme in Russian (the phonetically null affix of the category N) has no features other than its categorial features [+N, -V]. Therefore, in order to create a legitimate noun, it must attach to a form that already has all the features that a noun must be specified for. A schematic representation of the substantivization process is given below:

(16)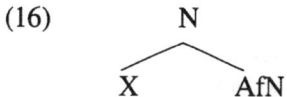

When this affix attaches to a LA, the category of the resulting form is determined by the category of the Affix (i.e., Noun), but all the other features must come from the LA base. In contrast, if the substantivization affix attaches to a SA, the resulting form will lack the specification for Case (and animacy) since both the SA and the substantivization affix lack it. Thus, the substantivized SA form is "still-born"; it is not a legitimate object and cannot be involved in any further computation. In other words, only LAs can undergo substantivization in Russian since only LAs are specified for all nominal features. On the other hand, neither SAs nor verbs can undergo category conversion, and all deverbal nouns are derived by overt affixation.

So far, we have considered the constructions where LAs behave essentially as Nouns. These phenomena have been explained by the fact that LAs are specified for the same features as Nouns. However, we have also seen a context where LAs can appear but nouns cannot: nominal modifiers. On the other hand, SAs cannot function as nominal modifiers. The explanation for these facts will once again rely on the morphological specifications of different adjectival forms. However, in order to arrive at this explanation, we have to consider some facts about modifier-head and subject-predicate agreement first.

4.2. On the two types of agreement in Russian

If we compare the way predicates agree with their subjects and the way modifiers agree with the heads they modify, the following generalization emerges: the two types of agreement are not the same. Subject-predicate agreement operates on the basis of the semantic features of the referent, whereas modifier-head agreement relies strictly on the grammatical features of the head noun. In order to show the difference between the two kinds of agreement, I will use the so-called nouns with inconsistent agreement patterns (the term is from Corbett 1989). In particular, consider masculine nouns that can refer to females. Some examples of such nouns from Graudina et al. (1976) are given below:

(17) agent   donor   pilot
      administrator minister   professor
      angel   operator   sculptor, etc.

As shown in the examples below, these nouns trigger feminine agreement on the predicate (either verbal or adjectival), but masculine agreement on the nominal modifier.

(18) a. Otvažnyj   / *otvažnaja   pilot   pogibla / *pogib.
         brave   / *brave   pilot   perished / *perished
         NOM_M / *NOM_F NOM(M)   F   / *M
         'A brave [female] pilot perished.'
     b. Agent   M. umnaja   / *umnyj.
         agent(M) M. intelligent$_{F.NOM}$ / *intelligent$_{M.NOM}$
         'Agent M. [referring to a woman] is intelligent.'

Therefore, I propose to distinguish two types of agreement: SEM-agreement (i.e., semantic agreement) and MORPH-agreement (i.e., morphological agreement). SEM-agreement is associated with subject-predicate agreement, whereas MORPH-agreement occurs phrase internally, between a head and its modifiers. SEM-agreement, but not MORPH-agreement, allows mismatches in grammatical agreement features, such as gender. In fact, SEM-agreement allows mismatches in all agreement features. The following example illustrates such a mismatch in number:

(19) Italjanskie studenty   –   narod   veselyj.
     Italian$_{PL}$ students$_{PL}$ people$_{SG}$ cheerful$_{SG}$
     'Italian students are cheerful people.'

4.3. On partial agreement

The analysis proposed here makes an interesting prediction: since MORPH-agreement requires full agreement in all relevant grammatical features, but SEM-agreement does not, partial agreement (i.e., agreeing in certain features in some contexts and in other features in other contexts) is predicted to be possible only in the case of subject-predicate agreement. This prediction appears to be borne out.

First, it is well known that in some languages (including Russian) different verbal forms may agree with their subjects in different sets of features. For example, in Russian past tense forms (historically, participial forms) agree in gender and number, whereas present and future forms agree in person and number. In Hebrew, another language with partial agreement, present tense forms agree in gender and number, whereas past and future forms agree in all three features, namely, person, gender and number. Another type of partial agreement is the phenomenon of the so-called agreement loss. Thus, "in some languages agreement with post-verbal subjects exhibits only a subset of features active in the agreement with preverbal subjects" (cf. Samek-Lodovici, 1996:135). Some example of agreement loss from Samek-Lodovici (1996:136) are given in the table below:

language	spec-head agreement	agreement under c-command
Standard Arabic	num, ps, gen	ps, gen
Fassan, Genoese, Ampezzan, Romagnol	num, ps, gen	(num), ps
Conegliano, Trentino, Fiorentino	num, ps, gen	ps

On the other hand, no language seems to exhibit the same phenomena with respect to nominal modifiers. Thus, all modifiers, whether pre-nominal or post-nominal, must agree in the same set of features. Moreover, if we compare adjectival agreement for adjectives in the predicative and modifier positions, the following generalization emerges: modifier-head agreement is always equally or more strict than subject-predicate agreement. For example, in some languages, such as Spanish and Italian, both the modifier-head and the subject-predicate agreement is in all the features. In other languages, including Russian, German, Greek and Hebrew, the modifier-head agreement is full, whereas the subject-predicate agreement is partial or absent. In yet other languages, such as English, neither modifier nor predicate adjectives exhibit any overt agreement. However, the fourth logical option, namely, a language where modifier-head agreement is partial or absent but predicative adjectives agree fully is predicted to be impossible, and is in fact unattested (to the best of my knowledge).

4.4. Modifier-head agreement and adjective forms in Russian

Crucially, in order to be able to function as a nominal modifier, a given item must agree with the head it modifies in all the features, including (for Russian) case and animacy. The following examples show that when a nominal modifier disagrees in case (and/or animacy), the sentence is ungrammatical. In the following sentence, the adjective is either inanimate accusative or animate nominative (or inanimate nominative). In either case, it does not agree with the head it modifies, which is animate accusative. Therefore, the sentence is ungrammatical. (The animate accusative form of the adjective is krasivogo).

(20) *On videl krasivyj mal'čika.
      he saw   beautiful boy
    'He saw a/the beautiful boy.'

Further support for the generalization that nominal modifiers must agree with the heads they modify in all features comes from comparatives in Russian. In this language, the choice of analytic vs. synthetic form of comparatives does not depend on the phonological properties of the adjective (as in English), but on the syntactic position in which the comparative is used. In particular, synthetic forms are used only in the post-copular position, whereas analytic forms can be used both as modifiers and as predicates (more rarely).

(21) a. bolee glubokaja reka   b. *glubže reka
        more deep   river   deeper river
        'a deeper river'
     c. Èta reka bolee glubokaja.   d. Èta reka glubže.
        this river more deep   this river deeper
        'This river is deeper.'

This is because only analytic forms (consisting of an adverb bolee 'more' and a LA) can agree in such nominal features as gender, number, animacy, and case. In contrast, synthetic forms do not inflect for nominal features and therefore cannot be used as nominal modifiers.

Recall now that SAs do not inflect for Case (or animacy). Therefore, they cannot agree with a head in these features (vacuous agreement being disallowed). Since SAs cannot agree properly, they are not allowed as nominal modifiers.

To sum up so far, a distinction is made between SEM-agreement (corresponding to subject-predicate agreement) and MORPH-agreement (corresponding to modifier-head agreement). The former type of agreement does not rely on the grammatical features of the nouns and allows partial agreement. In contrast, the latter type of agreement relies on grammatical features of the nouns and does not allow partial agreement. The ungrammaticality of Russian SAs in the nominal modifier position is explained by the lack of specification for Case and animacy features, that is two of the four features that a modifier and a head must agree in.

5. Consequences and conclusions

So far, I have argued that lexical categories must be distinguished by at least two sets of features: the categorial features [±N] and [±V], which, following Baker (2000), I assume to stand for the thematic properties of the category, and agreement feature specifications. The specifications for different lexical categories in Russian are given in the table below:

features	N	LA	SA	V
±N	+	+	+	−
±V	−	+	+	+
gender	√	√	√	√ (past)
number	√	√	√	√
animacy	√	√	−	−
Case	√	√	−	−

As can be seen from this table LAs and SAs share the same categorial features, which is in accordance with the claim (made in section 3.1.) that the two kinds of adjectives have the same thematic properties. In contrast, LAs and SAs are distinguished by their agreement feature specifications: as discussed above, only LAs are specified for the same set of features that the nouns are specified for, which explains their more nominal distribution. In contrast, SAs are specified only for a subset of these features (i.e., gender and number); therefore, they cannot appear in some of the positions where LAs can appear.

To reiterate the main claim of this paper, the categorial features (i.e., thematic properties) of lexical items are not sufficient in determining their morphological and syntactic behavior. Rather, other properties, such as specification for certain morphological features, must be taken into account.

Note, however, that in the majority of languages, the categories defined by categorial features alone and those defined by agreement feature specifications coincide (Italian and English being two examples mentioned above). Thus, the situation in Russian is special: the two sets of features divide lexical items into categories in a different way. In particular, categorial features group LAs with SAs and agreement features group LAs with Nouns.

I suggest that this mismatch between the ways two sets of features define lexical categories results in a diachronic change aimed at resolving the mismatch. This diachronic change is a gradual loss of the distinction between LAs and SAs that has been happening across Slavic languages in general and in Russian in particular. This loss of the distinction occurs through gradual loss of either set of forms. Here, I will enumerate only a few facts pointing in this direction; for a more detailed discussion of the diachronic aspects of the SA/LA distinction in Slavic see Nichols (1973).

For example, in South Slavic languages the LAs are being lost, so that in Slovene LAs exist only for masculine singular nominative forms (Mario Fadda, p.c.). In contrast, in West and East Slavic languages, it is the SAs that are being lost. For example, in West Slavic languages, including Polish, Czech, and Slovak, short forms are not productive; there are only a few remnant forms usually analyzed by traditional grammars of these languages as deficient verbs. East Slavic languages, including Belorussian, Ukrainian, and Russian, also exhibit a gradual loss of SAs, even though they are behind West Slavic languages in this process. For instance, Grannes et al. (1995:335) note that Ukrainian and Belorussian have largely lost short forms, which are now used "only in a limited and decreasing number of adjectives." With respect to Russian, Cohen (1988:100) notes that "the short adjectives are a system in decay." Furthermore, typological, historical and generative studies of Nichols (1973), Grannes (1990), and Bailyn (1994) all note that SAs are being lost in modern Russian. For instance, short forms of active participles have been lost altogether in the last 150 years or so.

To sum up, the differentiation of lexical categories is language-specific. In particular, many languages distinguish only three major lexical categories on the basis of their thematic properties: Nouns, Verbs, and Adjectives. Yet, other languages, including those of the (East) Slavic family, distinguish more than three categories on the basis of not only the thematic properties but also agreement feature specifications. Even though such systems tend to be unstable in the long run, they appear to happily exist for century after century. In other words, many generations of Russian speakers have successfully acquired a system that makes categorial distinctions not present in other languages. This fact argues against the Universal Category Hypothesis, namely the idea that the same lexical categories are distinguished universally, and in support of Culicover's (1999:37) Contingent Category Hypothesis, which claims that the learner acquires category distinctions through comparisons of words in the language with one another and finding similarities between them. A detailed study of the acquisition of nominal and adjectival systems by Russian children is beyond the scope of this paper; for some initial observations the reader is referred to Voeykova (1997).

References

Abney, Steven Paul (1986) *The English Noun Phrase and Its Sentential Aspect*, Ph.D. dissertation, MIT.

Babby, Leonard H. (1975) *A Transformational Grammar of Russian Adjectives*, The Hague: Mouton.

Bailyn, John F. (1994) The Syntax and Semantics of Russian Long and Short Adjectives: An X'-Theoretic Account, in Jindrich Toman (ed.) *Annual Workshop on Formal Approaches to Slavic Linguistics*, Ann Arbor, MI: Michigan Slavic Publications, 1-30.

Baker, Mark C. (2000) *Categories and Category Systems*, ms., Rutgers University.

Bittner, Maria and Ken Hale (1996) The Structural Determination of Case and Agreement, *Linguistic Inquiry*, 27, 1-68.

Chomsky, Noam (1995) *The Minimalist Program for Linguistic Theory*, Cambridge, MA: MIT Press.

Cohen, Gerald L. (1988) The Accentuation of the Short Adjectives in Slavic: Controversy and Insight into General Linguistics, in Gerald L. Cohen (ed.) *Pursuit of Linguistic Insight*, Rolla, MO, 97-108.

Corbett, Greville G. (1989) An Approach to the Description of Gender Systems, in Doug Arnold, Martin Atkinson, Jacques Durand, Claire Grover and Louisa Sadler (eds.) *Essays on Grammatical Theory and Universal Grammar*, Oxford: Clarendon, 53-89.

Culicover, Peter W. (1999) *Syntactic Nuts: Hard Cases, Syntactic Theory, and Language Acquisition*, Oxford: Oxford University Press.

Falk, Yehuda N. (1997) *Case Typology and Case Theory*, ms., Hebrew University, Jerusalem, also available from <http://pluto.mscc.huji.ac.il/~msyfalk>.

Galkina-Fedoruk, E. M. (1958) *Sovremennyj russkij jazyk – Syntaksis* (= Modern Russian language – Syntax), Moscow.

Grannes, Alf, Ksenija Klochkova, and Kolbjörn Slethei (1995) Morphosyntactic Variation in Predicative Adjectives Used with the Imperative of the Copula Verb *byts'* in Belarusian, *Zeitschrift fur Slawistik* 40:335-48, Berlin.

Grannes, Alf (1990) Morfosintaksicheskoe var'irovanie v ob"ektnom predikative v russkom literaturnom iazyke XIX veka, *Wiener Slawistischer Almanach*, 25-26:161-182, Munich.

Graudina, L.K., V.A. Ickovich, and L.P. Katlinskaja (1976) *Grammaticheskaja pravil'nost' russkoj rechi. Opyt chastotno-stilisticheskogo slovarja variantov* (=Grammatical correctness of Russian speech. An experimental frequential stylistic dictionary of variants), Moscow: Izdatel'stvo Nauka.

Milsark, Gary L. (1977) Toward an Explanation of Certain Peculiarities of the Existential Construction in English, *Linguistic Analysis* 3(1):1-29.

Moro, Andrea (1997) *The Raising of Predicates: Predicative Noun Phrases and the Theory of Clause Structure*, Cambridge: Cambridge University Press.

Neeleman, Ad and Fred Weerman (1997) *Flexible Syntax: A Theory of Case and Arguments*, Utrecht Institute of Linguistics, OTS.

Nichols, Johanna (1973) *The Balto-Slavic Predicate Instrumental: A Problem in Diachronic Syntax*, PhD dissertation, UC Berkeley.

Pereltsvaig, Asya (in press) Are All Small Clauses Created Equal? Evidence from Russian and Italian, in Myunghyun Yoo and and Jeff Steele (eds.), *McGill Working Papers in Linguistics* 15(1), McGill University, Montreal.

Pesetsky, David M. (1982) *Paths and Categories*, Ph.D. dissertation, MIT.

Samek-Lodovici, Vieri (1996) *Constraints on Subjects: An Optimality Theoretic Analysis*, Ph.D. dissertation, Rutgers University.

Samek-Lodovici, Vieri (1999) *The Internal Structure of Arguments: Evidence from Italian Nominalization-based Complex Predicates*, ms., UCL.

Voeykova, Maria D. (1997) Acquisition of Adjectival Inflections: Secondary Paradigms in Child Russian, *Papers and Studies in Contrastive Linguistics*, 33:141-151, Poznan, Poland.

Asya Pereltsvaig
Department of Linguistics
McGill University
1085 Dr. Penfield
Montreal, PQ, Canada H3A 1A7
<aperel@po-box.mcgill.ca>

Clausal Functional Projections in Serbian

Ljiljana Progovac
Wayne State University

1. Introduction

It is widely assumed in the GB framework, as well as in its Minimalism descendent, that a clause is headed by several functional projections, which hierarchically dominate the lexical projection of the V, VP. These functional projections are responsible for the representation and interpretation of Tense, Agreement, Aspect, Polarity, etc., and are usually named accordingly. Although there is no complete agreement as to which projections exactly dominate VP, there is nonetheless substantial agreement that the structure of a clause is hierarchical in this way, and the number and nature of the assumed projections vary little from analysis to analysis. Since functional projections of a clause constitute the skeleton for syntax, it is important to be able to determine their nature, hierarchical arrangement, and possibilities for variation, if any, from language to language. This paper addresses these questions, using Serbian as a point of departure. Looking at Serbian functional projections in depth opens up an interesting way of restricting the number and nature of functional projections in UG.

The following functional projections are initially postulated to constitute an extended projection of the verb in Serbian: CP, Asp_SP, EP (Event Phrase), Agr_SP, TP, Asp_OP, Agr_OP, and PolP. The argument for EP, an Event Phrase, is based on novel evidence from Serbian, namely, from the distribution and interpretation of the event pronominal *to*. The two Aspect Phrases reflect the analysis of Serbian aspect according to which one type of aspect, perfective aspect, is associated with completion, and with the object layer of the clause, while the other type of aspect, imperfective aspect, may be associated with the subject layer of the clause. Obviously, the choice of the labels for the two AspPs is by analogy with the two AgrPs.

The possibility of having more than one functional projection associated with the subject vs. object layer of the clause opens up a rather intriguing possibility, explored gradually in the course of the paper. Namely, it would be possible to consider CP as a subject-layer Polarity Phrase, i.e. a Pol$_S$P. In that case, of course, the PolP above the VP would correspond to a Pol$_O$P, which is the old NegP:

(1)

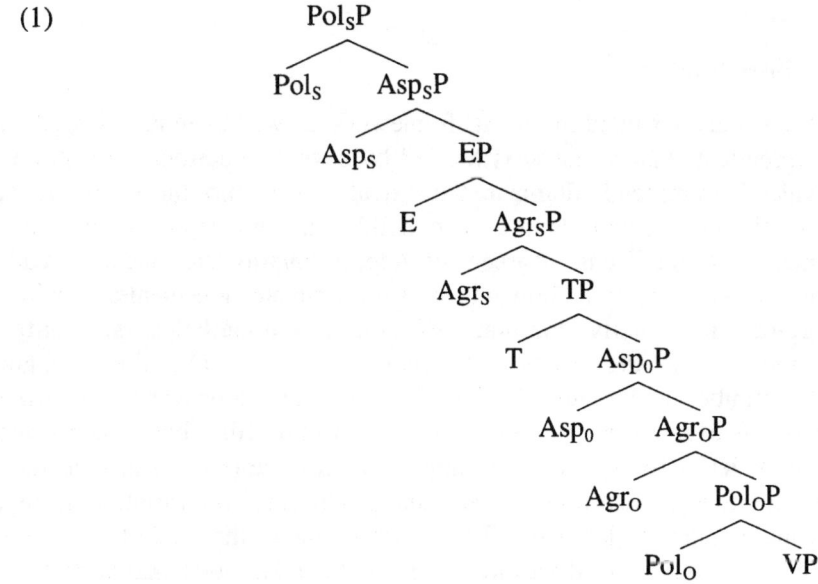

Empirically, this move would do justice to the long noted observation that CP hosts information about the truth-value of the clause. Theoretically, this move would substantially reduce the inventory of possible functional categories. In addition, it would go a long way toward constraining the projections only to those which involve clearly established grammatical cagegories, such as tense, agreement, aspect, and polarity, while eliminating the categories which are not associated with such grammatical concepts, such as CP.

Of course, this still leaves the question of EP unanswered, a rather stipulative concept, with no obvious connection to a grammatical category. While this issue will not be explored in this paper, it may indeed be possible to argue that EP is a layer of another projection, perhaps TP. If this line of reasoning is on the right track, then perhaps the number of distinct functional projections dominating VP is much more restricted than usually assumed. Perhaps there are only four such projections, with each coming in two realizations: in the subject and in the object layer of the clause: PolP, AspP, TP, and AgrP. All of these categories are well established cross-linguistically, and often have overt morphological manifestations.

It is due to these considerations that I conclude in this paper that Serbian does not offer enough independent evidence for functional projections such as Topic Phrase or Focus Phrase. It may well be, however, that other languages do. It may also be that the two projections are instances of one, corresponding to the subject vs. object layer of the clause.

Moreover, it is also suggested in this paper that each of the functional projections can "split" into two, as Chomsky (1995) suggested for VP and Radford (1997) for CP. Serbian provides evidence for at least split CP (or Pol_SP). Splitting independently motivated projections into two is a much more restrictive mechanism than proliferating various stipulative functional projections.

2. CP Layer(s)

2.1. Split CP

This section presents evidence from Serbian for a split CP projection, namely CP and cP. The outer segment, cP, hosts question formation, including *wh*-formation, while the lower segment, CP, hosts truth-conditional adverbials, as well as negative inversion in English. A clear connection between polarity of the clause and the CP layer of the clause is evident, both with Serbian adverbs and with English negative inversion. Section 2.2 explores an alternative analysis in which CP is reanalyzed as a PolP.

It is widely assumed that (at least) embedded and interrogative finite clauses are dominated by a CP projection, usually held to be the highest of the clausal projections. In English, the head C of such projection is associated with the category of complementizers, introducing embedded clauses, as well as with question formation. The same is true of Serbian. Serbian has two base-generated instantiations of C: the complementizer *da*, and the question particle *li*.

(2) Ne verujem *da* je Stefan stigao.
    not believe-1SG that AUX Stefan arrived
    'I do not believe that Stefan has arrived.'

(3) Voli *li* Stefan da putuje?
    likes Q Stefan that travels
    'Does Stefan like to travel?'

In addition to embedding and yes/no question formation, *wh*-movement is also widely held to target the CP projection as its landing site. *Wh*-movement in Serbian can target the specifier of CP, as in (4) below. It is argued in Bošković (1995, 1997, 1998) that *wh*-phrases in Serbian move to SpecCP only if the head of CP is realized, that is, if *li* is present. If true, the analysis implies that the *wh*-word is lower than CP layer in (5).

(4) Koga li je Ana videla?
    whom Q AUX Ana seen
    'Who(m) (on earth) has Ana seen?'

(5) Koga je Ana videla?
    'Who(m) has Ana seen?'

At first sight, this analysis seems also to extend to *wh*-questions formed with a *wh*-word followed by a complementizer *da*, as in (6)—(7). Thus, it appears that *da* in these cases occupies the head of CP position, while the *wh*-phrases are in the specifier position of CP.

(6) Kada da dodjem?
    When that come-1SG
    'When should I come?/When to come?'

(7) Koga da dovedem?
    whom that bring-1SG
    'Who should I bring with me?/Who to bring with me?'

The opposite order of *da* and *wh*-words is not possible, which would be consistent with the analysis. However, the following facts contradict the assumption that *wh*-words and *da* are in the same projection:

(8) ?Koga li da dovedem?
    'Whoever should I bring?'

(9) Koga ću da dovedem?
'Whom will I bring?'

If the clitics in Serbian occupy the highest functional head of the clause, as recently argued by many, including Bošković (1997), Caink (1997), Franks (1998), Progovac (1999), then the clitics in (8)—(9) would be in cP, that is in c, supported by the *wh*-word in the specifier of cP. The fact that *da* follows the clitics in (8) and (9) suggests that *da* is not in the same projection. The data provide an argument for a split CP.

There is another category in Serbian that seems to require a CP layer. A group of adverbs are obligatorily or optionally followed by the complementizer *da*, as illustrated below:

(10) Naravno   *(da)   ću   doći.
     of-course   that   will-1SG   come
     'I will certainly come.'

(11) Svakako   (da)   ću   doći.
     certainly that   will-1SG   come
     'I will certainly come.'

Their ability to take a *da* clause as their complement suggests that these adverbs can be in the specifier of CP. It may be that such adverbs are associated with C by virtue of relating to the truth-value of the clause. C is standardly assumed to be the projection that pertains to the truth-value of the clause, such as factivity, interrogative vs. declarative force, polarity, etc. Cinque (1999) has argued that each class of adverbs is associated with a distinct functional projection, and appears in the specifier of such functional projection. Thus, the conclusion that the adverbs in (10) and (11) are associated with C not only provides empirical support for Cinque's hypothesis, but also provides a rationale for the fact that this class of adverbs would be accompanied by a complementizer in Serbian.

It is also important to point out here that the clitics, italicized below, must follow the adverbial selected *da*. This is in sharp contrast to the examples of *wh*-words followed by *da* in (8) and (9).

(12) Naravno/Svakako   da   *sam*   *ga*   videla.
     of-course/certainly that AUX   him   seen
     'Of course I have seen him.'

(13) *Naravno/Svakako *sam ga* da videla.

If, indeed, second-position clitics are located in the head of the highest extended projection of V, the data above are not surprising. The clitics in (12) are in the head of the highest clausal projection; the reason why they are not in second position is the result of the unusual situation in which both the head and the specifier of this projection are overtly realized. Note that the adverbs are the integral part of the clause — there is no pause after them. (12) differs from (8)-(9) above in that (12) hosts only one CP projection, while (8)-(9) host two CP projections. This interaction with clitics strengthens the proposal that the adverb and the complementizer are in the same projection, realized as a spec and a head of that projection, respectively. Presumably, this is the CP layer.

A need for CP recursion, or for a double layer of CP, has also been noted for English. Inversion in English is triggered both by *wh*-raising and by Neg-Preposing, as illustrated below.

(14) When will he accept their offer?

(15) Under no circumstances would he accept their offer.

In both cases, the landing sites for the inverted verbs have been associated with C. Given this, examples like (16) below call for a CP-recursion analysis since they exhibit both inversion and an overt complementizer in a single clause (see e.g. Authier 1992). Radford (1997) reanalyzes CP recursion into CP split, arguing that the complementizer in (16) is in the higher segment of CP, while the inverted auxiliary and the negative phrase are in the lower segment, as represented in (17).

(16) John swore that under no circumstances would he accept their offer.

(17) John swore [$_{cP}$ that [$_{CP}$ under no circumstances [$_{C'}$ would [$_{IP}$ he accept their offer.]]]]

If the lower segment, CP, is where negation can occur in English, it may well be that CP is a PolP (see also Culicover's (1991) argument that PolP is a second complementizer-type position.) As argued in Laka (1990), a PolP is associated with either negative or positive truth-value indicators, including adverbials, such as *indeed* in English. As pointed out above, some adverbs of this type in Serbian are followed by a complementizer. If the adverbs in (10)—(11) are associated with PolP by virtue of their meaning, then identifying PolP with CP provides a rationale for the fact that this class of adverbs would be accompanied by a complementizer.

While one can certainly argue that English negative inversion and Serbian polarity adverbs occur in a projection distinct from CP, the most restrictive view of the data presented here would be that both phenomena are associated with the lower segment of CP. This would be the most restrictive view for the following reasons. Empirically, it would allow one to say that Serbian *da* only occurs in C heads, whether C or c, and that English inversion only targets C heads, C or c; c in the case of *wh*-inversion, and C in the case of negative inversion. Theoretically, if split functional projections are allowed in principle, then it is best to make use of this mechanism, rather than to introduce an ad hoc projection. Third, it has been long noted or assumed that the complementizer layer of the clause is somehow associated with the truth-value of the clause. The following section explores the possibility that CP itself is a PolP.

2.2 An Alternative to CP

Given the connection between the CP layer of the clause and its polarity, it was argued in the previous section that the lower segment of CP may in fact be a PolP. This connection is established by the argument that Serbian adverbs of assertion appear in this position, as well as the English negative inversion. One may wonder, however, why one layer of CP would be related to polarity, but not the other. Perhaps both layers of CP can be reanalyzed as layers of a PolP. More precisely, cP would correspond to polP, while the CP layer would correspond to PolP. The outer segment, polP, would then be associated with *wh*-movement and question formation in general, in both Serbian and English, while the inner layer, PolP, would host negative inversion in English and truth-conditional adverbials in Serbian, as follows:

(18)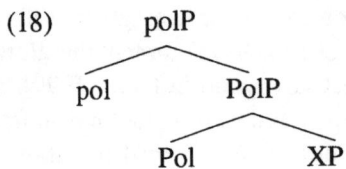

This raises (at least) three questions. The first question has to do with the position of regular clausal negation and the need for yet another PolP much lower in the tree. The second question is what evidence there is that the question layer of the clause should be in the same projection as the polarity layer of the clause. Finally, the question remains as to what advantage there is to treating CP as PolP, as opposed to leaving it as a separate CP projection.

To address the first question, there is a clear need for a PolP much lower in the tree, in both English and Serbian, namely the phrase in which regular negation occurs:

(19) John does not understand the question.

(20) Jovan ne razume pitanje.
Jovan not understands question

Zanuttini (1991) adopted a NegP for the analysis of negation in Italian, while Brown (1996) adopted it for Russian. In Progovac (in preparation) the NegP analysis is also adopted for negation in Serbian. In other words, there are two positions in which negation can occur: before the subject, as in (15), and after the subject, as in (19)—(20). On analogy with AgrPs, I propose that these two projections associated with polarity are Pol_SP and Pol_OP, i.e., subject and object PolPs, respectively, as represented in (21). Pol_OP is what has traditionally been called NegP, and Pol_SP is what has traditionally been called PolP.

(21)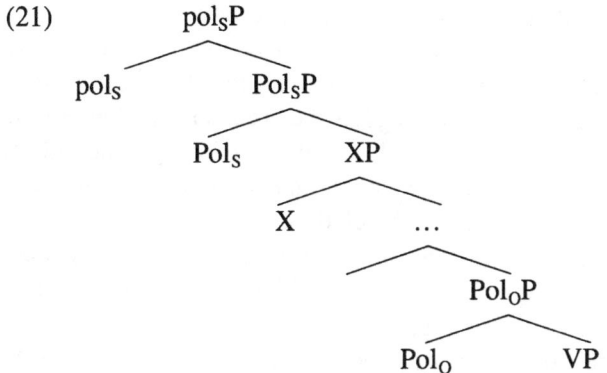

Still, one would wonder what motivates the object/subject sub-labels on the two PolPs. Motivation for Agr_OP (and, as will be argued in section 5 motivation for Asp_OP) stems from its association with the accusative case marking of the internal argument. In fact, like agreement (and aspect), negation also seems to have a connection with case. The so-called genitive of negation in Slavic may be a case in point. For example, in Russian, "genitive of negation" is optionally assigned to the object of a transitive verb (22), as discussed in Brown (1996):

(22) a. Ja   ne   čitaju   žurnalov.
        I   NEG   read   magazines-GEN
        'I don't read (any) magazines.'
     b. Ja   ne   čitaju   žurnaly.
        I   NEG   read   magazines-ACC
        'I don't read magazines.'

Although genitive of negation would not be grammatical in Serbian in the examples illustrated above, Serbian also shows some case sensitivity to negation in existential constructions, such as:

(23) a. Nema   Marije.
        NEG-has Maria-GEN
        'Maria is not there/not coming.'
     b. *Nema   Mariju
        NEG-has Maria-ACC
     c. *Ima   Marije.
        Has   Mary-GEN

Brown (1996) argues that NegP is directly involved in case checking of the genitive case feature. Brown's analysis provides an argument for positioning NegP below AspP or AgrP. The fact that PolP can actually assign case to the internal argument makes the argument for Pol$_o$P more credible. In this paper, I do not address the possibility that indirect objects may also have their own agreement projections, as pointed out by Tracy King. I leave this for future research to resolve.

The second question to address is the connection between polarity and the question layer of the clause: why should they be in split segments of a single projection, as opposed to in two distinct projections? It seems to me that there are both empirical and theoretical advantages to this move. The arguments are the same as those pointed out for split CP. Empirically, there is a real connection between the two positions in both English and Serbian. In Serbian, the complementizer *da* can appear in either position. If this is a single projection, then the distribution of *da* is captured in a uniform way: *da* occurs in a single projection, although in either split segment of this projection. The same rationale holds for English inversion, which would target one single projection, although either split segment of this projection: the outer segment for *wh*-inversion and the inner segment for negative inversion. Theoretically, as pointed out above, it is more economical to have a single projection and allow it to split into two segments, than to allow two distinct projections. Conceptually, there is no hard-and-fast evidence that CP and PolP are distinct.

The third question is "Why PolP, and not CP?" First, while polarity is a clear and well-defined grammatical concept, with overt morphological manifestations probably in every language, "complementizing" is not. Moreover, it is clear that (at least) one segment of this projection has to do with polarity, since it hosts negative inversion and affirmative adverbials. However, even question formation has a connection to the truth-conditions of the clause. In the next section, I argue that *wh*-phrases have a polarity feature that they check in a PolP (see also Progovac, in preparation). This feature arguably explains the positive presuppositions of *wh*-questions, as well as providing a rationale for *wh*-fronting of non-initial *wh*-phrases, which do not go to the top layer of CP.

2.3. The Wh/Polarity Connection

Serbian word order provides subtle support for the neg-raising analysis of *n*-words (cf. Zanuttini (1991) and Brown (1996)). As shown in Progovac (in preparation), overt raising of *n*-words occurs in Serbian (24)—(25). The unmarked order for an *n*-word is preverbal, that is, before negation, as in (24a), while (24b) is somewhat emphatic. On the other hand, the unmarked word order for an object is otherwise postverbal, as illustrated in (25b), *Mariju* in (25a) being interpreted as a topic.

(24) a. On *nikoga* ne voli.
    he no-one neg loves
    'He loves no one.'
  b. ?On ne voli *nikoga*.

(25) a. ?On *Mariju* ne voli.
    he Mary not loves
    'He does not love Mary.'
  b. On ne voli *Mariju*.
    he not loves Mary

This would follow if *n*-words raise to a projection which is higher than where objects otherwise go; for example NegP can be above VP or Agr$_o$P (but see Brown (1996) for different ordering).

However, it is not only *n*-words that show this kind of word order pattern. Other words associated with polarity show similar behavior, such as positive polarity items (PPIs), as in (26), and negative polarity items (*i*-NPIs), as in (27); see Progovac (1994) and references therein for discussion of PPIs and *i*-NPIs in Serbian:

(26) a. On je *nekoga* uvredio.
    he AUX someone insulted
    'He hurt somebody's feelings.'
  b. ?On je uvredio *nekoga*.

(27) a. Da li je on *ikoga* uvredio?
    that Q AUX he anyone insulted
    'Did he hurt anybody's feelings?'
  b. ?Da li je on uvredio *ikoga*?

In Progovac (in preparation) I argue that the raising analysis for *n*-words extends to PPIs and *i*-NPIs as well. This can only be possible if polarity features other than negation are also checked in this projection. Very roughly, the argument is that *n*-words have [+neg] features, PPIs [−neg] features, and *i*-NPIs in Serbian [−neg, −pos] features. Moreover, the scope restrictions on PPIs and *i*-NPIs suggest that their features can be checked in a PolP higher than NegP, providing a strong argument for two polarity phrases.

It is well known that *wh*-words contribute positive presuppositions to *wh*-questions, that is, they presuppose the existence of the event, as well as of the participants in the event:

(28) When did Peter ask Mary out?
(Presupposition: Peter asked Mary out sometime.)

(29) Who told Peter about the party?
(Presupposition: Someone told Peter about the party.)

Suppose then that the *wh*-words come with a corresponding polarity feature, say [−neg], as argued for PPIs or indefinites, which is then necessarily checked in a PolP. This conclusion is reinforced by the fact that *wh*-words can be used as indefinites in Serbian (cf. also Chinese, Japanese, Korean), as also pointed out in Citko (1998).

(30) Da   li   je   on   *koga*   uvredio?
     that Q   AUX he   whom   insulted
     'Has he insulted someone?'

This analysis would thus explain the requirement on *wh*-words to raise, whether or not they ultimately go to SpecCP. If on the right track, this analysis provides a rather straightforward rationale for the *wh*/polarity connection.

This section thus provides an argument that there are two PolPs in a clause, $Pol_S P$ and $Pol_O P$. The former is higher in the tree, and subsumes what was CP. The latter is lower in the tree, and is essentially the NegP of the previous accounts.

3. Agr$_S$ and Agr$_O$

Serbian provides morphological evidence for two agreement phrases in the clause, one in which the subject checks its nominative feature, or Agr$_S$P, and another in which the object checks its accusative feature, or Agr$_O$P. Moreover, an argument is made for a split Agr$_S$P based on the split subject agreement facts.

3.1 Agr$_S$ Phrase

Agr$_S$ is a projection assumed to have two basic roles: to check agreement features on the verb and to check Nominative case on the subject. It is commonly accepted that the [Agr$_S$,T] amalgam checks nominative Case; see e.g. Chomsky 1995.

Subject agreement in Serbian targets three features: person, number, and gender. While any tense, whether simple or complex, exhibits person/number agreement, only complex tenses formed with past participles also show gender agreement. In fact, the participle shows gender and number agreement, while the auxiliary shows person and number agreement, which means that number is checked twice. This is illustrated in the following examples:

(31) Ja   sam   peva-la / peva-o.
     I   AUX-1SG   sung-SGF / sung-SGM
     'I sang.'

(32) Mi   smo   peva-le/peva-li.
     we   AUX-1PL   sung-PLF/sung-PLM
     'We sang.'

Since in both cases agreement is with the subject, we are dealing with a "split" case of subject agreement, in a rather literal sense of the word. One may speculate that participle agreement is checked in a split version of Agr$_S$P. If so, the main segment of Agr$_S$P would check person/number agreement on the auxiliary, while the split segment, agr$_S$P, would check gender/number agreement on the participle. That subject agreement can surface on two different verbal categories is a powerful argument for a split Agr$_S$P.

If, indeed, the participle is specified for subject agreement, it will have to raise to Agr$_S$P to check these features, which will in turn enable the participle to support the clitics. Bošković (1997) has argued, based on data as in (33), that participles adjoin to the auxiliary verb.

(33) Odgovorio je   Milen-i.
     answered   AUX   Milena-DAT
    'He answered Milena.'

I interpret this movement in the following way, however: the auxiliary moves into the main segment of Agr_SP, in which person/number features are checked. On the other hand, the participle moves into the split segment, agr_SP, where gender/number features are checked. This analysis provides motivation for participle movement in terms of feature checking, which is in the spirit of the minimalist program.

In sum, Serbian data make a case for a split Agr_S projection. Subject agreement in Serbian can surface in two distinct places in the clause, namely, on the first auxiliary (person/number agreement), and on the participle (gender/number agreement). I briefly return to Agr_S in Section 3.2, where I argue that the reflexive pronoun *se*, typically associated with Agr_O, can also occupy the Agr_S position in impersonal sentences in Serbian.

3.2 Agr_O Phrase

According to Chomsky 1995, verbs that have the feature [+Case] will check this feature in the [Agr_O,V] amalgam. The Case associated with Agr_O is the accusative Case. Objects move from their base-generated position to the specifier position of Agr_OP to check their accusative features. This renders accusative and nominative feature checking essentially parallel: they are both achieved by movement, and they are both achieved through Spec/Head agreement in a functional projection — an Agr phrase.

One piece of evidence for the Agr_O projection in Serbian comes from Bošković (1995). He argues that the scope possibilities in the following examples can only be accounted for if one assumes that the object moves to a projection higher than VP:

(34) Jovan je   namerno   dvaput   oborio   Petra.
     John   AUX on-purpose   twice   failed   Peter
    'John failed Peter on purpose twice.'

(35) Jovan je   oborio Petra namerno   dvaput.
     John   AUX   failed Peter on-purpose twice
     'John failed Peter on purpose twice.'

In (34), the adverbs are to the left of VP, and the adverb *namerno* necessarily takes wide scope with respect to *dvaput*. On the other hand, (35) is ambiguous. Bošković argues that this ambiguity can only be derived if one assumes that the adverbs in (35) are either to the left or the right of VP. More specifically, on the reading on which the adverbs are still to the left of VP, it must be that the object (and the verb) have moved out of VP. The most natural assumption would then be that the object has moved into Agr_O, where it checks its accusative case.

The second argument for Agr_O comes from the analysis of the reflexive clitic *se* in Serbian as an Agr_O pronoun, checking accusative Case (see Franks 1995, Progovac 1998a). Progovac 1998a makes an additional claim that *se* is an expletive pronoun, whose sole purpose is to check Case, and that it is neither reflexive nor referential. If indeed *se* checks accusative Case, then any internal argument will have to check its Case against Agr_S, thus giving rise to reflexive (36), reciprocal (37), null-object (38), or passive interpretations (39), as illustrated below:

(36) Milan   se   brije.
     Milan   SE   shaves
     'Milan is shaving.'

(37) Deca   se   tuku.
     children SE   hit
     'The children are hitting each other.'

(38) Milan   se   udara.
     Milan   SE   hits
     'Milan is hitting (someone/me).'

(39) Deca   se   grle.
     children SE   hug.
     'One hugs children.'

In fact, given the right pragmatics, a single sentence can be multiply ambiguous, exhibiting any of these readings:

(39') Deca se grle.
'The children are hugging ?themselves/ each other/ somebody else. / One hugs children.'

This supports the conclusion that *se* is neither referential nor reflexive. It is also not associated with any particular theta-role. All it does is eliminate one argument, whether external or internal. The remaining argument is then understood as either internal (passive interpretation) or external argument (a range of other interpretations). If the subject is interpreted as the external argument, it seems that all logical possibilities are exhausted for the internal argument: the subject can perform the (transitive) action on itself (reflexive), or it can be a reciprocal action if the subject is plural, or it can just be an action performed on another person (null object). This last option is most natural in a situation in which the object of action is salient in discourse, for example the person speaking, or some other person present. An expletive analysis of *se*, according to which *se* is only responsible for checking the accusative feature of the verb, captures the data in a unified and straightforward way.

Se can also be argued to occupy the only Agr projection in a clause with verbs that take only one argument. In that case, the sole argument does not surface at all, and the verb is default third person singular neuter, even though the implied agent is plural. These are so-called "impersonal constructions:"

(40) Plesalo   se   sve do   zore.
     danced-3rd-Sg-N SE   all till dawn
     'One danced until dawn.'

I assume with Laka (1993), Uriagereka (1995), and Chomsky (1995) that, when there is only one argument in a clause, its AgrP is just one general AgrP, unspecified for either Subject or Object agreement. This would imply that *se* can check the case feature of an AgrP that is not specifically an Agr$_S$P.[1] This flexibility would not be entirely surprising in an expletive pronoun. The English expletive *there*, which typically checks nominative case, is also grammatical as a subject in Exceptional Case Marking (ECM) constructions, which check accusative case:

(41) **There** seems to be a problem with expletives.

(42) I consider *there* to be many problems with expletives.

(43) *She* seems to be a problem.

(44) I consider *her* to be a problem.

If the analysis of *se* is on the right track, then *se* provides direct morphological evidence for the Agr$_O$P projection.

4. Event Phrase

In Progovac (1998b, 1998b) I argue that the clausal demonstrative *to* in Serbian (45) heads an Event Phrase (EP), between CP and TP (for Event Phrase as a syntactic projection see e.g. Borer 1994, Travis 1997, Cowper 1997, and Rosen and Ritter 1997).

(45) *To*   Novak   pliva.
     that   Novak   swims
     'That is (the event of) Novak swimming./What you see/witness is (evidence) that Novak is swimming.'

To shows the same range of functions shown by pronouns referring to individuals: demonstrative (as illustrated above), anaphoric, and bound-variable functions (see Progovac 1998b). The purpose of this section is to establish that a functional projection, located between CP and TP, is necessary to accommodate the distribution of *to*.

---

[1] Notice that some dialects of Croatian, as discussed in Franks (1995), allow *se* to check nominative case even when there are clearly two Agr projections:

(i) %Jede   se   kola«ce.
    eats   SE   cakes-ACC
    'Cakes are eaten.'

One can assume with Franks (1995) that *se* in (i) absorbs nominative, leaving accusative available for checking by the object. I do not know why this strategy is marked in Slavic. It may be that *se* originally had an inherent accusative feature, since it is historically the clitic form of the accusative reflexive.

First of all, *to* appears in a fixed and well-defined structural position, which seems to be located right below CP. Thus *wh*-words and question particles necessarily precede *to*:

(46) a. Ko   *to*   (tamo)   peva?
        who   that   there   sings
        'Who is singing over there?'
     b.   ?*To ko tamo peva?

(47) a. Da   li   *to*   Tea   pere   zube?
        that   Q   that   Tea   washes   teeth
        'Is that Tea brushing her teeth?'
     b.   *To da li Tea pere zube?

In addition, *to* is necessarily preverbal:

(48)   *Tea pere *to* zube.

(49)   *Tea pere zube *to*.

These facts are captured by placing *to* in a distinct functional projection located between CP and TP. In its demonstrative use, *to* basically has a function of pointing to a scene/situation which is described by the sentence, or to evidence of such a situation. According to Ivić (1983, 127), "adding such a *to* in a sentence has as its goal to emphasize/highlight the actuality of what the sentence reports on" (my translation).

I tentatively assume that the projection in which *to* is generated is distinct from any other projection, and call it EP, but I leave open the possibility that this projection may be a split counterpart of another independently needed projection, such as TP.

The need for a Tense Phrase (TP) is well established in the minimalist and pre-minimalist syntactic literature. It is widely assumed that TP is situated somewhere below Agr_SP but above Agr_OP. The data in Serbian are consistent with this assumption and I will not present further arguments here.

5. Aspect Phrase(s)

This section explores the following basic analysis of Aspect in Serbian, consistent with the grammaticalization of aspect envisioned in Rosen and Ritter (1997). Aspect involves grammatical features checked in the functional projections of the clause. Serbian can be analyzed as involving two such aspect projections: Asp_OP and Asp_SP. Asp_OP checks the features of aspectual prefixes, which render the verb perfective. All prefixes will check the [+delimit] feature of Asp_OP. In addition, completion prefixes will also check the feature [+completed]; [+completed] feature is tightly linked to the transitivity of the verb, as completion is associated with Asp_OP, according to Rosen and Ritter (1997). Arguably, the [+completed] feature on Asp_OP selects an Agr_OP, rendering the clause transitive. To accommodate multiple prefixation, which is possible in Serbian, one can argue that Asp_OP can have split segments, each accommodating one prefix.

On the other hand, the Asp_SP is argued to check the features of the aspectual suffixes, such as *iva*. The feature of *iva* is comparable to that of universal quantification, rendering the aspect iterative, occuring on repeated occasions, and thus imperfective. Since this kind of quantification is possible only with "countable" events, the suffixes can only attach to perfective verbs, whether derived or underived.

5.1. Perfective Prefixes and Imperfective Suffixes

Serbian is traditionally described as having two basic aspects, Perfective and Imperfective, the former denoting a completed action, and the latter denoting other types of actions. Imperfective actions can be roughly classified into durative (lasting for a certain period of time), as in (50), and iterative (repeated in certain intervals), as in (51).

(50) Milena peva. (Durative)
 Milena sings
 'Milena is singing./Milena sings.'

(51) Mesec svetluca na nebu. (Iterative)
 moon twinkles on sky
 'The moon is twinkling in the sky.'

On the other hand, Perfective shows three basic sub-types, according to Mrazović and Vukadinović (1990). It can be used for a momentarily completed action (52), for the initiation of action (53), and for the completion of action (54).

(52) Saša   mi   je   dao   knjigu.   (Momentary)
     Saša   me-DAT   AUX   given   book
     'Saša gave me a book.'

(53) Zapevao   je   iz   sveg   glasa.   (Initiation)
     sung   AUX   from   all   voice
     'He started singing in full voice.'

(54) Otpevao   je   celu   pesmu.   (Completion)
     sung   AUX   whole   song
     'He has sung the whole song.'

If a prefix is added to an imperfective verb, it changes the aspect to perfective, as illustrated in (53) and (54).

Prefixes are not purely grammatical/inflectional affixes, given that they also contribute substantially to the meaning of the root in ways that are unpredictable. Also, unlike the imperfective suffixes discussed below, which can only attach to perfective verbs, the perfective prefixes can attach to either perfective or imperfective verbs. It is only with the latter that they trigger a change in aspect. I am assuming that a prefix comes with the specification [+delimit], which implies a delimitation of the boundaries of an action (Rosen and Ritter 1997). An action can be delimited by bounding the beginning of the action (inception prefixes) or by bounding the end of the action (completion prefixes).

The function of completion prefixes is reminiscent of the completion particles in English, such as *up*. In fact, just as is the case with the completion prefixes in Serbian (see next section), the use of the particle *up* renders the predicate necessarily transitive (except in imperatives, as noted by Tracy King, personal communication):

(55) John ate (his dinner).

(56) John ate up his dinner.

(57) *John ate up.

On the other hand, the sole function of imperfective suffixes seems to be to change the aspect from perfective to imperfective. In fact, such suffixes can be added to inherently imperfective verbs only if they have first been transformed into perfective verbs by prefixation, as evident from the following contrast:

(58)   pisati   *pis*iv*ati

(59)   ispisati   ispis*iv*ati

One can assume that suffixes such as *iva* come with a quantificational feature of universal quantification, such as *every/many/several*. This feature is in turn checked in Asp_SP. If indeed quantificational, such suffixes need to take scope over a perfective characterization of a verb, over which they quantify, explaining why they need to be in a projection higher than Asp_OP.

5.2. Perfective and Transitivity

A rather unexpected property of most perfective prefixes is that they have a consistent effect on the transitivity of the verb (the exception are prefixes of inception). More precisely, perfective prefixes seem to have two grammatical functions: (i) to change aspect from imperfective to perfective, and (ii) to enforce transitivity on the verb. Thus, an intransitive verb like *spavati* (60) becomes necessarily transitive through prefixation (cf. the ungrammaticality of (63)), and the accusative feature is then either checked by the Agr_O expletive *se*, as in (61), or by the direct object, as in (62):

(60)   Jovan   je   spavao.
       Jovan   AUX   slept
       'Jovan slept.'

(61)   Jovan   se   naspavao.
       Jovan   SE   on-slept.
       'John has slept to his heart's content.'

(62)   Jovan   je   prespavao   doručak.
       Jovan   AUX   over-slept   breakfast
       'John slept through breakfast.'

(63) *Jovan je prespavao/naspavao.

There is thus a clear connection between perfectivity and the transitivity of the verb. Rosen and Ritter 1997 make a syntactic connection between aspectual prefixes and the valency of the verb. They argue that Perfective is associated with completion, with object, and thus with Asp_OP; on the other hand, Imperfective is associated with initiation of action, with subject, and thus with Asp_SP.

One exception to this general claim are the Aktionsart prefixes, which are associated with the initiation of the event. Even though such prefixes change the aspect into perfective, they do not transitivize the verb. All three verbs in the examples below can be used intransitively, whether prefixed or not.

(64) *za*pevati   (start singing)

(65) *pro*govoriti   (start talking)

(66) *po*trčati   (start running)

One possibility is to claim that these prefixes are not associated with Asp_OP, but perhaps with Asp_SP. This move, however, would have two undesirable consequences. First, it would do away with the otherwise elegant generalization that aspectual prefixes check their features in Asp_OP, while aspectual suffixes check their features in Asp_SP. Next, it would also undermine the claim that Asp_SP is associated with the quantificational side of aspect — inception prefixes are not characterizable in terms of quantification. The other possibility would be that even these affixes check their features in Asp_OP, but that the features to be checked are different. Notice that the inception prefixes, unlike the transitivizing prefixes, do not imply completion of the event, but rather only completion of inception. Suppose now that the difference between transitivizing prefixes, such as *pre* in (62), and inception prefixes, such as *za* in (64) is the following: the former prefixes check the feature [+completed], while the latter check the feature [–completed]. If we assume that both [+completed] and [–completed] features imply the feature [+delimit], then we would be able to explain why prefixation yields perfective aspect. As already established, delimitation with transitivizing prefixes affects the completion end of the event. On the other hand, with inception prefixes, the delimitation affects the initiation boundary of the event. I will assume that the feature [+completed] selects an Agr_OP, whose Case feature in turn needs to be checked, rendering the construction transitive.

I adopt this basic analysis for the following reasons. First, it can capture the relationship between valency and completed aspect by making a single assumption that the feature [+completed] on Asp_O selects an Agr_OP. Next, it can capture the fact that there are two basic types of aspect in Serbian and in other languages: perfective and imperfective. In addition, this dual representation of aspect comes at no theoretical cost — other projections have also been argued to have such dual manifestations, notably AgrPs. Next, this analysis allows a quantificational analysis of iterative aspect by associating quantificational suffixes with Asp_SP. This projection is structurally higher than Asp_OP, allowing quantificational suffixes to take scope over the aspectual properties of Asp_OP. Admittedly, this is only a sketch of an analysis that needs to be researched in much more detail.

6. Other Phrases

There have also been proposals for additional functional categories in Serbian, such as Topic Phrase and Focus Phrase. As for TopP, consider the following examples discussed in Tomić (1995):

(67) Mariju,   da   li   ste   videli?
    Maria-ACC that Q   AUX   seen
    'As for Maria, have you seen her?'

(68) Mariju,   molići   lepo,   da   li   ste   videli?
    Maria-ACC please   nicely   that Q   AUX   seen
    'As for Maria, please, have you seen her?'

(69) Noću,   ko   bi   ovde   došao?
    at-night who   would   here   come
    'At night, who would come here?'

The examples illustrate that topicalized phrases can appear at the very beginning of the clause, even higher than *wh*-phrases, as in (69). In a rather obvious sense, a position exists that accommodates these phrases. There are two possibilities here. First, one can assume that there is another functional projection above CP, say TopP, to which topicalized phrases move. This is the course taken in Tomić (1995). Another possibility is to assume that these topicalized phrases are adjoined to CP, as suggested for examples like (69) in Progovac (1993). Both approaches have virtues and problems. The problem with assuming a separate functional projection for topicalized constituents is that there is no morphological or other independent evidence for such a projection, at least not in Serbian. To put it another way, there is no well established morphological category that such a projection would instantiate. On the other hand, assuming an adjunction to CP in these cases is rather ad hoc and unexplanatory.

As for the Focus Phrase, non-initial fronted *wh*-words in Serbian are sometimes taken to target such a position. Rudin (1988) observes that there are two positions for *wh*-words in Serbian, as well as in some other Slavic languages. The first *wh*-word enjoys a special status in that it is the only one that can support clitics:

(70) Ko   je   (prvi) koga   udario?   (Rudin 1988)
      who   AUX   (first) whom   hit
      'Who hit whom (first)?'

(71) *Ko koga je (prvi) udario?

There is growing consensus that the first *wh*-word occurs in a structurally higher position, say SpecCP (although not always SpecCP for Bošković (1997, 1998)). The rest of the *wh*-phrases, which are also preposed from their original base positions, are then placed in a lower functional projection. What exactly this position is remains controversial. Rudin argues that this is an IP-adjoined position. Stjepanović (1995) and Bošković (1996, 1997, 1998) argue that *wh*-movement in SC is Focus Fronting in the sense that all *wh*-words move to check a focus feature. For Bošković (1998), the focus features are checked in AgrPs. These approaches do not necessarily require an additional functional projection to be generated, such as Focus Phrase. However, they both raise a question. Rudin's analysis raises the question of the motivation for movement to an IP-adjoined position. While this particular requirement is met in Stjepanović (1995) and Bošković (1998), that is, the feature checking motivation, it is still not clear why AgrPs would be the ones to check the focus feature. It is also not entirely clear if *wh*-phrases have such a feature.

Citko (1998) argues that non-initial *wh*-phrases reside in a separate functional projection, the Operator Phrase (OpP), located below C. Presumably, this is the position where all operators check their operator features. While this seems to be the right insight, it is not clear what an "operator" feature is, other than something to force raising, which renders the analysis circular. As argued in section 2.3, the *wh*-data can be captured without a new projection if Citko's OpP is my PolP.

In sum, I conclude that there is no hard-and-fast evidence for either a Topic Phrase or a Focus Phrase, at least not in Serbian. However, future research or evidence from other languages may prove otherwise.

7. Concluding Remarks

The following functional projections are argued to constitute an extended projection of the verb in Serbian: Pol_SP (once CP), Asp_SP, EP (Event Phrase), Agr_SP, TP, Asp_OP, Agr_OP, Pol_OP (once NegP).

There is growing evidence that projections can be split (cf. split VP of Chomsky 1995 and split CP of Radford 1997). This paper provides further evidence from Serbian for split CP, which has here been rethought as a Polarity Phrase, Pol_SP. An argument is also made for split Agr_SP, to accommodate two types of subject agreement marking in Serbian: person/number agreement, surfacing on finite forms, and gender/number agreement, surfacing on participle forms. Some of the projections indicated above may be reducible to a split counterpart of another — for example, TP and EP may be split versions of a single projection. Moreover, this paper builds a case for an argument that all clausal functional projections come in two counterparts: a subject and an object phrase. The object phrase, whether it be Agr_OP, Asp_OP, or Pol_OP, seems to have a connection with objective case marking.

A re-thinking of the inventory of functional projections in this way may lead to a more restrictive and elegant theory of UG. The tension between the need to accommodate a wealth of cross-linguistic data by appealing to new functional projections, and the need to keep UG restrictive, can be alleviated by allowing each projection to have two basic manifestations, an object phrase, and a subject phrase, as well as a split counterpart. At the same time, the inventory of functional projections should be restricted to well-established morpho-syntactic categories only, such as Tense, Agreement, Polarity, Aspect. This paper should be taken as a sketch for such a program.

References

Authier, J.-Marc. 1992. Iterated CPs and embedded topicalization. *Linguistic Inquiry* 23.2, 329-336.
Borer, Hagit. 1994. The projection of arguments. In E. Benedicto and J. Runner, eds, *Functional Projections*. University of Massachusetts Occasional Papers 17, GLSA, UMass, Amherst.
Bošković, Željko. 1995. Participle movement and second position cliticization in Serbo-Croatian. *Lingua* 96, 245-266.
Bošković, Željko. 1998. *Wh*-phrases and *wh*-movement in Slavic. Paper presented at the Comparative Slavic Morphosyntax workshop, held at McCormick's Creek State Park, Indiana.
Bošković, Željko. 2000. Second position cliticization: Syntax and/or Phonology? In Frits Beukema and Marcel Den Dikken, eds., *Clitic Systems in Eastern Central Europe*, 71-119. John Benjamins, Amsterdam.
Brown, Sue. 1996. *The Syntax of Negation in Russian*. Ph.D. Dissertation, Indiana University, Bloomington. A revised version published in 1999 as *The Syntax of negation in Russian: A Minimalist approach*. CSLI Publications, Stanford. [*Stanford Monographs in Linguistics*.]
Caink, Andrew. 1997. Extended projections in South Slavic. Paper presented at the Second Conference on Formal Approaches to South Slavic Languages (FASSL 2), Sofia, Bulgaria.
Chomsky, Noam. 1991. Some notes on economy of derivation and representation. In Robert Freidin, ed., *Principles and Parameters in Comparative Grammar*, 417-454. The MIT Press, Cambridge, MA.
Chomsky, Noam. 1995. *The Minimalist Program*. The MIT Press, Cambridge, MA.
Cinque, Guglielmo. 1999. *Adverbs and Functional Heads: A Cross-Linguistic Perspective*. Oxford University Press, Oxford.
Citko, Barbara. 1998. On multiple *WH* movement in Slavic. In Željko Bošković, Steven Franks and William Snyder, eds, *Formal*

Approaches to Slavic Linguistics: The Connecticut Meeting 1997, 97-113. Michigan Slavic Publications, Ann Arbor.

Cowper, Elizabeth. 1997. Grammatical aspect in English. Paper presented at the Events as Grammatical Objects Workshop, LSA Institute, Cornell Univeristy, Ithaca, New York.

Culicover, Peter. 1991. Topicalization, inversion, and complementizers in English. Manuscript, The Ohio State University, Columbus.

Franks, Steven. 1995. *Parameters of Slavic Syntax*. Oxford University Press, Oxford.

Franks, Steven. 1998. Clitics in Slavic. Position paper for Comparative Slavic Morphosyntax workshop, held at McCormick's Creek State Park, Indiana.

Ivić, Milka. 1983. Iskazivanje direktnog objekta u (standardnom) srpskohrvatskom. In Ivan Čolović, ed, *Lingvistički Ogledi*, 115-138. Prosveta, Beograd.

Laka, Itziar. 1990. *Negation in Syntax: On the Nature of Functional Categories and Projections*. Ph.D. dissertation, MIT, Cambridge, MA.

Laka, Itziar. 1993. Unergatives that assign ergative, unaccusatives that assign accusative. Manuscript, University of Rochester, New York.

Mrazović, Pavica, and Zora Vukadinović. 1990. *Gramatika srpskohrvatskog jezika za strance*. Dobra Vest, Novi Sad.

Progovac, Ljiljana. 1993. Clitics in Serbian/Croatian: Comp as the second position. Presented at the Workshop on Second Position Clitics at the LSA Linguistics Institute, Columbus, Ohio; published in Aaron L. Halpern and Arnold Zwicky, eds, *Approaching Second: Second Position Clitics and Related Phenomena*, 1996, 411-428. CSLI Publications, Stanford, California.

Progovac, Ljiljana. 1994. *Negative and Positive Polarity: A Binding Approach*. Cambridge University Press, Cambridge.

Progovac, Ljiljana. 1998a. Events in Serbian. In Mila Dimitrova-Vulchanova, Lars Hellan, Ivan Kasabov, and Ilyana Krapova, eds, *Papers from Second Conference on Formal Approaches to South Slavic Linguistics, Sofia 1997*, 79-116. University of Trondheim Working Papers in Linguistics, Norway.

Progovac, Ljiljana. 1998b. Event pronominal *to*. *Journal of Slavic Linguistics* 6.1, 3-39.

Progovac, Ljiljana. 1999. Eventive *to* and the placement of clitics in Serbo-Croatian. In István Kenesei, ed., *Crossing Boundaries: Advances in the Theory of Central and Eastern European Languages*, 33-44. John Benjamins, Amsterdam/ Philadelphia.

Progovac, Ljiljana. In preparation. Negative and positive feature checking and the distribution of polarity items. In Sue Brown and Adam Przepiórkowski, eds., *Negation in Slavic*. Slavica Publishers, Ann Arbor.

Radford, Andrew. 1997. *Syntactic Theory and the Structure of English: A Minimalist Approach*. Cambridge University Press, Cambridge. [*Cambridge Textbooks in Linguistics*.]

Rosen, Sara, and Elizabeth Ritter. 1997. Ergativity and event structure. Paper presented at the Events as Grammatical Objects Workshop, LSA Institute, Cornell Univeristy, Ithaca, New York.

Rudin, Catherine. 1988. On multiple questions and multiple *wh*-fronting. *Natural Language and Linguistic Theory* 6.4, 445-501.

Stjepanović, Sandra. 1995. Short-distance movement of *wh*-phrases in Serbo-Croatian matrix clauses. Manuscript, University of Connecticut, Storrs.

Tomić, Olga Mišeska. 1995. Conditions on topicalization. Paper presented at ESSE/3, Glasgow.

Travis, Lisa. 1997. What it takes to make event structure syntactic. Paper presented at the Events as Grammatical Objects Workshop, LSA Institute, Cornell Univeristy, Ithaca, New York.

Uriagereka, Juan. 1995. Aspects of the syntax of clitic placement in Western Romance. *Linguistic Inquiry* 26.1, 79-123.

Zanuttini, Raffaella. 1991. *Syntactic Properties of Sentential Negation. A Comparative Study of Romance Languages*. Ph.D. dissertation, University of Pennsylvania. A revised version published in 1997 as *Negation and Clausal Structure: A Comparative Study of Romance Languages*. Oxford University Press, Oxford.

Wayne State University
English Department
51 W. Warren
Detroit, MI 48202
l.progovac@wayne.edu

Case and Agreement in Polish Predicates[*]

Adam Przepiórkowski
Ohio State University/Polish Academy of Sciences

In a recent paper, Bailyn and Citko (1999) propose an analysis of case marking of predicative phrases in Russian and, to a lesser extent, in Polish. The principles given in (1)–(2) below, which rely on the presence of the Pred(ication) functional head (Bowers 1993), constitute the pivotal part of that analysis.

(1) **Universal C:** $Pred^0$ has strong Case features (instrumental in Polish).

(2) **Morphological Pred Rule:** Overt morphology in $Pred^0$ absorbs Instrumental Case.

According to these principles, *za* in (3) below, being an overt realization of $Pred^0$, absorbs the instrumental strong Case features, so the only way for the predicative NP *student-* to receive case is to raise to a position in which it may agree in case with the NP being predicated of, namely, *go*.

(3) Uważam go   za studenta / *studentem.
    I-consider him$_{ACC}$ as student$_{ACC}$ / student
    'I consider him (as) a student.'

In brief, the accusative case on the predicative NP *studenta* is the result of agreement with the NP *go*.[1]

The aim of the present paper is twofold. The first, relatively minor aim is to conclusively show that the accusative case on the predicative

---

[*] I wish to thank Steven Franks, Tracy Holloway King and the audience of FASL 2000 for their comments and support.

[1] To be more precise, it is the result of the predicative NP raising to a position close enough to that of *go* so that both NPs may receive the accusative case from the same source.

NP in examples such as (3) is assigned by the preposition *za*, rather than as a result of agreement with the higher NP. Since this conclusion seems irreconcilable with Bailyn and Citko's (1999) analysis, that analysis must be on the wrong track. The second, main aim is to resolve the clash between the common assumption that predicative NPs and APs receive their case via agreement (or are otherwise marked as instrumental), and the fact that predicative complements of prepositions such as *za* in (3) are assigned their case via 'non-predicative' case assignment mechanisms, probably by a rule which states that complements of prepositions are accusative (unless they are inherently case marked). More generally, the main aim of this paper is to delimit the boundaries of predicative case marking.

1. Apparent Overt Preds do Assign the Accusative

As mentioned above, Bailyn and Citko (1999) argue that *za* in (3) above is *not* a preposition, but rather an overt realization of Pred, absorbing the instrumental case and, hence, forcing the predicate to agree with its 'antecedent'. Similarly, the predicative AP in (4) is supposed to agree in case with its antecedent.

(4) Uważam   go   za   zdolnego.
    I-consider him$_{ACC}$ as   gifted$_{ACC}$
    'I consider him as gifted.'

There are, however, at least five good reasons why this analysis cannot be correct, reasons clearly showing that the case of the predicative complement of *za* is independent of the case of the NP being predicated of.

The first argument comes from considerations of the Genitive of Negation, a highly grammaticalized phenomenon in Polish (see, e.g., Przepiórkowski 1999, 2000 and references therein):

(5) a. Nie uważam   jej   za studentkę   / *studentki.
       Neg I-consider her$_{GEN}$ as student$_{ACC}$ / student$_{GEN}$
       'I don't consider her a student.'
    b. Nie uważam   jej   za zdolną   / *zdolnej.
       Neg I-consider her$_{GEN}$ as gifted$_{ACC}$ / gifted$_{GEN}$
       'I don't consider her a student.'

As (4) shows, negating the verb causes the case shift on the complement of the verb only; the complement of the preposition is unaffected. If the case on the complement of the preposition were the result of agreement with the complement of the verb, both should occur in the genitive case, and there would be no source of accusative on *studentkę* / *zdolną* in (5).

The second argument is based on the somewhat idiosyncratic agreement facts involving numeral phrases. As discussed in detail in Przepiórkowski (1999), APs agreeing with accusative numeral phrases either agree with the accusative numeral or with the genitive NP, as illustrated in (6).

(6) Pięć   kobiet   było zdolnych / ?zdolne.
    five$_{ACC}$ women$_{GEN}$ was   gifted   / gifted$_{ACC}$
    'Five women were gifted.'

Given this quirky behavior, and assuming that the case marking of the predicative complement of *za* is a result of agreement with the object of the verb, one should expect this predicative complement to similarly occur either in the accusative or in the genitive case when the object of the verb is such a numeral phrase. (7) below shows that this expectation is not fulfilled, again against the predictions of Bailyn and Citko's (1999) analysis.

(7) Uważam   tych   pięć   kobiet   za   bardzo
    I-consider these$_{GEN}$ five$_{ACC}$ women$_{GEN}$ as   very
    zdolne   / *zdolnych.
    gifted$_{ACC}$ / gifted$_{GEN}$
    'I consider these five women as very gifted.'

The logic of the third argument is similar to that of the previous two arguments. If the case marking on the predicative complement of *za* stems from agreement with the accusative object, then, once the object is raised to subject position in a passive construction and is marked as nominative, the predicative complement should also be marked as nominative. Again, this prediction is false:

(8) Ona   jest uważana   za studentkę / *studentka   /
    she_NOM is considered   as student_ACC / student_NOM   /
    zdolną   / *zdolna.
    gifted_ACC / gifted_NOM
    'She is considered (as) a student / gifted.'

It should be noted that, in the transformational set of assumptions which Bailyn and Citko (1999) adopt, there is no covert (phonologically empty) accusative NP in (8) that the predicate could agree with; passive morphology is assumed to absorb the accusative case.

The fourth argument is an argument of uniformity: in Polish, there are constructions which differ from (3)–(4) in that the predicative complement of a preposition predicates of the subject of a verb, instead of the object:

(9) Janek   uchodził   za studenta   / *student   /
    John_NOM was-taken as student_ACC / student_NOM /
    zdolnego / *zdolny.
    gifted_ACC / gifted_NOM
    'John was taken as a student / gifted.'

Another similar verb is *wyglądać na* 'look like, appear to be'. These constructions should probably be analyzed on par with (3)–(4). If so, then, according to a natural extension of the analysis argued against here, the predicative complement of the preposition should agree with the nominative subject, contrary to (9).

The final argument comes from the observation that the verb *uważać* may occur with an infinitival VP instead of an accusative object, cf. (10).

(10) Kto   uważa   za właściwe   nadal spierać   się
     who_NOM considers   as appropriate_ACC still disagree_INF Refl
     za   mną?
     with me
     'Who considers it appropriate to still disagree with me?'

This argument is similar to that from passive constructions: Although there is no accusative NP that the predicative complement of *za* could agree with, that complement still occurs in the accusative case.

In summary, the analysis of '*za* + predicative NP/AP' which posits that the predicative NP/AP receives its case via agreement cannot be maintained.

2. An Alternative Analysis of *Uważać Za*

Constructions such as *uważać za, brać za, uchodzić za, wyglądać na*, etc., are interesting because they violate what seems to be an often assumed generalization, namely:[2]

(11) **Case Assignment and Case Agreement** (imprecise):
- case-bearing (i.e., nominal or adjectival) **predicative** phrases receive their case either via agreement with their antecedents or via the 'instrumental of predication' rule;
- case-bearing **non-predicative** phrases receive their case via general case assignment rules (e.g., 'accusative of prepositional complement', 'nominative of sentential subjects', 'genitive of negation', etc.), or idiosyncratically (so-called inherent or lexical case, e.g., *pomagać* 'help' + dative).

Contrary to this generalization, the predicative argument of the preposition *za* in, for example, (3) receives its case via the 'non-predicative' rule which states that (structural) arguments of prepositions are accusative.[3]

So where is the dividing line between 'predicative' case marking (via agreement or instrumental) and 'non-predicative' case marking?

The hypothesis which I would like to defend here is:

(11) **Case Assignment and Case Agreement** (alternative):
- case-bearing phrases whose **subject is raised to the immediately higher (i.e., selecting) head (if there is one)** receive the predicative (agreeing / instrumental) case;
- **other** case-bearing phrases receive case via general syntactic rules or idiosyncratically (but cf. fn. 2).

---

[2] Here I ignore case agreement between attributive APs and the noun they modify, as well as semantic case assignment.

[3] That structural arguments of prepositions are accusative was suggested, e.g., by Franks (1995).

Since the categories of 'predicative phrases' and 'phrases whose subject is raised to the immediately higher head (if there is one)' are to a large extent co-extensive, (11) and (12) make similar predictions. However, as I will argue below, they differ for predicative complements of prepositions.

In the remainder of this section, I will assume Head-Driven Phrase Structure Grammar (HPSG; Pollard and Sag 1994) as the framework in which to substantiate hypothesis (12).

2.1. Basic Cases

Copula. According to the standard HPSG assumptions, the copula can be schematically described as in (13).

(13) The predicative copula *być* (schematic and simplified):

$$\begin{bmatrix} word \\ \text{PHON} \ \ być \\ \text{SUBJ} \ \ \langle \boxed{1} \rangle \\ \text{COMPS} \ \ \langle XP \begin{bmatrix} \text{PRD} \ + \\ \text{SUBJ} \ \langle \boxed{1} \rangle \end{bmatrix} \rangle \end{bmatrix}$$

According to this description, the copula *być* takes two arguments, the subject and a complement, the complement must be a predicative phrase (i.e., [PRD +]), and the (unrealized) subject of this predicative complement must be identical to (structure-shared with or token-identical with in the HPSG parlance) the subject of the copula. This identity is represented by the two occurrences of the variable '[1]' and it corresponds to raising in transformational grammars.

For example, the constituent structure of (14) is schematically shown in Figure 1 on the following page.[4]

(14) Janek jest w domu.
        John   is   at home

---

[4] The attributes SUBJ and COMPS indicate the *remaining* combinatory potential of a word or phrase so, for example, although they are both non-empty on the copula *jest*, COMPS is empty (saturated) on the VP *jest w domu*, and both are saturated (but still present) on the whole sentence *Janek jest w domu*.

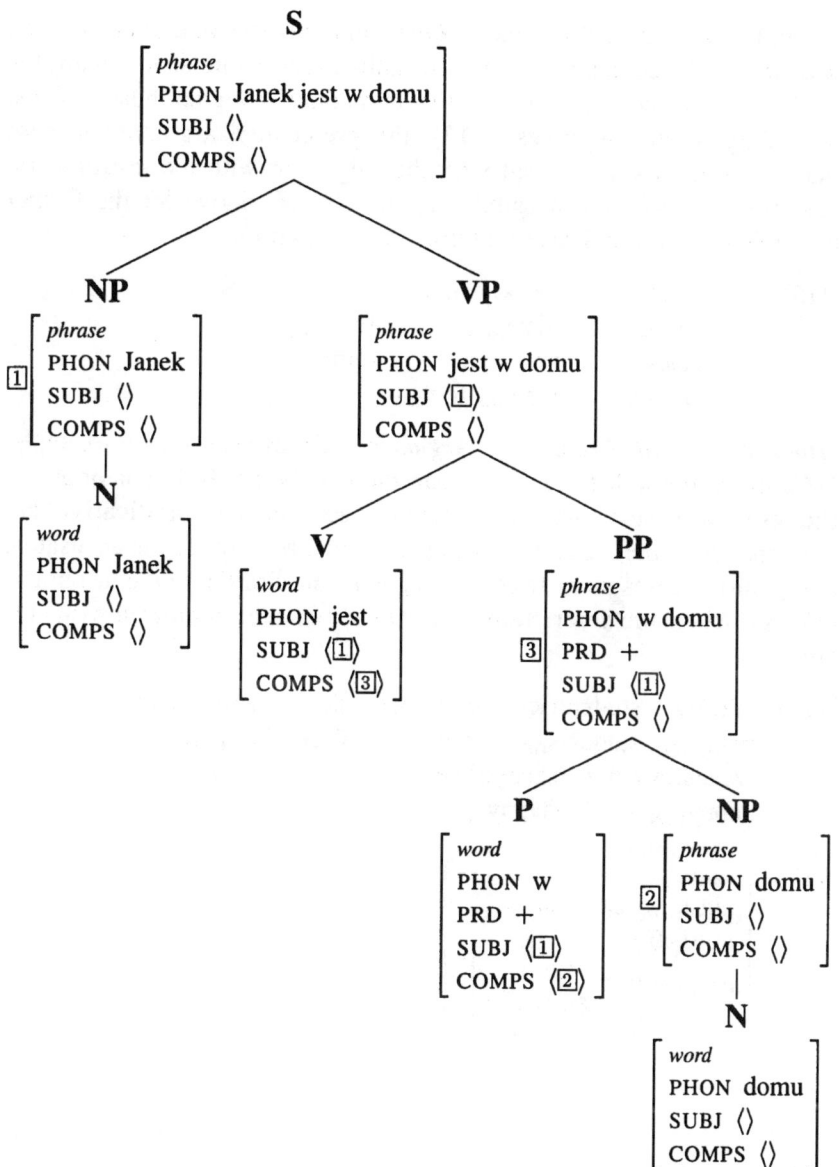

Figure 1: Schematic structure of (14)

In Figure 1, the subject (here, *Janek*) of a predicative argument (here, *w domu*) of the copula is raised to (or rather, is structure-shared with) the subject of the copula, i.e., 'to the immediately higher head'. Thus, according to the hypothesis (12), the predicative argument is case marked either via agreement with the subject or with the instrumental case (cf. (15) for both possibilities, and also (6) above for the former possibility),[5] if it bears case at all (in (14) it does not).

(15) a. Jesteś   zwykły dureń!
        you-are   mere$_{NOM}$ fool$_{NOM}$
     b. Jesteś   zwykłym durniem!
        you-are   mere$_{INS}$ fool$_{INS}$

Other Verbs with Predicative Arguments. Cases such as, for example, (16), involving a different verb than the copula, are fully analogous to the copula cases; the instrumental case on the predicative NP corresponds to the instrumental of predication rule, while the accusative and genitive cases stem from case agreement with the numeral phrase. (17) is a schematic description of *wydawać się*, to be compared with (13) above.

(16) Wiele   studentek   wydawało   się   ?szczęśliwymi /
     many$_{ACC}$ students$_{GEN}$ seemed   Refl   happy$_{INS}$ /
     szczęśliwych / ?szczęśliwe.
     happy$_{GEN}$ / happy$_{ACC}$

(17) $\begin{bmatrix} word \\ \text{PHON } wydawać\ się \\ \text{SUBJ } \langle \boxed{1} \rangle \\ \text{COMPS } \langle XP \begin{bmatrix} \text{PRD } + \\ \text{SUBJ } \langle \boxed{1} \rangle \end{bmatrix} \rangle \end{bmatrix}$

---

[5] Of course, there are additional constraints on when exactly 'predicative' case marking can be realized by case agreement, and when by the instrumental of predication. I have nothing to say about such constraints here, but see Przepiórkowski (1999) for some considerations.

Adjunct Predicates. Consider example (18).

(18) Lubiłem Janka trzeźwego / trzeźwym.
 liked$_{1.SG.MASC}$ John$_{ACC}$ sober$_{ACC}$ / sober$_{INS}$
 'I liked John (when he was) sober.'

There is a body of work within HPSG arguing for treating (at least some) adjuncts as arguments, at least from the point of view of argument / constituent structure.[6] Adopting this approach, *lubić*, as used in (18), can be schematically represented as in (19).

(19) $\begin{bmatrix} word \\ \text{PHON} \quad lubić \\ \text{SUBJ} \quad \langle NP \rangle \\ \text{COMPS} \quad \langle \boxed{1}NP, XP \begin{bmatrix} \text{PRD} + \\ \text{SUBJ} \quad \langle \boxed{1} \rangle \end{bmatrix} \rangle \end{bmatrix}$

Thus, here again the subject of the predicate is structure-shared with ('raised to') an argument position (here, object) of the immediately higher head.

Verb-less Predicative Constructions. The constructions above reflect the 'whose subject is raised to the immediately higher (i.e., selecting) head' part of the first clause of hypothesis (12). The environments exemplified below reflect the '(if there is one)' part.

(20) Wałęsa prezydentem! (Zwariować można!)
 Wałęsa$_{NOM}$ president$_{INS}$ go-crazy$_{INF}$ may$_{IMPERS}$

(21) On głupiec. / Starość nie radość. / Ja biedak,
 he$_{NOM}$ fool$_{NOM}$ / old age$_{NOM}$ not joy$_{NOM}$ / I$_{NOM}$ pauper$_{NOM}$
 a ty pan. (Klemensiewicz 1937, p. 105)
 and you$_{NOM}$ master$_{NOM}$

(22) Szofer, stary blondyn w siatkowej koszulce,
 chauffeur$_{NOM}$ old$_{NOM}$ blonde$_{NOM}$ in laced shirt
 (wysiadł sprawdzić motor.) (Pisarkowa 1965, p. 123)
 (got out to check the engine)
 'The chauffeur, an old blonde in a laced shirt, got out to check the engine.'

I assume that constructions such as (20)–(22) above do not involve any empty copula, and that their constituent structure is as represented schematically in Figure 2. Since there is no higher (selecting) head, the predicate in (20)–(22) is subject to the first clauseof (12) and may be case-marked either via agreement with its subject (as in (21)–(22)) or via the instrumental of predication rule (as in (20)).

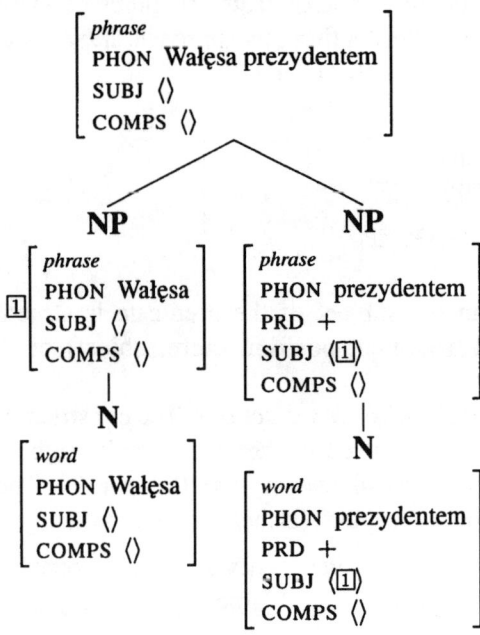

Figure 2: Schematic structure of (20)

No Raising. The most typical situation where the 'otherwise' clause of hypothesis (12) comes into play, i.e., where there is no raising to the immediately higher head, is when there is no raising at all. For example, in (23), all case-bearing elements are full NPs, which receive case via general case assignment rules (assign nominative to the subject, assign accusative to the object (of a non-negated verb), assign dative to the benefactive NP, etc.).

---

[6] See, for example, Miller (1992), van Noord and Bouma (1994), Przepiórkowski (1997, 1999), and Bouma et al. (1999), and references therein.

(23) Janek dał Marysi kwiaty.
John$_{NOM}$ gave Mary$_{DAT}$ flowers$_{ACC}$

The schematic HPSG structure of (23) is shown in Figure 3.

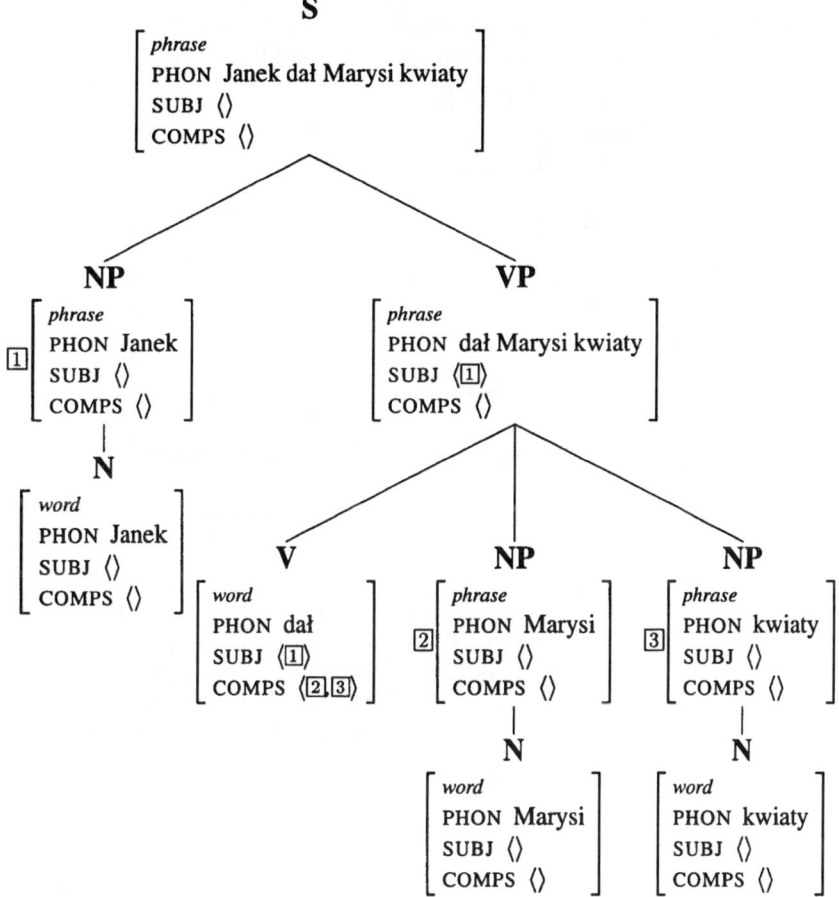

Figure 3: Schematic structure of (23)

2.2. Long Raising in *Uważać Za*

I claim that predicative phrases in constructions such as *uważać za* also satisfy the second clause of hypothesis (12), but not because they do not involve raising at all, but rather because they involve long raising over the immediately higher head (i.e., across *za*) straight to the second higher head (i.e., to *uważać*). In particular, I claim that (3), repeated below, has the structure as in Figure 4 and not the structure in Figure 5 on the following page.[7]

(3) Uważam   go   za   studenta / *studentem.
    I-consider him$_{ACC}$ as student$_{ACC}$ / student

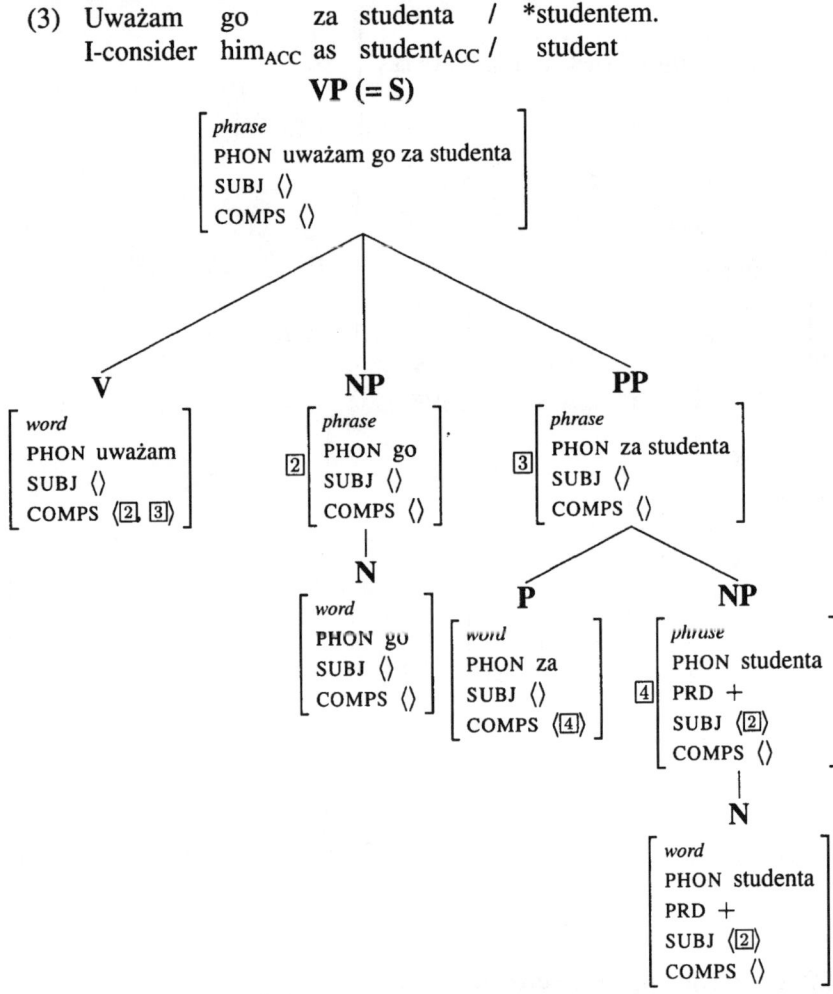

Figure 4: The structure of (3)

---

[7] I assume that the *pro*-dropped subject does not appear on the SUBJ list, but instead appears on the ARG-ST list, not shown or discussed here.

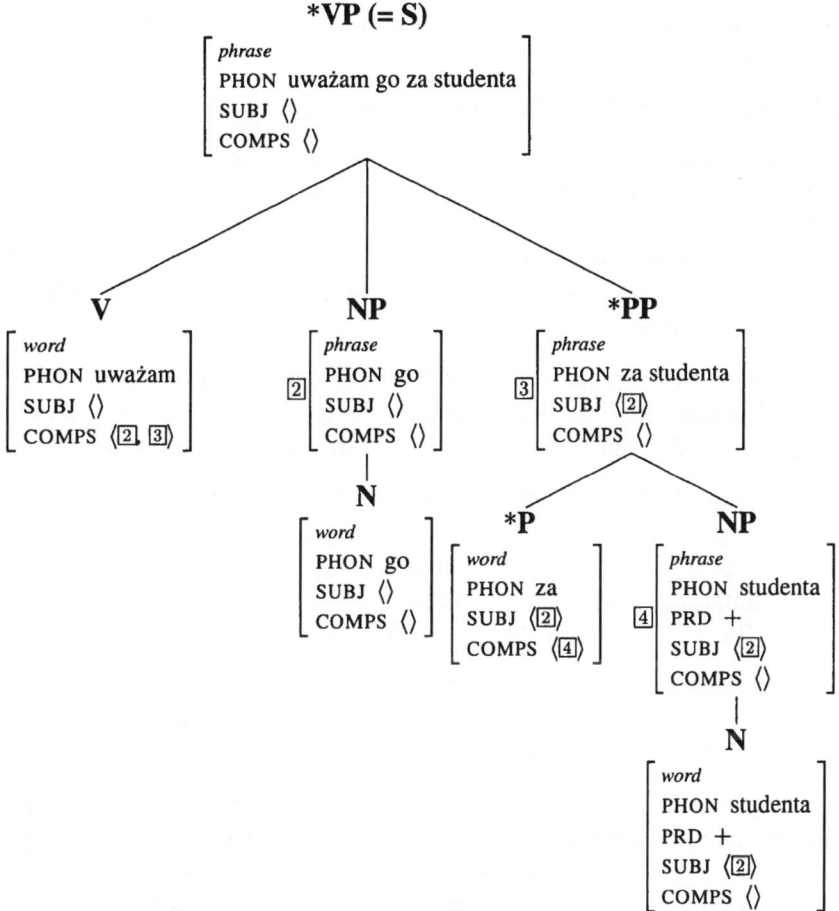

Figure 5: *Not* the structure of (3)

The assumption that Figure 4 presents the right structure for (3) explains the origin of the accusative case on the predicative complement of the preposition: the subject of this predicative complement is not raised to the immediately higher (selecting) head *za*, but rather to a still higher head *uważam*. This, however, means that, although the complement of the preposition is a predicative phrase, the second clause of hypothesis (12) applies, and this complement is assigned case in a 'non-predicative' way, probably via the rule 'assign accusative to structural complements of prepositions'.

2.3 Arguments for Long Raising in *Uważać Za*

Are there independent empirical arguments for the structure in Figure 4 and against that in Figure 5? This question is roughly equivalent to the following question: Are there arguments for the claim that *za* as used in (3) is a 1-argument preposition, as in Figure 4, in contrast to predicative (e.g., locational or temporal) 2-argument prepositions? There are at least two such arguments.

Subjects of Prepositions and Binding. There is a binding contrast between 2-argument prepositions, such as predicative prepositions (e.g., locational), cf. (24), and 1-argument 'case marking' prepositions, cf. (25):

(24) Nie można przecież położyć książki$_i$ na sobie$_{?i}$
Neg may but lay book$_{FEM}$ on Self
samej / na niej$_{?i}$ samej
Emph$_{FEM}$ / on her Emph
'But it is impossible to lay a book on itself.'

(25) Mówiłem jej$_i$ o sobie$_{*i}$ samej / o niej$_i$ samej.
talk$_{1.SG.MASC}$ her about Self Emph / about her Emph
'I talked to her about herself.'

Although the judgments in (24) are not very clear, the contrast between binding across a predicative preposition (24) and across a 'case marking' preposition (25) is clear: since in Polish only subjects can be binders, binding by the object in (25) is impossible, while binding by the object (24) is apparently acceptable, but only because the object controls the subject of the predicative preposition, which is the actual binder.

Now, the preposition *za* in (3) clearly patterns with the 'case marking' prepositions, such as *o* in (25), and not with predicative prepositions such as *na* in (24).

(26) (Nie pomyliłem się,) uważałem go$_i$ za
(I didn't make a mistake,) considered$_{1.SG.MASC}$ him$_{ACC}$ for
siebie$_{*i}$ samego / za niego$_i$ samego.
himself Emph / for him Emph
'(I didn't make a mistake,) I really considered him for himself.'

This is the first argument that *za*, as in (3), is a 1-argument preposition.

PP[za] is not Predicative. All prepositions seem to be partitioned into two classes: the class of 2-argument predicative prepositions and the class of 1-argument 'case-marking' prepositions. If so, then classifying *za* as a 2-argument preposition would amount to classifying it as a predicative preposition. In that case, the whole phrase *za studenta* in (3) would be predicative.

But there are good arguments that the PP '*za* + NP/AP' cannot be predicative; if it were predicative, it should be able to appear in other predicative environments, especially in those environments which do not posit particular constraints on the categorial makeup of the predicative phrase, such the complement of the copula, or exclamations. (27)–(28) show that this prediction is false:

(27) Janek   jest   szczery   / prezydentem   / w   domu... /
      John$_{NOM}$ is   sincere$_{NOM}$ / president$_{INS}$ / at   home...   /
      *za szczerego.
      as sincere
      'John is sincere / the president / at home... / *as sincere.'

(28) Janek szczery!   / Wałęsa prezydentem!   / Krokodyl w
      John sincere$_{NOM}$ / Wałęsa president$_{INS}$ / crocodile in
      klatce! / Obiad o dziesiątej! / *Janek za szczerego!
      cage   / dinner at ten   / John as sincere
      (Też   pomysł!)
      also   idea
      John (being) sincere! / Wałęsa (as) the president! / A crocodile in a cage! / Dinner at 10! / *John as sincere! (What an idea!)'

Although the copula in (27) could, in principle, impose an idiosyncratic constraint to the effect that its complement cannot be marked with *za*, such a constraint would violate the otherwise overwhelming generalization that the copula may combine with any predicative complement. Moreover, it is not clear that such a constraint could be imposed in (28), where there is no overt copula and no obvious reason to posit a phonologically empty one.

Thus, the PP '*za* + NP/AP' should not be analyzed as predicative and, hence, *za* should not be analyzed as a 2-argument preposition.

3. Summary

In this paper, I have critically examined the pivotal claim of Bailyn and Citko's (1999) analysis, namely, that Polish constructions such as *uważać za* involve a predicative NP/AP which receives its case via agreement with its antecedent (the phrase being predicated of). I have given five empirical arguments against this claim and I have suggested that the predicative complement of the preposition is case-marked in a regular 'non-predicative' way.

More generally, I have re-examined the dichotomy between case marking of predicative phrases and case marking of non-predicative phrases and I have proposed that it is not precisely predicative APs/NPs that are 'predicatively' case marked (i.e., that agree in case with their antecedent or are marked with instrumental case), but rather those APs/NPs, whose subject is raised to (structure-shared with) the immediately higher head. I have shown that this hypothesis explains the whole range of facts, including the troublesome *uważać za* construction.

Although I have illustrated this hypothesis with HPSG structures, I have not attempted to provide a complete HPSG analysis of predicative case assignment here. Such an attempt is made in Przepiórkowski (1999), which presents in greater technical detail the analysis only sketched here.

References

Bailyn, J. F. and B. Citko (1999). "Case and agreement in Slavic predicates". In K. Dziwirek, H. Coats, and C. M. Vakareliyska (Eds.), *Annual Workshop on Formal Approaches to Slavic Linguistics: The Seattle Meeting 1998*, Volume 44 of Michigan Slavic Materials, 17–37. Ann Arbor: Michigan Slavic Publications.

Bouma, G., R. Malouf, and I. Sag (1999). "Satisfying constraints on extraction and adjunction". To appear in *Natural Language and Linguistic Theory*.

Bowers, J. (1993). "The syntax of predication". *Linguistic Inquiry* 24(4), 591–656.

Franks, S. (1995). *Parameters of Slavic Morphosyntax*. New York and Oxford: Oxford University Press.

Klemensiewicz, Z. (1937). *Składnia opisowa współczesnej polszczyzny kulturalnej.* Kraków: Polska Akademia Umiejętności.

Miller, P. H. (1992). *Clitics and Constituents in Phrase Structure Grammar.* New York: Garland.

Pisarkowa, K. (1965). *Predykatywność określeń w polskim zdaniu.* Wrocław: Zakład narodowy im. Ossolińskich.

Pollard, C. and I. A. Sag (1994). *Head-Driven Phrase Structure Grammar.* Chicago, IL: University of Chicago Press / CSLI Publications.

Przepiórkowski, A. (1997). "Quantifiers, adjuncts as complements, and scope ambiguities". To appear in *Journal of Linguistics.* Draft of December 2, 1997. Available from: http://www.ling.ohio-state.edu/~adamp/Drafts/.

Przepiórkowski, A. (1999). *Case Assignment and the Complement-Adjunct Dichotomy: A Non-Configurational Constraint-Based Approach.* Ph.D. dissertation, Universität Tübingen, Germany. Available from: http://www.ling.ohio-state.edu/~adamp/Dissertation/.

Przepiórkowski, A. (2000). Long distance genitive of negation in Polish. To appear in the Journal of Slavic Linguistics, special issue on Polish, edited by Piotr Bański and Ewa Willim.

Van Noord, G. and G. Bouma (1994). "Adjuncts and the processing of lexical rules". In *Fifteenth International Conference on Computational Linguistics (COLING '94),* 250–256. Kyoto, Japan.

Ohio State University
Department of Linguistics
222 Oxley Hall
1712 Neil Ave.
Columbus OH 43210 USA
adamp@ipipan.waw.pl
http://www.ipipan.waw.pl/mmgroup/ap.html

Polish Academy of Sciences
Institute of Computer Science
ul. Ordona 21
01-237 Warszawa
Poland

Feature Movement Approach to Long-Distance Binding in Russian

Elena Rudnitskaya
CUNY Graduate Center & Institute for Oriental Studies, Moscow

1. Introduction: The Problems of Long-distance Binding

Example (1) illustrates long-distance (LD) binding in Russian.

(1) Marija$_1$ ne razrešaet Anne$_2$ PRO$_2$
Mary$_1$-N not allows Ann$_2$-D PRO$_2$
provodit' nad soboj$_{1/2}$ èksperimenty.
to-perform over self$_{1/2}$-I experiments-A
'Mary$_1$ does not allow Ann$_2$ to perform experiments on her$_1$/herself$_2$.'

LD reflexives pose serious problems for the standard Binding Theory and require major modifications to this Theory. There are two major theories which account for LD reflexives: the syntactic theory and the logophoric theory. The Binding Domain Parametrization framework (Manzini & Wexler (1987)) and the Head Movement framework (Pica (1987, 1991), Bailyn (1992), Cole, Hermon & Sung (1990)), and others advocate the syntactic approach; Zribi-Hertz (1989), Sells (1987), and others advocate the logophoric approach. My data support the syntactic account of LD binding.

I present a feature movement analysis of LD binding with reference to Russian. This analysis originates from Pica's (1987, 1991) Head Movement framework but is implemented in the Minimalist framework. I consider reflexive movement to be [+R] feature movement: [+R] is an interpretable feature of a reflexive attracted by a non-interpretable [+R] feature of an upstairs T head (whose subject is the antecedent). This movement is unbounded but since it is not contained inside one phase in the sense of Chomsky (1999) (it is successive-cyclic in the GB terms), it can only proceed when [+R] stops in all C heads which are on its way.

This derivation is schematically shown in (2) (all Spec positions are removed):[1]

(2)
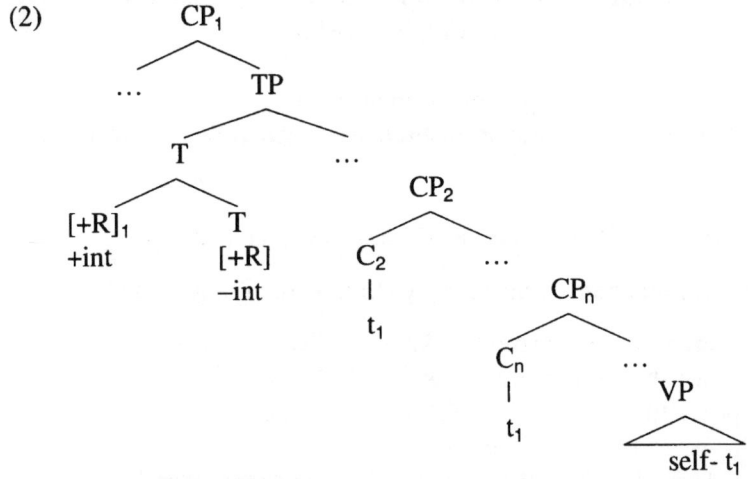

My account is crucially based on the distinction between interpretable and non-interpretable features: the result of the derivation with [+R] movement depends on the feature content of C. The [+R] feature cannot pass through C when C has *interpretable* features in it, but it can pass through C otherwise (if C has either no features or *non-interpretable* features). Thus, the data on binding provide independent support for the importance of the distinction between interpretable and non-interpretable features.

Finally, I adopt Kayne's (1994) Antisymmetry framework: I extend the Antisymmetry constraint on head adjunction to feature adjunction, and this allows me to derive the blocking effect of a C when it contains an interpretable feature. My analysis shows that the account for LD binding must adopt the Antisymmetry framework rather than the multiple specifier framework (Chomsky (1995)).

---

[1] According to this scheme, the ambiguity of (1) will be explained as follows: if the embedded T has the non-interpretable [+R] feature, the [+R] feature of *sebja* moves to this T and checks its feature (which yields index 2). If the matrix T has the [+R] feature, the [+R] feature of *sebja* moves to the matrix T and we have LD binding with index 1. See also note 3.

The article is organized as follows. In section 2.1, I give the data relevant for my analysis; section 2.2 presents the framework and proposal. In section 3, I show how my account works in relevant contexts; I concentrate on binding into overt Dative subjects vs. PRO infinitives and present the analysis of infinitives implicated by my framework in section 3.3. Section 4 gives the conclusions.

2. The Data, Framework and Proposal

2.1 The Facts of LD Binding in Russian

Russian, like Norwegian (Hellan (1991)), allows LD binding into infinitives but not into finite clauses (Rappaport (1986)). This is illustrated in (1) and (3) vs. (4)–(5).[2]

(3) Ivan$_1$ nanjal povara$_2$
John$_1$-N hired cook$_2$-A
PRO$_2$ gotovit' sebe$_1$ obedy.
PRO$_2$ to-prepare self1-D dinners-A
'John$_1$ hired a cook to prepare dinners for him$_1$.'

(4) *Ivan$_1$ ne velel Petru$_2$,
John$_1$-N not ordered Peter$_2$-D
čto-by on$_2$ gotovil sebe$_1$ obedy.
that-SUBJ he$_2$-N cooked self$_1$-D dinners-A
'John$_1$ did not order Peter$_2$ that he$_2$ would cook dinners for him$_1$.'

(5) *Marija$_1$ znaet, čto Ivan ljubil sebja$_1$.
Mary$_1$-N knows that John-N loved self$_1$-A
'Mary$_1$ knows that John loved her$_1$.'

The data above lead us to the conclusion that a finite T blocks LD binding (cf. Bailyn (1992)). However, non-finite clauses with a null subject do not always allow LD binding into them. PRO infinitives allow LD binding but participial clauses (PC-s), which always have a null subject in Russian, are ungrammatical with LD binding. LD binding is ungrammatical in both prenominal and postnominal PC-s:

---

[2] In all the following examples, I only give the indexing which corresponds to LD binding, that is, I omit the 'local' index 2 on *sebja*.

(6) a. On₁   smotrel   na   obed
       he₁-N looked   at   dinner-A
       [PartP gotovivšijsja   dlja   *sebja₁].
       [PartP being-cooked-PART.PAST-A   for   self₁-G]
    b. On₁   smotrel   na   [PartP gotovivšijsja
       he₁-N looked   at   [PartP being-cooked-PART.PAST-A
       dlja   *sebja₁]   obed.
       for   *self₁-G] dinner-A
       'He₁ looked at the dinner that was being cooked for him₁.'

As the following pairs of examples show, binding is allowed into all kinds of infinitives with a PRO subject (e.g. *wh*-infinitives) but not into corresponding infinitives with overt Dative subjects.

(7) a. (?)Andrej₁   objasnil   Petru₂,
       Andrew₁-N   explained   Peter₂-D
       čego   PRO₂   ne   rasskazyvat'   o   sebe₁.
       what-G PRO₂   not to-tell   about   self₁-P
       'Andrew₁ explained to Peter what not to tell about him₁.'
    b. *Andrej₁   objasnil   Petru₂,
       Andrew₁-N   explained   Peter₂-D
       čego   emu₂   ne   rasskazyvat'   o   sebe₁.
       what-G he₂-D   not to-tell   about   self₁-P
       'Andrew₁ explained to Peter₂ what he₂ must not tell about him₁.'

(8) a. (?)Anna₁   skazala   medsestre₂,
       Anna₁-N   told   nurse₂-D
       kuda   PRO₂   ukolot'   sebja₁.
       where   PRO₂   to-inject self₁-A
       'Ann₁ told the nurse where to give her₁ an injection.'
    b. *Anna₁   skazala   medsestre₂,
       Anna₁-N   told   nurse₂-D
       kuda   ej₂   ukolot'   sebja₁.
       where   she₂-D   to-inject self₁-A
       'Ann₁ told the nurse₂ where she₂ must give her₁ an injection.'

As (9) shows, overt dative subjects *per se* can occur in infinitives, so (7b)–(8b) are ungrammatical because of the 'self' reflexive in them.

(9) Anna   skazala   medsestre$_2$,
    Anna-N   told   nurse$_2$-D
    kuda   ej$_2$ ukolot'   Ivana.
    where   she$_2$-D to-inject   John-A
    'Ann$_1$ told the nurse where to give John an injection.'

Thus, not only a finite T but also an overt Dative subject can block LD binding, ([+R] movement). The fact in (7b)–(8b) is novel and doesn't straightforwardly fit into the scheme in (2). My account of the overt Dative subject blocking effect (section 3.3) is based on assuming that the Dative of the subject of the infinitive is structural (cf. Moore and Perlmutter (1999, 2000)) and checked by the C head.

2.2 The framework and proposal

As already mentioned in section 1, I regard reflexive movement as the [+R] feature movement. The interpretable (+int) [+R] feature of the reflexive (*sebja*) is driven by the weak non-interpretable (–int) [+R] feature of T which is the Tense of the clause whose subject is the antecedent.[3] The [+R] movement is movement of a single feature. Chomsky (1995, Ch. 4) mentions that movement of a single feature is impossible: any feature that moves pied-pipes all the other features of the same head. However, [+R] is the only +int feature of the *sebja* head. *Sebja* has no phi-features: it can be anteceded by a nominal with any phi-features. The only other feature of *sebja* is the Case feature. This feature

---

[3] In principle, it is possible that more than one of the upstairs T-s have the –int [+R] feature, for instance, the T of the embedded clause with *sebja* and the clause which embeds it. Then, the +int [+R] feature of *sebja* would be able to check both of these features. The structure will be the following:

(i)   ... [TP$_1$ [T$_1$-[+R]3] ...[TP$_2$ [T$_2$-[+R]3] ... self-t3]]

(i) would converge with a gibberish interpretation: *sebja* would have two antecedents. This problem is identical to the problem of the [+wh] feature of a *wh*-word, pointed out by Chomsky (1995: 291). If there are two [+wh] embedded clauses and the [+wh] feature of the *wh*-word in the second embedded clause is interpretable, this interpretable [+wh] feature can check both of the [+wh] features of the two C-s, as in (ii). The interpretation of the resulting well-formed structure will be gibberish: one *wh*-word will correspond to two *wh*-questions in two different clauses.

(ii) ... [CP$_1$ [C$_1$-[+wh]3] ...[CP$_2$ [C$_2$-[+wh]3] ... [DP ... t3]]]

is –int, and it must be checked by an Agr inside the same clause and deleted; it cannot undergo LD movement.

Pica (1989, 1991) assumes that C is the escape-hatch for the movement of the reflexive head. While proposing this, he brings in the similarity between successive-cyclic *wh*-movement and LD reflexive movement: both types of movement are long-distance and therefore have to proceed in steps through the SpecCP/C position. Chomsky (1999) proposes a *phase* derivation for successive-cyclic *wh*-movement. According to Chomsky, a feature F is not visible for attraction from outside a domain of H (which is C^4 in the case of successive-cyclic movement) unless F is in H (C) or in SpecHP (SpecCP). Consider a case of a LD movement. If the [+R] of the reflexive stays *in situ* (on *sebja*) without moving up to C, then it will not be visible for the attraction of [+R] by an upstairs T, as in (10a), as opposed to (10b). In the former derivation, the [+R] of *sebja* will not be able to be attracted, and the derivation will crash; in the latter, [+R] can be attracted, and the derivation will converge.

(10) a. ... [CP_1 [TP_1 [T_1-[+R]] ...[CP_2 [C_2] ... self-[+R]]]]
 b. ... [CP_1 [TP_1 [T_1-[+R]] ...[CP_2 [C_2-[+R]] ... self-t]]]

Thus, the requirement that [+R] move through each C on its way to the antecedent's clause (cf. (2) in the introduction) is well-grounded.

It is well-known that languages differ in their LD binding options. For instance, whereas Russian allows binding into infinitives but not into finite clauses; Icelandic allows binding into finite subjunctive but not indicative clauses. In Pica's framework, these parametric differences are accounted for by the blocking effect of C: Pica proposes that only head substitution but not head-adjunction of a reflexive head to C is allowed. Once C is filled at LF, the reflexive head cannot substitute into C and move through it.

I adopt Pica's idea about the blocking effect of C but implement it in another way. I propose that [+R] can adjoin to C but it cannot excorporate from C under certain conditions, and then reflexive movement is blocked. My account is based on Kayne's (1994:19)

---

[4] I do not consider *v* domains because I adopt Kayne's (1994) Antisymmetry framework, which is not consistent with the *v*P clause structure.

constraint on head adjunction. Kayne's constraint only allows one type of head adjunction: if two heads H1 and H2 subsequently adjoin to the head H, the second adjoined head H2 must adjoin to the first adjoined head H1 (11a) but not directly to H (11b): in the latter case, not every pair of the terminal nodes will be in the relation of the antisymmetric c-command (neither *k* nor *l* c-command each other).

(11)

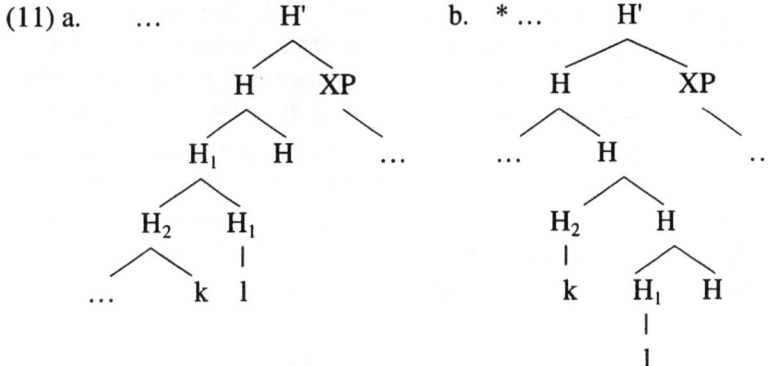

I propose to extend this constraint on head adjunction to feature adjunction. Adjunction of F2 to F1 (as in (12a)), but not of F2 to the head H (as in (12b)), is allowed.

(12)

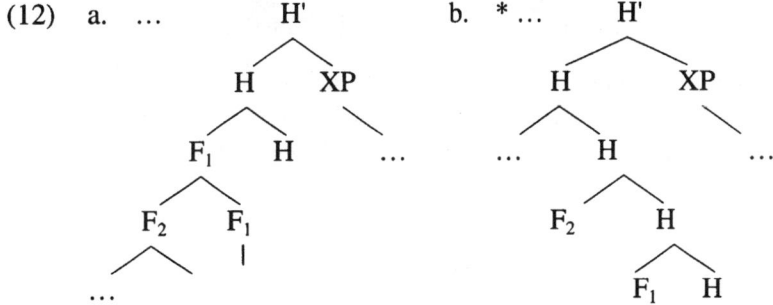

Based on the restriction on feature adjunction in (12a-b), I propose a unified account of constraints on LD binding in the contexts of LD binding in section 2.1. This account is the following. In order to be LD bound, [+R] must be able to move through the C position at LF (that is, adjoin to C and then excorporate from C). When C contains a +int feature, [+R] cannot move through it, and LD binding is blocked (cf. Pica's approach). This contrast is shown in (13) vs. (14).

(13) [$_{CP(MATR)}$ SUBJ$_1$ ... [$_{CP(EMB)}$ [$_{C'}$ [$_C$]] ... self$_1$-[+R]]]]

(14) *[$_{CP(MATR)}$ SUBJ$_1$...[$_{CP(EMB)}$ [$_{C'}$ [$_C$ [F[+int]]]] ... self$_1$-[+R]]]]

[+R] movement is blocked by a +int feature in C because excorporation of [+R] out of a C which contains [F[+int]] is disallowed. When [+R] moves to C, [+R] adjoins to [F[+int]] (as in (15a)), but not to C directly (as in (15b)). I propose the following constraint: if two interpretable features adjoin one to the other, only the less embedded feature is visible for further attraction. The more embedded feature is too deeply embedded to be visible from upstairs. In (15a), only [F[+int]] is visible for further attraction: [+R] can move up only pied-piped by [F[+int]]. Since [+R] cannot be attracted by the –int [+R] of a higher T, this –int [+R] feature cannot be checked, and the derivation will crash.

(15) a.

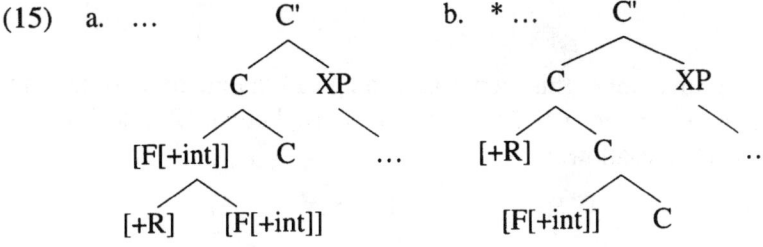

A very important question is why the [F[+int]] always moves to C first, before [+R]. If [+R] moved to C before [F[+int]], it would result in structure (16), and [+R] would be visible for further attraction.

(16)   * ...

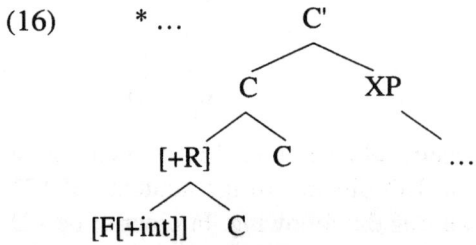

The following constraint makes (16) impossible. In all cases in which LD binding is banned (section 2.1), C has a –int feature that must be checked either by [F[+int]] or by another feature which pied-pipes [F[+int]] (see section 3 for details). I propose that if a movement of a feature F1 to a head H is driven by the need to check a –int feature (either F1 is –int or a feature F2 checked by F1 located in H, is –int), F1 moves to H before any other features.[5] Given this constraint, [F[+int]] will move to C before [+R]: [+R] does not check off any feature in C moving there to become visible to further movement.

In this section, I have shown how to account for LD binding using the mechanism of feature movement. The [+R] feature has to stop in every C head to satisfy the phase constraint on derivations. The distribution of LD reflexives is captured by the blocking effect of a C with a +int feature: [+R] cannot pass through such a C. The mechanism of the blocking effect of C is based on the constraint on feature adjunction along the lines of the antisymmetry framework.

3. LD Binding in Major Contexts in Russian

In this section, I will show how my analysis works in the three major contexts in Russian in which LD binding is blocked: in finite clauses (section 3.1), in PC-s (section 3.2) and in infinitives with overt Dative subjects vs. with PRO subjects (section 3.3).

3.1 Finite Clauses

As has been shown in section 2.1, infinitives allow LD binding, whereas finite clauses (either subjunctive or indicative) do not allow it (see examples (1) and (3) vs. (4)–(5)).

According to my account, there must be a difference between the feature content of a C of a (PRO) infinitive and the feature content of a C of a finite clause. I propose that the +int [PAST] feature of a finite T moves to C at LF. This movement is attracted by a weak –int [PAST] feature of C (this feature is present in C only if T has a [PAST] feature). Since the [PAST] feature of C is –int, the movement of the T features is driven by the need to check off this –int feature, and the T features move to C before [+R]. The [+R] feature has to adjoin to these features; so

---

[5] An alternative formulation of this constraint proposed by an editor ("it is cheaper to check a —int feature, so the system must try to do that first, and only when those exhausted, can it check +int features") wouldn't work because the [+R] feature doesn't undergo checking in C, it only gets there to become visible for further attraction.

[+R] is not visible to further movement, and its movement is blocked.[6] This relevant structure after the –int [PAST] feature of C is checked off is shown in (17).

(17) ... [$_{CP-MATR}$ [$_{TP-MATR}$ [T$_{MATR}$] ...[$_{CP-EMB}$ [[[+R]$_1$ [PAST]$_2$] [C$_{EMB}$]] [$_{TP-EMB}$ [T$_{EMB}$-t$_2$]... self-t$_1$]]]]

Infinitive clauses allow LD binding, in my account, since the T of an infinitive clause does not have a [PAST] feature (it can at most have an [UNREALIZED] tense feature, cf. Martin's (1992) proposal). C contains no –int [PAST] feature, and no T-to-C movement proceeds. [+R] adjoins directly to T and it can move further T.

This account of reflexives in finite clauses is partially based on Bailyn's (1992) proposal that a finite T blocks reflexive movement in Russian (implemented in the head movement framework). It is necessary to mention that my proposal of T-to-C movement is not related to Watanabe's (1993) proposal of T-to-C movement. In Watanabe's framework, T-to-C movement is contingent on Case-checking: both the Nominative Case and the Null Case of PRO are assigned by the combination of T and C. This Case-checking results in a –int [+F] feature in C which attracts the features of T. In my account, T-to-C movement is

---

[6] There is an alternative way to block the derivation with the [+R] movement in a finite clause, without stipulating that the TEMB features have to move to C first. Suppose, there is no such requirement that the TEMB features move to C before [+R]: then, both the configurations in (15a) and in (16) are possible. If (15a) occurs, the derivation will crash because [+R] will not be attracted to a higher TMATR, and the —int [+R] feature of the higher TMART will not be checked. If [+R] moves to C before the TEMB features, [+R] will be visible for further movement. It will be attracted to a higher TMATR and check off its —int [+R] feature. However, the [PAST] feature of TEMB, which is adjoined to [+R], will be pied-piped to TMATR. Since TMATR has its own [PAST] specification, TMATR will have two tense specifications: [PAST]EMB and [PAST]MATR. This is shown in (i).

(i) [CP-MATR [TP-MATR [TMATR-[PAST]EMB —...— [PAST]MATR ... [CP-EMB [CEMB-t] ... self-t]]]

If the matrix and the embedded tense specifications in (i) are different, the derivation will face an interpretation problem. If these two tense specifications are the same, the problem of "too much tense semantics" will arise. In both cases, the principle of FI will be violated. Thus, even if [+R] arrives to C before [PAST]EMB, the derivation will be ruled out in the end.

linked not to Case-checking but to the [PAST] feature of T and does not proceed in infinitives.

Thus, my account of the ban on binding into finite clauses is crucially based on movement of a finite T's [PAST] feature to C.

3.2 Participial Clauses (PC-s)

Examples (6a–b) in section 2.1 show that LD binding into pre/postnominal PC-s is ungrammatical.

My account of PC-s is similar to the account of finite clauses (section 3.1). My claim about PC-s is that they, unlike infinitives, have an +int [PAST] feature in T. This is because Russian has present and past participles with explicit tense morphology:

(18) a. gotov'-ašč-ij-sja
being-cooked-PART.PRES-SG.MASC.N
b. gotov-ivš-ij-sja
being-cooked-PART.PAST-SG.MASC.N

If the PC's T has the [PAST] feature, the C of PC-s has the –int [PAST] feature, which attracts T to C at LF. Then, the –int [PAST] feature of T in C will block [+R] movement: the account for PC-s is exactly similar to the account for finite clauses.

3.3 Infinitives

3.3.1 Infinitives with overt Dative subjects.

Examples (7a–b), repeated here, show the contrast in grammaticality between PRO infinitives and overt Dative subjects infinitives with LD reflexives.

(7) a. (?)Andrej$_1$ objasnil Petru$_2$,
Andrew$_1$-N explained Peter$_2$-D
čego PRO$_2$ ne rasskazyvat' o sebe$_1$.
what-G PRO$_2$ not to-tell about self$_1$-P
'Andrew$_1$ explained to Peter what not to tell about him$_1$.'

(7) b. *Andrej$_1$ objasnil Petru$_2$,
    Andrew$_1$-N explained Peter$_2$-D
    čego emu$_2$ ne rasskazyvat' o sebe$_1$.
    what-G he$_2$-D not to-tell about self$_1$-P
    'Andrew$_1$ explained to Peter$_2$ what he$_2$ must not tell about him$_1$.'

According to my account, a +int feature in C of overt Dative subject infinitives must block [+R] movement through this C. This feature cannot be any feature of T because an infinitive T has no [PAST] feature which would move to C. I propose that the +int features needed in C are the phi-features of the subject. The mechanism of how these features get to C at LF is the following.

I adopt the arguments of Moore and Perlmutter (1999, 2000) and assume that the Dative subject is a surface syntactic subject, unlike "Dative subjects" in finite clauses. So the Dative of the infinitive subject is structural. Which head checks this Dative (T or another head)? The LD binding data lead me to propose that this Dative is checked by C. Case-checking is done covertly because the Dative subject follows the complementizer in overt syntax, as in (19).

(19) Petr$_1$ zavel budil'nik,
    Peter$_1$-N set alarm-clock-A
    čtoby Marii$_2$ ne prospat'.
    in-order Mary$_2$-D not to-oversleep
    'Peter$_1$ set the alarm clock so that Mary$_2$ could not oversleep.'

C has a weak −int [Dat] feature which attracts the [Dat] feature of the subject. The phi-features of the subject move with the [Dat] feature. After the [Dat] features of C and of the subject delete, the phi-features stay in C, since nominal phi-features are +int. This derivation (with reference to (7b)) is shown in (20)–(21).

(20) ... [$_{CP-EMB}$ [$_{AdvP3}$ what] [$_C$ phi-ff$_{DP2}$-[Dat] [$_C$ [+wh][Dat]]] [$_{TP-EMB}$ [$_{DP2}$ he-t$_{ff-[Dat]}$] [T+V$_{EMB}$] ...t$_2$ t$_3$]]

(21) ... [$_{CP-EMB}$ [$_{AdvP3}$ what] [$_C$ phi-ff$_{DP2}$] [$_{TP-EMB}$ [$_{DP2}$ he-t$_{ff-[Dat]}$] [T+V$_{EMB}$] ...t$_2$ t$_3$]]

In (20), the [Dat] feature and the phi-features of DP2 move to C. In (21), the [Dat] features of C and of DP2 get checked and deleted. Only the phi-features of DP2 and the [+wh] feature are left in C. I assume (contra Chomsky (1995, ch. 4)) that the [+wh] feature is –int (see below). The [+wh] feature will delete at LF, whereas the +int phi-features of DP2 will stay in C. Then, [+R] will not be able to move through C blocked by the phi-features of DP2:

(22) ... [$_{CP\text{-}MATR}$ [$_{TP\text{-}MATR}$ [T_{MATR}] ...[$_{CP\text{-}EMB}$ [[[+R]$_1$ [phi-ff$_{DP2}$]] [C_{EMB}]] [$_{AGRSP\text{-}EMB}$ [DP$_2$-t$_{ff}$] ... self-t$_1$]]]]

3.3.2 Infinitives with PRO Subjects

The [+R] movement is blocked in overt Dative subject infinitives by the phi-features of the subject. Compare these infinitives with PRO infinitives. As (7a) shows, LD binding into PRO infinitives is possible. What is the difference between overt Dative subject infinitives and PRO infinitives?

Chomsky and Lasnik (1993) propose that the infinitive T checks the Null Case of PRO. Laurenćot (1997) and Babby (1998) consider Dative to be the Null Case in Russian. This conclusion follows from the data on agreement with secondary predicates *odin* 'alone', *sam* 'oneself', *ves'* 'entire'. In most infinitive constructions, these predicates show Dative (but not Nominative or Accusative) Case:

(23) Bylo   opasno   PRO$_{ARB}$ xodit'
      was   dangerous   PRO$_{ARB}$ to-walk
      tam   odnomu/ *odin.
      there   alone-D/ *-N
      'It was dangerous to walk alone there.'

I assume (following Franks and Hornstein (1992)) that secondary predicates agree in Case with the c-commanding subject. Then, these predicates agree with PRO. Therefore, PRO is checked for Dative.

If overt subjects and PRO are checked for the same Case, I propose that the same head checks this Case. My proposal is based on the principle of Case Uniformity and on Occam's Razor: in a certain configuration, one Case must always be checked for a DP by one and the same head, no matter what kind of DP is checked for Case in each instance of Case-assignment. Based on this principle, I cannot claim, following Babby (1998), Laurençot (1997), and others, that PRO is checked for Dative by T. This claim implies that Dative Case of infinitive subjects can be checked by two different heads: by C for overt subjects and by T for PRO. Hence, my proposal is that a null or overt C checks Dative for PRO similar to overt subjects.

The proposal must capture the fact that the null C that checks Dative for overt subjects blocks reflexive movement, but the null C that checks Dative for PRO does not block it (as in (7a) vs. (7b)).

As we saw in (20)–(21) (the derivation of (7b)), the C position is not empty in the LF structure of (7b); it contains the phi-features of the overt subject. I propose that the phi-features of a controlled PRO are *inherently non-interpretable*. That is, these features are only needed for agreement but not for interpretation. Thus, the phi-features of a controlled PRO delete at LF after checking.[7] Hence, no features remain in C after all the checking operations in PRO infinitives, and reflexive movement is not blocked.

I assume that the [wh] feature of C is –int and deletes at LF. This assumption (contra Chomsky (1995)) is based, first, on binding data in Russian (if [+wh] in C were interpretable, the contrast between [+wh] infinitives with and without overt subjects could not be explained). Second, we don't need the [wh] feature on C to be +int for selection purposes. A [+wh] C is not always selected by a particular matrix verb: for instance, verbs such as *know* can subca-tegorize both for [+wh] and for [–wh] C heads: *I know why/that he came*. Furthermore, *know* can select a yes-no question in a negative sentence or in a question but not in an affirmative sentence: *Do you know, whether he has come?* vs. **I know whether he has come*. So the [wh] feature cannot account for subcategorization of matrix verbs such as *know, ask* etc.; only a complex set of syntactic and semantic factors can account for [wh] clause selection. Thus, there is no evidence for considering the [wh] feature +int. Then, in the case of PRO *wh*-infinitives, the [+wh] feature of C

---

[7] I assume that PRO has no interpretable morphosyntactic features at all. That is, it has some interpretable features, such as theta-role features, but they are not morphosyntactic and thus cannot undergo movement and cannot be pied-piped to C by the [Dat] feature (also see the discussion in the main text).

deletes, no +int features are left in C, and the [+R] movement can proceed.[8]

It is necessary to mention that, first, my stipulation only concerns a controlled PRO but not an arbitrary PRO.[9] I assume that all morphosyntactic features of a controlled PRO, including phi-features, are copied from the PRO's controller (PRO has only an independent theta-role). The phi-features of a controlled PRO can delete at LF because they are recovered under the control relation with the PRO controller. Second, my claim that the phi-features of PRO are –int does not imply that no features of PRO are +int. In Chomsky (1995), features that can move are defined as morphosyntactic features. The phi-features of PRO are morphosyntactic, therefore they can be pied-piped by the [Dat] feature. However, a controlled PRO has non-morphosyntactic interpretable features. These +int features cannot move and thus [Dat] cannot pied-pipe these features when it moves to C. At LF, these features stay *in situ*, in SpecIP, and they cannot block reflexive movement through C.

Thus, a null complementizer that checks Dative for an overt DP blocks reflexive movement (because an overt DP has interpretable phi-features), but a null complementizer that checks Dative for a covert DP does not block reflexive movement (because a covert DP has non-interpretable phi-features). Here is the derivation of (7a):

(24) ... [$_{CP-EMB}$ [$_{AdvP3}$ what] [$_C$ phi-ff$_{DP2}$-[Dat] [$_C$ [+wh][Dat]]] [$_{TP-EMB}$ [$_{DP2}$ he-t$_{ff-[Dat]}$] [T+V$_{EMB}$] ...t$_2$ t$_3$]]

(25) ... [$_{CP-EMB}$ [$_{AdvP3}$ what] [$_C$] [$_{TP-EMB}$ [$_{DP2}$ he-t$_{ff-[Dat]}$] [T+V$_{EMB}$] ...t$_2$ t$_3$]]

---

[8] I assume that the [wh] feature is —int only on C but it is +int on a wh-word.

[9] Since the phi-features of an arbitrary PRO are +int, the prediction is that *sebja* cannot be LD bound when it is embedded into an infinitive with an arbitrary PRO. This prediction turns out to be true:

(i) Ivan$_1$ sprosil stjuardessu, čto PRO$_2$-ARB nadevat' na
John$_1$-N asked flight-attendant-A what PRO$_2$-ARB put-on on
sebja*$_{1/2}$ v slučae popadanija v vodu
self*$_{1/2}$-A in case of finding-oneself-G in water-A
'John$_1$ asked the flight-attendant what to put on oneself / *himself$_1$ in case of finding oneself in water'

The derivation in (24)–(25) is similar to the derivation in (20)–(21) The only difference is that the phi-features of PRO are –int and thus delete at LF. The –int [+wh] also deletes, and C is empty.

To conclude, I propose that PRO is checked for Dative by a null or overt C similar to overt infinitive subjects. There is a significant difference between a null C which checks Dative for overt subjects and a null C that checks Dative for PRO: the former blocks reflexive movement but the latter does not block the movement. I propose that a controlled PRO inherently has –int phi-features since these fea-tures can be recovered for interpretation under control. Then, in the case of overt subjects, C has the subject's phi-features after case checking, it is not empty and blocks movement. In the case of PRO, C is empty after case checking, and the movement is not blocked. That is, I can preserve both the uniformity of Dative Case checking and the blocking effect related to overt but not to PRO subjects.

4. Conclusions

In this article, I have introduced the feature movement account of LD binding. This account is based on syntax mechanisms and supports the syntactic approach to LD binding. Based on the derivation by phase framework, I explain the distribution of LD reflexives by the [+R] feature's need to go through every C on its way to the antecedent clause. I have shown that the feature content of C is crucial for the derivation with [+R] movement to converge. This derivation cannot converge if C has an interpretable feature: then, [+R] will not be able to pass through C. My account of the blocking effect of C is based on the antisymmetry constraint on feature adjunction. My account shows, first, that the distinction between interpretable and non-interpretable feature` s is crucial, and, second, that the [+wh] feature of C is non-interpretable.

The derivation of overt subject vs. PRO infinitives is crucially based on the proposal that the Dative for the infinitive subject (both overt subject and covert PRO) is checked by C but not by an infinitive T. I have shown that the phi-features of a controlled PRO are non-interpretable.

References:

Babby, Leonard: 1997, 'Subject Control as Direct Predication: Evidence from Russian', Bošković, S. Franks, and W. Snyder (eds.), *Formal Approaches to Slavic Linguistics 7, The Connecticut Meeting 1997*, Ann Arbor: Michigan Slavic Publications, 17-37.

Bailyn, John: 1992, 'LF Movement of Anaphors and the Acquisition of Embedded Clauses in Russian', *Language Acquisition* 2 (4), 307-335.

Chomsky, Noam: 1995, *The Minimalist Program*, Cambridge, Mass.: MIT Press.

Chomsky, Noam: 1999, *Derivation by Phase*, MIT Occasional Papers in Linguistics 18, MITWPL.

Chomsky, Noam, and Howard Lasnik: 1993, 'The Theory of Principles and Parameters', J. Jackobs, A. Van Stechow, W. Sternefeld, and T. Vennemann (eds), *An International Handbook of Contemporary Research 1,* Berlin: Walter de Gruyter, 506-569.

Cole, Peter, Gabriella Hermon, and Li-May Sung: 1990, 'Principles and Parameters of Long-Distance Reflexives', *Linguistic Inquiry* 21 (1), 1-22.

Franks, Steven, and Norbert Hornstein: 1992, 'Secondary Predication in Russian and Proper Government of PRO', R. Larson, S. Iatridou, U. Lahiri, and J. Higginbotham (eds.), *Control and Grammar*, Kluwer: Dordrecht, 1-50.

Hellan, Lars: 1991, 'Containment and Connectedness Anaphors', J. Koster and E. Reuland (eds.), *Long-Distance Anaphora*, Cambridge: Cambridge University Press, 27-49.

Kayne, Richard: 1994, *The Antisymmetry of Syntax*, The MIT Press: Cambridge, Massachusetts.

Laurençot, Elizabeth: 1997, 'On Secondary Predication and Null Case', M. Lindseth and S. Franks (eds.), *Formal Approaches to Slavic Linguistics 6, The Indiana Meeting 1996*, Ann Arbor: Michigan Slavic Publications, 191-206.

Moore, John, and David Perlmutter: 1999, 'Case, Agreement, and Temporal Particles in Russian Infinitive Clauses', *Journal of Slavic Linguistics* 7 (2), 171-198.

Moore, John, and David Perlmutter: 2000, 'What Does It Take to Be a Dative Subject?', *Natural Language and Linguistic Theory* 18 (2), 373-416.

Pica, Pièrre: 1987, 'On the Nature of the Reflexivization Cycle', J. McDonough, and B. Plunkett (eds.), *Proceedings of NELS* 17, 483-499.

Pica, Pièrre: 1991, 'On the Interaction between Antecedent-Government and Binding: The Case of Long-Distance Reflexivization', J. Koster and E. Reuland (eds.), *Long-Distance Anaphora,* Cambridge: Cambridge University Press, 119-135.

Rappaport, Gilbert: 1986, 'On Anaphor Binding in Russian', *Natural Language and Linguistic Theory* 4, 97-120.

Sells, Peter: 1987, 'Aspects of Logophoricity', *Linguistic Inquiry* 18 (3), 445-479.

Watanabe, Akira: 1993, *Agr-Based Case Theory and Its Interaction with the A' Theory,* PhD Dissertation, MIT.

Zribi-Hertz, Anne: 1989, 'Anaphor Binding and Narrative Point of View: English Reflexive Pronouns in Sentence and Discourse', *Language* 65, 695-727.

Elena Rudnitskaya
CUNY Graduate Center & Institute for Oriental Studies
Institute for Oriental Studies
The Language Division
12/1, Rozhdestvenka,
Moscow, 103753, Russia
e-mail: erudnits@mtu-net.ru

A Scrambling Analysis of Russian WH-Questions[*]

Natalya Strahov
Ben Gurion University of the Negev

1. Introduction

Although Russian seemingly has Wh-movement (both full and partial) as well as *Wh-in-situ*, I argue that Russian *Wh*-questions do not constitute a unique *Wh*-feature driven phenomenon, but are best analyzed as a product of other scrambling processes attested in the language. It follows that with respect to *Wh*-movement, Russian is an *in situ* language, just like Chinese. It is further argued that scrambling, including *Wh*-fronting, in Russian is triggered by the need to check a strong *Topic* or *Focus* feature of a *Top* or *Foc* head respectively (cf. Rizzi 1997). Therefore, there are actually two types of movement involved *Topicalization* and *Focalization*.

My arguments are based on the observation that Russian typologically patterns with *in situ* languages in that the question word is a variable which can be bound by a phonologically null question operator. Following Cheng 1991 and Tsai 1994 inter alia I assume that the question operator is universally generated as a null operator and that a *Wh*-word is universally a variable. Languages, however, differ with respect to whether or not the operator and the variable are integrated in the lexicon into one word. I illustrate that in Russian *Wh*-words may be used in a variety of non-question functions appropriate to a bound variable. These facts (among others) are used to argue that Russian is, in fact, an *in situ* language.

---

[*] Acknowledgements: I would like to thank John Bailyn, Robert Channon, Ariel Cohen, Steven Franks, Alex Grosu, Idan Landau, Luba Manto, Tova Rapoport, Michael Yadroff, audiences at FASL 9, Ben-Gurion University of the Negev and Tel-Aviv University for helpful comments and discussions. I am especially indebted for their help to Nomi Erteschik-Shir and Julia Horvath. All mistakes remain my own.

Following Cheng 1991, it is assumed that every clause must be typed. In case of *Wh*-questions there are two possible strategies of clausal typing: either with the help of a clausal typing particle, or by fronting a *Wh*-word to a position in which it forms a spec-head configuration with the [*Wh*]-feature. I incorporate Cheng's Clausal Typing Hypothesis (CTH) that says that the two options do not alternate, and in case a language possesses a clausal typing particle it must use this particle to type a clause. It is demonstrated that Russian behaves as a language of this class.

This paper is organized as follows: the strategies of *Wh*-question formation existing in Russian are presented in Section 2. Section 3 is devoted to the analysis of Russian as an *in situ* language. It starts with a discussion of a novel piece of evidence illustrating that *Wh*-elements in Russian may be used as variables bound by non-question operators (Section 3.1). Cheng's CTH is presented in Section 3.2. Section 3.3 demonstrates that Russian possesses a yes/no typing particle (*li*). Cheng's prediction is that Russian possesses a *Wh*-particle (which may or may not be overt). It is illustrated in Section 3.4 that this prediction is borne out in Russian.

A number of parallels between scrambling and *Wh*-fronting in Russian are outlined in Section 4. Section 5 introduces Rizzi's Split-CP hypothesis. After a minor refinement it is applied to the analysis of scrambling in Russian. It is argued that two different scrambling processes with distinct semantic properties should be distinguished in the language: Topicalization and Focalization (Section 6). Section 7 elaborates on the predictions of the analysis and their actual realization.[1]

Some advantages of the present proposal of similar approaches to *Wh*-fronting (Bošković 1998, 1999, 2000, Stepanov 1997) are outlined in Section 8.

2. *Wh*-Question Formation in Russian

Russian utilizes a number of strategies for *Wh*-question formation: it allows fully moved *Wh*-phrases with a *Wh*-phrase moved into its scopal

---

[1] This paper focuses on Russian mainly for the reasons of space. The analysis outlined here has broader cross-linguistic consequences some of which are discussed in Strahov (1998).

position (1), as well as *Wh*-phrases left *in situ* (2). Examples in (3) illustrate that a *Wh*-phrase is not obligatorily clause-initial:

(1) *Wh-phrases in initial position.*
   a. *Kogo* Marija vstretila *t* na ulice?
      who-acc Marija-nom met on street
      'Who did Mary meet in the street?'
   b. *Gde* on utverždaet čto videl ètu ženščinu t?
      where he-nom claims that saw this woman-acc
      'Where does he claim that he saw this woman?'

(2) *Wh-phrases in situ.*
   a. Ugadaj, Marija vstretila na ulice *kogo*?
      guess Mary-nom met on street who-acc
      'Guess, who did Mary meet in the street?'
   b. On utverždaet čto videl ètu ženščinu *gde*?
      he-nom claims that saw this woman-acc where?
      'Where does he claim that he saw this woman?'

(3) *Wh-phrase fronted to a non-initial position.*
   a. Ty *kuda* sejčas ideš?
      you-nom where now go
      'Where are you going now?'
   b. Marija *kogo* vstretila na ulice?
      Mary-nom who-acc met on street
      'Who did Mary meet in the street?'

Tsai 1994 schematizes the two strategies of *Wh*-question formation as (4):

(4) a. *Wh-in-situ is bound by the question operator, no movement*:
      $[_{X''} \Delta [_{X'}...WH...]] \rightarrow [_{X''} OpQ [x'...WH...]] \rightarrow$
      $[_{X''} Op_i Q [_{X'}...WH(i)...]$
   b. Wh-phrase in a scopal position, movement:
      $[_{X''} \Delta [_{X'}...WH...]] \rightarrow [_{X''} WHi [_{X'}...t_i...]]$

According to Tsai, (4a) should always have priority over (4b) for reasons of economy. Thus, apparent optionality of *Wh*-movement, like all optional movement rules, poses a serious problem for the Minimalist Program of Chomsky 1995, which sees movement as a "last resort".

I argue that *Wh*-fronting in Russian is neither optional, nor is it triggered by the need to check a strong *Wh*-feature. I propose that *Wh*-questions are best analyzed as a product of scrambling pro-cesses pervasively utilized by the language. It follows that with respect to *Wh*-movement Russian is an *in situ* language, and it is expected to pattern typologically with other *in situ* languages (e.g. Chinese). This hypothesis is explored in the next section.

3. Russian as an *in situ* Language

Cheng 1991 suggests that *Wh-in-situ* languages have the following characteristics:

(i) *Wh-in-situ*;
(ii) *Wh*-elements are indefinite pronouns (variables), not operators;
(iii) yes/no clausal typing particles;
(iv) *Wh*-clausal typing particle.

In this section I demonstrate that Russian exhibits all the properties of an in situ language.

3.1. *Wh*-in-situ and *Wh*-words used as bound variables

It has been observed (see the examples in (2)) that along with fronted *Wh*-phrases Russian allows for a *Wh*-phrase to stay *in situ*.

According to Cheng 1991, languages differ with respect to whether the variable and the Question operator are combined in the lexicon into one word. It has been illustrated that *in situ* languages (Chinese, Japanese) the question words are indefinite pronouns (i.e. variables) "that lack inherent quantificational force" (Cheng 1991:36). As a result, they can be bound by a phonologically null question operator, and their interrogative function is signaled by a *Wh*-particle. In addition, these words may be used in a variety of non-question functions appropriate to a bound variable as well. Examples in (5) illustrate that in Japanese *Wh*-phrases can have interrogative (5) universal (5) and existential (5) interpretation(s) (from Cheng 1991:36, (20)):

(5) a. *Dare*-ga ki-masu-ka.
       who-nom come-Q
       'Who is coming?'
    b. *Dare*-ga ki-te mo, boku-wa aw-a-nai.
       who-nom come-Q I-Top meet not
       'For all x, if x comes, I would not meet (x).'
    c. *Dare*-kara-ka henna tegami-ga todoi-ta
       who-from-Q strange letter-nom arrived
       'A strange letter came from god knows who (someone)'.

Thus, if Russian is an *in situ* language we expect it to behave similarly.

In fact, Russian *Wh*-words are used to form different types of indefinites. Importantly, in Russian just like in Japanese (Cheng 1991) it is also possible to use a bare form of the *Wh*-words with a non-interrogative (indefinite) meaning.

The examples in (6) illustrate that nominal (6a, 6b, 6d) and adverbial (6c) *Wh*-phrases may be bound by a non-interrogative operator *If*:

(6) a. Esli ty *kogo* vstretiš', to skaži emu,
       if you-nom who-acc meet then tell him-dat
       čto menja net doma.
       that me-Gen not home
       'For all x, if you meet x, tell x that I am not at home'.
    b. Esli *čto* slučit'sja, to zvoni mne nemedlenno.
       if what-nom happens then call me-dat immediately
       'If *anything* happens, call me immediately.'
    c. Esli *kogda* budeš' v našem rajone, to zaxodi,
       if when will be in our area then come by
       ne stesnjajsja.
       not (be) shy
       'If *sometime* you are in our area, drop in, don't be shy'.
    d. Esli *u kogo* est' osel, on vsegda b'et ego.
       if to who-gen is donkey he-nom always beats him
       'If *a man* owns a donkey, he always beats it.'

In summary, *Wh*-words have been shown to behave similarly to *Wh*-elements of other *in situ* languages in that they may be used as indefinites bound by non-question operators.

3.2. The Clausal Typing Hypothesis (CTH) (Cheng 1991)

As a point of departure I take Cheng's Clausal Typing Hypothesis (CTH) (1991:30), and assume that every clause must be typed. *Wh*-questions may be typed in one of the two ways: either with the help of a clausal particle, or by fronting a *Wh*-word to form a spec-head configuration with the *Wh*-feature. The two options do not alternate, and in case a language possesses a clausal typing particle it must use it to type a clause.

The CTH makes two points: (i) *Wh*-movement is seen as "a last resort"; (ii) there is no optionality involved in *Wh*-questions: the two methods of clausal typing should be in complementary distribution.

Thus, all languages are predicted to belong to one of the two groups: those with true syntactic movement, and those without such movement (i.e. *in situ* languages).

Based on the generalization concerning the latter group of languages, Cheng suggests (1991:21-23) that languages with special markings in yes/no questions are *in situ* languages, and predicts that such languages possess a *Wh*-typing particle (which may or may not be overt).

In the next section I demonstrate that Russian has a yes/no typing particle (*li*) which it uses to type a clause as a yes/no question.

3.3. Particle *li* as a yes/no Clausal Typing Particle

Example (7) illustrates that *li* is used in matrix and embedded questions:

(7) a. Čital   *li* Dima   ètu   knigu?
       read   Q   Dima-nom this   book-acc
       'Has Dima read this book?'
    b. Dima   sprosil čital *li* Aleks   ètu   knigu.
       Dima asked   read   Q   Alex-nom   this   book-acc
       'Dima asked whether Alex read this book.'

The particle *li* introducing general questions is in complementary distribution with the complementizer *čto* ('that'), which introduces a declarative embedded clause:

(8) a. *Dima sprosil čto čital li Aleks ètu knigu.
    Dima asked that read Q Aleks-nom this book-acc
  b. *Dima sprosil čto li čital Aleks ètu knigu.
    Dima asked that Q read Aleks-nom this book-acc

These observations allow me conclude that the particle *li* is a typing particle which is used to type a clause as a yes/no question.[2]

3.4 [wh Ø] Clausal Typing Particle

Note that the particle *li* is in complementary distribution not only with the complementizer *čto*, but also with *Wh*-phrases:

(9) a.* *Kto* li čitaet knigu?
       who-nom Q read book-acc
   b. **Kogo* li Dima priglasil v kino?
       who-acc Q Dima-nom invited to cinema

Under the assumption that *Wh*-fronting is an instance of true syntactic *Wh*-movement triggered by the need to check a strong *Wh*-feature the fact that *Wh*-phrases and the particle *li* are in complementary distribution in Russian is not problematic. However, the data in (9) pose a problem for the proposal I have been arguing for, i.e. that *Wh*-fronting in Russian is an instance of scrambling. The problem may be formulated as follows: if *Wh*-fronting is scrambling, then why should there be any difference between scrambling of *Wh*-phrases vs. scrambling of other constituents?

My claim is that Russian possesses a phonologically null clausal typing particle [wh Ø] that it uses to type a clause as a *Wh*-question. This particle is in complementary distribution both with the particle *li*, and with the declarative complementizer *čto* ('that'). Under this assumption the incompatibility of the particle *li* with the fronted *Wh*-phrases in interrogative clauses follows.

4. Some Parallels between *Wh*-fronting and Scrambling in Russian

Once we have established that Russian patterns typologically with other *in situ* languages, it is predicted that *Wh*-fronting is not an instance of

---

[2] A detailed discussion of the paticle *li* and its properties is beyond the scope of this paper. For an analysis see Franks 1998, King 1994 and Rudnitskaya 1999.

true syntactic *Wh*-movement, but rather that of scrambling. Therefore their behavior is expected to be syntactically in-distinguishable.

The term "scrambling" has been used to describe a number of unrelated phenomena with different properties. Sekerina 1997 demonstrated that scrambling to a sentence-initial position has properties of *A-bar* movement in Russian, while Bailyn 1995 argued that some instances of VP-internal scrambling have properties of *A*-movement. Sekerina 1997 further observed that there are certain parallels in the behavior of *Wh*-fronting and scrambling in Russian:

I. Both can be clause-internal and long-distance.

(10) a. *Clause-internal scrambling.*
[Èti ovošči]   on   ljubit *t*.
these vegetables-acc he-nom like
'He likes these vegetables'.
b. *Clause-internal Wh-fronting.*
Čto   ty   ljubiš *t*?
what-acc you-nom like
'What do you like?'

(11) a. *Long-distance scrambling* (from Zemskaja 1973).
Vy   [*posylku*   [videli [*t* [kak zapakovali *t*]]]?
you-nom package-acc saw   how   packed
'Did you see how they packed the package'?
b. *Long-distance Wh-fronting.*
Kogo   Dima   prosit Svetu   priglasit' *t*?
Who-acc Dima-nom asks   Sveta-acc to invite
'Who does Dima ask Sveta to invite?'[3]

II. Scrambling like *Wh*-fronting is not obligatorily to the clause-initial position:

(12) a. Ja   [èti ovošči]   ljublju *t*.
I-nom this vegetables-acc like
'I like these vegetables.'

---

[3] The sentence in (11b) can also mean 'Who does Dima ask *t* to invite Sveta?' This reading is irrelevant here.

(12) b. Ty   [*kuda*] sejčas ideš' *t*?
       you-nom where   now   go
       'Where are you going now?'

III. Scrambling and *Wh*-fronting are restricted by the same island constraints: sentential subject constraint, adjunct-island, complex NP constraint (Bailyn 1995, Sekerina 1997), but allow extraction from a *Wh*-island.

IV. Both multiple scrambling and multiple *Wh*-fronting exist:

(13) a. [*Èto*   *plat'e*]   [*mne*]   šila   podruga.
        this   dress-acc me-dat   sewed   friend-nom
        'A friend of mine sewed this dress for me.'
     b. [*Komu*]   [*čto*]   Dima   prines?
        whom-dat what-acc Dima-nom   brought
        'What did Dima bring to who?'

V. Fronted *Wh*-phrases do not form one constituent:

(14) *Komu*   Maša   *kogda*   zvonila?
     who-dat Masha-nom   when   called
     'Who did Masha call when?'

Based on Rizzi's 1997 Split-CP Hypothesis I argue that movement of the constituents to the left periphery of the clause in Russian is not optional, but is triggered by the need to check the Strong Top/Foc features of these functional heads in a spec-head configuration. I argue for two different scrambling processes in Russian: Topicalization and Focalization.

5. Rizzi's 1997 Split-CP Hypothesis

Rizzi 1997 (297:(41)) argues for the following clausal structure.

(15) [$_{ForceP}$ Relative Op [$_{Force}$ [$_{TopP*}$ [$_{Top}$ [$_{FocP}$ Question Op [$_{Foc}$ [$_{TopP*}$ [$_{Top}$ [$_{FinP}$ [$_{Fin}$ [$_{IP}$]]]]]]]]]]]

Among other things Rizzi proposes that Question Operators must move into *SpecFoc*. However, as he himself points out, in Italian other types of constituents may be focalized. Thus, according to Rizzi, Question Operators compete with other focalized constituents for this position. On considering these two types of Focalization Rizzi observes that movement of a *Wh*-phrase into *SpecFoc* triggers *I* to *C* movement of the verb, while focalization of other types of constituents does not. To account for this, he proposes that when *SpecFoc* is occupied by a *Wh*-element, the inflected verb carrying the *Wh*-feature must move to *Foc* to check the *Wh*-feature and to satisfy the *Wh*-Criterion. However, when a non-*Wh*-element is fronted, *I*-to-*C* movement of the verb is not induced. Rizzi suggests that in the latter case it is the Focus Criterion which is satisfied: the *Foc* head inherently possesses a Focus feature checked by the fronted elements in a spec-head configuration.

This proposal has two theoretical disadvantages. First, if we assume that the FocP is responsible for the satisfaction of two different criteria (the *Wh*-criterion and the Foc-criterion), then we have to set an artificial requirement that the *Wh*-criterion must override the Focus criterion in order to predict that in case a *Wh*-element and a non-*Wh*-element compete for the same position, it is the *Wh*-phrase which moves. Second, if we consider the complementizer system to be an interface between the propositional content (expressed by the IP) and the superordinate structure, then we expect the selectional restrictions of the immediately higher systems to be satisfied in ForceP, while the selectional restrictions of the lower system is satisfied in FinP. In other words, the selectional restriction of the verb subcategorizing for a [+*WH*] complement (such as *ask*, *wonder*) should be satisfied in ForceP, and not in FocP, as suggested by Rizzi. However, under the assumption that *Wh*-phrases move to SpecFoc this becomes a problematic issue, because the moved *Wh*-phrase is not in a spec-head configuration with the relevant (*Wh*) feature. Consequently, some additional mechanism (possibly feature-percolation) is required to satisfy the selectional restriction of such verbs. Although theoretically undesirable, this step would enable us to account for embedded questions such as (16) where no material intervenes between the embedding predicate '*wonder*' and the *Wh*-phrase *who*:

(16) a. John wonders *who* you invited *t* to the party.
     b. Io vorrei sapere *perche* Gianni ha portato via il mio libro.
(Italian)
'I would like to know why Gianni took away my book'.

However, some extra machinery is needed to account for sentences in which topicalized material appears between the embedding predicate selecting an embedded question *vorrei sapere*, and the *Wh*-phrase *perche* invoked to satisfy its selectional requirements in a spec-head configuration:

(17) Ora, io vorrei sapere [TopPil mio libro] *perche* Gianni lo ha portato via.
'Now, I would like to know my book why Gianni took it away.'

I suggest a minor refinement of Rizzi's original proposal which enables to avoid such an unnecessary complication of the grammar. Namely, in languages with the *Wh*-movement triggered by the need to check a *Wh*-feature, the Question Operators move all the way up to the Spec of *ForceP* where the *Wh*-feature is checked, thus satisfying the *Wh*-criteria.

(18) *Refinement of Rizzi 1997:*

[ForceP Relative Op/Wh Op [Force [TopP* [Top [FocP Wh=indefinite pronoun [Foc [TopP* [Top [FinP [Fin [IP]]]]]]]]]]]

This adjustment has a number of important consequences. On the one hand, it repairs a problematic account of the two instances of movement to *SpecFoc*, substituting them by movements into two distinct Spec positions (*SpecForce* and *SpecFoc*) where the *Wh*-criterion and the Focus criterion respectively are satisfied. On the other hand, it enables to extend Rizzi's analysis to account for those *in situ* languages which allow for optional fronting of *Wh*-phrases. That this option is available in some *in situ* languages has been mentioned by a number of linguists. For example, Dayal 1996:20 notes that fronting of *Wh*-elements is possible in Hindi, but this should be viewed as an instance of scrambling or Topicalization, rather then of "pure" *Wh*-movement. Recall that, according to Cheng 1991 and Tsai 1994, languages differ in whether a *Wh*-operator and a variable are integrated in the lexicon into one word or not. In the former case *Wh*-phrases are operators. Consequently, they must move to *SpecForce* to satisfy the *Wh*-criterion. This case of *Wh*-fronting is an instance of true syntactic *Wh*-movement. In the latter case *Wh*-elements are not operators but variables. They can either stay *in situ*, or move to some clause-initial position. Importantly, in spite of the fact that such movement of *Wh*-elements looks superficially like regular *Wh*-movement, it is not actually triggered by the need to check a *Wh*-feature.

In these languages the *Wh*-criterion is satisfied independently with the help of a typing particle (overt or not), which is inserted directly in *SpecForce*. Such fronting of *Wh*-phrases is indistinguishable from scrambling.

Therefore, in relation to the problematic example (17), I propose that Italian *Wh*-fronting is not an instance of true syntactic *Wh*-movement, i.e. the requirements of the higher system are satisfied independently (possibly by a non-overt *Wh*-question operator). As a consequence, an intervening topicalized Wh-phrase lower than *SpecForce* does not trigger a violation of the *Wh*-criterion. It follows that in Italian *Wh*-fronting is a case of Focalization.[4]

Note that this adjustment of Rizzi's Split-CP hypothesis not only enables us to account for the different types of *Wh*-fronting, but incorporates the insights that *Wh*-phrases in the two types of languages have distinct properties (operators vs. variables). In addition, Rizzi's Split CP may now be easily applied to those *Wh-in-situ* languages that allow for optional *Wh*-fronting. This problematic optionality is eliminated once such fronting is analyzed as an instance of movement to FocP or to TopP triggered by the need to check strong Focus or Topic features of the heads. I use Russian to have a closer look at this issue.

6. Scrambling as Topicalization and Focalization

Russian is notorious for its "free" word order. It is often argued that different linear orderings of the constituents result from scrambling. I view scrambling not as a uniform phenomenon, but as an instantiation of two distinct processes, Topicalization and Focalization. Following Rizzi 1997 I assume that these two processes are triggered by the Topic and the Focus criteria.

I argued above that *Wh*-fronting in Russian is an instance of scrambling. Thus, it ultimately follows that *Wh*-questions are derived by these two mechanisms. A proposal along these lines enables to syntactically distinguish between fronted *Wh*-phrases with different

---

[4] It may be further speculated that Wh-phrases in Italian may only be Foci, and not Topics. This would account for a notoriously known ban against multiple interrogations in the language (see the discussion of Russian Topics for further details). I leave this issue for further research.

semantic properties, and to provide an elegant account of the Superiority effects in multiple *Wh*-questions.

6.1. Wh-fronting in Russian as Topicalization and Focalization

Following Erteschik-Shir 1997, among others, I assume that two types of questions should be distinguished. A type of interrogations containing a non-D-linked (Pesetsky 1987) *Wh*-phrase asks for new information. Such *Wh*-phrases are viewed as foci, and this type of interrogation is derived by Focalization.

(19) *Kogo   ty   vstretil?*
     who-acc   you-nom   met
     'Who did you meet?'

Wh-phrases that belong to the second type ask for identification of an entity from a contextually given set. They are D-linked, or specific. According to Erteschik-Shir (1997:9) "the topic is used to in-voke knowledge in the pos-session of an audience", i.e. it is "old" information. Thus, D-linked *Wh*-elements display Topic-like properties. It is for this reason that they are considered topics, and this *Wh*-fronting is argued to be derived by Topicalization. This type of *Wh*-fronting is found in multiple *Wh*-questions.

6.2. Multiple *Wh*-fronting

It has been observed by Kiss 1993 that pair-list multiple *Wh*-questions do not have a singular interpretation, i.e., (20) cannot mean 'for which person did Dima bring something, and what was it', it can only mean 'for each person, what did Dima bring for him/ her?':

(20) *Komu   čto   Dima   prines?*
     whom-dat   what-acc   Dima-nom   brought
     'What did Dima bring to who?'

The outermost *Wh*-element acts semantically as a distributive universal quantifier: in a given context or situation it asks for the pairing of entities from a given set known to both the speaker and the listener with some other entity (possibly, but not obligatory from another given set).[5] Evidently, the outermost *Wh*-element can play this role only in case it is D-linked, i.e. possesses topic-like properties. This follows straightforwardly from the present analysis. Moreover, since multiple topicalization is allowed in Russian, multiple *Wh*-questions are predicted to be possible.

6.3. Superiority Effects in Russian

Blond 1996 argues that Russian exhibits Superiority effects. According to Blond the order of fronted *Wh*-words observes a certain grammatical hierarchy: Subject > IDO > DO > Adverb. Others claim that the order is completely free (King 1995, Stepanov 1997). The truth seems to lie in the middle. The order of *Wh*-phrases in multiple *Wh*-questions is free, but it is restricted by one requirement: the outermost *Wh*-phrase must be D-linked, or specific (Topic in our terms). My analysis easily accounts for this restriction.

6.4. Fronting to a non-initial position

We have seen in (3) (repeated here as (21)) that fronted *Wh*-elements do not obligatorily surface in the sentence-initial position, but may be preceded by other topicalized elements:

(21) Ty   kuda   ideš?
     you-nom where   go
     'Where are you going?'

Nor do fronted *Wh*-pharses form one constituent:

(22) Komu   Maša   kogda   zvonila?
      who-dat Maša-nom   when   called
      'Who did Masha call when?'

The analysis outlined above views *Wh*-fronting as indistinct from Topicalization/Focalization. Hence these data are accounted for.

---

[5] Stepanov 1998, in discussing multiple *Wh*-fronting, argues that questions like (20) can have either individual or pair-list readings. However, following Comorovsky 1996, Kiss 1993, among others, I assume that it is of crucial importance for any analysis to distinguish between two types of multiple Wh-questions: *pair-list* and *conjoined* question. In what follows I restrict the discussion to pair-list questions.

7. Predictions of the Analysis: Partial *Wh*-movement

Since Split-CP structure is available both in matrix and in embedded clauses it follows that fronting to the intermediate Spec positions should be possible. This prediction is borne out in Russian:[6]

(23) Ugadaj, Marina skazala čto *kogo*
  guess Marina-nom said that who-acc
  nužno priglasit' na večer?
  should invite on party
  'Guess, who did Marina say should be invited to the party?'

8. Similar Approaches to Russian *Wh*-questions

The suggestion that Russian (and possibly other Slavic languages) is an *in situ* language is by no means new. Recently, a similar approach to *Wh*-fronting in Russian has been advocated in a series of papers (Stepanov 1997, Bošković 1998, Bošković 1999, Bošković 2000).

One may wonder what is gained by present analysis and how it differs from the previous accounts. Abstracting away from many details, I concentrate here on one salient aspect: Whereas other approaches view *Wh*-fronting as purely Focus motivated, I set apart *Wh*-fronting triggered by Topic and Focus features. Importantly, the two proposals have a number of empirical consequences which can be tested.

Yadroff (to appear) points out that maintaining the view that *Wh*-fronting is purely Focus motivated results in (at least) two corollaries: (1) Multiple Focus Fronting (MFF) is not restricted to *Wh*-constituents; (2) It is impossible to split the sequence of fronted *Wh*-phrases by a topicalized constituent. As shown by Yadroff, both predictions turn to be empirically inadequate. As example (24) shows (from Yadroff (to appear)), Russian does not allow for MFF of non-*Wh*-constituents, and a topicalized constituent can interrupt the sequence of fronted *Wh*-phrases (see (14) above).

(24) *IVANU, KNIGU ja dam zavtra.
  to Ivan-dat book-acc I-nom (shall)give tomorrow

---

[6] I am grateful to M. Yadroff for his suggestion to embed questions with *Wh-in-situ* into matrix such as 'ugadaj' to make them unambiguously non-echo questions.

Since the idea of uniqueness of Focus and recursiveness of Topic is built into syntactic, these data are unproblematic for (and, in fact, follows from) my analysis.

Furthermore, the analysis advocated in this paper enables to account for an apparent contradiction (discussed in Yadroff (to appear)) that some *Wh*-phrases in Russian pattern with Topics (e.g. in allowing multiple *Wh*-fronting), but display Focus-like behavior with respect to WCO (25).

(25) *Kogo$_i$ ego$_i$ mat'   vsegda   uvažala t?
     who$_i$-acc his$_i$ mother-nom   always   respected

Treating *Wh*-fronting as a non-uniform phenomenon provides an elegant solution to this puzzle: multiple Wh-fronting is a result of Topicalization (thus its Topic-like properties), whereas simple Wh-questions in (25) are derived by Focalization. In the latter case they are expected to behave like bare quantifiers since Focus is quantificational, but Topic is not (Rizzi 1997, Yadroff (to appear)). Notice that WCO may be eliminated (or at least reduced) once a Wh-phrase is unambiguously a Topic:

(26) Kogo$_i$ iz   ètix   malčikov ego$_i$ mat'
     whom$_i$-acc from   these   boys   his$_i$ mother-nom
     vsegda   uvažala   t?
     always   respected
     'Which of these boys his mother always respected?'

References

Bailyn, John. (1995), A Configurational Approach to Russian "Free" Word Order. Ph.D. Dissertation, Cornell University.

Blond, Victoria. (1996), Multiple Wh-questions in Russian. M.A. Thesis, Bar Ilan University, Tel-Aviv.

Bošković, Željko. (1998), "*Wh*-phrases and *Wh*-movement in Slavic". Position paper presented at the Comparative Slavic Morphosyntax Workshop, Bloomington, Indiana.

Bošković, Željko. (1999), "On the interpretation of multiple *Wh*-Questions", ms. UConn.

Bošković, Željko. (2000), "What is special about multiple *Wh*-fronting". NELS 30.

Cheng, Lisa. (1991), On the Topology of Wh-Questions. Ph.D.Dissertation, MIT, Cambridge, Massachusetts.

Chomsky, Noam. (1995), The Minimalist Program. MIT Press, Cambridge, Massachusetts.

Comorovski, Ileana. (1996), Interrogative Phrases and the Syntax-Semantic Interface. Kluwer Academic Publishers, Dordrecht.

Dayal, Veneta. (1996), Locality in Wh-Quantification: Questions and Relative Clauses in Hindi. Kluwer Academic Publishers.

Erteschik-Shir, Nomi. (1997), The Dynamics of Focus Structure. Cambridge University Press, Cambridge.

Franks, Steven. (1998), "Clitics in Slavic". Position paper presented at *the Comparative Slavic Morphosyntax Workshop*, Bloomington, Indiana.

King, Tracy Holloway. (1994), "Focus in Russian yes-no questions". Journal of Slavic Linguistics, 2, 92-120.

King, Tracy Holloway. (1995), Configuring Topic and Focus in Russian. Stanford: CSLI Pub.

Kiss, É. Katherine. (1993), "*Wh*-movement and specificity". Natural Language and Linguistic Theory, 11, 85-120.

Pesetsky, David. (1987), "Wh-in situ: movement and unselective binding. E. Reuland and A. ter Meulen, eds. The Representation of (In)definiteness. Cambridge, MA: MIT Press, 98-129.

Rizzi, Luigi. (1997), "The fine structure of the Left Periphery". L. Haegeman, ed., Elements of Grammar. Kluwer: Dordrecht, 281-337.

Rudnitskaya, Elena. (1999), "The derivation of yes-no *li* questions in Russian: syntax or/and phonology?" Presented at Formal Approaches to Slavic Linguistics 8, University of Pensylvania.

Sekerina, Irina. (1997), The Syntax and Processing of Scrambling Constructions in Russian. Ph.D. Dissertation, CUNY.

Stepanov, Arthur. (1997), "On *Wh*-fronting in Russian". NELS 28.

Strahov, Natalia. (1998), The Typology of *Wh*-questions in Russian: a unified account. M.A. Thesis, Tel-Aviv University.

Tsai, W.-T. (1994), On Economizing the Theory of A-bar Dependencies. Ph.D. Dissertation, MIT.

Yadroff, Michael. (to appear), "What is the driving force for Multiple Wh-fronting". Proceedings of the Comparative Slavic Morphosyntax Workshop.

Zemskaja, E.A. (1973), Russkaja Razgovornaja Reč'. Moskva: Nauka.

nstrahov@bgumail.bgu.ac.il

Inertness of Sonorant [voice] in Polish

Yuki Takatori
Georgia State University

1. Voice Agreement in Polish

In Polish, two or more obstruents in a sequence must agree in voicing:

(1) [zb]igniew male name   [gd]y 'when'
     [tk]ać   'to weave'   [pš]y 'at'

Related to this general principle of cluster-building is a ban on voiced obstruents at the end of a word:

(2) chle[p] 'bread'   kre[f] 'blood'
     ló[t]   'ice'   nó[š]   'knife'

Voicing takes place only medially, when a voiceless obstruent comes to stand before a voiced obstruent within a derived noun (3a, b) or within a phrase such as (3c, d):

(3) a. pro[ś]+ić 'to request'   pro[ź]+[b]a   'a request'
     b. ja[k]   'how'   ja[g] [d]ługo   'how long'

In contrast with obstruents, the voice specification of sonorants changes little, as sonorants undergo devoicing only under very restricted circumstances: if, as illustrated in (4a, b), they follow a voiceless obstruent word-finally (regardless of whether the obstruent is underlyingly voiceless or has itself undergone devoicing), or, as in (4c, d), they appear between two voiceless obstruents. In all other environments, sonorants remain voiced (5):

(4) a. wia[tr]-u   wia[tr̥]   'wind' gen.sg/nom.sg.
     b. boja[źń]i   boja[śń̥]   'fear' gen.sg./nom.sg.
     c. [kr̥t]ań   'larynx'
     d. Pio[tr̥k]-a   'Peter' dim.gen.sg.

(5) a. do[m] 'house'   da[l]   'distance'
    b. poka[rm] 'food'   se[jm]   'parliament'
    c. wi[l]k 'wolf'   [r]tęć   'mercury'
    d. p[r]osić 'to request' ć[m]a   'moth'

Additionally, sonorants do not spread [voice] to an immediately preceding voiceless obstruent: *prosić (*[br]osić), ćma (*[dźm]a)*.

2. Representation of [Voice]

Having laid out the basic facts of Polish voicing phonology, I would now like to explore interactions among the phonological and morphological constraints that are responsible for the above alternations. But, first, I would like to reexamine the popular view on the status of [voice] in sonorants. On the basis of evidence garnered from a wide variety of languages, it has been suggested by many linguists that the feature [voice] be inherently unspecified in sonorants, for not only are sonorants voiced to an overwhelming extent in many of the languages studied, but it has been found that [+voice] is the normal status of the glottis in the articulation of sonorants (Chomsky and Halle 1968:301, Ladefoged 1971:108-11, Hyman 1975:44).This observation is substantiated by Kenstowicz (1994:36), who attributes voicing (and the lack thereof) to pressure differentiation in the oral cavity. In order for the voicing to occur, there has to be continuous airflow, which is possible only if the supralaryngeal pressure is smaller than sublaryngeal pressure. The stricture made for the articulation of obstruents increases the supralaryngeal pressure, inhibiting spontaneous airflow, whereas the stricture made for sonorants does not cause such interruption. This is why [+voice] is the natural status of the glottis for sonorants.

Leaving [voice] unspecified in underlying representations eliminates predictable, and therefore superfluous, information. Furthermore, it makes it possible to more adequately account for the "inertness" of sonorants in voice assimilation. As shown in (5d), sonorants do not take part in spreading [voice] to obstruents that precede them. If [voice] were present in sonorants, there would need to be a rule that spreads [voice] only from obstruents (Gussmann 1992). On the other hand, if it is absent from the underlying feature specification of sonorants, the lack of spreading can be explained quite naturally: it is impossible to spread that which does not exist.

This type of approach—coming up with representations from which rules naturally follow, rather than formulating rules which only apply in heavily restricted environments —had great appeal prior to the advent of Optimality Theory. However, such a strategy, based as it is on an input-specified [voice], does not mesh well with the tenet of OT that constraints are only about outputs. First of all, although positing an unspecified [voice] in sonorants may serve as an expedient way to account for their inertness, it is deceptive in that it neglects the reality that sonorants are unquestionably voiced. Furthermore, such a makeshift solution may lead to inconsistency (see Itô, Mester, and Padgett 1995 for the discussion about Compound Voicing in Japanese). A more convincing way to explain the inertness of [voice] would be to present straightforwardly the characteristic nature of [voice] in the representation of sonorants; to show, that is, that although from a phonetic point of view, sonorants have [voice] to the same extent that voiced obstruents do, that feature, nonetheless, does not spread.

3. Devoicing

There are two keys to a proper understanding of voicing phenomena. One of them is a constraint having to do with markedness and the other is one having to do with positional faithfulness (Beckman 1995, Steriade 1995). It has been observed that voiced obstruents are less prevalent than voiceless; that, in fact, most languages with a single series of obstruents have voiceless, rather than voiced, obstruents (Ladefoged and Maddieson 1996). A constraint that establishes [voice] as the marked value for obstruents would account for this prevalence. Lombardi (1999) proposes the constraint *LAR, which penalizes any voiced segment regardless of its position in a syllable:

(6) *LAR σ
         |
       [±son]
         |
       [voice]

The other constraint that plays a central role in voicing has to do with the position of release (Lombardi 1991):

(7) *Laryngeal* is licensed iff it occurs $[X\_\_ [+son] Y]_\sigma$

Since obstruents are released in this environment, one can go one step further and say that [voice] is licensed at the point of release. Lombardi's Laryngeal Constraint certainly applies here, but further analysis reveals a more satisfactory conclusion: this constraint is but one manifestation of a more general one, $IDENT_{Release}$, which demands that a released segment be left intact in an output:

(8) $IDENT_{Release}$: Preservation of underlying features must be enforced at the point of release.

It can be shown that the voice alternation in Polish emerges as a result of interactions between these two constraints, that is, between a markedness constraint banning voiced obstruents categorically and an IDENTITY constraint mandating that a released segment remain unchanged in an output.

In Polish, underlying voiced segments in codas become voiceless. This is a consequence of the dominance of the markedness constraint in relation to IDENT:

(9) *LAR >> IDENT

That voiced obstruents are more marked than their voiceless counterparts does not mean that devoicing can sweep across a word to eliminate all voiced obstruents, for devoicing at the point of release would result in an ungrammatical form. Therefore, the markedness constraint is outranked by $IDENT_{Release}$:

(10) $IDENT_{Release}$ >> *LAR

By transitivity, the overall ranking of $IDENT_{Release}$ >> *LAR >> IDENT obtains.

(11) IDENT$_{Release}$ >> *LAR >> IDENT
Syllable Coda: /bug/ <Bóg> 'God'

bug	IDENT$_{Release}$	*LAR	IDENT
a. bug		*!*	
b. ☞ buk			*

Syllable Onset

bug	IDENT$_{Release}$	*LAR	IDENT
c. puk	*!		*
d. ☞ buk		*	*

The same set of constraints accounts for devoicing word-internally before a voiceless obstruent (12). The /b/ in *żab-ka* 'frog' undergoes devoicing for the same reason the /g/ in *Bóg* does: the feature [voice] must be delinked due to a markedness constraint prohibiting voiced segments. In (12c), the feature [voice] propagates itself rightward to the immediately following released segment, a fatal violation:

(12)

żab+ka	IDENT$_{Release}$	*LAR	IDENT
a. żabka		*!	
b. ☞ żapka			*
c. żabga | [voice]	*!	**	*

By the same token, the devoicing of the prefix /v/ 'in, into' in *[f]pływać* 'flow in' occurs because /v/, even when part of a complex onset, is never released before another obstruent, and, when it is unreleased, its [voice] should be delinked:

(13)

[v+p]ływać	IDENT_Release	*LAR	IDENT
a. ☞ [fp]ływać			*
b. [vp]ływać		*!	
c. [vb]ływać |/ [voice]	*!	**	*

And, finally, the word-final consonant sequence in *gwia[zd]* 'star' collectively undergoes devoicing for precisely the same reasons:

(14)

gwia[zd]	IDENT_Release	*LAR	IDENT
a. ☞ gwia[st]			**
b. gwia[zd]		*!*	
c. gwia[zt]		*!	*

4. Internal Voicing

Voicing occurs only word- or phrase-internally:

(15) pro[ś] + [b]a pro[źb]a 'request' (*pro[śb]a)
 ja[k] [d]ługo ja[g d]ługo 'how long?' (*ja[k d]ługo)

In (15), the voiced obstruent spreads [voice] to the voiceless obstruent immediately preceding it. Without such spreading, the output would be ill-formed. What effects this transmission of [voice]? Padgett (1995:12) proposes a spreading constraint, which I adapt below:

(16) SPREAD(φ): Clusters must agree in Feature(φ).

Since SPREAD(Voice) must outrank IDENT (prohibiting any change in the output) and *LAR (prohibiting any voiced consonant in the output) in order for spreading to occur, and since the dominance of IDENT_Release over IDENT is a fixed one, the following ranking (as far as it goes) can be inferred:

(17) SPREAD(Voice) / IDENT_Release >> *LAR >> IDENT

The failed candidate (18a) does not change the input structure. The upshot of this inactivity is that the free-standing [voice] is associated only with /b/. This is precisely the kind of configuration which SPREAD(Voice) forbids. The other contender (18c) circumvents a SPREAD violation by eliminating [voice] altogether from the cluster. Unfortunately, this alters the released segment, a move which is more costly than preserving that feature, since it contravenes IDENT$_{Release}$:

(18)

	pro[ś+b]a	SPREAD / IDENT$_{Release}$	*LAR	IDENT
a.	prośba | [voice]	*!	*	
b. ☞	proźba \\| [voice]		**	*
c.	prośpa	*!		*
d.	proźpa | [voice]	*!*	*	**

The notion of [release] has very important consequences when applied to the analysis of voice assimilation. Devoicing and voicing are generally viewed as outcomes of neutralization and spreading, respectively, but such a way of seeing the process misses two things that have long been observed by Slavic linguists: (i) two (or more) obstruents in direct contiguity must agree in voicing; and (ii) the last of the contiguous obstruents determines the voice specification of the entire cluster. Consider the inputs and outputs of the following examples of assimilation:

(19) ża[bk]a → ża[pk]abk → pk
[vp]ływać → [fp]ływaćvp → fp
pro[śb]a → pro[źb]aśb → źb

In (19), each consonant sequence starts out with each of its two obstruents having a different voice specification, but ends up with both having the same one. The thing to note here is that when two obstruents disagree in voicing, it is always the unreleased segment, whether voiced or voiceless, that must change. Thus, what Slavicists refer to as the "last obstruent" is actually the released obstruent.

We can now discern a larger picture of voice assimilation, one in which several independent constraints "conspire" toward the common goal of unitary voice specification in any given sequence of obstruents. Should there be a difference in voice, it is the unreleased segment that must adopt the specification of the released segment. The constraint *LAR, dominating IDENT, prevents voiced obstruents from surfacing except where $IDENT_{Release}$, which ensures that the [voice] of a released segment remains as it is, overrides it. Hence, voice assimilation provides one more argument for the prominence of the released position.

5. Inertness of Sonorants

In contrast with that of obstruents, the [voice] of sonorants changes very little—in essence, it is inert, for it neither influences its environment nor is influenced by it. As stated earlier in this paper, [voice] in sonorants has two properties: (i) on the phonetic level, [+voice] is the natural status of the glottis for sonorants, with the result that the overwhelming number of the world's languages have voiced sonorants only; (ii) however, the [voice] of sonorants differs from that of obstruents in that it does not spread. To capture the predominance of [voice], I will concur with Lombardi's specification of [voice] in sonorants (1999). But, as for its unavailability for spreading, I will take issue with her unnecessary restriction of SPREAD to the [voice] of obstruents only.

Based on the formalization of SPREAD given earlier, it follows that both configurations shown in (20), in which [voice] fails to spread either from an obstruent or a sonorant, are forbidden.

In the remainder of this paper, I will argue that the inability of sonorants to influence their environment stems from their compliance with the IDENTITY constraint.

(20) a. *k d   b. *k n
         | |
       [voice]   [voice]

6. Inertness and Identity Requirements

The inertness of [voice] in sonorants can be seen in its inability to propagate itself to a preceding voiceless obstruent. Examples of allowable Obs-Son clusters, taken from Puppel, Nawrocka-Fisiak, and Krassowska (1977), are presented below:

(21) a. [sm]aczny 'delicious' [zm]artwić 'worry'
    b. ka[pw]an 'priest' o[bw]ok 'cloud'

In derived environments, too, sonorant [voice] remains inactive. For instance, a stem-final voiceless obstruent does not become voiced when it stands before an adjectival suffix, such as -*ny*:

(22) nastę[p]+[n]y *nastę[b]+[n]y 'next'
    smu[t]+[n]y *smu[d]+[n]y 'sad'

6.1. Word-Initial Obs-Son Clusters

We can see the absence of change in voice specification quite clearly when we take a closer look at word-initial Obs-Son clusters:

(23) a. [sm]aczny 'delicious' *[zm]aczny
    b. [zm]artwić 'to worry' *[sm]artwić
    c. [kn]edel 'dumpling' *[gn]edel
    d. [gń]iewać 'to anger' *[kń]iewać

What is the reason that [voice], though overtly specified in sonorants, does not spread from them? In the previous section, dealing with word-internal voicing, I proposed the ranking in (17), in which SPREAD(Voice) and IDENT$_{Release}$ remained unranked in relation to each other (owing to their lack of interaction in word-internal voicing). Now, however, the behavior of word-initial Obs-Son clusters allows a determination of the relative ranking between SPREAD(Voice) and IDENT$_{Release}$.

To take *[sm]aczny* as an example, [s] is a released segment occurring immediately before a tautosyllabic sonorant, and, therefore, the absence of spreading is due to IDENT$_{Release}$ overriding SPREAD(Voice):

(24) IDENT$_{Release}$ >> SPREAD >> *LAR >> IDENT

smaczny | [voice]	IDENT$_{Release}$	SPREAD	*LAR	IDENT
a. ☞ smaczny		*	*	
b. zmaczny	*!		**	*

In (24), the first of the two candidates, with its free standing sonorant [voice], fails to satisfy the requirement imposed by SPREAD. On the other hand, the second candidate, in an attempt to comply with SPREAD, alters the [s], a released segment, thereby earning a mark under the highest ranked constraint, IDENT$_{Release}$. Furthermore, as shown in (25b) below, an attempt to devoice the initial obstruent results both in a released segment which has been altered and a [voice] which has been left free-standing:

(25)

zmartwić \\| [voice]	IDENT$_{Release}$	SPREAD	*LAR	IDENT
a. ☞ zmartwić			**	
b. smartwić	*!	*	*	*

To sum up, word-initial Obs-Son clusters remain unchanged because to modify them to any degree would be to disregard the highest ranked constraint, IDENT$_{Release}$.

6.2. Word-internal Clusters

Word-internally, too, Obs-Son clusters are impervious to change. What is particularly interesting is the difference between Polish and German in regard to how medial Obs-Son clusters behave in syllable-final devoicing. Consider the following examples from German (Lombardi 1991:3):

(26) a. We[g]e   'way' (dat.sing)
     b. We[k]   'way' (nom.sing)
     c. We[k.b]ereiter 'pioneer'
     d. We[k.m]arkierung 'road marker'

The method of syllabification observed is one in which word-internal clusters, whether Obs-Son or Obs-Obs, are split into a coda and an onset: in other words, German does not follow "Maximize Onset" principle. Based on this observation, Lombardi (1999) limits SPREAD to obstruent clusters only, and puts forth the ranking of IDENT$_{Release}$ >> *LAR >> SPREAD to explain why a syllable-final obstruent in German undergoes devoicing regardless of what follows it:

(27) SPREAD: Obstruent clusters agree in voicing
     IDENT$_{Release}$ >> *LAR >> SPREAD (German)

Her version of SPREAD forbids the configuration shown in (28a), in which the [voice] of an obstruent fails to spread, but does not penalize (28b):

(28) a. *k   d   b. k   n
          | |
         [voice]   [voice]

(29) Obs-Obs

	we[g.b]ereiter	IDENT$_{Release}$	*LAR	SPREAD
a.	we[g.b]ereiter		**	
b. ☞	we[k.b]ereiter		*	*
c.	we[k.p]ereiter	*!		

Obs-Son

	we[gm]arkierung	IDENT$_{Release}$	*LAR	SPREAD
d.	we[g.m]arkierung		*!*	
e. ☞	we[k.m]arkierung		*	*

Polish differs markedly from German in two ways: (i) it does not allow a cluster like [kb] anywhere within a word or a phrase; and (ii) it does not permit an underlying sequence like [gm] to become [km] either initially or medially. Lombardi (1999) classifies Polish as a language characterized by voice spreading and syllable-final devoicing, proposes a ranking of SPREAD >> IDENT$_{Release}$ >> *LAR, and asserts that the hypothetical word /pigmen/ would surface as /pikmen/. However, the actual data do not support this assertion. Bethin (1984:18), for instance, finds that a voicing distinction must be maintained before sonorants, and data given in Puppel, Nawrocka-Fisiak, and Krassowska (1977) corroborate her findings.

To summarize the difference between German and Polish, it may be said that, in German, word-internal voiced obstruents are subject to syllable-final devoicing in pre-sonorant and pre-obstruent positions alike, but in Polish, they are "protected" in pre-sonorant positions:

(30)   Polish: IDENT$_{Release}$ >> SPREAD >> *LAR >> IDENT

	po.[gn]ać	IDENT$_{Release}$	SPREAD	*LAR	IDENT
a. ☞	po.[gn]ać \\| [voice]			**	
b.	po.[kn]ać | [voice]	*!	*	*	*

The reason for this crucial difference lies in the location of syllable boundaries, rather than in the ranking among constraints, for, as we have seen earlier in this paper, medial Obs-Son clusters in Polish are bundled together into complex onsets. For instance, in Polish, the medial cluster [gn] constitutes a complex onset, and, therefore, [g] is a released segment. If [voice] were delinked from [g], then both SPREAD (the original version) and IDENT$_{Release}$ would be disobeyed, resulting in the worst possible violation.

From the foregoing discussion, it is now evident that there is no need to impose any restriction on the applicability of SPREAD, in German or in Polish: a singly associated [voice], whether in an obstruent or a sonorant, is a SPREAD violation. And the failure of sonorant [voice] to influence neighboring segments in Polish, whether word-initially or medially, has to do with compliance with IDENT$_{Release}$: in both (25) and (30), the ill-formed candidates do not surface because of their violation of IDENT$_{Release}$. In German, on the other hand, the [voice] of sonorants does not spread for a different reason: in German, *LAR dominates SPREAD, making it less costly to suppress spreading (29e) than to increase the number of laryngeal features (29d).

For completeness, I will show that, in Polish, word-internal Obs-Obs clusters, in which the syllable boundary is located mid-cluster, never undergo devoicing.

(31)

ni[g.d]y	IDENT_Release	SPREAD	*LAR	IDENT
a. ☞ ni[g.d]y			**	
b. ni[k.d]y | [voice]		*!	*	*
c. ni[k.t]y	*!			**
d. ni[g.t]y | [voice]	*!	*	*	*

In (31), every ill-fated candidate commits a violation of IDENT_Release and/or SPREAD, either by altering the released segment or by leaving [voice] linked singly to an obstruent. In (31b), a free-standing [voice] associated with an obstruent constitutes a SPREAD violation; in (31c), eliminating [voice] altogether is as much of a disadvantage as a single-linked [voice], for the collective devoicing violates the highest constraint IDENT_Release.

7. Conclusion

In Slavic languages, it has been observed that two obstruents in direct contiguity always agree in voicing. Traditionally, such voice agreement was considered to be the outcome of spreading [±voice]. In this paper, following the lead of Lombardi (1999), I have shown that obstruents undergo devoicing as the result of a markedness constraint, *LAR, dominating IDENT. On the other hand, I have shown that internal voicing, which creates marked (= voiced) obstruents, is effected by SPREAD(Voice) overriding *LAR. These constraints are "cooperative" in nature: they affect only an unreleased segment, by spreading [voice] to it or delinking [voice] from it, thus achieving their common goal of a unitary voice specification without an alteration of the released segment.

I have also addressed the issue of inactive [voice] in sonorants. My proposal has shown that the inability of [voice] to spread is simply due to

IDENT$_{Release}$ overriding SPREAD, thus, preventing any change to the input structure. One by-product of this dominance by IDENT$_{Release}$ is the elimination of a stipulation that SPREAD(Voice) applies only to obstruent clusters.

8. Residual Problems

I would like to point out three problems that remain to be solved. The first problem concerns *LAR, which penalizes any voiced segment, whether a sonorant or an obstruent, regardless of its position in a syllable. Since it is indisputable that sonorants and obstruents differ in their preference for voicing, it is somewhat doubtful if such a categorical ban on voicing has a place in UG.

The second problem is the long-standing one that has to do with /v/ (Hayes 1984). In Polish, as well as in other Slavic languages, the voiced obstruent /v/, spelled <w>, is historically derived from the sonorant /w/ and, due to its non-obstruent origin, its behavior shows some deviation from that of other voiced obstruents: it undergoes devoicing not only before a voiceless obstruent (e.g. *[f]pływać*), but also, since it fails to trigger voice assimilation, after one (e.g. *t[f]ój* 'your,' not **[dv]ój*). How [v] should be represented is a problem that has aroused a great deal of interest among Slavic linguists, but since no acceptable solution has been arrived at, I will not discuss the issue further.

The third problem has to do with regional variations. Polish speakers seemed to be divided as to whether or not sonorants are really devoiced in (4). I find the judgment in this regard by Gussmann (1992) to be persuasive, but Schenker (p.c.), has stated that the sonorants in (4c) and (4d) are voiceless, but the ones in (4a) and (4b) are not. The latter conclusion, at least regarding, (4c,d) may be based upon phonetic implementation. For example, the /r/ in /krtań/ 'larynx' is [voice] at the end of the derivation, but is realized as [−voice] when actually pronounced. That is, due to the inherent mechanical difficulty the vocal folds have in switching rapidly from voiceless to voiced and then back to voiceless again, [krt] remains voiceless from beginning to end. Such lack of consensus may be due to regional variations, but I am unable to provide any suggestion as to how to represent them.

References

Beckman, Jill. 1995. Shona height harmony: Positional identity and markedness. In *University of Massachusetts occasional papers in linguistics* 18, 53–75. GLSA, University of Massachusetts, Amherst.

Bethin, Christina. 1984. Voicing assimilation in Polish. *International Journal of Slavic Linguistics and Poetics* 29: 17–32.

Chomsky, Noam, and Morris Halle. 1968. *The sound pattern of English.* Cambridge, Mass.: MIT Press

Gussmann, Edmund. 1992. Resyllabification and delinking: the case of Polish voicing. *Linguistic Inquiry* 23.29–56.

Hayes, Bruce. 1984. Russian voicing assimilation. In *Language sound structure*, ed. Mark. Aronoff and Richard Oehrle, 318–328. Cambridge, Mass.: MIT Press.

Hyman, Larry. 1975. *Phonology: theory and analysis.* New York: Holt Rinehart.

Itô, Junko and Armin Mester. 1986. The phonology of voicing in Japanese. *Linguistic Inquiry* 17: 49–73

Itô, Junko, Armin Mester and Jaye Padgett. 1995. Licensing and underspecification in Optimality Theory. *Linguistic Inquiry* 26: 571–613

Kenstowicz, Michael. 1994. *Phonology in generative grammar.* Cambridge, Mass.: Blackwell.

Ladefoged, Peter. 1971. *Preliminaries to linguistic phonetics.* Chicago: University of Chicago Press.

Ladefoged, Peter. 1975. *A course in phonetics.* New York: Harcourt Brace Jovanovich.

Ladefoged, Peter, and Ian Maddieson. 1996. *The sounds of the world's languages.* Cambridge, Mass.: Blackwell.

Lombardi, Linda. 1991. Laryngeal features and laryngeal neutralization. Doctoral dissertation, University of Massachusetts, Amherst.

Lombardi, Linda. 1999. Positional faithfulness and voicing assimilation in Optimality Theory. *Natural Language & Linguistic Theory* 17: 267–302.

Puppel, Stanisław, Jadwiga Nawrocka-Fisiak, and Halina Krassowska. 1977. *A handbook of Polish pronunciation for English learners.* Warszawa: Państwowe Wydawnictwo Naukowe.

Steriade, Donca. 1995. Underspecification and markedness. In *A handbook of phonological theory*, ed. John Goldsmith, 115–174. Cambridge, Mass.: Blackwell.

Padgett, Jaye. 1994. Stricture and nasal place assimilation. *Natural Language & Linguistic Theory* 12: 465–513.

Padgett, Jaye. 1995. Partial class behavior and nasal place assimilation. In *Proceedings of the Arizona Phonology Conference Workshop on Features in Optimality Theory*, 1–35. Department of Linguistics, University of Arizona, Tucson.

Department of Modern and Classical Languages
Georgia State University
Atlanta, Georgia 30303-3083
foryyt@panther.gsu.edu

On the Typology of Russian Comitatives

Masha Vassilieva
State University of New York at Stony Brook

1. Introduction

All languages have a way of expressing accompaniment. Language structures used for this purpose are called 'comitative constructions'. Russian has three types of comitative constructions, all of which use the word *s* 'with':

(1) a. Maša   igrala   [s   **Petej**]   v   karty.
Masha.NOM played.3rd.SG [with P.INSTR] in cards
'Masha played cards [with Peter].'
b. Maša   [s   **Petej**]   igrali   v   karty.
Masha.NOM [with P.INSTR] played.PL in cards
'Masha [and Peter] played cards.'
c. My   [s   **Petej**]   igrali   v   karty.
we.NOM [with P.INSTR] played.PL in cards
(i) 'We played cards [with Peter].'
(ii) 'I [and Peter] played cards.'

In (1a), the *with*-phrase is a VP adjunct with the comitative meaning 'together with'. The subject-verb agreement is determined solely by the subject (*Masha*). I will refer to such *with*-phrases as "*with*-adjuncts".

The *with*-phrase in (1b) contributes to the subject-verb agreement. The construction expresses comitativity but with a possibility for equal or independent participation of both Masha and Peter in the action of playing cards. While in (1a) Masha has Peter as her partner, in (1b) Masha and Peter do not necessarily play with each other. I will refer to such *with*-phrases as in (1b) as "*with*-conjuncts" because of their coordinative meaning.

The *with*-phrase in (1c) is known as the Plural Pronominal Construction (PPC). PPC has been frequently analyzed as an instance of coordination[1] (Camacho 1996 and 2000, McNally 1993 and 1988, Progovac 1997). There are, however, significant differences in syntactic behavior and semantic interpretation between PPC (1c) and the true comitative coordination (1b) as well as between PPC and the regular *and*-coordination. Because of these differences I will propose a non-coordinative analysis of PPC. For the three-person interpretation (1c-i), I argue for an adjunct analysis analogous to (1a). For the two-person reading of PPC, where it seems that *my* 'we' means 'I' (1c-ii), I develop an analysis, which treats the *with*-phrase as a comitative *complement* to the plural pronoun. Three types of *with*-phrases will therefore be distinguished: *with*-adjuncts (1a, 1c-i), *with*-conjuncts (1b) and *with*-complements (1c-ii).

This paper is organized as follows. I begin with a discussion of some syntactic differences between *with*-adjuncts and *with*-conjuncts (1a vs. 1b). I show the similarity between *with*-coordination and regular *and*-coordination. Then, having establi-shed a distinction between the two types of *with*-phrases (adjuncts and conjuncts), I will argue for the existence of a third type of *with*-phrases, namely *with*-complements that are found in the Plural Pronominal Construction. I will conclude with a brief note on factors that may determine the distribution of comitative constructions in different languages.

2. Comitative adjuncts vs. comitative conjuncts

The meaning of *s* 'with' – that of active accompaniment – sometimes makes it difficult to distinguish between the adjunct reading (2a) and the conjunct reading (2b):

(2) a. Maša ušla s Petej domoj. **(adjunction)**
 M.NOM went.SG with P.INSTR home
 'Masha went home with Peter.'
 b. Maša s Petej ušli domoj. **(conjunction)**
 M.NOM with P.INSTR went.PL home
 'Masha and Peter went home.'

---

[1] Ladusaw (1988) analyzes PPC as an adjunct structure in *both* interpretations.

The semantic difference between (2b) and (2a) is very subtle. Yet there are ways to disambiguate a construction, forcing a coordination-only meaning, when both conjuncts necessarily bear the same theta-role.

First, there are non-collective verbs that do not take *with*-modifiers, such as *znat'* 'to know' (3a). However, *with*-phrases with coordinative meaning are acceptable with these verbs (3b), just as are regular coordinated subjects (3c):

(3) a. *Maša znala s Petej nemeckij.
 M.NOM knew.3rdP.SG with P.INSTR German.ACC
 *'Masha knows German with Peter.'
 b. Maša s Petej znali nemeckij.
 M.NOM with P.INSTR knew.PL German.ACC
 'Masha and Peter knew German.'
 c. Maša i Petja znali nemeckij.
 M.NOM and P.NOM knew.PL German.ACC
 'Masha and Peter knew German.'

The ability of a *with*-phrase to occur with a verb like '*to know*' will henceforth be considered a diagnostic for comitative coordination.

Another hallmark of coordination is the plurality of the verb despite the singularity of the conjuncts. When '*s*' (*with*) connects two singular nominals and the verb is marked for plural (3b), the aforementioned nominals must be interpreted as comitative conjuncts. Therefore, plural marking on the verb can also serve as a diagnostic of coordination, although a much less straightforward one, because there are cases when singular agreement marking on the verb is possible despite the obvious plurality of its coordinate subject. One such case is exemplified by the so-called Conjunction Agreement[2] when the verb only agrees with the nearest conjunct; another is represented by examples like "*Bread and butter is my favorite breakfast*". Considering these cases, I will take the *possibility* of plural agreement in a structure as another diagnostic of coordination in this paper.

---

[2] The term 'conjunction agreement' (CA) was coined by Babyonyshev (1996). See the paper for a discussion of conditions on CA and a syntactic analysis. For my purposes, the important point is that the comitative coordination shows the same kind of sensitivity to the verb placement as regular *and*-coordination does, that is, singular marking on the verb is possible despite the coordinative meaning of the subject.

There are other syntactic contexts in which *with*-conjuncts differ from *with*-adjuncts and pattern with regular *and*-conjuncts. They involve, for example, *wh*-extraction, contiguity, and binding of anaphors.³

Let us begin with *wh*-extraction. The following sentence is ambiguous with respect to the meaning of its *with*-phrase (underlined) which can be interpreted either as adjunct or as conjunct:

(4) Maša   govorila   o   Pete   [s   Lenoj].
    M.NOM   talked.SG about P.LOC   with   L.INSTR
    a. 'Masha talked [to/with Lena] about Peter.'   **adjunction**
    b. 'Masha talked about Peter [and Lena].'   **coordination**

It is a well-known fact about coordination that conjuncts resist *wh*-extraction. If *s Lenoj* 'with Lena' is a *with*-adjunct to the verb in (4a) and a *with*-conjunct in (4b), as I have argued so far, then only the (a)-reading (adjunction) should be available when the *with*-phrase undergoes *wh*-movement. This prediction is borne out, as we see in the following example:

(5) [S   kem]   Maša   govorila   ob   Ivane?
    [with who.INSTR]   M.NOM   talked.SG   about I.LOC
    a. '[With whom] did Masha talk about Ivan?'
    b. *'[And whom] Masha talked about Ivan?'⁴

The inability of certain *with*-phrases to undergo *wh*-extraction under coordinate interpretation provides us with an argument for analyzing them as regular conjuncts.

An additional argument involves contiguity of coordina-tion. Neither in comitative coordination (6a) nor in *and*-coordi-nation (6b) can the conjuncts be separated by the verb, whereas comitative adjuncts occur either after or before the verb (6c):

---

³ Similar examples are discussed in McNally (1993).

⁴ As in English, it is possible to substitute an in-situ *wh*-phrase for the moved one in echo-questions. In this case, the ambiguity of the *with*-phrase is preserved, as expected:

(i) Maša   govorila   o   Pete   s   kem?
    M.NOM   talked.SG   about P.LOC   with   who.INSTR
    (a) Masha talked about Peter and whom?
    (b) With whom did Masha talk about Peter?

(6) a. *Petja pojut s Mašej.
     P.NOM sing.PL with M.INSTR
     'Peter and Masha sing.'
  b. *Petja pojut i Maša.
     P.NOM sing.PL and M.NOM
     'Peter and Masha sing.'
  c. Petja pojot s Mašej.
     P.NOM sings.SG with M.INSTR
     'Peter sings with Masha.'

In (6a), the *with*-phrase cannot be moved when the verb is plural and the intended interpretation is coordinative. If both (6a) and (6b) are instances of coordination, the ungrammaticality of the post-verbal positioning of one conjunct is due to a ban on movement out of coordination. Since VP-adjuncts can appear either to the right or to the left of the verb, the sentence in (6c) is grammatical when the *with*-adjunct follows the verb. Again we see that certain *with*-phrases exhibit a common pattern of syntactic behavior with regular conjuncts, distinct from the one shown by *with*-adjuncts.

Comitative conjuncts and comitative adjuncts exhibit different properties with respect to binding: *with*-conjuncts team up with regular *and*-coordination in their ability to bind anaphors. The following examples contain a coordinated phrase and an anaphoric pronoun bound by it:

(7) a. [Maša$_i$ i Petja$_j$]$_k$ pojut **svoju** $_{*i/*j/k}$ pesnju.
     [M.$_i$ and P.$_j$]$_k$ sing.PL **refl** $_{*i/*j/k}$ song
     '[Masha and Peter]$_k$ sing their$_k$ song.'
  b. [Maša$_i$ s Petej$_j$]$_k$ pojut **svoju** $_{*i/*j/k}$ pesnju.
     [M.$_i$ with P.$_j$]$_k$ sing.PL **refl** $_{*i/*j/k}$ song
     '[Masha and Peter]$_k$ sing their$_k$ song.'

Both types of nominal coordination can antecede the possessive reflexive pronoun *svoju* 'self' in (7). Such co-reference is, however, impossible in structures involving *with*-adjuncts such as:

(8) [Maša$_i$ s Petej$_j$]$_k$ pojot **svoju**$_{i/*j/*k}$ pesnju.
    [M.$_i$ with P.$_j$]$_k$ sing.SG **refl**$_{i/*j/*k}$ song
    'Masha$_i$ sings her$_i$ song with Peter$_j$.'

The contrast between the *with*-phrases in (7b) and (8) becomes clear if we assume that an XP-analysis of coordination[5] (9) applies to both comitative and regular coordination.

(9)   [&P conjunct A, [&' &°, conjunct B]]

In coordination, only the &P as a whole can antecede the reflexive (10). In adjunction (11), the subject does not form a constituent with the verbal adjunct; therefore the reflexive can only be anteceded by the subject:

(10) a. Maša [i   Petja] / [s   Petej] pojut   svoju pesnju.
         Masha [and Peter] / [with Peter] sing.PL refl song
         'Masha and Peter sing their song.'
     b.

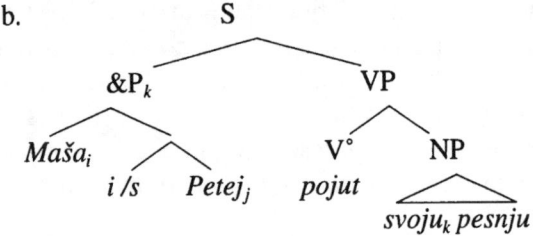

(11) a. Maša s   Petej pojot   svoju pesnju.
         Masha with Peter sing.SG refl song
         'Masha sings her song with Peter.'
     b.

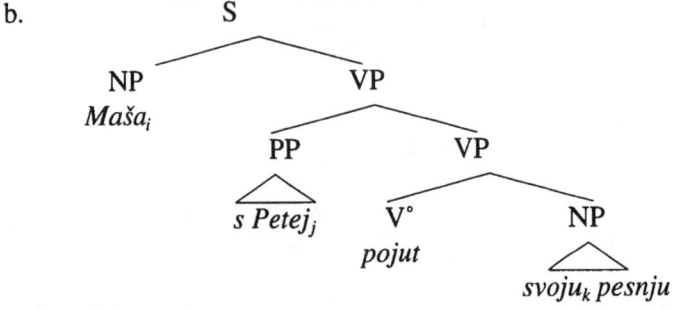

To summarize, comitative coordination differs from comitative adjunction in many syntactic contexts. It blocks extraction, exhibits a distinctive word order, co-occurs with predicates that otherwise do not allow *with*-modifiers, triggers plural verb agreement, and is able to

---

[5] Cf. Johannessen (1998) and references therein, as well as Zoerner (1995).

antecede plural reflexives as well as to have a uniform theta-role assignment by the predicate to both conjuncts. Having established the distinction between the two types of *with*-phrases, the adjuncts and conjuncts, I will now turn to another type of comitative *with*-phrase, namely the Plural Pronominal Construction.

3. Comitative complements

Languages as diverse as Fijian, Old Norse, Spanish, Navajo, and many Slavic and African languages[6] use a specific construction to refer to a group of people. It typically involves a plural pronoun, a comitative element and a nominal. This construction is known as the Plural Pronominal Construction (PPC) and is usually analyzed as an instance of comitative coordination.[7] However, PPC possesses syntactic and semantic properties that are in contrast with those exhibited by coordination. In this section I will compare PPC to other types of *with*-phrases to determine its place in the typology of Russian comitative constructions.

In many languages, including Russian, PPC is ambiguous with respect to the number of people who participate in an event:

(12) My   s   Petej   tancevali.
      we.NOM   with   P.INSTR   danced.PL
   a. 'We danced with Peter.'
   b. 'Peter and I danced.'

These two interpretations[8] should correspond to two distinct structural representations. I will begin with the interpretation that involves at least three participants, exemplified in (12a).

---

[6] Afro-Asiatic, Niger-Kordofanian, Uralic, Austronesian, and Indo-European language families have PPC (Progovac 1997:217). See also Urtz (1994).

[7] For example, Camacho (1996) assumes that the structure for PPC (in his notation, *pro*+NP) is identical to that of comitative coordination (NP+NP).

[8] The interpretation in (12b) is more natural and frequent. Ladusaw (1989:3) suggests the following explanation: the preference "should follow from a kind of Gricean reasoning. 'You have gone to the trouble of adding more information to the pronoun, so I will assume that you have given me all the relevant individuals'". The interpretation in (12a) requires some kind of focus intonation.

3.1. Three-person interpretation

In section 2, I have discussed a number of strategies that help to distinguish comitative coordination from comitative adjunction. In particular, *with*-conjuncts were shown to co-occur with predicates like *znat'* 'to know' and to resist movement. None of these properties are exhibited by PPC in the three-person interpretation. When PPC co-occurs with the verb *znat'* 'to know', the intended 3+ interpretation is impossible:

(13) *My   s   Petej   znaem   nemeckij.[9]
     we   with   Peter   know.1stPL   German
     'We and Peter know German.'

The behavior of PPC with respect to movement also sets this construction apart from comitative coordination. The following examples show that a verb can intervene between the elements of PPC (14) and that *with*-phrases in PPC can undergo *wh*-extraction (15):

(14) My   pošli   s   Petej   domoj.
     we   went.PL   with   Peter   home
     'We went home with Peter.'

(15) a. My   s   Lenoj   pošli   domoj.
        we   with   Lena   went.PL   home
        'We went home with Lena.'
     b. [S   kem]   my   pošli   domoj?
        [with whom]   we   went.PL   home
        'With whom did we go home?'

Since *with*-conjuncts were previously shown to block movement (cf. (5) and (6)), the *with*-phrases in (14) and (15) cannot be analyzed as an instance of coordination.

In addition, PPC differs from coordination in its ability to bind anaphors. Consider the following sentence:

---

[9] The sentence is grammatical, but only on the interpretation that involves two people: "Peter and I know German."

(16) My$_i$ s   Petej$_j$ čitaem   svoju$_{i/*j/*i+j}$ knigu.
     we$_i$ with Peter$_j$ read.PL   refl$_{i/*j/*i+j}$ book
     'We$_i$ read our $_{i/*j\ /\ *i+j}$ book with Peter$_j$.'

On the 3+ interpretation, the antecedent[10] of the possessive reflexive *svoju* is understood as *my* '*we*', without the inclusion of Peter. Since true comitative *with*-conjuncts must be included in the reference of the possessive (cf. (7) and (10)), the *with*-phrase in (16) cannot be a conjunct.

As I have shown, when PPC refers to at least three people, its *with*-phrases in PPC does not act like a *with*-conjunct but patterns in its syntactic behavior with *with*-adjuncts. On the basis of the linguistic evidence presented above, I propose that PPC is not an instance of coordination but of comitative adjunction on the interpretation that involves at least three participants.

3.2. Two-person interpretation

Now let us consider the interpretation of PPC (17b) that involves the speaker and whoever is denoted by the *with*-phrase. In spite of the possibility for this construction to involve more than two people (when the *with*-phrase refers to more than one person), I will refer to this interpretation of PPC as 'dual', for convenience, to emphasize the peculiar interpretation of 'we'.

(17) My s   Petej pojom.
     we with Peter sing.1stPL
     a. 'Peter and we sing'
     b. 'Peter and I sing.'

Unlike any coordinate or adjunct structure discussed previously in this paper, this construction requires the referent of the *with*-phrase to be included into the reference of the plural pro-noun. This is, however, not the only difference between dual PPC and coordination, because PPC imposes a number of restrictions on its components that are unparalleled in coordinate structures.

---

[10] In Russian, possessive reflexives agree in number and gender with the noun they modify. Nothing in their form reflects the antecedent.

First, PPC allows its components to be connected by *s* 'with' (17b) but not by *i* 'and' (18a), whereas comitative coordination permits such substitution (18b):

(18) a. My [i Petja] pojom. (cf.17)
we [and Peter] sing.1st.PL
   i. 'Peter and we sing.'
   ii. * 'Peter and I sing.'
b. Maša [s Sašej] / [i Saša] pojut
Masha [with Sasha] / [and Sasha] sing.3rd.PL
'Masha and Sasha sing'

Second, plural agreement, the possibility of which was argued to be a hallmark of coordination, is impossible in PPC when the order of components is changed (19). In contrast, the order of conjuncts can be freely changed in both comitative (20a) and regular (20b) coordination:

(19) a. My s Petej pojom.
we with Peter sing.1st.PL
'Peter and I sing.'
b. *Petja s nami pojom / pojut.
Peter with us sing.1st.PL / 3rd.PL
'Peter and I sing.'
(20) a. Maša s Petej (= Petja s Mašej) pojut.
Masha with Peter (= Peter with Masha) sing.3rd.PL
'Masha and Peter sing.'
b. ?Ty i ja (= ?ja i ty) pojom.
you and I (= I and you[11]) sing.1st.PL
'You and I sing.'

Third, pronouns cannot participate in comitative coordination in Russian (21). In addition, native speakers tend to avoid even *and*-coordination of pronouns (20b), giving preference to PPC (22) as 'more natural'.

---

[11] Russian has no preference on the order of pronouns in coordination.

(21) *Ty   so   mnoj   pojom.   (cf. 20b)
     you   with me   sing.1st.PL
     'You and I sing.'

(22) My   s   toboj   pojom.
     we   with you   sing.1st.PL
     'You and I sing.'

While pronouns are banned from comitative coordination and 'disliked' in regular coordination, PPC *requires* its first element to be a pronoun. This sets PPC apart from other types of *with*-phrases as well as from coordination in general.

Fourth, there is a restriction on the order of elements in PPC with respect to the person hierarchy. While English requires the 1st person pronoun to come second in a coordinate structure (*he and I* vs. **I and he*), Russian does not have any preference (cf. 20b). However, in dual PPC the plural pronoun must be higher in the hierarchy (1>2>3) than the (pro)noun in the *with*-phrase. Therefore, (23b) cannot have two-person reading even when the verb agrees with the plural pronoun in person:

(23) a. My   s   nej   pojom.
        we   with her   sing.1st.PL
        'She and I sing.'
     b. *Oni   so   mnoj   pojom   / pojut.
        They with me   sing.1st.PL / 3rd.PL
        'She/he and I sing.'

The strict selectivity imposed on the constituents and their order is unique to dual PPC and does not apply to other comitative constructions. This supports my hypothesis that this type of PPC is not an instance of coordination. Additional evidence comes from the tests that we used to distinguish comitative conjuncts from adjuncts. With respect to these tests, dual PPC patterns with neither of these constructions. PPC is similar to the adjuncts because it allows a verb to separate its constituents.

(24) My   znali   s   Petej, čto   Ivan   –   vor.
     we   knew.PL   with   Peter   that Ivan   thief
     'Peter and I knew that Ivan is a thief.'

On the other hand, two-person PPC patterns with comitative coordination (and not with adjunction) because PPC: (i) blocks *wh*-movement (25a-b), (ii) allows its constituents to jointly antecede reflexives (25c), and (iii) is possible with the verb 'to know' (24):

(25) a. [$_{PPC}$ My s Petej] tancevali.
       we with Peter danced.PL
   'Peter and I danced.'
   b. *S kem [$_{PPC}$ my *t*] tancevali?
      with whom we *t* danced.PL
   'With whom did I dance?'
   c. [My$_i$ s Petej$_j$]$_k$ čitaem svoju$_{*i/*j/k}$ knigu.
      [we$_i$ with Peter$_j$]$_k$ read refl$_{*i/*j/k}$ book
   '[Peter$_j$ and I$_i$]$_k$ read our$_{*i/*j/k}$ book.'

I have argued that while dual PPC shares some properties with comitative adjuncts and comitative conjuncts, it also exhibits a number of features not found in other *with*-constructions. Since dual PPC does not clearly pattern with any of these categories, it is logical to assume that its syntactic structure is neither adjunction nor coordination. In the next section, I will argue for an analysis of dual PPC as comitative complementation and show how this analysis explains its properties.

3.3. "Dual" PPC as comitative complementation

An important property of dual PPC is the inclusion of the reference of the *with*-phrase in the reference of the plural pronoun. This explains why PPC obeys a person hierarchy. When the plural pronoun is 3rd person, the *with*-phrase cannot contain a 1st person pronoun, because the latter cannot be included in the reference of the former. Another striking feature of PPC is that the plural pronoun appears to have a singular referent. In other words, *my* 'we' in PPC seems to mean 'I'. Assuming that the interpretation of 'we' is 'speaker (I) plus some other people', I propose that the *with*-phrase in PPC specifies who these 'other people' are. The corresponding syntactic structure involves a head (plural pronoun) that takes the comitative *with*-phrase as its complement.

(26)

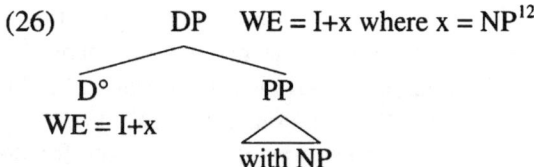

The proposed semantic interpretation of 'we' involves the speaker (I) and an unspecified variable x.[13] The function of the *with*-complement in PPC is to fix the reference of x within the pronominal head.

The complement analysis of dual PPC can account for the unique properties of PPC discussed earlier in this section. I will begin with the restrictions on word order and on the constituents of PPC. First, the impossibility of substituting *i* 'and' for *s* 'with' can be explained as the selectional preference of the pronominal head to take a PP rather than an &P'. Second, the fixed order of elements in PPC is due to the head parameter. In head-initial languages like Russian the plural pronoun would always have to come first. Third, the person hierarchy in PPC follows from the inclusion of the reference of the *with*-complement in the reference of the pronoun. For example, when the *with*-phrase has a 2nd person pronoun (you-SG), the head-pronoun cannot be 3rd person (they) because 'they' does not include 'you', nor can it be 2nd person (you-PL) because that would involve double reference to the same person within one pronoun (you-PL = you$i$+x, where x = you$i$).

In addition, there are three properties that dual PPC has in common with comitative coordination: co-occurrence with the verb *znat'* 'to know', serving as a complex antecedent for anaphors, and blocking of *wh*-movement. First, PPC can co-occur with verbs like 'to know' as do *with*-conjuncts. Since the *with*-phrase is located within the pronominal DP, the selectional restrictions of the verb do not apply as long as the verb can take a plural pronoun as its subject. In coordination, on the other hand, the verb takes the whole &P as its subject. Second, the two

---

[12] This informal notation does not represent an attempt at a formal semantic analysis.

[13] While 1st and 2nd person plural pronouns can be argued to have a core reference as "I" and "you-SG" respectively, no such analysis is possible for the 3rd person plural pronouns. "They" cannot be analyzed as 'he + other people". Therefore I suggest that 'they' is different from the other pronouns in having two rather than one variable in its head. For example, 'we' is interpreted as "I + x", while 'they' is interpreted as "y+x". In both cases, x can be determined by the comitative complement.

parts of PPC can act as a single antecedent for an anaphor. Again, this is not surprising since the antecedent DP (as well as &P in coordination) is a single constituent. Third, the blocking of *wh*-movement out of PPC is similar to the ban on movement of PP out of a quantified DP. Whatever bans *wh*-movement of the PP in (27) is presumably responsible for the same phenomenon in PPC.

(27) *Iz   kogo   ty   vsex   ____   predstavil   Petru?   DP
      of   whom   you   all.ACC   ____   introduced   Peter.DAT
      'All of whom did you introduce to Peter?'

Note, however, that while the movement of PP is banned for both PPC and quantified DPs, the D-head can undergo *wh*-movement only in the latter:

(28) a. Kto   iz   vzroslyx   znal,   čto   Petja – vor?   DP
         who   of   adults   knew   that   Peter   thief
         'Who of the adults knew that Peter was a thief?'
     b. *Kto   s   Ivanom   znal,   čto   Petja – vor?   PPC
         Who   with Ivan   knew   that   Peter   thief
         'Who including Peter knew that Peter was a thief?'

I have argued above that PPC is subject to very strict restrictions with respect to the types of elements that can participate. The example (28b) must be ungrammatical because its head is a *wh*-word and not a plural personal pronoun. Note that when a pronoun heads a PPC, the movement is allowed (24). Except for the *wh*-movement, the contiguity requirements on PPC seem to be the same as for the quantified phrases with a PP complement of the type shown in (28a). Both allow a verb, an adverb, or both, to intervene between the head and the complement. The space limitations do not allow me to dwell on this in any detail; therefore, the only point I would like to make here is that PPC behaves like a quantified DP with respect to contiguity.

Languages differ with respect to the types of comitatives they use. All three kinds are found in Russian. Other Slavic languages, such as Bulgarian, Macedonian, and Slovene[14] have no *with*-conjuncts, but allow *with*-adjuncts and *with*-complements. Kashubian and French, on the

---

[14] Judging from the language sketches in Comrie and Corbett (1993).

other hand, allow *with*-conjuncts but not *with*-complements. An important question to ask is which property of a language allows one or the other of these three separate constructions.

For comitative coordination, I assume that languages lacking it do not have a comitative conjunction that determines the properties of this construction. I have argued here that *and*-coordination and *with*-coordination share a number of properties, but they also exhibit differences. While my investigation of these differences is still in progress, it is already possible to see that differences stem from the different properties of the two respective conjunctions. The absence of a lexical item with the properties of a comitative conjunction in a given language makes comitative coordination impossible in this language.

An absence of the comitative conjunction does not mean that a language will automatically lack PPC. I have argued that PPC is separate from comitative coordination. We do not need, therefore, to posit constraints on coordination to explain why there are languages with PPC but without comitative coordination and vice versa. Without such separation, it would indeed be difficult to explain why comitative but not regular coordination allows the inclusive interpretation of its plural pronominal element, or why singular pronouns cannot be the first element of comitative coordination. It would be even more difficult to explain the cross-linguistic distribution of such restrictions. Keeping the two constructions apart allows a simpler explanation of their (non)co-occurrence in world's languages.

I take the internal structure of plural pronouns to be the factor that determines presence or absence of PPC in a given language. In a PPC-less language like English (29a), the variable argument of 'we' is presumably 'lexically saturated' (cf. Rizzi 1986). In a language with PPC, like Russian, the argument of 'we' is a *pro* (29b). It can either be silent or expressed by a comitative phrase, but it is not saturated in the lexicon.

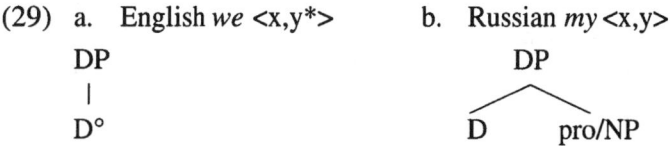

(29) a. English *we* <x,y*>   b. Russian *my* <x,y>

I conclude that the variation among languages with respect to a presence or absence of PPC stems from the specification of their plural pronouns in the lexicon.

4. Summary

I have proposed a three-fold typology of Russian comitative constructions that include adjunction, coordination and complementation. While distinguishing the first two classes is relatively uncontroversial, the third class has, to my knowledge, not been suggested previously as a separate entity. I have argued for its existence on the basis of evidence from the Plural Pronominal Construction which has typically been analyzed as an instance of coordination. I have shown that PPC differs in its properties from both regular and comitative coordination. I suggested that the two interpretations of PPC involve either comitative adjunction or comitative complementation.

Comitative constructions are unevenly distributed in languages. Most languages allow comitative adjunction. In order to allow comitative coordination, a language must possess a comitative conjunction whose properties are responsible for the differences between the regular and comitative coordination. Languages that allow PPC must have internally-complex plural pronouns whose complement can be either a *pro* or an overt NP.

References

Babyonyshev, Maria. 1996. Structural Connections in Syntax and Processing: Studies in Russian and Japanese. Doctoral dissertation, MIT, Cambridge, MA.

Cardinaletti, Anna. 1994. On The Internal Structure Of Pronominal DPs. *Linguistic Review* 11: 195-219.

Camacho, José. 1996. Comitative coordination in Spanish. In *Aspects of Romance Linguistics,* ed. Parodi, Claudia et al, 107-122. Washington, D.C.: Georgetown University Press.

Comrie, Bernard and Greville G. Corbett. 1993. *The Slavonic Languages*. Routledge, London.

Dalrymple, Mary, Irene Hayrapetian and Tracy Holloway King. 1998. The Semantics of the Russian Comitative Construction. *Natural Language and Linguistic Theory* 16: 597-631.
Johannessen, Janne Bondi. 1988. *Coordination.* Oxford University Press, New York.
Ladusaw, William A. 1988. Group Reference and the Plural Pronoun Construction. Paper presented at the LSA Annual Meeting in New Orleans.
McNally, Louise. 1988. Comitative Coordination in Russian. Paper presented at the LSA Annual Meeting in New Orleans.
McNally, Louise. 1993. Comitative Coordination: A Case Study In Group Formation. *Natural Language and Linguistic Theory* 11: 347-379.
Progovac, Ljiljana. 1997. Slavic and the Structure for Coordination. *Proceedings of FASL 5: The Indiana Meeting:* 207-223.
Rizzi, Luigi. 1986. Null Objects in Italian and the Theory of *pro*. *Linguistic Inquiry 17*, 501-558.
Urtz, Bernardette Jean. 1994. The Syntax, Semantics and Pragmatics of a Nominal Conjunction: The Case of Russian *S*. Doctoral dissertation, Harvard University, Cambridge, MA.
Zoerner, Edward. 1995. The Syntax of &P. Doctoral dissertation, University of California, Irvine.

mvassili@yahoo.com

Appendix: Properties of comitative constructions

PROPERTIES	comitative adjuncts	comitative conjuncts	comitative complements
ability to co-occur with the verb 'to know'	no	yes	yes
wh-extraction allowed	yes	no	no
both elements can serve as an single antecedent for anaphors	no	yes	yes
a verb can intervene between the elements	yes	no	yes
an adverb can intervene between the elements	yes	yes	yes
both a verb and an adverb can intervene	yes	no	yes
'and' can substitute for 'with'	no	yes	no
the agreement with the verb is plural even if one of the elements is singular	no	yes	yes
the order of elements can be switched without bringing a difference in interpretation	no	yes	no
the first element can be a pronoun	yes	no	yes
the first element must be a plural pronoun	no	no	yes
the reference of the second element is included into the reference of the first element	no	no	yes